The Foreign Press

THE FOREIGN PRESS

JOHN C. MERRILL

CARTER R. BRYAN

MARVIN ALISKY

The Foreign Press

by

John C. Merrill

Carter R. Bryan

Marvin Alisky

Louisiana State University Press

To

Dorothy, Annemie, and Beverly

Copyright 1964
BY LOUISIANA STATE UNIVERSITY PRESS
Library of Congress Catalog Card Number: 63-16659
Printed in the United States of America

Foreword

Even an elementary knowledge of the press of the world is not possessed by many Americans. This void in their information not only diminishes their understanding of events elsewhere than in their own country, but it also diminishes their understanding of the press of the United States.

The authors of this book have undertaken a most useful service. Students and general readers will put it down with a better comprehension of the variety of conditions under which newspapers are published and a clearer understanding of the different roles accorded the press under varying systems of government. The better they understand these variations, the more expertly they will put upon each newspaper that comes into their hands the estimate of credibility necessary to read any printed material with a proper perspective.

No single volume could tell a student of the press all that he would like to know or all that he ought to know about the many thousands of publications involved. It would be difficult to give a reader not otherwise informed a good understanding of a single great newspaper in a volume of this size. It therefore is a virtue of this effort that it presents a glimpse of the world press in a way intended to convey the basic information and in a manner calculated to excite an interest that will lead the student to fuller examination of particular aspects of the problem. More cannot be expected of a publication that has to deal with so large a subject.

James Russell Wiggins
Editor, The Washington Post

Preface

While there is certainly no paucity of excellent material concerning the foreign
press today, there has been since World War II a notable absence of any type of systematic synthesis of this information which might be used as a textbook or reference
book for persons interested in the broad aspects of international communication.
This book has grown out of a sincere desire to provide such a synthesis.

The serious student of the foreign press might very well be able to find much of
the material which is contained in this book scattered through dozens of existing
publications; indeed this is one major reason for the book's existence. For in this
single volume a great amount of pertinent data has been made readily accessible to
the person desiring a comparative study of foreign systems of printed news dissemination.

This book deals chiefly with the newspaper press of the principal foreign nations,
with some emphasis given the magazine press. It does not go deeply into the electronic media--radio and television--although in many parts of the world these media
are exceptionally pervasive and influential. Nor does this book pretend to be an
exhaustive treatment of the foreign press; such a treatment would, of course, necess-
itate many volumes and would defeat the purpose of this work--to serve as a survey or
introduction to the foreign press. This book might be used advantageously in a
course dealing with the foreign press specifically or as a supplemental book for
several existing basic journalism and social science courses.

We contend that every journalism student needs at least an introduction to the
foreign press so that he may better appreciate and evaluate the press of his own
country. Such an introduction should go a long way in helping the average student

shed his provincialism and think of his own press system in an international context. Probably within the next decade the foreign press will be emphasized to a far greater extent in schools and departments of journalism than it is today. For it is becoming obvious that an American studying journalism should no more limit himself to American journalism than a history student should study only American history. This survey book, then, is presented as such an introduction to the foreign press, and if used intelligently with collateral readings, should give the student a good insight into the foreign press situation.

Circulation figures given in this book are of course approximate. It is realized that all such figures change constantly, and they are included in this volume only so that the reader might have a general conception of the potential reading public of the various publications and might have the opportunity to rank them with other publications throughout the world.

The objective of this book is to present a panoramic picture of the world's press systems with a minimum of distortion and to bring to the student who desires a more intensive study many excellent sources for further investigation. Information in this volume has been obtained from innumerable sources, e.g., from analysis of the foreign publications themselves, and from lectures, conversations, letters, governmental pamphlets, embassy materials, journals and magazines of all types, newspapers, and various types of books. Most of these sources are referred to in the notes; others are identified in the bibliography. Much data has also come from our first-hand contacts with the press sytems of other countries.

We are indebted to many persons, known and unknown, for their valuable help in making this book possible. Encouragement, suggestions, and material have been supplied by so many persons (both in and outside the United States) that it is impossible to make individual acknowledgments here. We do, however, wish to express to all of them our sincere appreciation.

John C. Merrill
Carter R. Bryan
Marvin Alisky

Table of Contents

Authors

JOHN C. MERRILL, a native Mississippian and presently Associate Professor of Journalism at Texas A&M, has long had an interest in international communications. His Handbook of the Foreign Press (LSU Press, 1959) was the first full-fledged survey of the press systems of the world's major countries to be published in the United States. A Navy veteran of World War II, he saw action in both the Atlantic and Pacific theaters of operation.

He received the B.A. in English and history from Mississippi Delta State College, the M.A. in journalism from Louisiana State University, and the Ph.D. in mass communications from the State University of Iowa. He has worked for both daily and weekly newspapers in the United States and has served as special correspondent for several in Latin America. Dr. Merrill has also taught English and journalism at two colleges in addition to his present position at Texas A&M.

He has written numerous articles in academic journals and is co-author of Modern Journalism (1962) for which he wrote the chapter on foreign mass media. He is also the author of Gringo: Mexican Journalists Look at the U.S. (1963). He holds membership in the Association for Education in Journalism, Kappa Tau Alpha (honorary journalistic society), and Phi Kappa Phi (national scholarship society). He is listed in Who's Who in American Education.

CARTER R. BRYAN, B.A. (University of California), Ph.D. (University of Vienna); Associate Professor of Journalism at University of Maryland. He was Vienna correspondent of the London Times and of the New York Times (1938-40); Editor of Foreign Commerce Weekly (1940-42); Chief Economist of the American Republics Unit, U.S. De-

partment of Commerce (1942-43); Chief Information Specialist, Office of War Informa-
tion (1943); Chief of the Italian Section, Chief of the Balkans Division, Chief
Economist of the Austrian Mission (successively), Foreign Economic Administration,
Washington and Europe (1943-46); Economic Editor, World Report (1946); Foreign Trade
Advisor, U.S. Military Government in Korea (1946-47); Chief of the Printing and
Publishing Unit, SCAP, Tokyo, Japan (1947-48); Chief of Political and Economic
Intelligence, European Command, Berlin and Heidelberg (1948-50); Planning and Review
Staff for War Industry Expansion, National Production Authority, Washington (1951-52).
Since 1955 he has been teaching and writing at the University of Maryland. In 1958,
he visited Europe to study the press of various countries.

MARVIN ALISKY, chairman of the Department of Mass Communications at Arizona State
University, holds the Ph.D. degree in Latin American political science and journalism
from the University of Texas.

  He has been a news correspondent in most of the Latin American republics and Spain
for the Christian Science Monitor, the NBC network, the Copley News Service, and
freelance for various magazines.

  As the U.S. delegate to the UNESCO Conference on Journalism in Ecuador in 1960, he
helped found Latin America's first graduate school in journalism in Quito.

  The ASU professor is active in the Inter-American Press Association and the Inter-
American Broadcasters Association.

  Dr. Alisky has been a visiting lecturer at the national universities of Mexico,
Guatemala, and Peru, and was the first Smith-Mundt visiting professor in Central
America. He founded the School of Journalism of the National University of Nicaragua.

  His studies of various facets of the Latin American mass media over a period of
years have made his writings on the subject standard references.

Part I

The General
Foreign Press Picture

World
Crisis
and the Press

Distrust and misunderstanding among peoples
everywhere are commonplace today, and in this
period of Cold War the greatest problem facing the entire world is the prevention of the
ruinous recurrence of a Hot War. Men of
many nations are seated at peace tables talking of this problem. But seated with these
men are deep-rooted prejudices and suspicions,
and beneath the smooth patina of their words
are fundamental misunderstandings and traditional power politics. And all the while,
the media of mass communication throughout
the world are pouring a glut of messages over
vast audiences. The world press--the giant
organism holding together cultural and nationalistic groups--is busy "reporting" and "in-
terpreting" the constant succession of world
crises to the jittery populations.

✳ The press wields tremendous power today as
a purveyor of vital information. It has the
potential to help erase erroneous impressions
and stereotypes and to ease tensions; it also
can create fears or needlessly perpetuate
anxieties. It can shake people from com-
placency, or it can lull them into an un-
thinking and dangerous sleep. With psychological warfare raging fiercely, the press
finds itself in a place of tremendous responsibility today. Modern technology has
created a small world, and mankind is locked
together in the same tiny room where everyone is forced to share the consequence of
another's action.

Physical means of communicating news and
interpretation throughout the world are well-
developed and capable of providing the
quantity of messages needed for proper understanding among peoples. But while messages
flow more rapidly and in greater bulk than
ever before, questions of quality, of impact,
of significance, and of motive come to the
forefront. And while on the surface there
appears to be adequate information moving
from even the most remote areas of the world,
governmental pressures, secrecy, censorship,
and propaganda impede the meaningful and free
flow of news.

An informed public opinion is needed
throughout the world if judicious decisions

are to be made; a free-flowing and intelligent supply of news and interpretation must
nourish this public opinion. Lester Markel,
Sunday editor of the New York Times, said in
1956:

"We live in a mine-trapped and fog-bound
world, a world in which facts are few and
hunches difficult....We shall not be able to
reach sound judgments that are so urgent unless we have an informed and alert public
opinion, unless our information is good....
For an informed opinion is a weapon without
which we cannot be truly armed, a torch without which we cannot find our way through the
darkness."[1]

And, speaking out again in 1960 on his
favorite subject, Markel stated concerning
the concept of the "flow of the news":

✳"We cannot have understanding--and thus
peace--among the peoples of the world unless
they come to know one another better, unless
they have better, truer, information about
one another; the main instrument for communicating such information, for bringing
about such understanding is the newspaper;
it is not the Voice of America, the BBC,
Radio Moscow, that matters in the long run;
it is the day-by-day flow of the news."[2]

On the world scene as on the national scene,
a truthful and unfettered press can best
serve the people. It can go far to mend differences among nationalities, classes and
groups; it can frustrate the plans of war-
hungry leaders and rulers. The accomplish-
ment of these possibilities is a prodigious
task for the press, one that requires the
acceptance and application of the free press
theory; for only under such a theory can
people have more than a foggy or lopsided
picture of what is happening around them.

When one looks at recent history, he sees
what has happened to freedom of the press in
countries controlled by such men as Mussolini,
Hitler, Perón, Trujillo, Rojas Pinilla,
Franco, Khrushchev, Mao Tse-tung, and more
recently, Castro. Throughout the world tight
restrictions on the press prevail, even in
countries which do not receive much publicity
for their totalitarian activities. India
constantly meddles in press affairs and newspapers find themselves in danger if their
stories reflect adversely on a government
official; opposition papers in Pakistan can
be dealt with in many ways, one of which is
government refusal of newsprint to critical
journals. Newspapermen in Turkey may find
themselves in jail for "insulting" a government official. In South Korea an editor had

better make sure his paper does not "disturb people's minds," and in Greece an editor endangers himself and his paper if he causes the public to become restless. In many other nations the press is only partially free to report and interpret the news. This situation, existing in varying degrees in all parts of the world, makes it extremely difficult for the press to fulfill its responsibility under the free press theory; in fact, it would seem to make it an impossibility.[3]

In the light of the foregoing facts, the idea of free access to factual and significant information by the press audiences may understandably appear to many thoughtful persons as only a dream of unrealistic optimists. Certainly, few observers could fail to see the difficulties of implementing such an idea in these days when the world is divided into numerous nationalistic camps, each with its own governmental and press philosophy.

Even the casual observer will note that the world press today is subjecting men's minds to a ceaseless and terrific bombardment of messages calculated to influence and control.[4] Internally a nation's press tries to mold the state into a consolidated, smooth-running machine ready to repel any outside danger, and externally the press directs its broadsides at potential enemies. This may be a practical course in times of danger, but it does not make for objective, information-oriented communication within or among countries. Perhaps the press has come in for too great a share of blame for this situation. Press responsibility to all men of all nations is a fine concept, but a responsible press in an irresponsible social or government context is hardly to be hoped for except by those too uninformed or too idealistic to know better. And it may be, as has been pointed out, that the individual citizen is to blame for the bias and government propaganda which permeates large segments of the world press today.[5]

Many critics say that the press is actually hindering world understanding and cooperation, and that the world press is stretching animosities among nations to dangerous dimensions and thereby worsening the international psychic crisis. This does not seem an unlikely thesis. It would imply great amounts of propaganda in the news stream--propaganda aimed at perpetuating the psychological tug of war among nations and peoples; it would also imply that "exceptional" incidents which are even further exaggerated by the newspapers are disseminated as important news; it would further imply that "eccentric" and "dangerous" people are the subject of much of the news. In short, it would imply that the "unreal" and "alarmist" news dominates the newspaper columns. It is not difficult to see how critics feel this to be the case.

When one examines the world press today, he gets the feeling that the jangled nerves of the world's populations can hardly be eased by the newspapers. On the contrary, anxieties are created, magnified, and perpetuated; religion is set against religion, social class against social class, and nationality against nationality. Instead of being conveyors of enlightenment, the national press systems tend too often to be "press agents" for individual countries or special groups, thus doing a good job of increasing irritations and suspicions among governments and giving distorted pictures of various nations.

Very few observant critics of the press would deny that news media--printed and electronic--are mainly instruments of propaganda seeking to create and destroy images. Certainly the world's communication channels have been all but choked in recent years by inflammatory and slanted messages concerning explosive situations in the emerging nations of Africa, in divided Berlin, in communist Cuba, in northern India, and in such American racial crises as the Ole Miss rioting. The reader, listener or viewer searching for truth and the "real story" is left oftentimes in bewilderment. He notes contradictions in the news, discrepancies among world news agencies, and opinion in news columns and network newscasts. He is indeed puzzled-- and frustrated.

All indications are that the world's consumers of news and views are in for a long siege of ideological messages. There have been few truces in international psychological warfare. As technology pushes mass messages into the more remote regions and saturates ever-growing populations, the world's psychosis is bound to spread. Truth in the messages is no assurance of enlightenment or psychological stabilization; recent history has shown clearly that even the most truthful statement can boomerang, or it can appear as something quite different when viewed from the perspective of a particular audience's traditional beliefs, desires, and expectations.

The mass media, either the quantitative or the qualitative, should not be looked upon as a panacea for the world's problems or as a quick end of the Cold War. The most powerful radio transmitters and the most enterprising and honest newspapers and magazines will not be able to substitute for international cooperation and progress on the diplomatic level. Mass communication is obviously no substitute for direct involvement of persons and their technologies in the world crisis; international action certainly speaks louder than mass-oriented words.

World-wide envy, resentment, suspicion, and hatred build emotional walls against the most objective and well-meaning printed word and erect mental jamming stations against the most honest broadcast. And when one considers that in every nation the government uses news as a weapon, with no real attempt at honesty and objectivity, the task of the mass media in the fight for peace and understanding appears dismally hopeless. As government management of the news (even in the U.S. and other libertarian nations) grows, the more dismal the future looks for world journalism.

However, regardless of this dismal picture, there is always hope. There are indications that the concept of "press freedom" in the Western sense is gaining slowly in certain parts of the world. There are still plenty of vigorous voices crying for freedom in deserts of red tape and insistent hands groping for truth in diplomatic darkness.

Increasing pressure is being exerted on totalitarian press systems by organizations such as the International Press Institute and the Inter-American Press Association. Varied national journalistic groups such as Sigma Delta Chi in the United States and the Royal Commission on the Press in the United Kingdom are fighting for unhampered news collection and dissemination.

More and more the importance of international communication to world understanding is being stressed. Journalists and journalism teachers are visiting and studying in other countries in greater numbers every year. At least through these regional and world press organizations and through the international exchange of ideas by traveling journalists, the world press is becoming ever more homogeneous. One can only hope the end product of this increasing homogeneity will be maximum freedom of information.

World Press at a Glance

It can be estimated from reliable information furnished by UNESCO that some 45,000 newspapers are being published throughout the world, having a total circulation of over 300 million. This would mean that about 95 copies per 1,000 persons in the world are printed every day. Of the dailies (about 8,000), two-thirds are morning papers and one-third are evening papers. The nondaily newspapers have a total circulation of perhaps 200 million.

The actual readership of newspapers, however, is difficult to estimate, since in many nations there is the practice of passing copies on to others for reading or of having them posted in public places. When one considers that in addition to the dailies (with which this book mainly deals) and the less-frequently-published newspapers, there is a magazine and assorted periodical press of gigantic proportions, he can readily see that the printed media of mass communications have the potential of great power and influence in creating, stabilizing, and changing world opinion. And if one takes into consideration the potent electronic media of radio and television that gird the globe and reach even the illiterates, the communications impact on international thought is magnified almost beyond conception.

✳ At least one-third of all newspapers are found in North America; another third are in Europe (including the U.S.S.R.), and the other third are scattered throughout the remainder of the world. Europe probably accounts for almost half of the world's total newspaper circulation, North America for a quarter, and the rest of the world for another quarter.

In many of the world's press systems all types of periodicals are being hampered by the high price of newsprint. Advertising and subscription rates are not increasing sufficiently to keep pace with rising costs in production. This is leading to (1) closing down of publications, (2) curtailment in size and quality of publications, (3) increased reliance on private and government subsidies, and (4) mergers and chain ownership of publications.

Countries with the highest newspaper readership rates are Britain, Norway, Denmark, Sweden, Japan, and the United States.

Britain's rate is slightly more than 600 copies of dailies published per 1,000 persons; the other five nations have rates which are somewhat behind that of Britain. The average circulation of dailies per 1,000 persons (for the world as a whole) is between 90 and 100.

About 40 nations and territories of the world are without daily newspapers. In most countries dailies are very small, having only four pages; only in some 25 nations can dailies be found with as many as 12 pages.

More than 25 per cent of the world's daily newspapers are English-language publications. Next to English the greatest numbers of dailies appear in Chinese, followed by German, then Spanish.

The press is growing especially rapidly in Africa, South America, and Asia. Not only are new publications springing up everywhere in these continents, but serious and well-edited journals are reaching new segments of the population. In large areas of these continents newspapers are commonly found today where as late as 1950 there was almost total illiteracy.

The European press is still expanding, but more slowly than in other parts of the world. The West German press has risen to a leading position in continental Europe since its new start after World War II. With the possible exception of the North American press, the European press is the most vigorous and most economically sound in the world. Europe probably has the freest (Sweden) and the most captive (Spain) press systems found anywhere in the world today.

The Asiatic press has grown greatly in recent years and from all indications is still growing. Most of the papers (outside Japan) are small and circulate to limited audiences. The problems presented by geography, economy, illiteracy, and a multiplicity of languages are hindering the press development throughout this vast continent.

In the strategic Middle East, even with increased government restrictions due to the region's international "crises," the newspapers are growing steadily. Most marked advances in the technical and quantitative aspects of the press are visible in the Arab states of North Africa where Arab nationalism and the emergence of several new nations have served as a spur to communications. Israel and Lebanon are also witnessing significant improvement in their press systems. The latter country probably has the freest and most "westernized" press in the Middle East.

The press of Turkey, a country which is often classed as part of the Middle East, is certainly a technically good one, and is improving in this respect all the time; morever, with the reduction of government pressures on the publications since the fall of the Menderes regime, the press is able to function in an atmosphere of increased freedom.

Daily newspapers of the world usually considered "international" newspapers because of their world-wide readership (though small), their stability, high standards, and consistent quality, follow: the London Times, Manchester Guardian, Le Monde, Neue Zürcher Zeitung, La Prensa, the New York Times, and the Christian Science Monitor. And of course, from the standpoint of "influence" or "prestige" others of a more specialized nature might be added to this list, including such leading dailies as Russia's Pravda and Izvestia, Red China's Jen Min Jih Pao (People's Daily), Italy's L'Unita, and Vatican City's L'Osservatore Romano.

In a second group of "quality" daily papers of general excellence or wide influence, one could expect to find the following: the Daily Telegraph (England), the Scotsman (Scotland), the New York Herald Tribune, the Washington Post, Frankfurter Allgemeine and Die Welt (West Germany), Il Corriere della Sera (Italy), Le Figaro (France), Berlingske Tidende (Denmark), Dagens Nyheter (Sweden), Nieuwe Rotterdamse Courant (Holland), Aftenposten (Norway), Le Journal de Geneve (Switzerland), Die Presse (Austria), the Times of India and the Hindu (India), Asahi (Japan), the Toronto Star and Globe and Mail (Canada), the Age (Australia), Excélsior (Mexico), El Tiempo (Colombia) and La Nación (Argentina).

Cities of the world which might be considered the chief press centers because of the number and quality of the newspapers printed there include: London, New York, Paris, Moscow, Amsterdam, Copenhagen, Stockholm, Brussels, Rome, Hamburg, Vienna, Zurich, Peiping, Tokyo, Cairo, Johannesburg, Toronto, Melbourne, Havana, Mexico City, Rio de Janeiro, Buenos Aires, and Bogotá.

The world's largest daily papers are found in Britain, Japan, and the Soviet Union, with Britain's Daily Mirror and Daily Express, Japan's Asahi and Mainichi, and the U.S.S.R.'s Pravda having the greatest circulations. Nations having at least one daily newspaper with a circulation of three million or more are Great Britain, Japan, and West Germany. (The United States has one daily with a circulation of as much as two million--The New York Daily News).

Following are the cities of the world which have the greatest number of daily newspapers: Tokyo, Buenos Aires, Beirut, Djakarta, Karachi, Lahore, Rio de Janeiro, São Paulo, Bombay, Istanbul, Mexico City, Havana, and Berlin (East and West combined) have 20 to 30 papers; Paris, Tel Aviv, Taipei, Hong Kong, London, New York, Moscow, Rome, Milan, Amsterdam, Vienna, Copenhagen, Stockholm, Lisbon, Rangoon, Singapore, Manila, Osaka, Calcutta, Cairo, Warsaw, Montevideo, and Santiago have 10 to 20 papers.

The largest-circulation dailies in some of the major nations are Daily Mirror (Britain); Bild-Zeitung (West Germany); Il Corriere della Sera (Italy); Asahi (Japan); Jen Min Jih Pao (Red China); Pravda (U.S.S.R.); Times of India (India); France-Soir (France); ABC (Spain); New York Daily News (U.S.A.); La Prensa (Argentina); Toronto Daily Star (Canada); Excélsior (Mexico); O Globo (Brazil); Le Soir (Belgium); Berlingske Tidende (Denmark); Het Vrije Volk (Holland); Aftenposten (Norway); Dagens Nyheter (Sweden); Rand Daily Mail (Union of South Africa), and Sun News Pictorial (Australia).

Among the most influential weekly newspapers in the world are the following: Die Zeit (West Germany); Manchester Guardian Weekly (Britain); Die Weltwoche (Switzerland); Ecclesia (Spain); La Patrie du Dimanche (Canada); Weekly Star (Canada); Dagbreek and Sunday Times (South Africa); and the Nation (Burma). Britain has the greatest number of large weekly newspapers of any nation in the world. There are four British weeklies (Sunday papers) which have circulations of two million or over. The News of the World, with about 7.5 million circulation every Sunday, is the largest of these Sunday papers and has the largest circulation of any paper in the world today. Having world-wide prestige among the British Sundays are The London Observer, and London's Sunday Times. Very similar to these two quality weeklies of Britain is the National Observer of the United States, a weekly begun in Washington, D.C. in early 1962.

The periodical press of the world is extremely varied in scope, quality, and general purpose. Magazines and journals range from the popular "illustrateds" of many nations (e.g., Stern of Hamburg, Germany) to the ultraserious journals of comment and news (e.g., Swiss Review of World Affairs of Zurich). There are also well-written quality "humor" or "satire" magazines of the New Yorker type such as Britain's Punch and Italy's Il Borghese and offbeat varieties such as the Soviet Union's Krokodil.

There are newsmagazines of the Time and Newsweek pattern such as West Germany's Der Spiegel, Mexico's Tiempo, Turkey's Akis, and Colombia's Semana, and newsmagazines of a more pictorial and colorful nature such as Oggi of Italy or Aktuell of Norway. Magazines of the Life or Look variety abound throughout the world, with the majority of leading nations having a journal like Paris-Match of France, O Cruzeiro of Brazil, Tempo of Italy, Illustrated London News (really a type unto itself) of Britain, or Eikones of Greece. There are the quality pictorials such as Mundo Hispánico of Spain, the "general-pictorials" with a political emphasis such as Hoy and Siempre of Mexico, the broadcasting journals like the Listener of Britain and Se Og Hør of Denmark.

Also published throughout the world in surprisingly large numbers are serious journals of intellectual discussion exemplified by Britain's Economist, New Statesman, and Spectator. And there are specialized "professional" journals of the Editor & Publisher (U.S.) variety such as World's Press News of Britain and Sovetskaya Pechat (Soviet Press) of the U.S.S.R. On through the periodical spectrum into the purely entertainment magazines, confessions, hobbies, comics, off-beat "art" journals and romance and adventure journals runs the international publication pattern. The world reader in most every country has a wide assortment of periodicals to choose from if he desires to supplement his newspaper reading.

Electronic Media: A Survey

Of the 130 independent nations of the world (republics, kingdoms, democracies, dictatorships, dominions), almost half of them-- approximately sixty countries--are broadcasting not only internally but also externally.

That is, these nations not only have a broadcasting system for the domestic audience but also deliberately beam programs to one or more foreign countries.

We tend to think of international broadcasting in terms of the two most famous exponents: the Voice of America of the United States and Radio Moscow Shortwave Services of the U.S.S.R. Of course, we remember from time to time the pioneering of the BBC of Britain in global radio with its Overseas Services. And more recently, Cold War pressures make us aware of the international broadcasting by Red China.

But we must not forget the various foreign broadcast schedules of CBC in Canada, of the Spanish-language programs Czechoslovakia beams to South America, of the many French-language programs France sends directly to Africa, and the twenty-four-hour-a-day propaganda aired in Arabic from Radio Cairo to listeners throughout the Middle East and North Africa. Yugoslavia utilizes Italian music to try to win friends in Italy with broadcasts from Belgrade. Spain broadcasts in both English to North America and Spanish to South America, trying to improve the image of the Franco dictatorship. Poland tries to soften the harsh fact of its Communist regime by airing German-language cultural programs to West Germany.

In addition to governmental foreign broadcasting, there are external commercial radio services too. Europe's political enclaves, especially, epitomize this type of programming. Britain has commercial television (ITA networks) to rival its BBC-TV, but no commercial radio. Therefore, English-language commercial programs are beamed into the United Kingdom from Radio Monaco, Radio Luxembourg, Radio Andorra, and similar principality transmitting sites.

Nongovernmental private radio stations also parallel our Voice of America in Cold War broadcasting. Radio Free Europe's transmitters beam to the Communist satellites of Eastern Europe. RFE laughs at the Communists, reveals truths they try to hide in Hungary, Bulgaria, Rumania, Poland, and Czechoslovakia. Even daily serialized dramas--soap operas, in American slang--are utilized. Similarly, Radio Free Asia confronts Red China.

GOVERNMENTAL INTERNATIONAL BROADCASTING. Late in 1961, the Voice of America increased its broadcasting time to improve its position in the competitive field of international propaganda.[6] But in 1962 the Soviet Union still led in the number of hours of air time--1100 hours per week. Communist China ranked second with 700 hours per week; the United States was third with 650 hours; and Britain, fourth, broadcasted 600 hours per week to court world opinion.

Each year the world's total of radio receivers rises 50,000 to 100,000 sets, a tempting target. With the advent of cheap, portable transistor sets, the world now has almost 450 million radios in daily use.

With more than half of the adults in the world not able to read well enough to decipher a newspaper headline--some of them are arbitrarily classified as "literate" because they can read and write their own name--the importance of radio communication becomes self evident.

DIFFERENT SYSTEMS. The system of broadcasting enjoyed by the United States--privately-owned commercial radio and television stations--has been copied by the Latin American republics.

The British system, the famed public trust called the BBC, has been adapted with modifications by France, Italy, and several other European and Commonwealth nations.

The governmental broadcasting system run directly by the regime in power and symbolized by the Soviet Union and Communist China, has been copied with modifications by many African and Asian nations.

Canada, with its private stations and its BBC-like Canadian Broadcasting Corporation, combines the British and American systems.

American influence can be evidenced with the coming of regional, commercial privately-owned networks to Britain, existing alongside the BBC-TV. Conversely, British influence can be found in the spread of educational or cultural noncommercial television stations in the United States.

Like Britain, Australia has set up a public broadcasting trust. The Australian Broadcasting Commission is a public authority from which radio and television networks stem, but neither BBC nor ABC are government-operated systems like that of the Soviet Union. Ultimate ownership of the BBC and the ABC are the British and Australian people, but the operations are handled by semiautonomous nonpartisan agencies, instead of the government in power. No cabinet member intervenes in programming as in the Communist world or in non-Red authoritarian nations such as Spain, Portugal, or South Africa.

For an insight into British, Canadian, and Australian broadcasting concepts of the public-trust agency, study should be made of Burton Paulu's two volumes on the subject.[8]

Even though from time to time France has claimed that its RTF (Radio Télévision Française) resembles the BBC, it differs in one big respect. The BBC is removed from political parties and regimes in office, while the RTF is tied to the Minister of Information, a cabinet member of the government in power.[9]

Another variation on broadcasting systems is that of the Dutch. In Holland, listeners' societies own stations on a cooperative basis. There is a labor union broadcasting society, and both Catholic and Protestant societies. Radio listening and television viewing in Holland measure lower than they do in other European countries, but book and magazine reading and theater attendance rates are among the world's highest.[10]

LANGUAGES WHICH DIVIDE. A country with several languages cannot use radio to integrate and inform as readily as a monolingual nation can. Of course, Switzerland has no trouble broadcasting in German, French, and Italian. Nor does Belgium, broadcasting in Flemish and Walloon to its German and French-speaking citizens.[11]

But in an underdeveloped, overpopulated nation such as India, the problem of languages becomes acute. Switzerland and Belgium are highly literate, industrialized, and contend with only two or three languages. But the 480 million people of India are mostly illiterate, poor, and recognize sixteen different official languages, not counting minor dialects by the dozens.

All Indian Radio (known as AIR) is a state-owned, governmentally-operated system, AIR being a separate cabinet ministry of its own, distinct from other communications, postal service, or transportation agencies.

AIR broadcasts in each of the sixteen official languages, but tends to emphasize English, Hindi, and a few other of the largest linguistic groups. Though only two million Indian homes have radios, there are more than 90,000 community listening posts. Group listening brings broadcasts, especially at news time, to millions of Indians who do not have their own radio receivers.[12]

Considering just Asia, India seems meagerly endowed in terms of radio and television when compared with modern, industrial Japan, literally bristling with antennas. But relatively, India seems well off when compared to Laos, where rudimentary communications often range from erratic to nonexistent. Every major city in India has a radio transmitter; the same cannot be said for Laos. Every major urban center in India has community listening facilities. In Laos these centers do not exist.

INFORMATION, ENTERTAINMENT. Radio around the world has more music than news, but it has sufficiently large segments of air time devoted to informational programs, including news bulletins. Television utilizes more air time for entertainment than for information, though in the United States the amount of news programmed steadily increases.

Eurovision, which links together twelve or more European nations for special telecasts, has great potential for expanding into global video, as Telstar and similar satellite aids may permit in the future.

On June 2, 1953, television stations in France, Holland, Belgium, and West Germany hooked up to the BBC-TV to present simultaneously the telecast of the coronation of Queen Elizabeth II at Westminster Abbey. After this successful hookup, Eurovision presented a view of Paris from the Eiffel Tower, a tour of the Louvre, an address by the Pope in Vatican City, the 1956 Winter Olympics, the 1960 Summer Olympics from Rome, and similar special events.[13] Finally, on July 10, 1962, Telstar began to link North America and Europe with televised spot news.

For the world as a whole, radio is truly global but television still is received principally in the urban centers. However, Japanese and U.S. portable TV receivers--small, lightweight, transistorized--are already on the market. Once their price goes down as it did for radio receivers, TV will globalize too. Needed in the near future will be a corresponding rise in the quantity of news and informational-type programs in television.

Despite jamming, censorship, and inadequate reporting, radio news echoes within nations and across borders. If freedom of information--press and radio--existed in a majority of the world's nations, then broadcasting indeed would be a genuine hope for spreading information and news instantly everywhere.

But the number of free-radio nations are in the minority. And because of this, a crowded, semiliterate, impoverished world will continue partially informed, partially propagandized.

Broadcasting can jump mountains, can diminish the isolation of villages without roads, can penetrate the minds of those who cannot read. But just as with the press, the transmitting medium must be free of governmental and private restraints for reporters and editors to fully accomplish their professional mission, to inform.

Even in its less-than-good state, world broadcasting does reach millions of people who otherwise would have no link with the mainstream of the world. And with group listening multiplying manyfold the millions reached by individual receivers inside homes, broadcasting deserves the close attention of correspondents and editors, both from the fields of radio-television and from newspaper-magazines, news agencies, and from all those seriously concerned with the basic significance of mass media in our time.

Current Press Theories

The world today is a giant arena in which large and small press systems are actively engaged in a strange kind of game. It is obvious to the onlooker that the participants are not certain just what it is they are supposed to be doing. Some are fighting among themselves; others are parading placidly about, oblivious to the rather frenzied activity about them. Some appear to be rushing madly about, shouting and kicking at their less active neighbors. Others stand in neat rows awaiting an order which will send them marching as one toward a certain goal, and some-- their rows sagging rather wearily--seem to be ready to give up independent action and join the ranks of a bigger neighbor.

What is guiding these activities? How do the participants--press systems and units thereof--know what it is they are trying to do? In the main, they all have rather specific sets of directions, but these directions vary considerably. However, it may be said that all of these participants--regardless of their peculiarities--have guiding concepts which are tied rather tightly to the traditional types of governments they represent. These concepts or theories--in many cases unwritten--serve to give some type of reason for the participants being in the arena.

Probably as many press concepts or theories exist in the world today as there are publishers and editors; certainly an observer can see many, and often quite significant, variations in basic newspaper and magazine types from country to country and in many cases among sections of one country. However when he looks down on the giant arena--to continue the metaphor--he will notice that out of the wide and intricate press design a few ideological patterns take form and stand out. Four such principal patterns have been isolated and have been fully discussed in a highly interesting and scholarly book by three journalism professors.[14] Called "theories," these ideological patterns formed among the world's press systems, are classified as (1) the authoritarian theory, (2) the communistic theory, (3) the libertarian theory, and (4) the social responsibility theory.

The first two of these theories are really quite similar, and it is difficult to differentiate many of the basic characteristics; for example, both are primarily totalitarian in their insistence on control and careful regimentation of the press. The press systems of Hitler's Germany in the 1940's and of Franco's Spain in the 1950's are good examples of the authoritarian theory in practice; in a totalitarian sense they differ little from today's prime example of a communistic press system--that of the Soviet Union.

The other two theories--the libertarian and the social responsibility--overlap also in many respects. In fact, most nations which accept the libertarian theory today consider responsibility of the press to the public a part of this theory. Of course, the idea of social responsibility brings up many philosophical questions which cannot be taken up here; but since in any country the organization of society--its social and political structure--determines to a large extent what responsibilities the press (and the citizen) owes this society, one must conclude that every country's press quite naturally considers itself as being socially responsible.

If it is realized that these four theories have evolved over many years and are still evolving, and they overlap in many respects when applied, then as a method of systematizing a discussion of press concepts this four-way classification is quite helpful. Very briefly, here are a few important aspects of the four theories:

AUTHORITARIAN THEORY. Under the authoritarian theory which made its appearance in a clear form in sixteenth century England, the press was to support the government in every respect and advance the programs of the national leadership. A press system which serves in the main capacity of a governmental propaganda agency under a "strong man" type of government might be called an authoritarian press system. The theory revolves around the idea that a person engaged in journalism is so engaged as a special privilege granted by the National Leader. It follows that this journalist is under an obligation to the Leader and his government. This press philosophy has formed, and now forms, the basis for many press systems of the world, and may be observed currently in Spain and Portugal, several Latin American countries, and in weaker versions elsewhere. Having had the longest tradition, the authoritarian press--although functioning as a private enterprise within the individual country--owes its existence to the state and must operate to support and perpetuate the authority of that state which permits it to survive. The press, in such an authoritarian country, has just as much freedom as the national leadership wants it to have.

COMMUNIST THEORY. Karl Marx might be called the father of the communistic press theory which took its roots during the first quarter of the present century. In a communist society, according to Marx, the functions of the press should come from the central function--the perpetuation and expansion of the socialist system. Means of communication should exist to transmit social policy and not to aid in searching for truth. Media of communication under this theory are simply instruments of the government; as such they are integral parts of the state. The press must be owned and used by the state and directed by the Communist party or its agencies. Within the communist press system, however, self-criticism (i.e., criticism of failure to live up to communist planning) by the press is permitted; in fact, it is encouraged. The communist theory is based on the premise that the masses are too fickle and too ignorant and unconcerned with government to be entrusted with details of its operation. Such ideas as "man's inherent rationality," "minority rights," and the "fundamental right of every citizen to know government business" are considered unrealistic and simply "bourgeois concepts" by those adhering to the communist press philosophy.

This communist theory is much like the authoritarian one previously discussed; the one big difference in the two in practice is that while the communist press is owned and operated by the state, the authoritarian press is privately owned. Another difference is that control by government in the communist system is constant and uncompromising, whereas government control in an authoritarian system can change considerably with the particular leader in power.

LIBERTARIAN THEORY. The concept of the "libertarian" press can be traced back to the seventeenth century where it took roots in England and on the "new" continent of America. The philosophy of the time which viewed man as a rational being having inherent natural rights gave rise to the libertarian press theory. Man, according to this new rationalistic philosophy, had the right to pursue truth, and would-be interferers with this right should be restrained. Exponents of this libertarian press movement during the eighteenth century--characterized by John Milton and John Locke--insisted that governments keep hands off printed material. Individual liberties were emphasized by these philosophers, and these liberties have manifested themselves in the American Declaration of Independence and the constitutional guarantees of free speech, free press, and free religious pursuits.

Under the libertarian theory, the press functions to uncover and present the truth, and it cannot so function if it is controlled by some authority outside itself. The free press in theory will produce reportorial truth because it is regulated by all members of a free society who express their wishes in a free market where they can support or refuse to support certain newspapers or magazines. Rather than this being a freedom especially for the press, it is really a right of the people to be informed, or to choose by whom they desire to be informed; this freedom belongs to the people rather than to the editors and publishers. However, since the press must serve as the informational link between government and people, the freedom automatically extends itself to the press. If this informational link is broken by governmental censorship or secrecy-- or by other means such as "doctored news" released by a government press agent--the concept of freedom of information is largely invalidated.

Today the libertarian press measures its social utility by how well the public is kept abreast of government activities. Theoretically at least, the libertarian press is a "fourth estate," supplementing the executive, judiciary, and legislative branches of government. This, according to the theory, is the one principal way the libertarian press accepts its social responsibility.

SOCIAL RESPONSIBILITY THEORY. A midtwentieth century concept, the "social responsibility" theory of the press as it is recognized in the Western World had its roots in the libertarian press system. It goes beyond the libertarian theory, however, in that it places a great many moral and ethical restrictions on the press. Instead of emphasizing "freedom," it stresses "responsibility." The theory has been drawn largely from a report published in 1947 by a private group which studied the American press; further elaboration on the theory was made in another book published the same year by a member of the Commission on Freedom of the Press, as the group called itself.[15] According to this commission (often called the "Hutchins Commission" after its chairman, Robert M. Hutchins), the mass media, because of their pervasive impact in all areas, have gone beyond such "libertarian" concepts as "the search for truth," and the "press's right to access to information." The new theory, as expressed by the commission, maintains that the importance of the press in modern society makes it absolutely necessary that an obligation of social responsibility be imposed on the communication media.

According to the Hutchins Commission, press freedom is limited by a social responsibility to report facts accurately and in a meaningful context. Such thinking, of course, leads to the advocation of a regulatory system to watch the actions of the press and to keep it functioning properly; the Commission on Freedom of the Press did not overlook this, and in its report suggested that some type of government regulation might be needed to assure that the press accepted its responsibility. It was even suggested that the government go into the communications business to properly inform the citizens if the private media did not accept their obligations to the public. The social responsibility theory implies a recognition by the media that they must perform a public service to warrant their existence. The main parts of the Commission's report which seemed to have antagonized many American editors and publishers were those that intimated government interference in the press system. Journalists generally advocate social responsibility by the press, but they see the government's role of enforcement as a definite trend toward socialism and a danger to the free press.

Government and the Press

Freedom of expression is the continuation and practical manifestation of freedom of thought and is, therefore, one of the most fundamental human rights. Consequently, the principle of such freedom is set forth more or less explicitly in every social covenant, regardless of the political system it establishes.[16] Such covenants--whether in the form of written constitutions or, as in the United Kingdom, derived from custom--acknowledge the fundamental nature of this right and assert the right of freedom of expression and, more specifically, freedom of the press.

Nevertheless, throughout the world--regardless of what press theory a country might accept--the right to publish and to read the truth is either denied or under constant attack. Limitations imposed on such rights are often undisguised, but they can be quite subtle. The complex nature of gathering, publishing, and disseminating news is such that the press is brought constantly into contact with the government. In addition, because of the pervasive role of the government in determining the affairs and destinies of men, the press is increasingly dependent on government for a major portion of its most significant news.

Wherever in the world the courageous newspaper exists, serving its reader as the guardian of his interests and the protector of his rights, exposing abuses of power and criticizing failures and wrong decisions, it is a thorn in the side of government--or could be. It is an ever-present source of concern for government officials; it is a power that must be kept under control if the government is touchy about criticism or adverse news presentation. All this makes press-government relations difficult, and the only place where harmony seems the rule is in the Communist or Fascist nations where frictions are not long tolerated.

In the "libertarian press" nations, government pressures[17] are usually a gradual application of legal,[18] political and economic restraints with the lid of secrecy opening and closing from time to time. In the "authoritarian press" countries, the government pressures are more direct, less subtle, and press freedom varies (if at all) with the individual "strong man" leader. In the Communist nations, of course, the press-government relationship is most stable, for both parties know what to expect of the other. After all, "both parties" are in reality the "same party." Government pressure in Communist press systems amounts to constant and pervasive editorial, economic, and policy direction.

CONSTITUTIONAL GUARANTEES. While some constitutions guarantee freedom of expression, others mention only the freedom of the press, which, of course, is the oldest of the great media of news dissemination. Generally speaking, freedom of expression is not guaranteed so fully (for technological reasons) to radio and television media as it is to the press.

The principle of freedom of expression, as proclaimed by Milton's "Speech for the Liberty of Unlicensed Printing," was first included as part of a social contract in Article 11 of the French Declaration of the Rights of Man in 1789 and two years later in the First Amendment of the Constitution of the United States.[19] Today, it is included, in only slightly varying form, in the constitutions of nations with widely differing political and press systems.

Despite these patent differences, it is none the less necessary to take these constitutional guarantees and their declared permissives as the starting point of any study of government-press relationships. A doctrine officially recognized as the basic premise of a system, even if it remains theoretical, serves as an ideal to which all men may aspire regardless of the resultant political and press systems. It represents an acknowledgment, a "bending of the knee," by that system to the human right that it professes to grant.

The preamble of the Constitution of the Fifth French Republic (1958) "solemnly proclaims its attachment to the Rights of Man... Declaration of 1789, reaffirmed and complemented by the Constitution of 1946." The preamble of the French Constitution of 1946 declared that "the unrestrained communication of thoughts or opinions being one of the precious rights of men, every citizen may speak, write and publish freely."

The First Amendment to the Constitution of the United States adopted in 1791, declares that Congress "shall make no law...abridging the freedom of speech, or of the press."

Article 125 of the Constitution of the

U.S.S.R. says, "...the citizens of the U.S.S.R. are guaranteed by law (a) freedom of speech, and (b) freedom of the press. These civil rights are ensured by placing at the disposal of the working people and their organizations printing presses, stocks of paper...communications facilities and other material requisites for the exercise of these rights."

Article 12 of the Spanish Charter of July 13, 1948 states that "all Spaniards may freely express their ideas."

The constitutions of more than eighty other countries contain similar guarantees, and while the United Kingdom has no written constitution, the principles of freedom of expression and of the press are fundamental to most of the systems prevailing in the British Commonwealth. The principle of freedom of expression, which in the United Kingdom was first proclaimed by Milton, is the very keystone of its constitutional system of unwritten law.

The traditional definition of the British attitude has been succinctly put by Lord Kenyon: "A man may publish anything which 12 of his countrymen (a jury) think is not blamable, but he ought to be punished if he publishes that which is blamable." (Rex vs. Cuthill). The statement emphasizes the responsibility of the press and the penalties that may be incurred by abuses of its freedom.

Obviously it would be unrealistic to assume simply because of the similarity of all these declared (de jure) principles and common law (de facto) practices that the newspapers of these countries operate under like conditions. What are some of the reasons for these differences and why have the presses of many countries lost freedoms once enjoyed--freedoms envisioned by their countries' constitution framers?

a. Many constitutions contain no sanctions or provisions for enforcement.
b. The inferior position of the judiciary in its relations with the executive and legislative branches has made it difficult to bring violations to the bar of justice.
c. Lack of a tradition of freedom and responsibility has resulted in excesses by the press.
d. Need for defense against certain forms of propaganda inspired by foreign sources has led to an extension of the concept of public order and safety beyond that foreseen by the framers of the constitution.
e. Constant pressures are brought by strong executives.

Government pressures on the press of the world can be placed in the following categories:

(A) legal pressures
(B) economic and political pressures
(C) secrecy
(D) direct: censorship and force

LEGAL PRESSURES

These consist of:

1. constitutional provisions
2. security laws
3. press laws
4. penal laws[20]

1 CONSTITUTIONAL PROVISIONS. While almost every national constitution traditionally provides for press freedom, in many cases the same constitutions place certain restrictions on this freedom. In almost identical words the Soviet Union, the People's Republic of China and the various communist people's republics of Eastern Europe guarantee the freedom of the press. But in every case the constitutional guarantee or its economic adjunct limits the guarantee and the means (communications facilities, printing equipment, paper, and other materials) to the "working people." Since the Communist party in each of these countries is the self-appointed spokesman for the working people, the effect has been to limit the proclaimed freedoms to itself.

As we have seen, Article 12 of the Spanish Charter of July 13, 1945, one of the fundamental documents of the Spanish Constitution, declares that "all Spaniards may freely express their ideas." Appended to this statement, however, is an additional passage that says that this right can be maintained only as long as these ideas "do not advocate the overthrow of the fundamental principles of government." Article 33 of the Charter states additionally, "the exercise of the rights that are recognized in this Charter may not prejudice the spiritual, national and social unity of the community."

Article 35 of the Spanish Charter further stipulates that the principles embodied in Article 12 "may be temporarily suspended in part or in whole by the government by means of a decree which must define the scope and duration of this measure." Article 36 of the Charter warns, "any violation of any of the rights proclaimed in this Charter will be punished by laws which will determine, in each case, the actions that may be taken in its defense before the competent jurisdictions."

Almost as clearly defined is the situation in Portugal. Under Section (IV) of Article 8, the Constitution of the Portuguese Republic lists as one of the rights that Portuguese citizens enjoy: "The free expression of thought in any form...." But Paragraph 2, attached thereto, says: "Special laws shall govern the exercise of the freedom of expression of opinion, education, meeting and of association. As regards the first item (expression of opinion), they shall prevent, by precautionary or restrictive measures, the perversion of public opinion in its function as a social force." Paragraph 3 of the same says, "imprisonment without formal charge is permitted in cases of flagrante delicto and in cases...committed...against the safety of the state...." Articles 22 and 23 further limit the rights and define the duties of the press with respect to the state.

In Greece, the birthplace of democracy, Article 14 of the 1911 Constitution as revised by the Fourth Revisionary Assembly and readopted on January 1, 1952 says: "Any person may publish his opinion orally, in writing or in print with due adherence to the laws of the state. The press is free. Censorship and every other preventive measure is prohibited. The seizure of newspapers, either before or after publication, is likewise prohibited.

"By exception, seizure after publication is permitted (a) because of insult to the Christian religion or indecent publications manifestly offending public decency, in the cases provided by law, (b) because of insult to the person of the King, the successor to the Throne, their wives or their offspring, (c) if the contents of the publication according to the terms of the law be of such a nature as to (1) disclose movements of the armed forces of military significance or fortifications of the country, (2) be manifestly rebellious or directed against the territorial integrity of the nation or constitute an instigation to commit a crime of high treason."

Similarly, the Constitution of Ireland by way of exception says, "the publication or utterance of blasphemous, seditious or indecent matter...shall be punishable according to law." The Belgian constitution reserves the "power to suppress offenses committed in the use of (this) liberty." The constitution of Norway prohibits publication in contempt

of religion, morality, or the constitutional power, or false or defamatory accusations against any other person. While the constitutions of Germany, Mexico, Cuba, Nicaragua, Venezuela, and India explicitly forbid the publication of libel, obscenity or other material harmful to public morality, other constitutions make provision for such restrictions through a phrase as, "except as provided by law."

In the Constitution of Brazil, adopted 1946, Article 141 (Paragraph 5) sets limits to the freedom of publication in the following terms: "Freedom of thought is guaranteed and is not subject to censorship except as to shows and public spectacles;...publication shall not depend on permission of the authorities. However, propaganda (1) of war, (2) of violent methods to overthrow public order, and (3) of prejudice of race or class, shall not be tolerated."

Article 2 of the Nicaraguan law of July 31, 1948, places the following limits on the freedoms set forth in Article 1: "There shall be no censorship of such a nature as to restrict the diffusion of thought, unless it be intended to safeguard morals or decency, or to prevent the incitement to war or violent attacks on public order, whether political or social. In such cases the censorship shall be established by a decree signed by the President of the Republic at a meeting of the Cabinet. This decree must specify the form to be taken by the censorship and the means of diffusion to which it is to be temporarily applied."

The Indian Constitution acknowledges that there cannot be any such thing as absolute and uncontrolled liberty and makes provisions authorizing the state to restrict the exercise of the freedom guaranteed under Clause 1, Article 19, within the limits specified. Thus, Clause 2, Article 19, as subsequently amended under the First Amendment to the Constitution, enables the Legislature to impose reasonable restrictions on the exercise of freedom of speech and expression in the interests of the security of the state, friendly relations with foreign states, public order or decency or morality or in relation to contempt of court, defamation or incitement to an offense.

Press restrictions found in the laws of all countries, regardless of their press systems, fall into the following categories:

a. protection of individuals against libel and slander
b. protection of society against dissemination

of obscenity

c. protection of the state against internal disorder

d. protection of the state against external agression

2 SECURITY LAWS. No country allows the press total freedom in the publication of information. Even the publication of truth is not always in society's interest. The publication of news which might endanger national security is everywhere prohibited.[21] Infringement of such prohibition may constitute the crime of treason or espionage, or that of divulging the secrets of national defense, secrets involving relationships with other states, or other official secrets.

All states punish treason, espionage, and violations of state security. Such offenses are of many different kinds including: betrayal to a foreign power of personnel, military installations, war matériel and strategic or technical information pertaining thereto; disclosure of information concerning the government's espionage and counterespionage apparatus and/or activities; and the communication of documents, plans or other information relating to the national defense or to the safety or order of the country.

Such offenses may occur in times of peace or war. In the latter case the penalties are more severe; the list of prohibited information is longer, but the nature of the offense remains the same. Some of these crimes or violations are such as can be committed by the press, either knowingly or unknowingly. Such security laws are used in all parts of the world as a legal method of press control and are widely accepted as both necessary and right.

It can be argued, however, that even in genuine offenses, publication lessens rather than increases the danger present, for publication reveals internal security weaknesses of which the government may not have been aware, and the worst danger for a state is when it is unaware that its secrets have been revealed to a foreign power. If this has been done through the press, the government is alerted to the danger and can take steps to counter the damage and to check security weaknesses thus revealed.

Many states, therefore, while severely punishing treason, espionage, or violations of security, by whatever other means committed, often regard disclosures through the press as a somewhat different form of offense. Press violations which may be unintentional, but are none the less harmful, are often adjudged less severely than in the more usual instances of such offenses. But this is not always the case, and frequently when a regime has reason to fear the press such offenses, "violations of state security," are used as an excuse to destroy the freedom of the press to publish.

3 PRESS LAWS. These deal specifically with the rights and restrictions of the press. Most of the press laws throughout the world are more restrictive than protective, as exemplified by those in such countries as Turkey, India, and many of the Middle Eastern and Latin American countries. However, some actually stress the press' rights and make them explicit, as is the case in Sweden. Typical of the stricter press laws are the "desacato" laws of Latin America which prevent the press from being "disrespectful" to government officials.[22] The United States, Belgium, Switzerland, and Britain have no press laws.

4 PENAL LAWS. These are usually just and require the press to accept responsibility for its published material, but they do not require censorship. These laws can be restrictive, however, when such phrases as "incitement to disorder" are too strictly interpreted or when provisions dealing with defamation are too harsh, or when the stamp of "immoral publication" is applied too widely and often. Moreover, in some nations inaccurate news can be the basis of immediate press punishment.

Freedom of the press exists in varying degrees in most countries, but in all these the journalist who abuses it and goes beyond certain limits commits an offense under civil and/or criminal law. No country allows the press total freedom with respect to information. Prohibition to publish is found to a greater or lesser degree in the press and/or penal laws of every country.

In most countries the law forbids malicious slander or libel; that is, statements-- whether true or false--maliciously intended to damage the honor or reputation of private individuals. The Mexican Press Law, Article 9, goes quite far in this matter; it prohibits the publication of information dealing with adultery, indecent behavior, rape, attacks on private life, divorce, paternity or maternity, or annulment of marriage. As is also the case in many states of the United States, Mexican law does not allow the publication of the names of the victims in cases of rape or indecent behavior. Many jurisdictions make it illegal to report offenses committed by juveniles.

In Japan both civil and criminal codes prohibit both libel and obscenity and provide penalties therefor. By the Juvenile Law of 1948, Article 61, Japan prohibits publication of any material identifying juvenile delinquents, and, by Article 148 (Paragraph 2) of the Election Law, Japan forbids the publication of news designed to influence an election. Article 148 (Paragraph 3) of the same law prohibits the publication of the results of election polls.[23]

In nearly all countries it is forbidden to publish information likely to impede the course of justice. In some countries it is forbidden to publish evidence until it is heard in open court, but in every country where the press is free it is permitted to publish the actual proceedings. Among the severe restrictions found in most countries is publication of news or comment likely to bring a court of law into contempt. In some countries the press may not criticize any legal decision before, during, or after the hearing.

To ensure that the press shall inform the public truthfully, certain countries recognize two kinds of offense: the publication of false news and the publication of biased news. The United Arab Republic, Luxembourg, Sweden, Uruguay, Brazil, Chile, Colombia, and Mexico, all have laws prohibiting the publication of false news.

Still other publication that is more or less widely held as culpable is subversive propaganda and incitement to revolt; defense of anarchy, crime, and felony; propaganda against a race or faith; propaganda against the public credit and advocating the refusal to pay taxes; propaganda in favor of foreign countries and propaganda in favor of class warfare, incitement to mutiny and incitement to other crimes punishable by law.

Another form of propaganda, of quite a different sort, that is punishable in a large number of countries is incitement to abortion. Some countries go beyond this and forbid birth-control propaganda. Article 34 of the Japanese Pharmaceutical Affairs Law (1951) says, "the statements or diagrams which suggest abortion...shall not be used in connection with drugs devices or cosmetics." In France a law of July 21, 1920 punishes any person, "who...to propagate the practice of birth control, shall publicly describe or divulge, or offer to disclose, any process calculated to prevent pregnancy...." The terms of this law are so broad that it has been humorously suggested that should the

press advise young persons to enter certain religious orders it would become liable to its penalties.

ECONOMIC AND POLITICAL PRESSURES

One of the less apparent means of abridging the freedom of the press is through economic controls and pressures.[24] Governments have exerted these economic pressures by offering bribes and subsidies to newspapers and journalists, by granting pro-government publications special favors and privileges, by placing official advertising in "friendly" papers and withholding it from antigovernment papers, by selectively distributing newsprint, by restricting newspaper distribution in the case of antigovernment papers, and by giving grants of various kinds to selected newspapermen. One or more of these techniques are common in most parts of the world, and are especially prominent in Southeast Asia, Latin America, and the Middle East.

Regulation of the press enterprise and the material resources usually presents either of two aspects. It may tend toward or result in giving full force to the concept of free information--either by giving free play to the economic system which is considered necessary, or by helping to remove the obstacles to free information that system might create and founding or assisting the special organizations needed for the proper exploitation of material resources. Or, such regulation may be motivated by the wish of the political authorities to restrict the right of expression and to make the press a channel of control by political leaders.

In either case the regulation of the enterprise and the material resources necessary for the publication and dissemination of information profoundly affects the freedom of such enterprises in the conduct of their activities.

Because of the high costs of production and distribution the governments of many countries with economies based on private enterprise make available to the press both direct and indirect subsidies. In the United States and most other countries newspapers and periodicals enjoy lower postal rates. In Italy and several other countries of Europe, journalists are granted reduced railway fares, and publications occasionally receive subsidies and reductions in taxes. Grants are also made to news agencies. In other countries publications often receive preferred exchange treatment, government subsidized newsprint imports, advertising subsidies, etc.

Obviously all these measures of economic assistance can be used as instruments to exert pressure on the press. The exercise of such pressures is common in many countries of the world and is especially prominent in Southeast Asia, Latin America and the Middle East.

While it is true that paper is the material most essential to printing, it has been only during periods of extreme economic disruption (war and early postwar periods) that shortages of newsprint have posed serious problems for the paper industry. Today (1963), there is a plentiful supply of newsprint, although the cost has risen about 200 per cent since the outbreak of World War II. With the price of newsprint at about $135.00 a ton, import licensing, exchange and newsprint allocation, and other forms of governmental intervention have been found necessary in a few countries that are chronic sufferers of exchange shortages.

But there are countries with authoritarian regimes,[25] e.g., Spain, Portugal, the United Arab Republic, Cuba, and Indonesia, or with authoritarian tendencies that use such economic intervention as an instrument of control. In Spain the government has used its powers of price regulation and allocation of newsprint in controlling the press. It can also regulate the circulation of papers and their number of pages. It has regularly used these methods in favoring the Falangist press, which also enjoys fiscal and postal privileges.

Portugal also uses restrictive or discriminatory measures such as subsidies to government papers and the inequitable distribution of newsprint. The decree of May 14, 1936 limits the number of pages of newspapers, yet exceptions can be granted by the authorities and these obviously tend to favor government organs since these papers can claim a special allowance of pages for space occupied by official texts.

Authoritarian regimes in Latin America also have found economic regulations useful in controlling the press. In Argentina the Perón regime used a wide range of such powers, and in Colombia the dictator, Rojas Pinilla, chose these quieter and more subtle methods of muzzling the press, notably through the control of newsprint. By decree of August 23, 1955, all orders for the importation of newsprint had to have the approval of the Empresa Nacional de Publicaciones which issued licenses. If these were granted, the orders could be made at the official exchange rate of 2.50 pesos per dollar with a stamp tax of 3

per cent. Without the license the tax automatically rose to 30 per cent and the exchange rose to 4 pesos to the dollar. This peculiarly capricious system, abolished by the liberal regime of Lleras Camargo, was consciously designed not only to control opinion but also to prejudice the circulation of independent newspapers in favor of the Diario Official.

In Bolivia, the government's actual control of newspapers is chiefly exercised through its control of newsprint which is used as a sword of Damocles over the heads of editors who might be tempted to criticize the government or its officials. The government office for the control of the news is copied from the similar institution created by Perón. Bolivia's state controlled trade unions (COB) have also been used against nonconformist newspapers, and it is often from this quarter that demands for suppressions and closures originate.

As has been seen in the discussion of the legal position of the press in communist countries, the economic adjunct of the constitutional guarantee limits the means of production (plant, equipment, paper, and other materials to the Communist party or its auxiliaries. These provisions represent the economic implementation of the principles laid down by Lenin when he wrote:

"True freedom (of the press) will be found only in that future system...in which any worker (or group of workers) will be able to possess and exercise the right, enjoyed equally by all, of using the public printing works and the public paper...."

A Soviet law of 1932 that interprets and implements the economic corollary of the constitutional guarantee states that printing offices of any kind, including those using duplicating machines as well as those dealing in printing equipment, may be maintained only by government agencies, cooperatives, and public organizations. Moreover, even government agencies must obtain special permits to acquire printing equipment or to use printing offices and are held strictly accountable for supplies of paper, inks, type metal, and other necessities.

The distribution of newspapers to the appropriate sections of society is also regulated. Only 10 per cent of a newspaper's edition is sold in the street. The rest is distributed according to a detailed plan. Each republic and region of the country receives a fixed quota of papers appearing in Moscow. Local distribution is arranged so that Party and Komsomol officials are first to receive newspapers, and administrative and economic units are next. It is almost impossible for a private person to subscribe to one of the chief newspapers. A Soviet citizen cannot simply buy or subscribe to the paper of his choice; he receives the paper that is specified for him according to the plan.

In Communist China and the communist states of Eastern Europe the governments have taken firm control of the press, and a major part of this control is exercised by economic means. In each country the regime or the Party has taken ownership of the principal and best printing plants. And even in those nominally independent printing plants all the materials needed for printing--paper, inks, metals--are owned by the state and may be obtained only by allocation, much in the Soviet pattern.

Certain principles that have characterized the economic evolution peculiar to Yugoslavia since 1948 also apply to the press. Each newspaper is operated by its employees, but it is owned by what Yugoslavs call "society." They insist that "ownership by society" is not the same as ownership by the state. The system of self-administration applied to the press by the law of June 26, 1956, has had the effect of freeing the Yugoslav press from the financial control of the state which originally, as in every communist society, provided the necessary funds and equipment for the press' enterprises. The result has been a greater degree of independence with considerably broader possibilities of expression than in other communist countries.

SECRECY

"The people's right to know," says James Russell Wiggins,[26] distinguished editor of the Washington Post and Times-Herald, "really is a composite of several rights. It has at least five broad discernible components: (1) the right to get information; (2) the right to print without prior restraint; (3) the right to print without fear of reprisal; (4) the right of access to facilities and material essential to communication; and (5) the right to distribute information without interference by government acting under law or by citizens acting in defiance of the law.

"Of these rights, the first in order of its exercise, and perhaps the first in order of its importance, is the right to get information.

"Secret arrest, secret trial, and secret punishment are the three prerogatives of arbitrary government that most menace the rights of individual citizens.

"The right of citizens to know about the conduct of their own government, to see for themselves the public records of the executive departments, certainly seems implicit in all theories of democracy and self-government upon which (such a) system rests.

"The people will not obtain information if those to whom they look to supply it live under the threat of reprisal for innocent publication, or if the penalties for wrongful publication are such as to make the risks of publishing unbearable.

"Freedom of the press exists in theory in a society where citizens have a right to get information, and a right to print it without prior restraint or unwarranted punishment subsequent to publication.

"The right which thus exists in theory will not exist in fact, however, if to these constitutional rights is not added the practical right of access to the instruments of publication. Secrecy about government may still prevail, and silence about nongovernmental affairs may be enforced, if citizens cannot obtain the use of the facilities of publication.

"Private persons must be able to buy presses (or the use of them), paper (or the use of it), radio and television stations (or the use of them), and public halls and meeting places (or the use of them), without the interposition of governmental power if the ideal enjoyment of the liberty of utterance is to be afforded. The law must permit them to do it, and the economic means of doing it must not be such that the right is limited to and reserved for a privileged few in society.

"Of that whole process by which an idea is conveyed from the mind of an author to the mind of the auditor, the act of distribution is the culminating step.

"If it cannot be accomplished, the whole process fails. A government that has allowed citizens to get information, to print it without prior restraint, and to publish without fear of intimidation, and to have access to the means of publishing, can still maintain such secrets as it chooses to keep, and it can still keep the people in ignorance of the daily life about them that lies beyond the reach of their own immediate and personal observation.

"If the delivery of the printed work can be

stopped, the whole process that has gone before becomes just an enormous waste of energy, ending in the accumulation of so much spoiled paper.

"A government that intends this sort of interference in the machinery of mass communication, or proposes to allow its citizens to effect such intervention, might just as well play the tyrant from the beginning, except of course that there always is the hope that bad intentions may be circumvented."

GENERALIZATIONS

1 Governments are getting ever more cautious around newsmen and increasingly wary of the press.

2 Increasing numbers of governments are regarding press expression of antigovernment opinions as an "unpatriotic" act.

3 Legal measures and laws aimed at papers thought to be harmful to national "prestige" or "interests" are becoming more common.

4 There is a growing tendency to protect government officials from press criticism.

5 Through press directors, secretaries and other such representatives, and through planned press conferences, governments are increasingly controlling the government news which reaches the press and the people.

Of the various forms of secrecy limiting the people's right to know, interference with the right to get information ("first in order of its importance") is the most subtle and at the same time the most erosive. This type of indirect pressure, taking the form of hindering press access to government sources and records, is quite common throughout the world press systems. Governments attempt this in varying degrees everywhere. It has been, and is today, a special irritant to the "libertarian" press which tries to inform the citizens of government activities. The United States and other libertarian press nations in recent years have seen increasing government evasiveness and over-classification of documents and papers. "Press conferences" scheduled and directed by the government are becoming ever more popular; government may use these to channel such news as it desires to the readers. This tends to place government

in the position of news determiner and relieves the press of most of its initiative and independence in the investigation of government affairs. This situation is often attributable to the press' own inertia; for example, Marquis W. Childs (American columnist) has said that although government "constantly threatens to circumscribe and curtail the right of the people to know" and "secrecy becomes an end in itself," this freedom is "threatened not so much from without as from within."[27] He adds: "The corrosive blight of conformity has spread where nonconformity was once the measure of courageous performance."

DIRECT CENSORSHIP AND FORCE[28]

This is common in the Communist and other dictatorial nations. There are various forms of this type of forceful pressure such as official censorship, warnings and instructions to publishers and editors, obligation of the press--as in Spain--to publish government "handouts," use of harassment and violence in dealing with the press--as exemplified by politically inspired mob actions, strikes and demands for direct intervention of Cuban and Bolivian trade unions and Perón's tactics in dealing with hostile Argentine newspapers like La Prensa.

PROFESSIONAL SECRECY AND THE JOURNALIST[29]

Intimately related to the principle of freedom of the press but not nearly so widely recognized in law is the right of journalists to professional secrecy. Freedom-of-press guarantees in democratic libertarian societies are recognition that the basic function of the press in such a society is to present that information necessary for the democratic process to operate efficiently. To obtain that information, the press, as we have seen, must have access to the facts and then be free to publish them without interference or harassment.

In providing information for the people and acting in their behalf, the press seeks information about the administration of the government and about all other matters related to the public welfare. Limits still exist even in free countries, relative to access to some such information. Also, as might be expected, when inefficiency, corruption, or selfish interests are involved in the conduct of public or private affairs, or where intolerances exist, the investigative and reporting function of the press frequently encounters obstacles. Information is often difficult to obtain even though the public welfare may be seriously involved.

Because of the obstacles that may be met in the obtaining of legitimate information, a responsible press may be forced to get information outside normal channels. This information may be of such a nature and involve such powerful interests, e.g., crime organizations, movements of racial or religious intolerance, or organized economic groups, that the sources of the information--for their own protection--may want to remain anonymous. This wish arises from the fact that an individual providing information that these interests prefer to have withheld might well become the target for retaliation taking any imaginable form up to and including murder.

An essential part of the news-gathering process is the ability of the reporter to obtain information from every source likely to provide him with information. Usually the information can be attributed to the source and the reporter identifies the source, particularly if credibility depends on the source of the information. But occasionally, as we have noted, there are circumstances under which an informant may not want to be identified. Under these conditions the information is given "in confidence," or "not to be attributed," or "off the record."

The ethics of journalism, written or oral, are such that a journalist receiving such "confidential information" will respect that confidence. The relationship in such situations is called "professional secrecy."

While many states recognize "the right of professional secrecy" as it pertains to the clergy, physicians, and lawyers, no Latin American nation nor any country under a British system of law and only a few European states and the Philippines have extended this right to journalists. Nevertheless, all journalists who pretend to adhere to a code of ethics claim such a right, and in some few additional countries courts have shown consideration for such claims before requiring disclosure of information.

But neither courts nor jurists are agreed in terms of society's interest as to whether it is more important that such potential channels of information be kept open through the legal assurance of anonymity or that such evidence which might thereby be unavailable to litigants before the courts not be foreclosed. Dean John Henry Wigmore, jurist and professor of law and recognized authority on evidence (who disapproved of the Maryland law granting such a right for journalists), contended that four fundamental conditions are necessary to justify "the establishment of a privilege against disclosure of communications between persons standing in a given relation." These he listed:[30]

1. The communication must originate in confidence that it will not be disclosed.
2. The element of confidence must be essential to the full and satisfactory maintenance of the relation between the parties.
3. The relation must be one which in the opinion of the community ought to be sedulously fostered.
4. The injury that would injure the relation by the disclosure of the communication must be greater than the benefit thereby gained for the correct disposal of litigation.

Most professional journalists, including some trained in law, contend that an analysis of these "four tests" suggests that they do, in fact (although this was not Dean Wigmore's view), justify the extension of such a right to journalists.[31]

International News Flow

The flow of international news in the modern world is not only highly important to the international press picture; it is actually the starting point, the basic requisite, of a communications system geared to better understanding among races, nationalities, and cultures. Regardless of high transmission costs, elaborate equipment, the necessity of large staffs, and the constant governmental barriers thrown up at national borders, the world consensus among journalists today seem to be that the news flow is satisfactory--at least in a quantitative sense.

The main links in the world news system are the international and national news agencies which supply the bulk of the foreign news to newspapers (and many magazines) of all countries. The big providers of world news are the five world agencies which have their communications network spread around the globe--the Associated Press and the United Press International (U.S.); Reuters (Britain); Agence France-Presse (France); and TASS (Soviet Union). Most of the larger nations of the world can also make use of their own national news agencies, many of which are doing excellent jobs of intranational collection and distribution of information.

Most of the news transmitted throughout the world is what is generally referred to as "headline news," "straight news," or "spot news" and there has long been a realization among world journalists that too little "interpretive" or "explanatory" writing finds its way into the international communications stream. Most news agencies are trying to remedy this situation, and increasingly the "why" of the news is being emphasized by international reporters as they try to put their communiques into a meaningful context for the reader.

There are three main foreign news sources used by the press of the world. They are news agencies; special news services, syndicates, and "stringers;" and staff correspondents of newspapers. The news agencies account for more than three-fourths of the news transmitted internationally. Only the larger and more progressive of the world's newspapers can maintain full-time correspondents abroad, but scores of journals have special assignment correspondents or roaming reporters throughout the world or have writers on a "stringer" basis in various countries. Many newspapers also share correspondents with other publications.

```
        SOME PRINCIPAL NATIONAL*
          NEWS AGENCIES TODAY

Argentina        Agencia Noticiosa
                 Saporiti, f.1900.

Australia:       Australian Associated
                 Press, f.1935; Australian
                 United Press, f.1932.

Belgium:         Agence Belga, f.1920.

Canada:          Canadian Press, f.1917.

China (Red):     Hsin Hua (New China)
                 News Service, f.1944.

China (Formosa): Central News
                 Agency, f.1924.

Denmark:         Ritzau Agency, f.1866.

Germany (East):  Allgemeiner Deutscher
                 Nachrichtendienst, f.1946.

Germany (West):  Deutsche Presse-
                 Agentur, f.1949.

Greece:          Agence d'Athenes, f.1905.

India:           Press Trust of India,
                 f. 1905.

Italy:           Agenzia Nazionale Stampa
                 Associata, f.1945.

Japan:           Kyodo, f.1945; Jiji Press,
                 f.1945.

South Africa:    South African Press
                 Association, f.1938.

Spain:           Agencia Mencheta, f.1882;
                 Agencia Efe, f.1938.

    *The big international agencies
     are not listed here, although
     they serve also as "national"
     agencies.
```

The bulk of the world news flow is made up of political, military, and foreign relations items, as might be expected. "Human interest" news follows in fourth place. In the 1953 study called The Flow of the News,[32] the International Press Institute found that readers desire certain changes in foreign news coverage. They feel, for example, that (1) there should be more pictures, (2) there should be better physical presentation of foreign news in newspapers, (3) the news should be more accurate, (4) the news should be more simply and understandably written, and (5) the "human side" of foreign news should be given more emphasis. Other students and critics of the international flow of news have pointed out that too great a proportion of foreign news originates in five major nations--the U.S., the United Kingdom, France, Germany, and the Soviet Union. Most journalists feel that international news could be improved, but few are more critical than Lester Markel, Sunday editor of the New York Times, who said in 1958 that "the information that passes among nations is not good. We do not have a very accurate picture of other nations, nor they of us...."[33]

Making possible the great glut of international press messages are three main communications systems--submarine cables, telegraph and telephone lines, and radio (including radio-telephone, point-to-point radio, and omni-directional radio). In addition, of course, many feature stories and background articles are sent through the mails.[34]

There are certain cities throughout the world, which because of their location, size or political importance, are especially prominent as collecting centers and transmission points for world news. These cities are London, Paris, Zurich, Madrid, Rome, Copenhagen, Stockholm, Berlin, Bonn, Brussels, Amsterdam, Tokyo, Calcutta, Bombay, New Delhi, Peiping, Hong Kong, Moscow, Cairo, Ankara, Sidney, Brisbane, Montreal, Toronto, Havana, Buenos Aires, Rio de Janeiro, Caracas, Mexico City, Honolulu, Manila, San Francisco, New York, and Washington, D. C.

All of the big news agencies have bureaus in these cities, or in a few cases, special correspondents who cover them regularly. In addition, most of the larger newspapers of the world keep their own men in these strategic centers.

In conclusion, it would seem safe to say that quantitatively the news flow is adequate, although unbalanced and spotty from time to time, and the big job facing the world press is the improvement of the quality of news as it moves in increasing bulk from country to country.

World News Agencies

The modern, systematic gathering of international news has developed and grown along
with communication facilities. From courier-
carried newsletters sent by persons and groups
across national boundaries, special messenger
services and the slow transmittal of news by
horseman and coach, international news gathering and disseminating has made slow but
tremendous advances. In the early 1800's
light signals and the use of carrier pigeons
made their advent, but it was the telegraph's
appearance on the communications scene a
little before mid-century that did most to
clear the way for a speedier and freer flow
of news among nations and to precipitate the
growth of the news-gathering organizations.
By the late 1860's, continents had been linked
by undersea cables, and land and submarine
telegraph communication had caught the interest
of governments and business enterprises; and,
of course, newspapers were fascinated by this
chance to send their news by this new and
speedy telegraphic method. Great Britain
early took the lead in international communication, and even in the first part of the
present century her cable interests exceeded
those of all the rest of the world combined.

With the advent of the telegraph in the mid-
1800's, the modern news agencies came into
existence. The Havas agency of France appeared first, and by 1840 the organization
had joined its continental service to Britain
by carrier pigeons, and after the coming of
the telegraph expanded its services rapidly.

A Havas employee, Israel J. Beer (later
known in Britain as Paul Julius Reuter), left
the agency and in 1848 began his own service,
first in Aix-la-Chapelle and soon afterward
in Brussels. In 1851 he moved his headquarters
across the English Channel to London, where
after a slow beginning he secured the respect
and cooperation of the British press. By the
end of the nineteenth century, Reuter's
agency (as it was then called) was the world's
most important.

Another Havas worker who deserted the
French agency (in 1848) to set up his own
was Bernard Wolff. He returned to his native
Germany, and by 1860 his agency was regularly
sending commercial news and political dispatches to German business firms and newspapers. The Wolff agency (Wolffische Tele-
graphen-Büro--WTB) thereby took its place
among the early news-gathering organizations
of the world.

In 1870 the big agencies (Havas, Wolff, and
Reuters), after a period of heated competition, entered into an agreement by which each
was to have "news rights" in certain areas of
the world and must share with the others its
daily news file.[35] These areas were actually
"news preserves" in which each of the agencies
(the U.S.'s Associated Press soon became a
part of the plan) had a collecting and distributing monopoly.

The "news preserves" of the alliance
(generally known as the "European Agency
Alliance" or the "International News Cartel")
were as follows: Wolff would operate in
Germany, Scandinavia, Austria, Hungary, the
German colonies, and in parts of the Balkans
and Switzerland; Havas would cover France and
the French colonies, Spain-Portugal, Italy,
Belgium, Rumania, Serbia, Turkey, and most of
Latin America; Reuters had the biggest slice
of the world--the Middle and Far East, most
of Africa and part of the Balkans, the East
Indies, and part of South America; and The
Associated Press (of the U.S.) got North and
Central America as its special area.

This alliance broke up in the 1930's because
of pressure from many sources and because it
was directly challenged by the American
United Press, which early in the post-war
period was expanding its world news service
into such "cartel" areas as Latin America
and Japan. Actually the alliance began to
dissolve in 1924 when Mussolini took the
Italian agency (Stefani) from French control;
the cartel further crumbled a few years later
when Hitler's government bought the Wolff
agency and turned it into a propaganda instrument. The final blow was given to the
alliance in 1934 when the Associated Press
declared complete independence of the news
cartel; this opened a new era in world news
gathering in which all agencies became independent and free to operate anywhere.

The agencies Wolff and Havas kept their
names until World War II. Wolff's agency
became Hitler's Deutsches Nachrichten-Büro,
and France's postwar agency emerged under
the name of Agence France-Presse.

In the twentieth century, with the help of complex networks of telegraph, telephone, radio, radiotelephone, and radio-telegraph facilities, the news-gathering organizations have become tremendously powerful on the international scene. A "world news agency" is an organization, comprehensive in scope, which offers extensive world news coverage and large-scale distribution to subscribers in many nations. A strictly "national" agency on the other hand is mainly local in scope, offering news coverage and distribution to the press of the country in which it is based, or serving as a disseminating agency for news coming from a world agency. At present there are five major world news agencies; they represent four major nations of the world, two being based in the U.S. and one each in Britain, France and the Soviet Union. These five agencies will be dealt with in more detail in the following section. Since they handle the great bulk of international news that appears in the newspapers of the world, they have a power and responsibility unsurpassed in the modern world of communications.

World News-Gathering Development

Five news-gathering and transmitting organizations with headquarters in four different nations can be classified as "world news agencies." A world news agency is one which has a network of correspondents to gather news in a large number of countries and a headquarters staff to edit this news and transmit it to (1) the agency's bureaus abroad for local distribution, (2) national news services with which it has an agreement, and (3) subscribing printed and electronic media abroad. These agencies make extensive use of telecommunications in receiving and transmitting their messages. All having originated in nations where the press was highly developed, these agencies came into being between 1835 and 1918. One, the United Press International, was created in 1958 with the merging of the United Press and the International News Service. Together these five agencies serve at least 150 nations and territories which have more than nine-tenths of the world's total population.

REUTERS. This agency was founded by Paul Julius Reuter in 1851 in London. The agency was a family concern until 1916 when it was formed as a private company with Sir Roderick Jones serving as managing director until 1941. It then became a cooperative agency owned by the British press (with the Australian and New Zealand dailies also owning stock). Reuters became a trust in 1941 and since has been governed by 11 trustees, eight of whom represent the press of the United Kingdom.

Reuters is a nonprofit agency, with operating costs derived from subscribing media. Its service is received in almost every country. Its largest offices are in New York, Paris, Rome, Buenos Aires, Cairo, Frankfurt, Stockholm, and Geneva. The agency has a world-wide staff of 500 full-time and some 4,000 special correspondents. It relies heavily on the American AP for its news of the U.S. which it distributes abroad; in return it furnishes AP with its domestic news file. Reuters is known for its reliable, alert reporting; its writing is not as colorful and lively as is some of its competitors', but it has a quality of seriousness and conciseness that has long made it a leader in its field. All of the

Reuter service is transmitted in English.

TASS. Telegrafnoie Agenstvo Sovetskavo Soiuza (TASS) was founded in 1918 under the name of ROSTA; it took its present name in 1925. This agency, like Agence France-Presse and the two U.S. agencies, acts as a national agency as well as a world news agency. TASS is state-controlled and is the sole organization for collecting and transmitting news within the Soviet Union. As a government agency, TASS is dependent on the Council of Ministers of the Soviet Union for its economic and editorial direction. Its headquarters are in Moscow, and its sprawling network of thousands of full-time and part-time correspondents stretches throughout the Soviet Union. It maintains bureaus or correspondents in all the major countries of the world. TASS has arrangements, sometimes informal, to exchange domestic news with several other world agencies.

TASS is the main source of news for national agencies in nations politically associated with the Soviet Union, such as Hsin Hua (New China News Agency) and national agencies in the Eastern European satellite nations. TASS also provides news to agencies outside the Soviet bloc, such as Pars (Iran), Kyodo (Japan), and Bakhtar (Afghanistan). For news collection, TASS uses mainly ordinary commercial telecommunication channels, and for news distribution it relies heavily on voice radio. As the official Soviet news agency, TASS is widely quoted in the world press.

ASSOCIATED PRESS. The oldest of the American agencies, AP was founded in 1848 and was called the New York Associated Press. The New York AP went out of business in 1892 and a new AP--founded in the Middle West and incorporated in Illinois--took over and became the present Associated Press. In 1900 it reorganized and incorporated in New York, where its headquarters have been ever since.

Today the AP, a cooperative agency owned by its newspaper members, has some 7,200 members and clients and provides news to subscribers in some 80 nations (it has more subscribers in Germany, Japan and Italy than in any others). AP news from Latin America, Canada and Europe is sent through its New York office and news from the Pacific is channeled through its San Francisco bureau. AP has about 50 bureaus in foreign countries and has exchange agreements with agencies of nine countries. The bulk of AP's news traffic is routed by radio or cable from London, the world's greatest communications hub.

AGENCE FRANCE-PRESSE. This French agency was

28

founded in 1835 by Charles Havas as Agence Havas with headquarters in Paris. In 1840 it used carrier pigeons to speed up transmission of news. By 1860 the agency had subscribers in most parts of Europe, and had drawn up contracts with Reuters and the German agency Wolff for cooperative news exchange. In that year the agency began using transoceanic and international cables. In 1875 Havas signed a news-exchange agreement with the New York Associated Press, its first contract outside Europe. In 1879 the agency became a joint stock company; by 1939 it had made agreements with about 30 other agencies throughout the world and had weathered a serious financial crisis.

Faced by Nazi agression in 1940 the French government bought the agency's information branch and set up a propaganda office at Vichy. When the Germans came in they took over the agency and turned it into a part of the official Nazi news agency, Deutsches Nachrichten-Büro.

After France was liberated at the end of World War II, several interim war agencies were merged to form the Agence France-Presse, which was set up in the old Havas headquarters and took over most of the prewar agency's employees.

In 1944 AFP was forced to ask for financial aid from the government--with subsequent government slanting of news--because the struggling Paris dailies could not finance its operating costs. Thus, until 1957, Agence France-Presse was the only major wire service of the free world to be largely government-supported. In January, 1957, AFP got an autonomous board of directors, controlled by editors of French newspapers. To compensate for lost state subsidies (50 per cent of the agency's budget in 1956), France's nearly 150 dailies had their AFP service charges boosted about 30 per cent.

Agence France-Presse currently has a staff of some 2,000 and about 2,500 clients in almost 50 countries. Transmission is principally by wire, but radio is being used increasingly. The agency has 15 bureaus in France and some 60 abroad. It has radio-teleprinter links with North and South America, the Middle and Far East, and South Africa. Nearly half of AFP's daily transmission is world news. It has exchange agreements with agencies in some 30 nations, including agreements with the international agencies AP, Reuters, and TASS.

UNITED PRESS INTERNATIONAL. In May, 1958, the United Press International (UPI) was formed in the United States when the United Press Association (f.1907) and the International News Service (f.1909) were consolidated. This merger reduced the number of major world news-gathering agencies to five, and put the new UPI on the same international footing with the U.S.'s Associated Press and Britain's Reuters. UPI is a commercial profit-making agency.

When the UPI was created in 1958, Frank H. Bartholomew, president of the United Press, became president and general manager of the new global agency, and Kingsbury Smith (who was president of INS) was named vice president. Bartholomew listed "economics" as one of the chief reasons for the UP-INS merger. Shortly after the formation of UPI, he said:

"Economics was an important factor in the creation of the great new news network. Costs of covering the world's news fronts have risen steadily with rapidly improving means of transmitting both news and pictures by leased wire and electronic processes."

Most of UP's personnel were retained by the UPI; however, the majority of INS's approximately 500 editorial employees were out of a job after the merger. UPI now has about 7,500 clients, a number slightly above that of the Associated Press; the agency operates in 85 countries.

The UP was formed in 1907 by E. W. Scripps to assure anyone who desired to begin publishing a newspaper that he could obtain "an adequate national and international news service." This privately-owned corporation grew into a highly-respected world agency, and shortly before the merger in 1958 it was furnishing news, features and pictures to some 5,000 clients. The UP was especially strong in Latin America and the Far East. Noted for its lively featurized writing, the UP exerted great influence on the other news agencies. A few UP innovations were (1) transmitting feature stories by leased wire, (2) the use of by-lines, and (3) supplying news to radio (1935).

INS was established in 1909 by William Randolph Hearst. It entered the international field about 1930 and greatly expanded its foreign service by 1958. Although often in the red financially, INS was a vigorous agency boasting some of the world's great reporters (e.g., H. R. Knickerbocker, George R. Holmes, Frank Coniff, Richard Tregaskis, James Kilgallen, Inez Robb, and Bob Considine). By the time of the merger, it was servicing some 3,000 clients throughout the world.

Foreign Papers: Early Pioneers

In this brief section the attempt is made to present simply and concisely a chronological picture of the development of foreign newspapers up to the present century. No attempt at completeness has been made; only the publications which might be called "pioneers" of special note have been included. It would certainly be wrong to consider all these publications (especially the earlier ones) as "newspapers." They served many purposes: relaying government information to the people, publicizing commercial and legal transactions, presenting royal proclamations and bulletins, giving an outlet to literary offerings, acting as a forum or sounding board for varying viewpoints in science and politics. In fact, up until the nineteenth century very few of these journals emphasized nongovernmental news as we think of it today.

The following news sheets (in the sixteenth and seventeenth centuries called newsletters, Zeittungen, mercuries, courriers, journaux, avisos, gacetas, hojas volantes, nouvelles, gazzettas, and relaciones) and early newspapers are presented to give the reader a quick survey as to when and where the foreign press developed.

FOREIGN NEWSPAPER FORERUNNERS. Acta diurna ("Daily Acts," begun 60 B.C.)--posted in the Roman Forum and sent to major cities in Rome's Empire; earliest known ancestor to the newspaper.

Tching-pao (or "News of the Capital," ca. 500 A.D.--1935)--mainly a government or court bulletin of offical news; published in Peking. At first handwritten; later printed from carved wooden blocks, irregularly published during the early period (in T'ang dynasty).

Ti Chau ("Peking Gazette," ca. eighth or ninth century A.D.)--first printed news sheet of which there is a record.

Notizie Scritte (Venice, 1566)--official news sheets at first posted in public places where they could be read by those paying a small coin called a "gazzetta"--a term later applied to a newspaper itself; this accounts for the great number of "Gazettes" and "Gacetas" published early in printing history.

Extraordinari-Zeitungen (Germany, 1568-1604)-- news sheets similar to Notizie Scritte of Italy; irregularly published.

Mercurius Gallo-Belgicus (Cologne, Germany, 1588?-1594?)--irregularly-published news sheet.

Relación...(Lima, Peru, 1594)--irregularly published.

Historische Relatio (Augsburg, Germany, 1597)--irregularly published.

Nieuwe Tijdingden (Antwerp, Belgium, ca. 1605-29)--irregularly-published news sheet typical of many such sheets in Europe at the end of the sixteenth and the beginning of the seventeenth centuries; another was Mercurius Britannicus (1625) in England.

EARLY FOREIGN "NEWSPAPERS". Avisa Relation oder Zeitung (Strasburg, Germany, 1609)-- weekly; first printed and regularly-published news sheet on record; a single sheet dealing with only one item.

Frankfurter Journal (Frankfurt, Germany, 1615; suspended, 1902)--weekly; first real newspaper in the world. Founded and published by Egenolph Emmel who was the first person to conceive of a newspaper presenting several items presented in a "news-book" form.

Frankfurter Oberpostamtszeitung (1615 or 1616); as the Frankfurter Postzeitung, this paper lasted until 1866; it was an ancestor of the famed pre-World War II Frankfurter Zeitung.

Weekly Newes (1622-41)--first regularly-published newspaper in England.

Magdeburgische Zeitung (Magdeburg, Germany, 1626)--ceased publication only in 1955; was one of Germany's (and the world's) oldest newspapers.

Gazette de France (Paris, 1631)--France's first newspaper; at first a weekly, then semiweekly; founded by Theophraste Renaudot, a physician.

Gazeta (Barcelona, 1641)--weekly; usually considered Spain's first newspaper.

Ordinarie Post-Tidende (Stockholm, 1643)-- first real newspaper in Sweden.

Gazette Burlesque (Paris, 1650-65)--French "popular" paper; first of the world's "yellow" journals; played up scandals, crime, gossip, etc.

Courant (Haarlem, 1656)--Holland's first newspaper.

Leipziger Zeitung (Leipzig, Germany, 1660)-- first a weekly, then daily; generally considered the first daily journal in the world. However, it was mainly a polemic organ and gave almost no space to news.

Oxford Gazette (1665)--first English newspaper (semiweekly) in a real sense; first to use term "newspaper"; became London Gazette in 1666 under which name it still publishes twice weekly as a government journal.

Le Journal des Scavans (Amsterdam,1665)-- usually considered the first magazine in the world; founded by Dexis de Sallo; dealt mainly with scientific and literary subjects.

Den Danske Mercurius (Copenhagen, Denmark, 1666)--first Danish newspaper.

Gazeta de México...(Mexico City, 1679)-- Mexico's first newspaper.

Worcester Postman (1690)--weekly; first British provincial paper.

The Daily Courant (London, 1702)--first English daily; small sheet printed only on one side, founded by Elizabeth Mallet. Printed "news" instead of "views" and government announcements.

Viedomosti (Moscow, 1702)--first newspaper in Russia; ordered published by Peter the Great to report Russia's war with Sweden.

Wiener Zeitung (Vienna, 1703)--the world's oldest newspaper still publishing; except during the Nazi occupation of Austria, it has been published continuously since its founding.

The Review (London, 1704)--weekly then tri- weekly; published by Daniel Defoe, first English journalist of national renown; fore- runner to the Tatler (founded 1709 by Daniel Steele), and Spectator (begun 1711 by Steele and Joseph Addison). The Review was founded the same year as the first newspaper in Britain's American colonies--Boston News- Letter.

Der Hamburgische Correspondent (Hamburg, Germany, 1714)--noted as the paper having the world's first foreign correspondent (a French refugee living in London).

Diario di Roma (1714)--leading Italian newspaper for over a century.

Petersburgskija Viedomosti (1728)--one of

the earliest Russian general newspapers; published in St. Petersburg by the Academy of Sciences.

Gaceta de Guatemala (1729)--first Guate- malan newspaper.

Berlingske Tidende (1749)--one of Denmark's earliest newspapers; today it is generally considered one of the leading journals in Scandinavia and is noted as the world's oldest "family" paper.

Halifax Gazette (1751)--one of the first Canadian newspapers; the first one of pro- minence.

Christiana Intelligentssedler (Bergen, 1763)--first Norwegian newspaper. Also known as Norske Intelligenz Seddeler.

Journal de Paris (1777-1819)--first daily newspaper in France.

Neue Zürcher Zeitung (1780)--founded in Zurich, Switzerland; still publishing, and is considered one of the most courageous and dependable dailies in the world; an inter- national "quality" paper.

The Times (London, 1785)--at first called the Daily Universal Register; from its earliest days one of the world's "quality" papers; always vigorous and enterprising, yet dignified. Usually The Times is placed among the top two or three papers of the world today in general excellence.

La Gaceta de Santa Fé (1785)--Colombia's first newspaper.

Diario de Barcelona (1792)--began "political" journalism in Spain; considered one of the all-time "greats" of Spain.

Indian World (Calcutta, 1794)--first news- paper in India.

Allgemeine Zeitung (Augsburg, 1798; later moved to Munich)--was a distinguished political organ and for decades one of the foremost news- papers of Germany and all Europe.

Gazette (Sydney, ca. 1800)--Australia's first newspaper.

El Telégrafo Mercantil (Buenos Aires, 1801)--first Argentine newspaper.

La Gaceta de Caracas (1808)--Venezuela's first newspaper.

Manchester Guardian (1821)--since its

beginning has been one of the top British "quality" (liberal) papers; one of the most-often quoted newspapers in the world today. In 1962 it dropped the "Manchester" from its name, and is now called simply the Guardian.

The Sunday Times (London, 1822)--one of the oldest British "Sunday" newspapers; still publishing.

News of the World (London, 1843)--one of Britain's older "Sunday" papers; a sensational, gossipy standard-format paper; now has the world's largest circulation (more than 7 million).

La Presse (Paris, 1850)--first French paper aimed at the masses; general news of a serious nature in addition to a heavy offering of feature material.

Le Figaro (Paris, 1854; daily, 1866)--well-known French "popular" paper; still publishing; influenced the mass-circulation press of Britain and elsewhere; has been called the modern "journal de scandale," although in recent years it has become a complete paper (probably the most thorough news coverage in France) and is gaining wide prestige at home and abroad.

Daily Telegraph (London, 1855)--first London penny paper; cooperated with New York Herald in sending Henry M. Stanley to Africa in search of Dr. David Livingstone. Extremely popular mass-appeal paper in its early days; today one of the three more serious British dailies.

Frankfurter Zeitung (Frankfurt, Germany, 1856)--first called Frankfurter Handelszeitung. For many years recognized as one of world's highest quality and most courageous dailies; mainly a paper for the intelligentsia, with strong emphasis on politics

and economics. Even in 1933 it was known as a "resistance" (anti-Nazi) paper, but was allowed to publish until 1945 because of its international prestige. Many of its old staff members now work for the Frankfurter Allgemeine (probably the best modern German daily newspaper) and attempt to continue in the tradition of the old "Frankfurter" as it was generally called.

Le Temps (Paris, 1861)--solid, highly respected throughout the world; after World War II its name was changed to Le Monde, which is today the principal "quality" paper of France and one of the top "prestige" papers of the world.

La Prensa (Buenos Aires, 1869)--with La Nación (1870) of the same city, is one of Argentina's all-time great papers, considered a "quality" paper throughout the world; today is still published by members of its founding family.

Mainichi Shimbun (Tokyo, 1871)--first of the big Japanese dailies; still thriving, with one of the world's largest daily circulations.

Corriere della Sera (Milan, Italy, 1876)--one of Italy's earliest important dailies. Today is the country's largest newspaper and by far its most enterprising. It has a tradition of short hours, high wages, and great respect for newsmen. The paper today has a news staff of about 150, nearly 20 foreign correspondents ("special envoys") and some 650-700 stringers in countries throughout the world.

Daily Mail (London, 1896)--founded as a sensational daily at a popular price by Alfred Harmsworth; its very first edition was one of 395,000 copies; today one of Britain's leading popular dailies--paradoxically, probably its most serious.

Part II

The
Specific Press Situations

Europe: Overview

There is a shift in the European press today away from the older "opinion" press and a trend toward one which, like that of the United States, is "information-oriented." However it might still be said that the press in Europe is an "opinion" press with an overlay of "information." Overall, the press of this continent is not as political as before World War II, with only about 20 per cent of the papers controlled by or affiliated with specific parties. Before the war more than 60 per cent of the papers fell into this category. Another trend in many of the European countries is toward larger and more thorough provincial papers; this is partly due to mergers brought about by high costs of publication (which continue upward).

The amount of foreign news used in newspapers throughout Europe is growing, and the typography and makeup of European publications--newspapers in particular--have shown great improvement in recent years. Magazines, newspapers and other periodicals thrive in all parts of the continent. Britain, Norway, Denmark, Belgium, and Switzerland have kept their readership rates high (all over 300 copies daily per 1,000 citizens). The West German press has grown amazingly in the last few years and today is one of the healthiest on the continent. European newspapers enjoy considerable freedom, with notable exceptions being found in Spain and Portugal, and, of course, in the communist nations of Eastern Europe behind the Iron Curtain (not dealt with in this section).

Of all European nations, Britain has the largest newspapers, both weekly and daily; France, West Germany, and Italy follow Britain in the number of large papers published. Britain's largest daily is the Daily Mirror (circ. about 4.5 million) and its largest weekly is the Sunday News of the World with a circulation of more than six million. The country has at least eight other dailies with circulations of more than a million. The largest daily in France is the afternoon France-Soir with a circulation exceeding a million. In France there are about a dozen dailies with circulations in excess of 200,000 (four of these have circulations of more than 400,000). West Germany's illustrated tabloid daily Bild-Zeitung (circ. about 3 million) is the nation's largest and leads all other continental European dailies; this specialized daily is followed by some 25 other dailies with circulations of more than 100,000. Italy's largest daily is Il Corriere della Sera of Milan (circ. about 500,000), followed by about 20 dailies with circulations exceeding 100,000.

In other European countries circulations may not be as high, but newspapers are well-read and popular and the press in general is thriving.

Austria

This nation of some seven million inhabitants and a literacy rate of between 95-99 per cent has about 35 daily newspapers circulating approximately 1.5 million copies. In addition, and occupying an important place in the press, are about 115 weeklies.[1] Two characteristics have marked the Austrian press since World War II: the growing number of journals owned by political parties, and the increasing importance of the provincial press. Most of the papers today are owned by two political parties--the People's party and the Socialist party. There are very few truly independent newspapers in the country today.[2] As one observer noted recently: "Practically all of them (the newspapers) are either owned or influenced in more subtle ways by a political party, or parties; one is beholden to both the major parties and to the Communists, and if its harried editor lives long enough he may well achieve fame as the most nimble journalistic acrobat in history."[3]

In Austria, not only is freedom of the press (limited only as provided by liberal law) guaranteed, but the right of professional secrecy in its reference to journalists is more clearly established in Austria than in any other country in the world. The right of professional secrecy is understood to mean the right of journalists to refuse to reveal the sources of their information in civil and in criminal courts, as well as in administrative proceedings.[4]

From the end of World War I until 1933 the number of papers in Austria grew steadily (68 dailies in 1933 compared to 40 in 1914). After 1934 the number decreased, and this decrease was accelerated by the Nazi occupation of Austria in 1938. In 1944 there were only 14 dailies--all of them dependent on the government for their livelihood. After being liberated in the spring of 1945, Austria saw her press begin to recover and grow. In 1957 the government gave the total circulation at 1.5 million daily, about two-thirds of which came from the Vienna papers.[5] By 1962 total circulations were estimated at 1.6 million.[6]

The nation's press is centered in Vienna; however, other important newspaper cities are Graz, Salzburg, and Innsbruck. Although most of Austria's large circulation dailies are published in Vienna, provincial papers are increasing in importance; they are generally considered very good and devote much space to foreign news. The oldest Austrian newspaper is the daily Wiener Zeitung (f.1703 and the oldest daily paper publishing in the world today); it is owned by the government and is given preferential treatment through state advertising and other benefits.

Arbeiter-Zeitung, a Socialist party daily of Vienna, is the nation's largest circulation paper. Two of the outstanding non-Vienna dailies are Innsbruck's Tiroler Tageszeitung, and Salzburg's Salzburger Nachrichten. An important weekly is Die Wochen-Presse of Vienna, which calls itself "the Austrian news-magazine." It is actually a tabloid-size newspaper like most others of the country; however, it does present news categorized under label headings in the Time and Newsweek style. Most of the journalists of the country receive their training at the School of Journalism at the University of Vienna.

DAILY NEWSPAPERS.[7] Ten dailies are published in Vienna. These are all morning papers except two which are published at noon. The largest of the dailies is the noon paper Der Neue Kurier of Vienna with a daily circulation

of about 300,000 and a week-end circulation
of 400,000. Next is Express (180,000) followed by Arbeiter Zeitung with 109,000 circulation. Other influential dailies published
in the capital are Das Kleine Volksblatt with
107,000, Die Presse (52,000), Neues Österreich
(62,000), and the Communist party's Volks-
stimme (39,000).

Other leading dailies in Austria, published
outside Vienna, are Kleine Zeitung (83,000)
and Neue Zeit (53,000) of Graz, Salzburger
Nachrichten (36,000) of Salzburg, and Tiroler
Tageszeitung (41,000) of Innsbruck.

WEEKLY NEWSPAPERS.[8] Leading weeklies of
Austria are the Monday papers Welt am Montag
(170,000) and Wiener Montag (120,000) of
Vienna and the Grazer Montag (100,000) of
Graz. Other influential weeklies are Die
Wochen-Presse (40,000) of Vienna, Sonntagspost
(33,000) of Graz, Der Wochenspiegel (25,000)
of Ried im Innkreis, Tiroler Bauernzeitung
(25,000) of Innsbruck, and Neuland (15,000)
of Salzburg.

Weeklies of Austria having more of a national
circulation are the following: Neue Illustrierte Wochenschau (398,000; circulation
leader), Wiener Wochenausgabe (266,000), Das
Kleine Blatt (145,000), Wiener Samstag
(123,000), and Der Erzahler (75,000). Also
quite popular among the weeklies are the
illustrated magazines such as Wiener Illustrierte (82,000) Wiener Wochen-Magazin (40,000),
Wiener Bilderwoche (30,000), and the humor
weekly Der Igel which claims to present "die
Welt in der Karikatur."

NATIONAL NEWS AGENCY. Austria's national news
agency is the Österreichische Presse-Agentur
(Austrian Press Agency). It is owned by the
press of the country. ÖPA's main office is
in Vienna, and it has six branch offices
throughout the country and about six correspondents outside Austria. The agency has
exchange agreements with Reuters, which supplies most of its foreign news, and with AP,
AFP, and TASS. It also has agreements with
a number of European national agencies.

SOME NEWSPAPER CHARACTERISTICS.[9] A few of the
leading Austrian journals are briefly described below to give the reader an idea of
the appearance and tone of the country's newspapers.

Neue Kurier, with a daily circulation of
300,000 and 400,000 on weekends, is Vienna's
top newspaper. Even at the height of the
Austro-Hungarian empire, no Austrian paper
ever attained such a large scale. Originally
published by the U. S. occupation forces, it
was taken over by Dr. Ludwig Polsterer; the
Kurier is now published in three editions
with the main final appearing at noon.[10]

Die Wochen-Presse, which calls itself "the
Austrian newsmagazine," is really a weekly
tabloid newspaper. It has no counterpart in
the American press, since it is both a newspaper and a newsmagazine. Its news is generally categorized in the Time and Newsweek
tradition under label heads such as "Österreich" (Austria), "Rundfunk" (Radio),
"Vereinte Nationen" (United Nations), "Internationales" (international), and "Bücher"
(Books). It also has special articles which
are boxed and generally signed à la Newsweek.
It usually presents a few pages of entertainment in addition to its serious news
coverage. It uses color (usually blue) sparingly on its front page (in its nameplate)
and as a box generally on its last page.
This weekly is published in Vienna and contains very little advertising.

Arbeiter-Zeitung (Socialist, f.1889, circulation about 109,000) is the country's third
largest circulation daily. It is a four-
column tabloid publication. It presents a
particularly heavy fare of world news, and
its photographs and special picture pages
are exceptionally fine. It, like most
Austrian dailies, carries attractively-laid-
out feature pages, and on Sunday several
pages of cultural articles under the heading
"Kunst und Kultur" form an important section.
The last page is usually a sports page. This
newspaper does not carry as much advertising
as Die Presse and some of the other dailies.

Die Presse (Independent, f.1948, circulation about 52,000) is one of the best-informed
of Austrian dailies. Its usual 14 pages (and
its special Sunday edition often reaching 36
pages) are filled with a wide variety of
national and foreign news and features. This
four-column tabloid has an especially good
coverage of cultural affairs. It also contains an unusually thick classified advertising section, usually in the last several pages
which are divided into eight narrow columns.
International news is given considerable
emphasis in Die Presse; however, the paper
seems to focus on national affairs. Daily
the paper runs a few attractive "feature"
pages, and on Sunday at least eight pages
are given over to light or background-type
articles which comprise its fine arts
("Feuilleton") section. Die Presse is Vienna's
most serious and comprehensive daily newspaper. It derives its name from the renowned
pre-war Neue Freie Presse and upholds the same
principles of freedom.[11]

Wiener Zeitung (government paper, f.1703; circulation unknown) is not as thick as most of the other dailies of Austria. In typical tabloid format, this carefully edited and printed paper uses color very conservatively on its front page. It also uses photographs very sparingly. Normally it publishes eight-page editions. The last two of these four-column pages are usually given over to classi-fied advertisements and program listings for radio, theater, and movies, and to government financial items.

Neue Öesterreichische Tageszeitung (People's party, Vienna local paper, f.1950, circulation unknown) is a very neatly made-up and printed four-column tabloid daily, averaging from eight to ten pages. It carries few photo-graphs (about three per issue). Foreign news is found on pages 1 and 2; local news and editorials on page 3; columns and features on pages 4, 5, and 6 with some news interspersed. Financial and industrial news is generally on page 7; radio-movie-concert news and schedules on page 8; advertising on page 9, and sports on the back page (10).

Salzburger Nachrichten (Independent, f.1945, circulation 36,000) of Salzburg is considered by many observers to be the best paper in the country. It is a four-column tabloid but made up more conservatively than most other dailies. It uses photographs sparingly but effectively. Normally, it contains at least three pages of foreign news and about one page of national news. There are many "kultur" articles in daily editions, and a special attractively presented Sunday feature called "Gesprächthemen." It is heavy with advertis-ing, and display and classified advertising accounts for about one-half of the total space.

Belgium

Belgium shares with Holland and Germany one of the oldest periodical press traditions of Europe. There is in the British Museum a <u>Mercurius Gallobelgicus</u>, the work of D. M. Janson, of Cologne. A fairly thick octavo book, giving a Latin chronicle of events from 1587 to 1594, it is really an annual news summary. <u>Mercurius Gallobelgicus</u> was continued down to 1635, and it is chiefly interesting to British and American press historians, because, by circulating in England, it started the idea of a periodical providing foreign news, and the title <u>Mercurius</u> or Mercury--as representing a messenger of the gods--thus became a common one for English and later American periodicals.

With a population of nine million only about 3 per cent of the Belgian people of reading age are illiterate. A nation of high newspaper readership (nearly 400 copies per 1,000 inhabitants), Belgium has 54 daily newspapers[1] (including a group of six controlled by one Brussels publication house) with a total circulation of more than 3.5 million. These dailies are published in fourteen cities. There are also about 15 weeklies with a combined circulation of 1.625 million.[2] Ten of the newspapers have circulations upward of 100,000; however, Belgian newspapers range from small papers like <u>Le Courrier du Soir</u> of Verviers with a circulation right at 7,000 to the nation's biggest papers (<u>Le Soir</u> and <u>Het Laatste Nieuws</u> of Brussels) with circulations of about 300,000.

Belgium is bilingual, and dailies are widely distributed in the two official languages of the country--Flemish and French, with most printed in the latter. The press is centered in Brussels, the capital and chief city, but the provincial press is developing rapidly. Brussels' newspapers circulate throughout the nation and those in three other cities--Antwerp, Liege, and Ghent--might be called "national" papers as well. The nation's two largest dailies are published in Brussels; one is in Flemish (<u>Het Laatste Nieuws</u>) and one is in French (<u>Le Soir</u>). The nation's third largest daily is <u>La Meuse</u> of Liege with a circulation of some 200,000.

The national news agency of the country is Agence Belga, with headquarters in Brussels and branch offices in Antwerp and in Leopold-ville, the Congo, where it is known as Agence Congolaise de Presse. It distributes about 50,000 words daily in Flemish and French, about half of which is foreign news. Agence Belga has foreign subscribers in the Congo and in Luxembourg. Communications facilities are "adequate," and during the Congo crisis when the government realized that coverage was poor because of high cable tolls (thirty-two cents a word) it reduced then to four cents a word. Agence Belga has exchange agreements with Agence France-Presse, Reuters, and several European agencies.

LEADING DAILIES		
Brussels:		
Le Soir	303,000	Independent
Het Laatste Nieuws	295,000	Liberal
Het Nieuws van den Dag	185,000	Catholic
La Dernière Heure	170,000	Liberal
La Libre Belgique	170,000	Catholic-Conservative
Le Peuple	126,000	Socialist
La Lantern	60,000	Conservative
Antwerp:		
Volksgazet	111,000	Socialist
Gazet van Antwerpen	152,000	Catholic-Labor
Ghent:		
Het Volk	224,000	Catholic-Labor
Liege:		
La Meuse	205,000	Independent
Charleroi:		
La Nouvelle Gazette	70,000	Liberal
Le Rappel	70,000	Catholic

Newspapers in the country are almost all "journals of opinion," but few of them are official party organs. Of the 20 important dailies in the country six are controlled by political parties.[3]

LEGAL POSITION OF JOURNALISTS. The Belgian constitution specifically states that "the press is free." Belgian journalists and newspapers jealously guard this right, and, because the title "journalist" occasionally has been misused "to the damage of the reputation and moral code of journalism," Belgian newspapermen have sought to have the use of

this title put on a legal footing. In 1962
the Belgian cabinet approved the text of a
bill presented by the Prime Minister and the
Minister of Justice dealing with the protection of the right to use the title of professional journalist.

The bill provides that the title of professional journalist may be used only by people
over the age of twenty-one, enjoying full
civil and political rights, who do not take
part in commercial activity other than the
directorship of a newspaper or news agency.
Their principal source of income must be
through the exercise of the journalistic profession with the exception of direct or indirect income from any publicity activity.

Necessary qualifications include that of
attachment with regular remuneration as
editor, subeditor, photographer, newsreel
cameraman or correspondent in Belgium, to one
or several newspapers or news media and the
exercise of the profession for at least two
years.

The bill also provides that anybody who
publicly uses the title of professional journalist without being entitled to do so is
liable to a fine of between 200 and 1,000
francs. Enactment of the bill into law is
expected.[4]

THE PERIODICAL PRESS. The periodical press of
Belgium is very important. In searching for
knowledge in politics and for information of
a cultural, technical and religious nature,
the Belgian people devote about the same
amount of money to buying periodicals as they
do the purchase of daily newspapers. An
average of six million periodicals (copies)
are sold per month, and this in a nation of
only eight million people. Nearly 2,000
different titles circulate within the country.

Periodicals are published in French and
Flemish; some of them are bilingual. Women's
weekly magazines are very popular and many
have a Parisian flavor. Also extremely
popular are sports, literary, art, music, and
children's magazines. Many of the periodicals
are exceptionally well made-up, although their
layout and general presentation vary widely--
from dignified pages with few pictures to
colorful photographic display pages.

A few of the most influential information
weeklies are Europe-Magazine, La Gazette de
Huy, Germinal, Samedi (in French), and De
Post Ons Volk, De Zweep, Zondags Vriend, De
Zeewacht, and Zondagsblad (in Flemish).
Two of the most important women's magazines
are Elle and Les Bonnes Soirées.

A BRIEF LOOK AT A FEW PAPERS.[5] Het Laatste
Nieuws has the largest daily circulation of
any Flemish language paper in Belgium. Its
page size is about average for the country's
papers (just slightly smaller than the page
size of the New York Times). This Liberal
newspaper is a well-printed seven-column
paper which uses the same technique on its
front page as the Christian Science Monitor
(stories, not columns, are separated by
column rules and cutoff rules). Make up,
though dignified, is lively and interesting;
pictures and some bold-face story leads give
"color" to the pages. A typical edition runs
to 20 pages, about the last five of which are
given over to advertising. Inside pages (no
column rules used) are quite attractive,
dignified, and loaded with serious national
and foreign news and features. Three or four
comic strips appear in various parts of the
paper, adding their amusement content to such
features as crossword puzzles. This paper
has an especially large and attractive sports
section (averaging four to six pages). It
uses AFP, UPI, and AP foreign stories.

Le Peuple is a Brussels afternoon paper
which is over 75 years old. It uses a
slightly larger page size than does the New
York Times and has eight columns to the page.
Like most Belgian papers, it is well-printed,
neat, carefully-edited and has interesting
make up. Usually running to only eight pages,
it makes use of some color--mainly on the
back page which is known as the "Magazine
Page." It uses an average of three photographs daily on its front page. Le Peuple
carries an average of one page of sports, one
page of stories devoted to movies, radio-TV
and other popular entertainment, and several
pages of national and international news and
commentary. For its foreign news it relies
mainly on AFP and AP.

De Nieuwe Gids of Brussels is representative of the Belgian tabloids. It is a five-
column (usually 16 pages) paper which presents its information and commentary in the
German or Austrian fashion--horizontally--
with most headlines of the one-line spread
variety. This paper has conservative, dignified make up and serious intellectual treatment of news and views. This paper usually
has no advertising. It has especially fine
financial and economic coverage. It uses
very little news agency material.

Volksgazet of Antwerp is another small five-
column tabloid. It uses color but very conservatively on its front page and sometimes
on an inside page. It uses column rules on
some pages and leaves them out of others.

Britain

Britain (or the United Kingdom), with 53 million inhabitants and an illiteracy rate of only 2 per cent, has some 130 daily newspapers circulating about 30.5 million copies every day.[1] This gives Britain the world's highest newspaper readership--about 575 copies of dailies per every 1,000 citizens (Norway and Sweden: about 500; United States: about 340). At least 90 per cent of adult Britons buy at least one morning daily paper. Although Britain has a tremendous daily readership, it has comparatively few daily papers; however, several are among the world's circulation leaders (seven have circulations of more than a million. In addition to the great daily circulation, the national Sunday papers circulate about 30 million copies each week. The provincial weeklies add another 12 million copies to the total. This means that some 225 million copies of newspapers are published each week in Great Britain. The high circulation in Britain is due chiefly to the concentration of population and the well-developed distribution system for the "national" papers. These are the big dailies published in London (one in Manchester) and the mass-appeal Sundays which circulate throughout the country. The size of the United Kingdom, with London as its main hub, allows for a system of rapid distribution; a gigantic population close to London makes it possible for nearly everyone in the United Kingdom who wants to read a "national" paper to do so.

Although newspapers dominate the publications picture in varying degrees in all countries, in Britain they have a very special place. When a person speaks of "the press" in Britain, he refers first of all to newspapers or "papers." (Even such weekly reviews as The Spectator are referred to as "papers.") Magazines are not nearly as important to the British as they are to readers in the Scandinavian countries, France, and the United States. Although daily papers account for the bulk of the British circulation, weekly papers are extremely important in the total press picture. Generally these weeklies fall into one of two general categories: local weeklies (about 1,200) and national Sunday papers (about 15).

BRITISH PRESS: AN OVERVIEW. The press of Britain is privately owned. Large chains, however, are tending to dominate the newspaper picture. In 1962, for example nearly 75 per cent of the 30 million papers sold daily came from printing presses owned by four organizations: Associated Newspapers, Beaverbrook Newspapers, the Daily Mirror group, and the Roy Thomson group. The four major chains together control about half of Britain's principal dailies and weeklies. Mergers in 1958, 1959, and 1960, the struggle between two of the four publishing giants for control of a fifth group, the resultant public concern for press freedom, and the investigation by the Royal Commission on the Press that followed made the five years ending in 1962 notable in the twentieth century history of the country's press.[2]

Chief contestants in the struggle were Cecil King of the Daily Mirror group and Roy Thomson, a newcomer to the British press scene, whose press empire was started in Canada and the United States and was extended to Britain by way of Scotland. In 1958 King bought Amalgamated Press, Ltd., the big women's and trade magazine publishing group. In 1959 Thomson bought Kemsley Newspapers, Ltd., publishers of four national Sunday papers, several important provincial dailies, and a number of country weeklies. In 1960 both King and Thomson set out to buy the Odhams-Newnes group, publishers of the Daily Herald (circulation, 1.5 million), the Sunday People (5.3 million circulation), and about 200 women's, trade and technical, and special interest magazines. Amid a barrage of comments from Parliament and the press, bidding climbed until King's Daily Mirror group offered and paid £38,500,000 ($111,000,000). Meanwhile, the Beaverbrook group had acquired title to the News Chronicle when that paper ceased publication in 1960.

Although the Royal Commission on the Press (in a study made in 1949) reported that chain growth posed no danger to freedom of the press, as a consequence of the described mergers and the furor that they evoked the government launched a new inquiry into the workings of Fleet Street (the press's own designation for "the press"). After two years (February, 1961--September, 1962) of extensive investigation the Commission issued a 239 page blistering report on the economics of the British newspaper business.[3] The Commission in its report to Parliament found (1) "gravely inefficient" production methods in newspaper plants, most of it due to union featherbedding, restrictive union practices, and extravagant union demands which have made weaker or less efficient units vulnerable to assimilation by

more efficient competitors and chains. In
this connection it called for a joint pub-
lisher-union study to find ways of increasing
efficiency in the production of newspapers.
It charged that employers "lack unity and pay
insufficient attention to the industry as a
whole;" declared (2) that there is still a
range of opinion in the British press but less
than there was in 1949, and "it would be
better if there were more." Concentration of
ownership threatens the variety of opinion,
and chain ownership in the provincial press
may deprive the local press of its local
character. It said no newspaper organization
should be allowed to get a controlling interest in television stations; (3) opposed
all proposals to aid the press economically,
including reductions in postal charges, tax
relief, wider spread of government advertising, subsidization of printing facilities by
government or industry, and various schemes
that would penalize large papers through
limitations on advertising or a graduated
scale of taxes on advertising volume the
proceeds of which would be used to provide
subsidies to help keep smaller, weaker, or
less efficient papers alive; urged (4) that
the Press Council, established in 1953, be
given more authority to police the abuses of
ownership, concentration of power, influence
by advertisers on the editorial policies of
newspapers, and unprofessional conduct. It
urged the Council to conduct continuous research in the long-term social and economic
developments, report and publish all facts
about ownership, control, and growth of the
press; and (5) proposed that mergers involving publications whose aggregate weekly circulations exceed 3,000,000 copies either before
or after the merger be submitted to a Press
Amalgamation Court with authority to give or
withhold permission on mergers and sales of
such newspapers. Such mergers would be permitted "only if it is established by means
of statutory criteria that the transaction
is not contrary to the public interest."

The reaction of the British press while
generally favorable showed a strong tendency
to agree with the first points of the findings above, and to ignore or deride the
latter. For example, it was pointed out that
the proposal contained in point 5 would not
affect the merger of two papers such as the
London Times and the Guardian, whose circulations do not aggregate three million copies,
although the disappearance of either as an
independent voice would constitute a far
graver loss to the diversity of opinion available than would the merger of any two papers
that would be subject to such review.

"The truest truism about British journalism,"

writes John Tebbel in the Saturday Review,
"is that it produces some of the best and
some of the worst newspapers in the world."
In the United States there are many grada-
tions between the "quality" papers and the
sensational papers, but in Britian the papers
tend to cluster to the extremes. The quality
of the Times, Guardian, Daily Telegraph, the
Sunday Times the Sunday edition of the Telegraph, and the Observer, to name some of the
best but not the only excellent papers, is
matched in the United States by only four or
five papers including the New York Times,
the Wall Street Journal, and the Christian
Science Monitor.

The general editorial trend in Britain
today appears to be toward a more popular
type of newspaper which stresses entertainment rather than news and commentary, although
between the end of 1960 and the middle of 1961
a redesigned, more newsy, less sexy, News of
the World had gained 700,000--a 10 per cent
rise that brought its net sales to over 6.75
million. Typical of the mass-appeal papers
are the Daily Mirror, Daily Express and Daily
Mail among the morning papers, Reveille among
the weeklies, and News of the World, the
People and Sunday Pictorial among the big
national Sunday papers. These "popular"
papers provide daily and weekly diets of
scandal, gossip, and sex-interest to their
millions of readers. Such sex-and-scandal

These mass-appeal or "popular" papers provide daily and weekly diets of scandal,
gossip, and sex-interest to their millions
of readers. They are far more extreme
than anything in America.

sheets in London are far more extreme than anything in America, where sensational journalism has been declining steadily since the Twenties.

On the other hand, the "class" or "quality" papers circulate throughout Britain and, indeed, in most countries of the world. Foremost among these are the Times, the Daily Telegraph, and the Guardian (formerly the Manchester Guardian) of London. Of these three the Times is the soberest and the Daily Telegraph is the liveliest. Although most of Britain's papers stress "information" or "entertainment" or a little of both, there are some notable examples of newspapers giving considerable space to commentary, opinion, and background-interpretation pieces. Chief among these are probably the Scotsman of Edinburgh and the Guardian, especially in their weekly editions. Dispatches from the Guardian, the London Sunday Times (not connected with the daily Times) and the London Observer are distributed in the United States through the Los Angeles Times-Washington Post News Service.[4] Some 3,500 periodicals are published in Britain, covering most vocations and special interests. London is the national publishing center of the United Kingdom, although Manchester has the largest single printing center in Europe.

British newspapers, with the exception of the Communist Daily Worker, the Labour party's Daily Herald and Sunday Citizen (formerly the Reynolds News), are independent of party control. This does not mean that British papers are free from political biases and opinions. In fact, most have political "leanings" well known to all readers, which partly accounts for the multiple-newspaper households and consequent high circulations in Britain. Financially, however, they are not tied to any political party. Political editorial policies, in general, are those of the owners; none is a career politician, and no paper is bound to any party line. In general, the conservative papers are more critical of the Conservative party when in power than are Republican papers in the United States when the Republican party is in power, and the Labourite press is more critical of the Labour party policies than U. S. papers with Democratic party leanings are of Democratic party policies.

Circulations in Britain generally have been decreasing since 1957. For example, recent figures indicate that the national dailies during 1961 were circulating about 16.5 million (a loss of some two million from five years before), the national Sundays were circulating about 27 million (a loss of some two million from five years before), and the

London PMs were circulating some 2.25 million (a loss of about 500,000 from five years before). The only important newspaper which showed an appreciable growth during the period was the Sunday Times[5] and the new "class" Sunday Telegraph.

In concluding this summary introduction, four main characteristics of the British press should be given. They are (1) the great contrast in circulation and contents between the "quality" newspapers and the "popular" newspapers; (2) the existence of large chains of national and provincial newspapers; (3) the concentration of circulation in the national dailies and Sundays published in London; and (4) the tremendous circulations held by the "popular" national dailies and the mass-appeal national Sunday papers.

BRITISH PRESS: BRIEF HISTORY. British newspaper history began in the sixteenth century with writers gathering serious news in London coffee-houses and sending it to provincial readers in the form of newsletters.[6] Printing, known in Britain in 1500, was licensed by the Crown; therefore, most of the early newsletters were hand-written. Laws were strict concerning what could be printed; however, these were relaxed by 1693 and weekly newspapers began to develop. Heavy taxation and stringent libel laws were obstacles to the development of the British press. Stamp, paper and advertisement taxes were finally abolished by 1861, making it possible for the press to become economically stable. Two other important factors contributed to the rapid rise of the press during the nineteenth century: the growth of the railway system between 1850 and 1900, making possible rapid and wide circulation of papers, and the introduction of free compulsory education, giving the papers a broad literate potential readership.

The first successful British daily paper, the Daily Courant, was founded in London in 1702; it was followed by the Daily Post in 1719. The Morning Chronicle was begun in 1769 and lasted three years. The Morning Post was founded in 1772 (absorbed by Daily Telegraph in 1937); in 1785 the Daily Universal Register was established (name changed three years later to the Times). Many provincials, mostly weekly, sprang up prior to 1800. Britain's first Sunday paper was the Observer, founded in 1791 and still publishing. Sunday papers, however, did not achieve much importance in Britain until after World War I.

In Scotland and Ireland the press development was similar to that in England. The

Mercurius (f.1661) of Edinburgh was the
first Scottish newssheet, and the first real
newspaper was the Edinburgh Gazette (f.1699).
In Dublin, Ireland, the first newspaper, the
Dublin Gazette, was begun in 1705. The Scotsman, one of Scotland's most influential papers
today, was founded in 1817 and became a daily
in 1855. The first newspaper established in
Wales was the Cambrian (f.1804).

The British popular press began with the
Daily Telegraph of London in 1855 when the
Stamp Act was repealed. In five years its circulation had doubled that of the Times, which
was sailing its conservative course with a
circulation of about 65,000. By 1870 the Daily
Telegraph had the world's largest circulation
(more than 240,000 daily). By the time Alfred
Harmsworth (Lord Northcliffe) exploded his
sensational Daily Mail on the British scene in
1896, a great new reading public composed
largely of the lower middle and working classes
was available. The Daily Mail took advantage
of this vast new audience and led the British
press (one segment of it at least) into a new
"popular journalism" era. Soon other papers
were imitating the Daily Mail whose human-
interest formula by 1900 had gained it a circulation of half a million.

The Daily Express was founded in 1900, followed by the Daily Herald in 1912. A new
type "popular" paper was created in 1903 with
the founding of the Daily Mirror, a picture
tabloid; it was followed by an imitator, the
Daily Sketch, in 1909. The Daily Mirror had
a circulation of 720,000 by 1934, and since
then has consistently held its own or led the
field in the circulation race among the big
"popular" dailies of Britain. Today it is
Britain's largest daily (about 4.5 million
circulation), slightly ahead of its nearest
rival, the Daily Express.

British newspapers today can be roughly
divided into two main types: quality, and
popular. Each of these types includes dailies
and weeklies. Other ways of classifying
British newspapers are the following: national
dailies and local dailies published in London,
Sunday nationals--serious and popular, provincials, and miscellaneous weeklies. The
various categories of the British press are
dealt with below:

THE "QUALITY" PAPERS. The Times of London and
the Manchester Guardian are representative of
the "quality" daily papers of Britain and of
a high type of serious journalism as it exists
in the world today. Their circulations are
small (Times, about 260,000; Guardian, about
235,000) compared with the mass-circulation
"popular" papers. The other daily in England

which would be classified as a "quality"
daily is London's Daily Telegraph (circulation: about 1.25 million). In Scotland are
published two important "quality" dailies,
the Scotsman of Edinburgh (circulation: about
70,000), and the Glasgow Herald (circulation:
about 87,000). About the only other daily in
this elite group is the Yorkshire Post (circulation: about 120,000).

The London Times and the Daily Telegraph,
two "quality" or "prestige" papers, devote much space to politics, government,
education, and the arts. Headlines are
usually small, dignified and not very
exciting. "Quality" papers are aimed at
the highly educated.

The "quality" papers are aimed at the highly
educated. They might also be called "prestige" papers. All devote considerable space
to politics, government, education, and the
arts. Headlines are usually small, dignified
and not very exciting (e.g., a headline in
the Manchester Guardian in 1958: "No News
Today From Iceland.")7

Besides the dailies there are several
"quality" Sunday papers typified by the
Observer and the Sunday Times (read largely
for book reviews, music and art criticism,
and feature articles). Their steady circulation rise indicates a growing public for
serious journalism. According to Francis
Williams (probably the best-known and best-

informed writer on the British press), "the number of those who want serious news seriously reported may still not be very large, but it is steadily increasing."[8]

THE "POPULAR" PAPERS. The British "popular" press is mainly composed of dailies and Sundays (there are a few "popular" weeklies, e.g., Reveille), all of which are mass-directed and have exceptionally large circulations. Dailies in this category range from the Daily Mail (the pioneer of mass-oriented dailies), which is rather sober and responsible, to the sensational tabloid Daily Mirror with its many pictures and large headlines set in a context of sex, crime, and gossip. The mass-appeal Sundays are led by News of the World, with 6.75 million sales, and Sunday Pictorial, with 5.35 million copies. They are basically like the popular dailies, but perhaps they go a step further in sensationalism.

In recent years the "popular" papers, especially certain of the more sensational of them, have received much criticism from the nation's Press Council, Parliament, and other groups feeling that the sensational papers were not what they should be. Foreign sources also add their uncomplimentary statements to those from Britain. For example, Time has described the London tabloid Daily Sketch as a "chronic boudoir skulker and chronicler of overcrowded love nests."[9]

The "popular" journals have been called "gutter" papers, "bloodhounds of circulation" and other such derogatory names. In 1957 Sir Linton Andrews, chairman of the Press Council, accused the mass-circulation-seeking papers of "seizing on the trivial."[10] Randolph Churchill, a frequent critic of both the British and American newspapers, has referred to the "popular" papers of Britain as a "cataract of filth" flowing through Fleet Street.[11] He goes on to say of them: "In circulation building time, stories about the royal family are the solid meat-and-potatoes of the diet. A good murder may be the hors d'oeuvre, and a juicy sex story may be the dessert, but the royal-family stories are what put flesh on the bones of the street-sale figures."[12] Again in 1958, Churchill, this time writing in a British weekly review, contended that the public was becoming increasingly concerned about the "abuse of power shown by the gutter press," especially, he said, as "it concerns intrusion into the lives of other people."[13] He added: "I can think of many rich men who control newspapers and whose private lives are much more interesting and spicy than that of the drab, unfortunate couple who have just been pilloried. How strange it is that we never hear about

their private lives."

Joseph Whitt, an American writing about the British press, has called these "popular" journals "non-U" papers to differentiate them from the "upper class" or quality papers. Whitt says these "non-U" papers are marked by "poor writing, amateurish layout and confused typography."[14]

Cecil H. King, chairman and managing director of the Daily Mirror Newspapers Ltd. in 1958 presented a defense for the popular press.[15] He contended that millions look to the "more sprightly papers" for "guidance in national and international affairs, as well as for entertainment." According to King, the Daily Mirror (probably the most maligned of the popular papers) and other of the mass-appeal journals have "filled with honour and a high sense of duty the part of friend, tutor, counsellor and entertainer" for the readers.

"The popular press," King continued, "has recently faced a barrage of ill-tempered and ill-founded charges reflecting on our attitude of private grief. The word 'intrusion' has been bandied about by mischief-makers... and has been falsely applied to responsible reporters and photographers....I take this opportunity of rebutting these charges."

Beyond all the heated words that have arisen for and against the "popular" press, the facts tend to indicate a new interest in the serious or "quality" press. During the last five years such papers as the Daily Sketch and the Daily Mirror, and the Sunday News of the World (which once published more than eight million copies) suffered losses or barely held their own in circulation. A redesigned, less sexy News of the World has won back part of its losses, and the "quality" papers generally held their circulations while in the case of the Times, the Guardian, and the Sunday Times circulations have grown steadily.[16]

NATIONAL MORNING PAPERS

THE TIMES. The Times is probably the best-known newspaper in the world. Although its daily circulation is only some 260,000--a mere dribble compared with other London dailies--its influence on the thinking of Britain's leaders is difficult to assess. The newspaper is definitely the journal of Britain's governing circles; it is written and edited for thinkers and opinion leaders-- for such people as civil servants, teachers, scientists, journalists, economists, clergymen, and labor officials. One writer has recently called the Times "sedate, unsensational,

indestructible, a little complacent, a little
dull and uninspired, well-mannered, and
impeccably turned out."[17] This is certainly
a colorful, as well as accurate, description
of the newspaper.

An important feature of the Times is its
letters from readers. These letters have

by the Times.

From its earliest days the Times attained
a high quality in its writing and editing.[18]
It probably reached its most prestigeful
position in the mid-nineteenth century when,
under its brilliant editor John Delane, it
became known as the "Thunderer." At the

always contained thoughtful and sparkling
pieces. "A letter to the Times" has become a
sort of institution in Britain. Today one
can find among the letters numerous essays of
the very highest type. Another outstanding
feature of the newspaper is its "fourth
leaders" which are excellently-written light
essays appearing in the fourth position on
the "leader" (editorial) page.

The Times was founded in 1785 by John Walter
as the Daily Universal Register, and took its
present name three years later. A series of
politically influential editors in the
nineteenth century established its reputation
so firmly abroad that the erroneous idea
developed that the Times was a government or
official paper. It does seem, even today, to
have an "official" flavor; this is mainly
because of its emphasis on government and
economic affairs. It is recognized for its
thoughtful and interpretive articles, for its
conservative news presentation and make up.
Its news coverage is thorough, although it is
highly selective compared to the New York
Times; it assumes the reader is already well-
informed and wants new information and interpretation to fill in the gaps. The style of
reporting used by the Times is restrained,
dignified, and unsensational; it has long been
known for its razor sharpness and its conser-
vation of words. All news stories are treated
with a certain detachment in a respectful
manner. The Times has never felt that when
personalities become news they lose their right
to respect. Movie stars, businessmen, bankers,
and Cabinet members who find themselves in the
news are handled in the same dignified manner

beginning of the twentieth century it was
rescued from an economic slump by Lord Northcliffe, who bought the paper in 1908 and devoted most of his attention to its financial
status. Although Northcliffe apparently
saved the Times from serious economic troubles,
it is generally thought that because of his
tendency to personally supervise everything
and his affection for sensation, he would
have distorted the paper's character completely had he lived longer. When he died
in 1922, the Times was sold to a combine
headed by John J. Astor. A "Times Trust" was
set up to govern the paper and to keep it out
of the hands of any individual owner. The
Trustees of the Times are five leading British
citizens who own no stock in the newspaper.

The Times speaks with authority on all
subjects through a staff of always anonymous
editors and writers. "With a byline, there's
always the risk of distortion, of injecting
one's own personality," explains one top Times
editor. So Times readers get their news from
"Our Correspondent," "Our Own Correspondent,"
"Our Special Correspondent," even "Our
Astronomical Correspondent."[19]

THE GUARDIAN. This world-famous quality newspaper was founded in 1821 as a weekly; it
became a daily in 1855. Today it ranks at
home and abroad very close to the Times. In
fact, it is actually quoted abroad more often
than any other British newspaper. Its readers
are mainly business and professional people,
yet its influence is great among the young
serious readers of Britain and among the
middle-aged. Its most influential editor was

the late C. P. Scott, who took over in 1872 and guided the Guardian for 57 years. Under his direction the paper assumed its strange position as the only non-London "national" daily. Its circulation is about 235,000 today, about four times as large as before World War II.

The Guardian is traditionally a Liberal newspaper. It has always been for reform, has argued forcefully but calmly for personal freedoms, high thinking, and consideration. As one writer has put it, "If the Times is the voice of God, the Guardian is the voice of conscience."[20] The paper has always enjoyed a literary prestige held by practically no other newspaper; it has a dignity of expression and an overall literary character given it by its top-notch writers and editors. Two of its foremost correspondents today are two who mainly report on the American scene: Max Freedman and Alistair Cooke. One of its best known writers on British political affairs is Francis Boyd. The newspaper's commentaries on world affairs are considered among the best anywhere. In Britain today most of the serious journalists still follow the principles on the function of a newspaper as defined by the Guardian's great editor C. P. Scott, who wrote in 1921: "Its (the newspaper's) primary office is the gathering of news. At the peril of its soul it must see that the supply is not tainted....Comment is free but facts are sacred."[21]

The Guardian is particularly influential in its dramatic criticism and book-reviewing and for its well-rounded and interpretive presentation of international news. The newspaper also publishes a weekly edition, the Manchester Guardian Weekly, which has a wide readership prestige throughout the world.

DAILY TELEGRAPH. The Telegraph has the largest circulation of the three national "quality" dailies (about 1.25 million). Politically it is Conservative. It was founded in 1855 and merged with the Morning Post in 1937; the combined paper has since been reliable, courageous, and journalistically competent. Its layout is neat, well-planned, sober, and perhaps even "old fashioned." Yet it is livelier than the Manchester Guardian and the Times. The paper stresses foreign, economic, and political news. Although it is one of the principal business papers, it is typically Conservative in its support of the Crown and the social hierarchy with its elaborate and ritualistic ceremonials.

DAILY HERALD, THE DAILY MAIL. The Daily Herald is the organ of the Trades Union Congress and the Labour party. Strangely, its

readership contains as many women as men. Until 1930 the Herald was a socialistic propaganda sheet; today it is rather typical general-information with a Labour bias. The Daily Mail is politically Conservative. It was the original British "popular" paper. Today it is considered less sensational and more reliable than its fellow Conservative Daily Express.

DAILY EXPRESS, DAILY MIRROR, DAILY SKETCH, DAILY WORKER. The Daily Express is Britain's largest circulation daily published in regular-size format. It is second only to the picture tabloid Daily Mirror in circulation among all British dailies. Owned by Beaverbrook Newspapers Ltd., it is a joint stock company. Although its basic policy is Conservative, it often deviates from the official view of the Conservative party. Its readership is great in every class of the population. It is an easy-to-read paper, with a certain well-planned brilliance which makes it acceptable to the educated as well as the uneducated Briton. Although it has many characteristics of a sensational newspaper (e.g., large photographs and headlines), it gives practically no space to sex and crime stories which are common in the Mirror and the Sketch.

The Daily Mirror was founded in 1903 by Lord Northcliffe. It appeals to the uneducated segments of the population; nearly half of its

PRINCIPAL LONDON NEWSPAPERS

London Sundays:

News of the World	6,734,000
Sunday Pictorial	5,335,000
The People	5,442,000
Sunday Express	3,767,000
Sunday Dispatch	3,767,000
Sunday Times	1,022,000
The Observer	728,000
Sunday Citizen	326,000

London Dailies:

Daily Telegraph	1,250,000
The Times	260,000
Financial Times	132,000
Daily Mirror (tab)	4,593,000
Daily Express	4,360,000
Daily Herald	1,418,000
Daily Mail	2,687,000
Daily Sketch (tab)	1,006,000
Daily Worker	60,000
Evening News (PM)	1,485,000
Evening Standard	761,000

readers are under 35 years old. Commonly
found on its tabloid pages are large headlines
over its short stories and many and large pictures of the human interest-sex-crime-gossip
type.

The Daily Sketch is another tabloid paper
which provides a steady and plentiful diet of
cartoons, photographs, gossip, and sensational
features in each morning's issue. Its readers,
like those of the Mirror, are mostly in the
lower income groups. The Daily Worker is
owned by numerous small stockholders in the
People's Press Printing Society, Ltd., a
communist group. The Worker is the official
daily organ of the Communist party of Great
Britain. Its circulation is small (about
60,000). In most respects other than its constant expounding of the Party line, the
Worker resembles the other popular nationals.
Rather strangely, its make up and headlines
are generally more conservative than many of
its morning competitors.[22]

THE SUNDAY PAPERS

About a dozen Sunday papers circulate a
total of some 30 million copies throughout
Britain each week.[23] These Sunday papers are
strictly weekly papers of an independent
nature and are not just editions of regular
newspapers as is the case in the United States.

Leading among these Sunday papers are News
of the World (with the world's largest circulation), and the Sunday Pictorial, both
published in London. Other big circulation
"popular" Sunday papers are the People, Sunday
Express, and Sunday Dispatch. The News of
the World is both a national institution and
an international phenomenon. It is easily
the "biggest" newspaper in the world, having
a circulation of 6.73 million and a readership estimated at more than twice that number.
It is read by every second adult in Britain.

The newspaper prints regular news, features,
and political articles, but what seems to
attract and hold its gigantic reading public
is its emphasis on crime mixed liberally with
sex. These stories are usually presented in
great detail, but are worded so as not to
offend puritan standards or the libel laws.

Outside London the main Sunday papers are
Glasgow's Sunday Post and Manchester's Empire
News & Sunday Chronicle, both with circulations
exceeding a million. Of the British Sunday
papers, the Sunday Times (no relation to the
daily Times) and the Observer of London represent the quality segment of the press,
give considerable emphasis to foreign news and

have their own foreign correspondents. Both
cover a wide variety of subjects competently
and print many special articles from distinguished contributors.

With the exception of the Sunday Times and
the Observer, the Sundays make a play for
gigantic circulations by appealing to lower
tastes of the masses. They present some
foreign news, but tend to play up the sensational elements. These Sunday papers are
basically of the same nature as the mass-
circulation popular dailies.

The reader of the Sunday papers of the
"popular" variety is given large amounts of
sensation, sex, horoscopes, puzzles, and
comics. The Sunday press apparently fills a
real need for the British people to "escape"
from the more serious affairs of the modern
world. More papers are sold on Sundays than
there are households in Britain, and more are
read each Sunday than there are adult Britons.
Letters to the editor, which take a prominent
place in the Sunday papers, indicate pretty
well what the reader of the Sunday popular
press likes to read. In the letters one can
find a surfeit of personal and intimate details; the letters are filled with information
about marital problems, about personal habits,
about amorous "escapades," and about household and gardening ideas. They also contain
jokes, requests for advice, complaints; some
of them even contain prayers.

THE PROVINCIAL PRESS

There are about 100 provincial papers in
Britain, with a total circulation of slightly
more than 10 million. In covering national
and international events, the provincial AM
press has to face the competition of London's
nationals which are circulated throughout the
British Isles. This may account for the fact
that the largest of the British provincials
are mostly afternoon papers. Provincials,
especially the PMs, concentrate on local and
national news, and might be called the true
British "grass roots" press. Most are owned
by big joint-stock companies; however, many
of the smaller ones are still family enterprises. Most of the provincial dailies, regardless of size, replate through three or
four editions and make a special effort to
keep their readers informed as to the last
minute news. British craftsmanship and
patience produce some fine papers on old
equipment, which is common in the provinces.
Writing and editing is good on the provincial papers, although few of the editors
and reporters are university-trained. Provincial newspapermen seek a high quality and

take a real pride in their papers.

```
┌─────────────────────────────────────────────┐
│              LEADING PROVINCIALS              │
│                                               │
│  (Morning "Qualities"):                       │
│                                               │
│  The Manchester Guardian      235,000         │
│  Yorkshire Post (Leeds)       119,000         │
│  Western Mail (Cardiff, Wales) 104,000        │
│  Glasgow Herald (Scot.)        87,000         │
│  The Scotsman (Edinburgh)      69,000         │
│                                               │
│  (Other Dailies):                             │
│                                               │
│  Belfast Telegraph            193,000         │
│  Daily Record (AM: Glasgow)   498,000         │
│  Liverpool Echo (PM)          410,000         │
│  Manchester Evening News      232,000         │
│  Birmingham Mail (PM)         294,000         │
│  Evening Times (Glasgow)      243,000         │
│  Evening Chronicle                            │
│       (Manchester)            281,000         │
│  Evening Chronicle                            │
│       (Newcastle)             257,000         │
│  Yorkshire Evening News       237,000         │
│  The Star (PM; Sheffield)     225,000         │
│  Evening Dispatch                             │
│       (Birmingham)            167,000         │
│  Leicester Mercury (PM)       155,000         │
│  Bristol Evening Post         158,000         │
│  Edinburgh Evening News       157,000         │
│  Daily Mail (PM; Hull)        125,000         │
│  Northern Echo (AM;                           │
│       Darlington)             102,000         │
│  Portsmouth Evening News      104,000         │
│                                               │
│  (Sundays):                                   │
│                                               │
│  Empire News and Sporting                     │
│       Chronicle (Manchester) 2,600,000        │
│  Sunday Post (Glasgow)      1,000,000         │
│  Sunday Mail (Glasgow)        610,000         │
│  Sunday Sun (Newcastle)       216,000         │
│  Sunday Mercury                               │
│       (Birmingham)            209,000         │
└─────────────────────────────────────────────┘
```

THE WEEKLIES

There are several types of weekly papers in Britain. They might be placed in the following categories: provincial weeklies, London suburban weeklies, miscellaneous weeklies, weekly editions of certain national dailies, and weekly reviews.

Over 1,000 provincial weeklies are published in some 630 towns; these are local-appeal papers carrying news of the town and its surrounding area. London weeklies are special types; for example, one is considered an authority on London municipal government, and another (London Weekly Advertiser) carries all types of classified advertising, and another is a tabloid sensational paper (Reveille). Some of the national dailies have weekly editions, chief among these being the Manchester Guardian Weekly, the Times Weekly Review, the Overseas Mirror, and the Overseas Mail.

There are also some weekly reviews which actually might be considered magazines as well as newspapers. These reviews, having circulations from 25,000 to 50,000, form an important part of the British press. Most of them contain political, literary, and economic essays and reviews. Spectator (nonparty) is the oldest of these journals. Others are the New Statesman (independent Socialist) and Time and Tide (right-wing). They carry an editorial, political and current affairs articles, letters to the editor, and book reviews. The Economist is a little different from these in that it gives a greater amount of space to news, comment, and statistics concerning politics and economics. Its scope is far wider than its name implies, and it is widely quoted throughout the world. The Listener is a BBC weekly subsidized journal, carrying broadcast commentaries and programs.

Three other weekly publications should be mentioned. Unlike the periodicals mentioned above which are printed on newsprint, these three are typical of the American magazines printed on a higher quality paper. The Illustrated London News, the closest thing in Britain to the U.S.'s Life, is a picture magazine of high quality devoted to general news and the arts. The famed British humor weekly is Punch, which has been poking fun in a highly literate manner since 1841. A great tradition has attracted to its roster of contributors Britain's keenest wits, cartoonists, and critics. It publishes some 1,000 cartoons a year--some in full color--which are highly thought of throughout the world and are reproduced regularly in journals of many nations. Probably the magazine in the U.S. most closely resembling Punch is the New Yorker. Of special interest to those working in the printed communications professions of Britain is World's Press News & Advertisers' Review (better known simply as WPN). This weekly equivalent of the U.S.'s Editor & Publisher is a well-written and well-edited journal serving the journalistic, printing, and allied fields.

NEWS AGENCIES. Great Britain has one of the world's most highly-respected international news agencies--Reuters, which is principally a British Commonwealth cooperative, jointly owned by the Press Association (a cooperative agency of weeklies and provincial dailies in the U.K.), the Newspaper Proprietor's Association (London papers), the Australian Associated Press, and the New Zealand Press Association. Reuters was the first agency to be established in Britain, being transferred to London from France in 1851 by its founder, Paul Julius Reuter. Reuters Ltd. came into its present trust status just after World War II.

Reuters has a "Home Service" which supplies foreign news to the British newspapers, and the "Overseas Service" which sends British news and foreign news to some 3,000 daily subscribers outside Great Britain. Reuters has correspondents in most of the world's capital cities. It has about 50 offices abroad and some 2,000 foreign correspondents and stringers. Reuters concentrates on British Commonwealth and foreign news, and has exchange agreements with some 35 to 40 news agencies outside the United Kingdom.

The other British news agencies are the Press Association (distributes the Reuters service to the Provincial press which owns it) and the Exchange Telegraph Co. Ltd. The PA distributes home news and is owned by the provincial newspapers of the British Isles. It has almost 175 full-time and more than 1,500 part-time correspondents. It also distributes the overseas news of Reuters to the provincial papers. The Exchange Telegraph Company distributes mainly domestic news, but does handle a few big foreign stories bearing especially on Britain. This public company of more than 100 stockholders has about 1,000 correspondents in Britain. It was established in 1872 mainly to distribute stock exchange news by tape machines, and although it now deals in all types of news it is still the only agency with the right to send telegraph messages directly from the "floor" of the London Stock Exchange. It is unlike the other two main British agencies in that it supplies private subscribers-- hotels, clubs, individuals--with news.

Two other sources of general foreign news in Britain are the Associated Press (a branch of the U.S.'s Associated Press), and the British United Press (a Canadian branch of the United Press International). Also in Britain are many small syndicates and agencies specializing in features, photographs, economics, sports, and the like.

Some of the larger newspapers of Britain and some of the newspaper groups supply news, features, and pictures to newspapers of foreign countries. The most important of these papers are the Sunday Observer, the Times, the Guardian, Daily Telegraph, Daily Express, Daily Mail, and Daily Mirror.

"CRISIS": BRITISH PRESS PROBLEMS. Britain today, like so many other nations of the world, is facing a real crisis. The possibility that the number of newspapers published in the nation will diminish in the next few years is not an unlikely one. Since the 1920's the number of papers in the U.K. has shrunk by 25 per cent, although the circulations have grown. A few of the reasons for the present "crisis"[24] are the rising cost of newsprint, the growing popularity of television and television advertising, and the unwillingness of newspaper production unions to accept promptly mechanization advances. The small circulation papers, with their ever-decreasing advertising revenue, appear to be the ones which will feel the greatest sting from the current situation which began to become severe in late 1956.

Until December, 1956, when the government allowed newspapers to run as many pages as they wished (newsprint restrictions were lifted), the biggest papers were unable to provide advertisers with all the space they desired; therefore much advertising was scattered among the smaller and weaker papers. The lifting of newsprint restrictions after nearly twenty years of rationing caused advertisers to turn to the mass-circulation dailies, giving them a temporary lift but increasing the economic problems of the smaller papers. More recently, with the development of commercial TV, advertising revenues are declining even among the mass-circulation dailies. With rising costs the outlook for many smaller independent papers is increasingly precarious.

Commercial television also has lured advertisers from the magazines, and with production costs, especially wages and paper, skyrocketing (newsprint in Britain in 1962 was six times as expensive as before World War II), many magazines and newspapers are having trouble staying in business. Although the majority of British publications continue to show a profit, it seems economically inevitable that the number of journals will decline in the next few years. Since rising wages account for most of the increase in production costs, and unions are fighting all attempts to economize through mechanization and the elimination of excess labor, the problem will continue to be the subject of much debate in press and government circles.

JOURNALISM TRAINING. Journalism in Britain is a reasonably well-paid profession and the best journalists are highly intelligent and able. However, in recent years there has been concern in British press circles about current training and recruitment methods. Most British journalists who are well-entrenched in the country's newspapers today entered the profession as copy boys and worked their way up. In recent years more and more of the British newspapers have been hiring university graduates; these, however, are still mainly used as leader writers or special columnists. Some newspapers and newspaper groups (e.g., Thomson Newspapers Ltd.) provide their own educational systems for budding newspapermen; these systems stress general education, travel, and technical newspaper work. The Commonwealth Press Union has an interchange system by which journalists can move from country to country and work on various newspapers.

Although today in Britain there is no organized preparatory training for those who would enter journalism as a profession, a national "training scheme," based on a three-year apprenticeship for young journalists who have a position with a newspaper, exists. Organized in 1952, the National Council for the Training of Journalists offers comprehensive training "of journalists," and by 1960 had awarded 820 certificates to young journalists and were training 80 per cent of the new personnel entering the profession.[25]

The London Times's well-known editor, Sir William Haley, dealt with the need for better-trained newspapermen in a 1958 lecture. He said: "We are going to have tremendous problems in getting the best people for journalists. The demand will be all the time for better and better, more qualified people, and all newspaper managers will have to pay more for their services. Where human beings are concerned, cheapness is death."[26]

GENERAL COUNCIL OF THE PRESS. This group, generally called the Press Council[27] in Britain, was set up on the recommendation of the Royal Commission on the Press in 1953. The object was to attempt to bring to the British press some sort of standard concept of press responsibility and performance. As might be expected, such a council was not greeted enthusiastically by certain segments of the press fearing the old monster of "control" was rearing its head.[28] However, after some initial concern and debate, the British press accepted the idea, and today the Press Council appears to be an important and permanent part of the British press system.

The Council is composed of 15 editorial and managerial representatives from British newspapers; there are no lay members. The chairman is elected each year. The Council considers press performance and can censure offenders;

it also investigates problems and squabbles within the press and between the press and the public.

Chief among the Council's purposes are to: preserve British press freedom; maintain high professional standards; promote and encourage methods of recruitment, education, and training of journalists; promote research; appraise press performance and issue regular reports; study developments in the press which may lead toward monopoly; review developments which may restrict the supply of information; and publish reports periodically setting forth its work and reviewing press developments. In the United States most of the functions of the Press Council are performed by private groups like the American Society of Newspaper Editors, Sigma Delta Chi, and the Association for Education in Journalism.

The following part of a story concerning Press Council "statements" is quoted below to indicate at least one important aspect of the Council's function. This is from a story in the Times:

"The council received numerous complaints from members of the public against a recent series of articles in the Sunday Pictorial dealing with the Setty murder case. The council had before it a letter from Mr. Colin Valdar, editor of the Sunday Pictorial. The council decided to issue the following statement:

The council, having considered numerous complaints from the public on the subject, strongly condemns the Sunday Pictorial articles by Donald Hume which appeared under the general heading: 'I killed Setty and got away with murder.' The council holds it to be against the public interest to give an atmosphere of successful crime to so sordid a story, or to allow criminals to justify or mitigate their crimes by romantic explanations which, never having been tested in a court of law, may or may not be true...."[29]

PRESS FREEDOM. Basically the British press has about the same restrictions on its freedom as does the American press.[30] The press in Britain has the same freedom as the individual to say what it pleases provided it does not break the law. There are no specific laws in Britain dealing solely with the press; however, the press is subject to such laws of libel, obscenity, and sedition as apply to all individuals of the country. Except for voluntary censorship during World War II, the

British press has not been subjected to censorship since 1695 when the Licensing Act expired. The British press, however, must be careful of what it prints. For example, an act passed in 1926 restricts statements in the press about divorce cases. A series of laws regulate the action of the press in respect to reporting trials. A British paper may be held in contempt of court if it publishes comments on judges or proceedings of the court which may prejudice their reputation for fairness or may interfere with a fair trial. Theoretically then, the British press is more careful in handling crime news and court proceedings than is the U.S. press. However, the sensational "popular" papers of Britain manage to pack their pages with editorializing and lurid accounts which in many cases would put a sensationalized U.S. crime story to shame. It should be noted, however, that the British journalists have developed a type of writing style which allows them to say about what they wish without actually stating the facts explicitly.

The Defamation Act of 1952, which presents an extended list of "privileged" subjects which may be reported on by the press and which gives more emphasis to "fair comment" and "truth" as defenses in libel actions than was theretofore the case, is generally considered a good law by the press. This law does differentiate between a "public official" and a "private individual," and a newspaper risks more when it attacks a public official. There are also certain laws in England and Scotland which place restrictions on publications which might deal with immoral or obscene material (e.g., the Children and Young Persons Act).

PROFESSIONAL SECRECY. The right of professional secrecy has no legal recognition in British law, and until recently there has been an almost complete lack of decided case law touching on the matter particularly as it affects journalists.[31] On January 24, 1963, however, the High Court of Britain handed down an historic ruling in the case of London Daily Sketch reporter Desmond Clough, who was found in contempt of court for his refusal to name sources for a story about Soviet spying in the British Admirality. To Clough's plea that he "would be breaking a firm trust," the Lord Chief Justice of the High Court, Lord Parker, said he sympathized with Clough's "point of princi-

ple," but "there must be emergencies and urgencies where all interests must be subordinate in a state." He added that while Parliament had granted some special privileges to the press "law has not developed and crystallized the confidential relationship" between newsmen and their sources "into one of the classes of privilege known to law." While holding that Clough must disclose his sources, Parker said that "it is still open to this court" to say whether in a special case "public policy did demand that journalists should be immune."[32]

SOME IMPORTANT NAMES IN BRITISH JOURNALISM. The history of British journalism is filled with names of men who have made significant and lasting contributions to the press. To list all these persons would be an exhausting task even in a study limited to press personalities. However, it might be well to name at least a few of the outstanding British journalists here; this list, while being highly selective and admittedly inadequate, will at least serve as a kind of "personality outline" of British journalistic history. These names are listed in such a way that they coincide generally with the chronological development of the press in Britain:

Daniel Defoe, Richard Steele, Joseph Addison, William Hazlitt, John Bell, John Walter, James Perry, John Wilkes, Richard Carlile, Paul Julius Reuter, John T. Delane, William Howard Russell, Herbert Ingram, Alfred Harmsworth (Lord Northcliffe), John Walter III, Henri de Blowitz, C. P. Scott, H. Wickham Steed, John Alfred Spender, and J. L. Garvin.

Journalists who have been leaders in the British press during the last decade include the cartoonists David Low, Viktor Weiss ("Vicky"), Michael Cummings, Leslie G. Illingworth, Carl Giles and Tom Webster; the correspondents Alistair Cooke, David J. Mathew, Rene MacColl, Donald Ludlow, Patrick O'Donovan, Denys Smith, Ralph Champion, Ross Mark, Christopher Lucas, D. Kimpton Rogers, Henry Brandon, Luis Eric Britter, and M. R. Werner; Columnists, J. B. Morton ("Beachcomber"), William Conner ("Cassandra"), and Francis Williams; and the editors Douglas McCray, R. W. Cudlipp, William Haley, Gordon Newton, W. L. Andrews, H. A. Hetherington, and Malcolm Muggeridge.

Denmark

Denmark takes a leading place among countries with high newspaper readership. Danish newspaper circulation is one of the world's highest in proportion to the population (about 400 copies published daily per 1,000 inhabitants). Denmark, too, has comparatively more newspaper plants than any other nation, with about 225 separate papers existing to serve the country's four million citizens. The press circulates more than a million and a half copies daily to some 1,200,000 households (some two million copies on Sunday), and at least one copy in five is passed on, some to as many as a half dozen persons. In 1962, there were 81 main daily papers published in Denmark.[1] Ten of them are in Copenhagen, the capital, and the rest are scattered rather evenly throughout the provinces. Morning papers account for the bulk of the circulation of the Copenhagen press; the provincials are mainly afternoon journals. The trend in Denmark, as in most nations, is toward fewer but larger newspapers.[2]

The high educational level and general interest in social and political affairs have enabled the daily press to reach out to broad segments of the population. The smallest farm house in the most remote rural area of the country will get at least one newspaper each day. In general, the Danish papers are less formal than those in other countries. They have a pleasing make up, attractive typography, interesting pictures and cartoons, and they try to present something for all the family. The papers generally have a certain wholesome appearance, informal yet not shallow; they probably reflect the characteristics usually associated with the Danes themselves. The overall tone of the newspapers is one of neatness and dignity, yet of friendliness and warmth. Stories are usually written in language that in the United States would be called "light" or "folksy." Another interesting characteristic of Danish newspapers is that the pages are agglutinated (glued at the fold) in the process of printing so that they hold together like magazines.

BRIEF HISTORY. The first Danish paper (Den Danske Mercurius) appeared in 1666 with the support of the Crown; it was the official organ whose principal purpose was to publish bulletins and to glorify King and government. The oldest existing Danish paper, Berlingske Tidende, was founded in 1749 by Ernst Henrich Berling.[3] It is still owned by the founder's family and has been a family paper longer than any other in the world. For the first two centuries of its history the Danish press was subjected to censorship; this rigid control was abolished by the liberal Constitution of 1849, and since then the Danish press has been one of the freest in the world.

Although freedom of the press and access to news is not as fully guaranteed in Denmark as in Sweden, the press-state relationship in Denmark has been delineated as follows:

"The chief characteristic of democracy is that its political will originates from the... people.... Democracy, which is based on the citizen's right to form his own opinions, cannot dissociate itself from freedom of the press.... Without the freedom of the press democracy simply ceases to function, ...and for this very reason (the press) must be independent of the government. The freedom of the press, therefore, is not a privilege granted to newspapers. For them freedom is an obligation, rather than a privilege."

The principle of press freedom is extended even to the laws governing military information where publication is prohibited only where the government has requested secrecy or such information as the government has been keeping secret.[4] Consonant with these freedoms is the right of professional secrecy. Journalists are not obliged by law to observe professional secrecy in Denmark as in Sweden whether with reference to sources or to content. Nor does any Code of Ethics exist within Danish journalist associations binding them to professional secrecy. Nevertheless, Danish journalists consider it an unwritten law they they must observe secrecy with reference to their sources of information, and that a wish for anonymity by a "source" must be respected in court or out. As far as is known, no Danish journalist during the twentieth century has complied with a court order to reveal his source, even under threat of punishment, and courts have generally respected this principle of ethics.[5]

THE PRESS TODAY. Copenhagen has 10 per cent of the nation's dailies and accounts for half of the total circulation. Denmark's largest daily is Copenhagen's Berlingske Tidende; the largest PM daily is Ekstrabladet of the same city, and the largest provincial daily is the morning Jyllands-Posten of Aarhus. About half of the 225 newspapers published in the country are local editions of larger papers. These local editions or "branch" papers began early in Denmark's

journalistic history. Still characteristic
of the country's press system, the papers
share general material with the parent papers,
but print their own local news and advertisements. They are quite similar to the regional
"Kopfblätter" of West Germany. Newspapers in
Denmark are still largely in the "opinion" or
"viewspaper" tradition of Europe, but the
trend seems to be toward a more "information-
based" press. According to a recent article
by Danish writer Paul Graae, the larger the
Danish newspapers become, the more they
emphasize straight news reporting.[6]

COPENHAGEN DAILIES. The nation's three
dailies are Berlingske Tidende, a Conservative
morning paper; Politiken, a Liberal morning
paper, and the midday B.T. These are the only

One of Scandinavia's leading dailies and
one of the oldest national papers in the
world, Berlingske Tidende was founded in
1749 as a 16-pager by Ernst Henrich
Berling in Copenhagen.

Danish dailies with circulations in excess of
100,000. Other important Copenhagen dailies
in order of size are the afternoon Ekstrabladet
(Liberal), the morning Aktuelt (Social-Democratic), the afternoon Berlingske Aftenavis
(Conservative) and Information (Independent),
the morning Kristeligt Dagblad (Independent),
and the morning Land og Folk (Communist).

These dailies range in circulation from
about 62,000 for Ekstrabladet down to about
8,000 for Land og Folk.

JOURNALISTS. In Denmark's long and colorful
press history there have been many important
journalistic figures who have helped evolve
the present excellent press of the nation.[7]
Three of the most important of these journalists are Christian Ferslew (1836-1910),
Henrik Cavling (1858-1933), and Vilhelm
Lassen (1861-1908). Ferslew, who founded
Aftenposten in 1873, introduced a new type
newspaper into the press picture; this was
a nonpolitical journal filled with an assortment of entertainment and how-to-do-it
features which still characterize the Danish
press to a great extent. He also brought to
Denmark the first rotary press (1875).
Cavling was famous for his highly literate
interpretive articles and foreign reportage;
it was he who made the Danish press conscious
of world affairs. He also turned Politiken
from a "literary" paper into a "news" paper
especially important for its international
reporting. Lassen exerted great influence
on Danish newspaper style, breaking down the
earlier academic sentence structure and intro-
ducing a direct, vivid style to journalism
which made use of fresh imagery.

A few other important Danish journalists
and the papers with which they are generally
associated follow: Christen Nielsen (1838-95),
Jyllands-Posten; Herman Bang (1857-1912),
Nationaltidende; Carl Carstensen (1837-1932),
Dagens Nyheder; Viggo Horup (1841-1902),
Politiken; and Emil Wiinblad (1854-1935),
Social Demokraten.

PROVINCIAL PRESS. Unlike the Copenhagen
press, the Provincial Press has retained a
keen interest in politics. It exercises
great influence on political thought throughout the provinces. Most provincial papers
have six to eight pages. They avoid sensationalism and have good national and international coverage. The style is more lucid
and is briefer than is generally found in
the Copenhagen papers. The Danish Provincial
Press makes use of many stringers throughout
the rural areas. Although there is no provincial paper in Denmark of the international
importance of France's La Voix du Nord of
Lille or England's Manchester Guardian, there
are many well-written and excellently-edited
provincial journals. Each newspaper in Denmark's provincial press system is rooted in
one town and its district; there are no
absentee owners.

Usually four dailies (representing each of
the four main parties) can be found in each

of the larger towns throughout the provinces.
However, this system has been on the decline
in recent years. The largest and most important of the provincials are the Conservative
morning dailies Jyllands-Posten of Aarhus
(circulation about 63,000; 143,000 on Sundays);
Aalborg Stiftstidende of Aalborg (circulation
about 40,000; 70,000 on Sundays); Fyns Tidende
(36,000 and 67,000) and Fyens Stiftstidende
(33,000 and 39,000), both of Odense, and the
Jydske Tidende of Kolding (circulation about
30,000).

ADDITIONAL PRESS FACTS. There is much mutual
trust between the press and the public in
Denmark, and journalists are highly respected
in Danish society. Newspaper readers are
highly loyal to their newspapers and generally
feel that they are being served well by the
press.

A large proportion of the newspapers are
publicly owned by joint stock companies.
Newspapers are financially independent.

The Labor press developed about 1870 in
Denmark and follows Germany as the oldest in
the world. Social-Demokraten is the principal
daily serving the laboring classes of the
country.

Danish newspapers get plenty of advertising,
and in this respect are generally considered
ahead of other papers in continental Europe.

A special daily, the Kristeligt Dagblad
("Christian Daily"), represents the Folk
church, the major religious group of the
country. The country also has a specialized
news organization called the "Kristeligt
Pressebureau" which distributes church "copy"
to the Danish newspapers.

The press has a great amount of freedom and
is truly considered the "fourth estate" of
government; it is generally agreed that the
Danish press is as free as any in the world.

Three leading weeklies (quasi magazines)
are the picture paper Billed-Bladet, a farm
illustrated Landet, and the mass appeal
Sondags-B.T., a Sunday publication extremely
popular in the cities. Se og hor, a big circulation radio and television picture review,
is one of the country's most popular monthlies.

Denmark has a well-known school of journalism
at the University of Aarhus. Newspapermen,
not only from Denmark but all through Scandinavia, study here.

Especially significant is the cartoon in
Danish newspapers.[8] The reader finds a wealth
of satirical, informational, and political
cartoons. These drawings add grace to the
news columns, variety to page makeup, and
a sense of intelligent humor to the entire
fare of the Danish press.

THE NATIONAL NEWS AGENCY. The country's
national news agency is Ritzaus, founded in
1866 by E. N. Ritzau. It serves government
departments but is not state controlled; since
World War II it has been owned by the press
as a whole, just as the British press owns
Reuters. It is the largest supplier of news
to the daily press, and also has an excellent
service for the provincials and for radio and
television stations.

DISTRIBUTION. Distribution of almost all
Danish newspapers is handled by A/S Bladkompaniet, a joint media distribution and
delivery cooperative. Owned and controlled
by five Copenhagen dailies, Bladkompaniet
serves all Copenhagen dailies and with few
exceptions all Danish periodicals and a
number of foreign papers. Every paper is
accepted, as are all magazines, unless pornographic in content.

Using about one-fourth the personnel that
would be necessary if every publisher organized his own distribution, the cooperative
delivers about 350 million papers to 7,000
newsstands in Denmark and to nearly four
million subscribers, each year. The organization is not set up to make large profits
for its owners but is serving the Danish
press nearly at cost which is certainly much
lower than the individual papers could hope
to reach even if they could find sufficient
personnel.[9]

LEADING DAILIES: A BRIEF COMMENTARY[10]

BERLINGSKE TIDENDE: (Copenhagen; Conservative
AM; f.1749). Denmark's leading paper; cir-
culation--163,000 daily and 320,000 Sunday.
It is "The Paper" to the great number of
middle class and upper middle-class Danes.
Runs an average of 24 pages, and up to 48
on Sunday. Carries more advertising than
any other Danish paper. Has plenty of
features, puzzles, special columns, drawings,
and photographs. Usually carries a large
cut on front page. Uses color on front page,
and often inside in display advertisements.
News and features scattered rather haphazardly
throughout the advertisement-loaded pages.
A big and varied daily, with make up and
typography not as attractive as other Copenhagen dailies.

POLITIKEN: (Copenhagen; Liberal AM; f.1884).
Denmark's third largest daily; circulation--

144,000 daily and 258,000 Sunday. Often
called the "organ of intellectual liberalism."
Usually runs 16 to 24 pages. Uses color and
often at least one large cut and rather heavy
type on front page. Many and large display
advertisements toward the front of the paper.
Usually has one sports page. Has an attractive editorial page, broken with pictures and
drawings. At least five pages of assorted
features daily and many more on Sunday. Excellent typography and make up. Though a
serious news medium, it probably carries more
entertainment in proportion to total space
than any other of the dailies.

B.T.: (Copenhagen: Conservative midday paper;
f.1916). Denmark's largest daily; circula-
tion--172,000. A lively and entertaining
lunch-time newspaper. One of the Berling
publications. Circulation growing faster than
any other daily in the country. Especially
good sports section. Clean, modern make up
and typography; good photographs. Carries
more advertising than any of the afternoon
papers.

BORSEN: (Copenhagen; Independent AM; f.1896);
circulation--7,500. Denmark's leading commercial and shipping daily. Usually runs 12
pages. Carries most of its advertisements
(display) on pages 2 and 12. Has an attractive editorial page (usually page 8). Might
be called Denmark's equivalent of the United
States's Wall Street Journal.

AKTUELT: (Formerly Social-Demokraten; Copenhagen; Social-Democratic AM; f.1872). Usually
runs 16 pages. Uses color in front and back
page nameplates. Rather gaudy use of type
similar to many French dailies. Generally
two or three large photographs appear on the
front page. Very attractive (conservative)
editorial page (usually p. 10). About seven
pages of features, and usually two full pages
of sports. Circulation--40,000 and 58,000 on
Sunday.

INFORMATION: (Copenhagen; Independent PM;
f.1943). Small in number of pages (usually
eight) and circulation (about 23,000). An
attractive, compact little daily. Skillful
and conservative use of color and typography
on the front page. Inside pages neat and well-
planned. Photographs also conservatively used
(most are one-column). Uses front page display advertisements (usually one), but this
practice fails to disrupt the neat page
appearance. Has normally one page of sports,
about three pages of features, and the rest
news and advertisements.

JYLLANDS-POSTEN: (Aarhus; Conservative AM;
f.1871). Leading and largest daily outside
Copenhagen. One of the most attractive and
best edited newspapers in the country. Especially good national news coverage. Plenty
of entertainment features; attractive editorial
and sports pages. Circulation--nearly 63,000
daily and 143,000 on Sunday.

Finland

Finland has about 200 newspapers of which 23 are dailies, 36 appear six times a week, two appear five times, three appear four times, 28 are triweekly, 11 biweekly, and the remainder are weeklies. These newspapers publish an aggregate of two million copies a day. Newspapers issued every day account for 40 per cent of the total press circulation while those that publish six times a week account for 35 per cent. Consequently, many newspapers are small, but they vigorously champion

dependence and are more or less strictly obliged to accept orders or direction from party authority. Among the bourgeois press the political bonds are generally less rigid.

In Finland as in many other countries, the number of newspapers and their circulations are not apportioned according to political parties in the same ratio as the popular vote in general or local elections. As in the Scandinavian countries, the Labor (Socialist), Agrarian, and Communist press in Finland is considerably smaller in terms of circulation figures than the strength and influence of these parties in parliament. On the other hand, the relatively large circulations enjoyed by the liberal bourgeois newspapers is not nearly reflected by the popular vote. The political right is also disproportionately

FINLAND

LEADING DAILY NEWSPAPERS IN FINLAND[1]

Name of Paper	Party	Circulation
Helsingin Sanomat (Helsinki)	Independent	256,000
Uusi Suomi (Helsinki)	Conservative	93,500
Aamulehti (Tampere)	Conservative	87,500
Turun Sanomat (Turku)	Independent	74,000
Hufvudstadsbladet (Helsinki)	Independent (Swedish)	69,000
Ilta-Sanomat (Helsinki)	Independent Liberal	64,500
Savon Sanomat (Kuopio)	Agrarian Union	55,000
Kansan Uutiset (Helsinki)	People's Democratic Union (Communist)	55,000
Vaasa (Vaasa)	Conservative	50,000
Satakunnan Kansa (Pori)	Conservative	42,500
Keski-Suomalainen (Jyväskylä)	Agrarian Union	48,000
Kaleva (Oulu)	Independent Liberal	40,000
Suomen Sosialidemokraatti (Helsinki)	Social Democratic	36,500
Karjalainen (Joensuu)	Conservative	36,000
Etela-Suomen Sanomat (Lahti)	Independent Liberal	35,500
Maakansa (Helsinki)	Agrarian Union	32,500
Ilkka (Vaasa)	Agrarian Union	25,000

local interests, although often the publishing organization is poor and limited in material resources.[2]

The press, with few exceptions as in the Scandinavian countries, is a party press, and there is no doubt of each newspaper's affiliation. The leading exception to the rule of party connections is Helsingin Sanomat with 256,000 circulation. Its nearest competitor, the Conservative Uusi Suomi, has a circulation of about 93,500. While the press is generally attached to political parties, the extent to which they are politically bound varies considerably. In general, the organs of the leftist parties have the least in-

represented in the press. It is estimated that about 85 per cent of the circulation of the Finnish press belongs to the bourgeois newspapers, but the total representation of bourgeois parties is generally less than 60 per cent. The combined circulation of Social Democratic (Labor or Socialist) newspapers is less than 10 per cent of the national total, but the Party controls almost 20 per cent of the seats in parliament. As for the Communists, although their newspapers account for about 6 per cent of the total circulation, the party controls 23.5 per cent of the seats in parliament.[3]

PERIODICALS. In 1962, there were 1,540

periodicals published in Finland. Of these
1,179 were published in the Finnish language,
130 in Finnish and Swedish, 183 in Swedish
and 48 in other languages. Of the general
interest weeklies the following lead in circulation: Apu (circulation 300,000); Seura
(186,000); Suomen Kuvalehti (150,000); and
Viikko-Sanomat (145,000). Three weekly
magazines put out by and circulated to the
membership of cooperatives are Yhteishyva
with 313,500 circulation, Kuluttaja with
233,000, and Elanto (112,000). Also among
the circulation leaders are two monthly
women's interest magazines: Kotiliesi with
a circulation of 200,000 and Eeva with 105,000.
The top magazine in point of circulation is
Pirkka, a monthly give-away distributed
through retail grocery stores. Two others
deserving mention are a triweekly (about 18
issues a year) magazine devoted to economic
discussions, Pellervo with 133,000 circulation and Valitut-Palat, a monthly general
interest magazine with 127,000 circulation.

HISTORICAL BACKGROUND. The first newspaper
to be published in Finland, Tidningar, utgifna
af ett sallskap i Åbo, published by the Aurora-
Society in Turku, was printed in Swedish and
appeared in 1771. The first Finnish-language
newspaper was Suomenkieliset Viikkosanomat,
published by Antti Lizelius in 1776. In 1820,
when Helsinki was made the capital, publication of an official newspaper, Finlands
Allmänna Tidning, was started, and four years
later Åbo Underrattelser, which is still pub-
blished in Turku under the same title, was
launched. During the next 20 years other
smaller papers were started from time to time
in such towns as Oulu, Viipuri, Vaasa, and
Kuopio.

Because of the severe censorship of the
Tsarist Russian government, the content of
newspapers were for the most part limited to
news of interest only to relatively uneducated
people or to literary articles. The first newspaper that dared to discuss subjects of more
general interest was Saima, founded by J. V.
Snellman in 1844 and suspended in 1846. There-
after Snellman published a monthly literary
periodical, first in Kuopio and later in
Helsinki.

The first newspaper published in Helsinki
in Finnish was Suometar (1847-66). In 1863,
the diet, which had not met in 56 years, was
convoked by Alexander II, and with the political developments of the 1860's more and more
newspapers were established. Helsingsfors
Dagblad, which became the organ of the Liberal
party, was launched in 1862, and in the following year Helsingen Uutiset was founded.
In 1864, Hufvudstadsbladet appeared and has

since remained the leading paper of the
Swedish party. In 1869, Uusi Suometar,
which became the organ of the Finnish party,
was started, and in 1919 it was replaced by
the Uusi Suomi.

Dissatisfied with the Finnish-language
newspaper of that time some younger journalists founded their own newspapers in the
1890's. Of these Päivälehti was the most
notable. When it was suspended by the
censors, it was replaced by Helsingin Sanomat
in 1904. Meanwhile, newspapers of labor
groups appeared, and their number increased
especially after the General Strike of 1905.
The leading paper of the Social Democratic
party was Työmies, published in Helsinki
from 1895 to 1918 and called Suomen Sosiali-
demokraatti from 1918 on. The Communists
also had their own paper, Tiedonantaja,
which was suspended in 1930, and since 1946
Työkansan Sanomat has been published in
Helsinki as the leading organ of the Communist party. After the constitutional reform of 1906, a new political group, the
Farmers' party was formed, and its leading
newspaper, Ilkka, was founded in Vaasa in
1906.

The first periodical published in Finland
was the Swedish-language publication, Allman
litteraturtidning, published by the professors
of the Turku University in 1803. The first
Finnish-language periodical called Mehiläinen
was published under the editorship of Dr.
Elias Lönnrot, the recorder and editor of
the great Finnish epic poem, "Kalevala."
Another periodical, Suomen Kuvalehti, first
appeared in 1873. It ceased publication in
1880, but was re-established under the same
title in 1894. In 1917 a new Suomen Kuvalehti
appeared and is still the largest circulating
periodical in Finland.[4]

FREEDOM OF THE PRESS. By the Form of Government for Finland--the constitution of 1919--
"the right of printing and publishing written
or pictorial representations without any
previous restraint being imposed," is
guaranteed, with "the exercise of these
rights" determined by law.[5] The Finns insist
that they enjoy freedom of the press in the
western sense. Further, they point to certain advantages denied in many other countries. As an example, they cite the law
governing the publication of public documents,
which guarantees with certain exceptions
freedom of access to public information, an
important supplement to freedom of the press.
Exceptions are allowed only in matters of
national security, relations with foreign
states, defense, prevention or investigation
of crime, commercial transactions or

administration of justice by state or local government, or when the vital interests of private persons in the spheres of religious worship, medical care charity, imprisonment, taxation, or official search demand secrecy.[6]

In practice, Finland has no press censorship; the authorities do not check printed matter before publication. Finland's laws, however, make it an offense to endanger Finland's relations with her neighbors, i.e., the U.S.S.R.[7] Moreover, newspaper editors sometimes complain that the government tends to impose a news blackout on subjects which might affect relations between Finland and the U.S.S.R. One editor writes, "these restrictions on information which the public ought to have distort the interpretation of events and are equivalent to a censorship."

While the press in Finland does not suffer abnormal restrictions based on law or on arbitrary measures taken by the authorities, the press has been told to take a moderate tone in discussing East-West disputes, and editors do not feel at ease in discussing international questions, owing to the country's geopolitical position. Because of their sense of civic responsibility, many editors feel enjoined to an attitude of tact toward the U.S.S.R. The result is often a distortion of the news or comment. Some information never sees the light of day, and some editorials are excessively watered down. Many newspaper editors feel restricted by these circumstances, but the fact is that Finnish newspapers can say a great deal. Newspapers may still criticize Russia, if they do it in an objective, restrained tone, and, in the view of some observers, they actually could be more outspoken than they are without running afoul of any law.[8]

Aside from the limitations described, there is no restriction on information in Finland, and the worst that happens according to some newspaper editors is that the party in power sometimes gives its party press a helping hand by letting them in first on official news. Such "leaks" serve the double purpose of giving the party's press a "beat" and assuring a favorable "first editorial reaction."[9]

In Finland there is film censorship, aimed at safeguarding the morals of the young, and this law also applies to television newsreel film. TV people in Finland say, however, that there have been no deletions in film supplied to them.[10]

In the matter of professional secrecy the Finnish law requires persons printing or publishing a newspaper or periodical to keep secret the name of the writer of anything appearing in print, unless the writer agrees that his name may be made known. But the law also requires a journalist to divulge the source of his information to a court of law, if the court rules that there are "important reasons" for demanding it. The journalist himself may consider it his clear duty to divulge the source of information if a major crime or matter affecting the security of the state is before a court. In other cases, he may refuse to divulge information, although the court may then order him to do so under pain of coercive penalty. The journalist may not be required to divulge the source of information to a legislative group, to administrative authorities, or to private persons.[11] In general, the Finnish law shows greater consideration for journalistic confidences than is the case in most other countries.

SOME NEWSPAPER CHARACTERISTICS. One of the most noticeable features of Finnish newspapers is the amount of space they devote to foreign news and, at the same time, the number of news items of a strictly local, small-town character. Because of Finland's geographical position--it is isolated from the main streams of world events and at the same time exposed to the unpredictable turns of Soviet policy-- Finnish readers are profoundly aware of the importance of foreign news, and their interest in such news is correspondingly high. Finnish newspapers therefore generally print more foreign news and give it better play than do U.S. dailies with but a few exceptions. Since the beginning of the growth of European tensions among European states in the 1930's the Helsingin Sanomat built its national standing in circulation on the quality and quantity of its foreign coverage, at the same time not neglecting its national, provincial, and municipal news. Helsingin Sanomat, Uusi Suomi, and Hufvudstadsbladet maintain correspondents in several European capitals and Hufvudstadsbladet,together with the magazine Viikkosanomat, has a correspondent in New York. Most Finnish newspapers subscribe to the Finnish News Agency (Finska Notis Byran) service, and many also get news from AP, UPI, Reuters, TASS, and other agencies.

Finnish newspapers give almost no space to crime news, sex scandals, divorces, etc., and never treat it in a sensational manner. On the other hand, proportionately more space is given in Helsinki papers to news of theaters, concerts, art exhibits, and to education and science than in most U.S. newspapers serving cities of equal population. The Finns are sports enthusiasts and Finnish newspapers provide good coverage for this interest.

While there is no "society page" such as is to be found in most U.S. papers, Finnish newspapers publish engagement and wedding notices and a peculiarly Finnish institution, the birthday notice. These notices are not limited to prominent persons or public figures. Birthday notices are of special interest to

the same amount of advertising. As in Sweden and Denmark, the pages of Finnish newspapers are glued at the fold.

Finnish newspapers run a number of photographs of good quality, and along with other entertainment material they generally use

Three leading Finnish newspapers showing the use of a number of photographs of good quality. The papers are glued at the fold.

all acquaintances, and press surveys show such personals to be among the top items of reader interest.

Finnish newspapers carry both display and classified advertising with the former taking the major part. The Helsingin Sanomat, usually running 20 pages, devotes about one-third of its space, including its front page, to advertising. Of the advertising space, about one-fourth is occupied by classified advertising. Uusi Suomi devotes two of its 14-page average to advertising while the smaller Maakansa with 8 pages carries almost

cartoons and comic strips, including several syndicated in the United States. Editorial commentary is run separate from the news, and since most of the papers are party papers, "canned" party editorials are common. Larger Helsinki newspapers generally devote a full page to editorials, editorial commentary, and opinion pieces by Finnish and foreign writers. Essays and feature material may also be found on the "editorial" page. Smaller papers limit editorials and commentary to one or two columns with the balance of the page devoted to news and feature material and an occasional advertisement.

France

The French press today is slowly evolving from an "opinion" press to an "information" press. Another notable trend is toward more and better provincial newspapers, with an accompanying drop in importance of the Paris press. However, it is wrong to think that the opinion press of France has disappeared. The Paris press is about as much an opinion press today as before World War II, and while the big French dailies are becoming more complete and objective organs of information, they are still largely concerned with commentary and opinion. Throughout the country the circulation of the daily press has been dropping slightly during the past several years; however, the weekly papers and the varied periodicals have had substantial increases in their circulations. There are more than 1,000 weeklies in France and about 2,500 other periodicals of a "nonnewspaper" variety.

There are about 120 dailies in some 70 French cities and towns today with a total circulation of some 10 million. In the nation of 44 million people with an illiteracy rate of 4 per cent, there are about 240 copies of newspapers printed daily for every 1,000 persons. The number of dailies has been steadily decreasing since World War II, and the French press generally is having a difficult existence. The high cost of newsprint, the outmoded plants, the heavy printing charges, and the increasing government control are causing the French newspapers considerable anxiety. Transportation is often slow and uncertain and hinders circulation; advertising is not easy to get, and production costs in general are higher than in any other European country. Two drastic price increases totalling 66 per cent in 18 months (1958-59) put an end to efforts by most French newspapers to increase their circulations. Since 1960 those French newspapers of both the Paris and the provincial press which have been able to survive, with but few exceptions have suffered substantial (20 per cent average) losses in circulation. Also, the rise of television is a matter of growing concern to the French press. Existing legislation forbids participation by the press in its development as has occurred in the United States.

In the postwar years there has been a definite move away from a strictly party press in France, and information papers have become strong--especially in the provinces where about 90 per cent of the papers are "information" journals.

POLITICAL AND INFORMATION NEWSPAPERS. Although the Paris papers (accounting for about a third of France's total circulation) generally support some party rather forcefully, even they are slowly changing from their role as party organs and polemic journals, and are taking on a more independent attitude. And while opinion is still mixed in large doses in the news columns, the ration is decreasing. The three best examples of "information" or nonpolitical dailies of Paris are the PMs France-Soir and Paris-Presse (mainly a feature paper) and the morning Le Parisien Libéré. However, there are still good examples of political papers in the nation's capital. For example, there are L'Aurore and La Croix far to the right-of-center and L'Humanité and Libération on the extreme Left. The best representative of the Paris political weeklies is the slightly left-of-center "opinion" paper L'Express. This lively weekly in 1955 tried to become a daily, but in so doing it lost its popularity and much of its circulation; in early 1956 it returned to its weekly status.[1]

PARIS PAPERS. The Paris daily papers (about 15) now have a total circulation of some 3.5 million. Biggest among them are France-Soir, Le Parisien Libéré, Le Figaro, L'Aurore, L'Humanité and Le Monde. One of the world's most highly-respected papers, Le Monde, has never failed to criticize the government when criticism was felt to be needed; it has always refused outside financial support (often badly needed), preferring to have complete editorial freedom. France-Soir is one of the largest dailies on the European continent. L'Aurore is the daily of the big businessman; it is conservative almost to the point of being reactionary. The four Paris papers with the largest circulations-- France-Soir, Le Parisien Libéré, L'Aurore and Le Figaro--account for nearly three fourths of the capital's total daily circulation.

Since 1959 circulations have generally been falling among Paris newspapers. Over a three year period Paris Soir, the largest of the French dailies, suffered a drop of 235,000 in its circulation. Only one paper, the jazzy tabloid Paris Jour (successor to the conservative, standard-sized but unsuccessful Paris Journal) is an exception to these falling circulations. Launched on September 24, 1959 (the day after the last issue of Paris Journal), it went heavily for splashy headlines, crime stories, gossip columns and

photos. Its success was immediate and by
1962 its circulation stood at 105,000.[2]

Usually considered the best weekly paper
in Paris (certainly the liveliest) is L'Express,
a political journal noted for its sharp writing and courageous editorial policy. It and
Le Monde were two of the most outspoken press
critics of Charles de Gaulle in his successful
bids for French governmental leadership in

any other city in the world.[5] Until after
the war the steel industry of the country
controlled many publications, financing them
to a great degree and even owning several
Paris dailies. (Though this situation still
exists, it is not as serious as it was.)
Before the war the government aided the
press with hidden subsidies, and in the case
of the news agency, Havas, even with "open"
subsidization. The French press was always

LEADING PARIS DAILIES[3] Showing Declining Circulations		1959	1962
France-Soir	(PM; independent.; mass appeal)	1,350,000	1,115,000
Le Parisien Libéré	(AM; independent.; mass appeal)	900,000	757,000
Le Figaro	(AM; independent.; moderate)	480,000	384,000
L'Aurore	(AM; Rightist)	472,000	355,000
Paris-Presse L'Intransigeant	(PM; independent.; mass appeal)	190,000	88,000
Le Monde	(PM; serious; neutral)	202,000	167,000
L'Humanité	(AM; official Communist)	200,000	142,000
La Croix	(PM; Roman Catholic)	132,000	89,000
Libération	(AM; pro-Communist)	110,000	67,000
Paris Jour	(Mass appeal)		105,000

1958 and 1962.[4] Another weekly Paris paper
of great influence is Journal du Dimanche
which gives exceptionally good economic coverage. France-Observateur and Tribune du Peuple
are two other Paris weeklies of note. Two
of the leading Communist weeklies in Paris
are L'Avant-Garde and France-Nouvelle.

PRE-WORLD WAR II PRESS PICTURE. It is probably safe to say that before World War II
the French press was the worst among those
of the major countries of the world. The
French press was certainly an "opinion" press
and made no attempt to present the facts or
to keep Frenchmen abreast of international
affairs. It was a press made up of many
"specialized" publications, each catering to
some particular class or to some special
interest of a reader group. Ethical standards
were not given second thought on most French
papers. What were the reasons for this situation? (1) the French press had a "literary"
origin rather than a "commercial" one, (2)
there was a tradition of low pay and bribes,
and little or no profit came to newspaper
executives, (3) the French press was accustomed to receiving subsidies from government
and business, (4) the press had been considered "Church-dominated" during its earliest
history and was accustomed to various outside
pressures. Although the press might have been
considered "free" of direct government censorship or control prior to World War II, there
was certainly no tradition of social responsibility among French newspapers.

Before the war Paris had more dailies than

amenable to pressures and aid, especially
of an economic nature. These came from
without, as well as within, the nation.
For example, before the outbreak of war in
1939, the Italian and German governments
bribed many French newspapers to be "sympathetic" to their cause.

Prior to the war, Agence Havas (forerunner
of today's Agence France-Presse) was one of
the great world news agencies. It controlled
another French agency--Agence Télégraphique
Radio, which specialized in political and
financial news. Havas also controlled the
chief prewar Spanish news agency--Fabra.
Havas had long been active in providing news
to Latin America, and its successor, the
modern AFP, still has great prestige there.
Another prewar French agency, Agence Fournier,
distributed mainly financial news.

There were five large-circulation papers
in France prior to the War.[6] Known as the
"Big Five," these Paris AMs with circulations
over a million, were Le Petit Parisien
(largest in France), Excelsior (society and
class paper), Le Matin (conservative, semiofficial), Le Journal (sensational, anti-
U.S.), and Le Quotidién (Socialist). The
outstanding political papers at this time
were Le Temps (influential among French
leaders), Le Journal des Debats (ultrareac-
tionary), Le Populaire (Socialist), La
Liberté (Catholic national paper), and
L'Humanité (Communist).

During the liberation period (1944-45) there occurred an extraordinary development from the press point of view. Old newspapers disappeared overnight to be replaced by an entirely new press. Some papers were revivals rather than newcomers. But the majority were entirely new. They were unknown to the general public and owed their generation and ability to survive entirely to the sudden disappearance of all competition. The result was a remarkable upsurge of newspaper launchings. For example, Troyes, a town of 58,000, had six dailies and in Paris and other cities new papers in comparable ratios appeared.

POSTWAR FRENCH PRESS. From the start it was certain that most of these papers would not prove economically viable, and the consequences were soon seen. In 1946 alone 10 Paris and 24 provincial papers closed down. Eventually four strong press groups formed with the four top circulation dailies, France Soir, Le Figaro, L'Aurore and Parisien Libéré each heading a group as its principal asset. There were other important Paris papers launched in the postwar period, e.g., Le Monde (which took over the old Le Temps) which has gained steadily in prestige, influence, and economic strength. With the decline of the French Communist party, its once potent paper L'Humanité has lost much of its immediate postwar prestige. More than half the Communist papers that existed in the French provinces in 1945 are now dead.

In the postwar period with its increased advertising, political parties have been losing their tight grip on the press. Consequently, drastic changes have been taking place in the fare that newspapers offer their readers. The dailies, freed from their need for subsidization, dropped politics and set out to inform and to entertain. Romantic publications and women's weeklies grew at fantastic rates with circulations exceeding a million. Also, science (Science et Vie), economic (La Vie Francaise), and cultural (Réalités) publications won front rank positions for their kind in the world. Paris is still the news center of all France and its shrinking empire and remains one of the main centers of European news. While much of the news of Portugal and Spain, Switzerland and Belgium, and even South America filters through the French capital, some news sources have disappeared, such as that of Parliamentary information. Against this, however, new ones have opened: science news with exploration of outer space and medical development--both intermittent and difficult to exploit. NATO and the Common Market are also difficult to put in popular terms, and while Algeria offered newspapers many temptations, a lack of public interest more than the Government's disapproval

of what was published accounted for the relatively minor play that it received. All these factors point to a future of change for the press of France.[7]

PROVINCIAL PRESS. The French provincial press, although only recently coming into a position of great influence, is an ancient institution, whose popularity was great even during the seventeenth century and even greater during the eighteenth.[8] The provincial papers of today (total circulation about 8 million) are powerful social instruments throughout rural France; they are close to their readers, and their editors understand the wishes and the needs of their readers better than do their counterparts in Paris. Most of the provincials receive news from one or more of the wire services AFP, UPI, AP, and Reuters, and give a well-balanced diet of local and foreign news, light features, and heavy interpretation. All of them in recent years have placed more emphasis on well-trained reporters, better editorial writing, and more "news-conscious" editors. Unfortunately, however, because of acute space problems these editors cannot provide as much news as they would like.[9] Most of the provincial papers are mainly "information" journals, giving very little attention to political commentaries and polemics. With but few exceptions there are no small-town newspapers in France. Special regional editions of metropolitan dailies satisfy the demand for local news in thousands of small and medium-sized communities within their circulation areas. One such large metropolitan daily puts out 19 regional editions. Paris newspapers, however, are not among the newspapers entering this field.[10]

Three of the most influential provincial papers, which in their scope and striving toward quality are rather typical of the whole provincial press, are Ouest-France of Rennes (with nearly 50 different editions), and Le Progrès de Lyon and Lille's La Voix du Nord, each with some 30 editions. These are the nation's largest provincials and strive for quality as well as for large circulations.

Without a doubt the French press of today is better than it was before World War II. Newspapermen are better trained; newspapers present a more thorough and more realistic picture of France and of the world; and newspapers are more objective and place more emphasis on "hard" news. Frenchmen read more today than before the war, but more reading is done in the provinces than in prewar days and less in Paris. French papers give the reader more than two and a half times as much foreign news as before the war and twice as much scientific and medical news. Newspapers, which before the war subscribed only to Havas, now receive local and international news from many sources.

```
┌─────────────────────────────────────────────┐
│           LEADING PROVINCIAL DAILIES          │
│                                               │
│  Ouest-France (Rennes)              535,000  │
│  Le Progrès de Lyon (Lyon)          355,000  │
│  La Voix du Nord (Lille)            337,000  │
│  Sud-Ouest (Bordeaux)               307,000  │
│  Dauphiné Libéré (Grenoble)         330,000  │
│  Depêche du Midi (Toulouse)         252,000  │
│  La Nouvelle République (Tours)     238,000  │
│  L'Est Républicain (Nancy)          225,000  │
│  La Provençal (Marseille)           194,000  │
│  Le Republicain Lorrain (Metz)      162,000  │
│  Le Midi Libre (Montpellier)        162,000  │
│  Nord-Matin (Lille)                 154,000  │
│  La Montagne (Clermont-Ferrand)     150,000  │
│  L'Union (Reims)                    139,000  │
│  Paris-Normandie (Rouen)            137,000  │
│  Derniers Nouvelles d'Alsace                 │
│     (Strasbourg)                    135,000  │
│  Nice-Matin (Nice)                  130,000  │
│  Le Telegram de Brest et                     │
│     P'Ouezt (Morlaix)               110,000  │
│  La France (Bordeaux)               100,000  │
└─────────────────────────────────────────────┘
```

THE FRENCH PRESS: A GENERAL SUMMARY. Foreign language publications in France are numerous; in 1958 there were about 80 of them being published in some 20 different languages. Today's French press gives much more play to pictures than before the war and is more concerned with typography and make up.

Large papers often serialize books. Women's magazines have seen a phenomenal rise since the war and account for nearly half of the periodical press (about 5,000 titles).[11] A few of the leading women's magazines are Echo des Francaises (with a circulation of more than 2 million), Echo de la Mode (circulation: about 1.5 million), Elle, Bonnes Soirées and Intimité. Two of France's leading general magazines (picture) are the weekly Paris-Match (patterned after U.S.'s Life magazine, and the monthly France Illustration. A few other popular general magazines are Réalités (a quality monthly), Le Canard Enchaine (humor-satire), Ici-Paris, Jours de France, Point de Vue, and La Presse.

The main distributing agency today for the press is called the "Nouvelles Messageries de la Presse Parisienne." Almost all the Paris circulation is carried out through the news-stands or "kiosks" as they are called in France. Publications-distributing groups such as the "Messageries" organization of Paris operate

throughout France.

There are no such bulky newspapers in France as are published in the U.S. and Britain; few of the French dailies or weeklies have more than 8 to 12 pages.[12] Le Figaro and France-Soir among the mass-appeal papers and the ultraserious Le Monde probably give the French reader more to read than any of the other dailies in the country. Although rather gaudy in make up and aimed at a larger audience than is Le Monde, Le Figaro and France-Soir consistently contain a large amount of national and world news of a serious nature. Le Figaro, especially, pro-vides a heavy diet of well-written foreign news and commentary. Although it may be termed a "popular" paper, it bears little resemblance to British "popular" papers such as the Daily Mirror or the Daily Sketch; it is similar, however, to the Daily Mail and other of the more conservative "popular" papers in treatment of the news. France-Soir, especially in many aspects of its make up and photographic treatment, resembles Britain's Daily Express.

La Croix, a PM daily with a circulation of about 155,000, is France's leading Roman Catholic paper. It is owned and edited by the Order of Assumption, and although a Catholic paper, it gives a good general news coverage and shows little religious bias.[13] As might be expected, however, it travels a far Right political road; in 1958 and 1962 it was one of the strongest press advocates of De Gaulle's rise to power in France.

Classified advertising is the dominant type of advertising in French papers; the French people have always been somewhat suspicious of display advertising, considering it "propagandistic." Display advertisements, many of which are full-page, are commonly found, however, in several of the larger Paris papers such as France-Soir and Le Figaro.

French law dating back to the last century permits the press to be censored in times of crisis, and after World War II, beginning with the war in Indo-China, from time to time the law was evoked.[14] Such a crisis occurred in late 1958 when the French government fell, and General Charles de Gaulle became premier. French newspapers were censored and issues were confiscated by the government.[15] Although such seizures had been made before, the Gaullist government, citing the war in Algeria, resorted to the frequent use of seizures and occasionally closed newspaper offices. More-over, the legal position of the government in such actions was strengthened by Article 16 of the Constitution of the Fifth Republic, adopted in 1959, which permits the head of state to take any action he feels necessary regarding the press. The effect of this "Sword of Damocles" has been to make newspapermen "think twice about printing some stories."[16]

With the end of the Algerian crisis French journalists hoped that such seizures would cease, but in this they were disappointed. Seizures continued through 1962, [17] and there is no sign of their termination. Such seizures inevitably result in losses to the publishers. As the London Economist pointed out in 1958, issues can be impounded if such issues are termed "undesireable" by the government. The government then "shows no hurry to prosecute," adds the Economist, and the "newspaper has no real redress."[18] The famed British political and economic weekly review then proceeds to issue this warning: "In modern times, any tampering with the rights of the Fourth Estate is a sign that democracy in a country is in serious danger." Finally, the government often uses many of the papers as propaganda instruments. It is not traditional in France for the press to be regarded as owing any special responsibility to the people, but there does appear to be a trend toward more social responsibility.

Most newspapers in France are well-written and well-edited. This is true of Paris papers, as well as those in the provinces. Generally the stories are concise and readable. French journalists in general appear to be well-informed, literate, and forceful. Newspaper readers in France do not have to worry about being bored; even stories which contain information of great significance are written in an interesting manner. In Paris there is no actual home delivery of newspapers. Instead, the papers are delivered to the "kiosks," where the Parisian traditionally expects to obtain them.

The French national news agency is Agence France-Presse (AFP). It was established in 1835 under the name of Agence Havas and took its present name after World War II. Most of the postwar agency's staff members were former Havas employees, and AFP has in most respects continued in the old Havas tradition. Until 1956 AFP received government subsidies; at this time the subsidies were replaced by subscriptions contracted with AFP by the public services and certain of the larger ministries, and, of course, by the press itself. According to the law of 1956 the agency now has its management in the hands of an administrative council under a director general. The Council is composed of 15 members from press, radio and government.

There are two schools of journalism in France. One is at the Catholic University of Lille; the other is an independent school in Paris called the Superior School of Journalism. Supplementing these two schools is the Institute of Industries and Graphic Arts in Paris; this school makes available courses for journalists interested in technical aspects of publications work.

Standards in French journalism appear to be improving constantly. The provincial papers are showing more rapid improvement than are the Paris papers. Paris is still the center of the French press and its papers are most all "national" journals since they circulate throughout the country; however, regional patriotism and the rapid improvement of the "local" papers have increased the readership of the provincial papers to an unprecedented extent.

This picture weekly has great prestige both in France and abroad. It has a circulation of nearly two million a week. Paris-Match is known for its thorough news coverage and imaginative methods of displaying its pictures. Its staff members are young (average age 30) and have high morale and loyalty to their publication. The magazine has about 100 photographers. Directing its pictorial news content toward the middle-brow, the magazine avoids both cheap cheesecake and philosophical subjects.

Paris-Match covers all big stories with many photographers. One rival has said, "Match men move in on a story like locusts. After they're through, there's nothing left for anyone else to reap." (Newsweek, Nov. 17, 1958, p.82).

France-Soir is France's largest circulation daily, selling 1,115,000 copies each day.

This PM paper concerns itself mainly with "news" and gives practically no space to opinion and commentary. Although its make up is a very lively "circus" type, it evidences careful planning and a flair for originality.

Generally an edition of this paper runs 20 to 24 pages, making it one of the thickest of French dailies. Its director is Pierre Lazareff, a dynamic journalist who worked for New York's Daily Mirror during World War II. This probably helps account for France-Soir's formula of "more news and features and less opinion."

Le Figaro, founded in 1854 (daily in 1866), chiefly represents the conservative bourgeoisie of France. This "morning bible of France's upper middle class,"[19] is regarded as the country's most pro-U.S. paper. It is a daily with a good reputation at home and abroad, giving much emphasis to foreign news, music, literature, art, and the theater. Pierre Brisson, its "Directeur," is one of France's most noted journalists. This daily has been called "one of the greatest--in some respects the very greatest" of French newspapers.[20] A copy of the paper usually runs 20 to 24 pages.

Le Monde, a PM with a circulation of some 200,000, is France's most serious newspaper and usually considered one of the top "quality" papers in the world. It is today's counterpart of France's prewar daily--the influential Le Temps.

The publisher of Le Monde is the colorful and temperamental Hubert Beuve-Méry, who writes under the pen name of "Sirius" and is considered one of Europe's most courageous and competent journalists.[21]

This tabloid "quality" paper is the main spokesman of the left-of-center intelligent

liberals. It never hesitates to criticize any regime or group or policy; often it has been critical of U.S. foreign policy and has blasted French government activities. It uses no art, and its grey masses of body type and lifeless pages make it improbable that it will win any make up awards. However, it is generally recognized as the best-written analytical paper in France.[22] Its pages are filled with weighty news and commentary.

Le Monde does not contain much advertising; it relies on newsstand sales and subscriptions for most of its income. It is often in serious financial difficulties but maintains its high quality and has a dedicated staff, who own a one-fourth interest in the paper.

L'Humanité, the official Communist party daily organ in France was founded in 1904 by Jean Jaures, strange as it may seem today, as an anti-Russian paper.

Although it has lost some of its immediate post-World War II prestige, it still ranks next to Italy's L'Unità as the Free World's leading Communist daily newspaper.

L'Humanité is better written and edited than the pro-Communist paper, Libération; however, the latter is more professionally made up than

L'Humanité. Both papers get outside subsidies.[23] At the end of 1958 L'Humanité had a circulation of about 200,000 and Libération was circulating some 110,000 copies.

Greece

dailies and a large number of weeklies scattered throughout the nation. Although the nation's newspaper circulations are among the lowest in Europe and the economic position of publishing is precarious, the press has great vitality, frequently shows courage, and among the newspapers are some that strive for a high intellectual level.

Greece, a country of 8.25 million people and a literacy rate of about 75 per cent has some 900 newspapers of which almost 100 are dailies with a total circulation of more than half a million. More than two-thirds of the dailies are published in the capital city of Athens.

GENERAL PRESS CHARACTERISTICS.[2] Today's journalism in Greece is a blend of politics, culture, and general news presentation, with a liberal portion of lively editorializing. The reader of an average Greek paper receives

```
PERIODICAL PUBLICATION IN GREECE[1]

Daily Newspapers . . . . . . . . . . . . . . . . . . . . . .   94
     Athens . . . . . . . . . . . . . . . . . . . . .   27
          News and Politics . . . . . . . . .   14
          Sports . . . . . . . . . . . . . . .    1
          Economics and Business . . . . . .    7
          Foreign Language . . . . . . . . . .    5
     Provincial . . . . . . . . . . . . . . . . . . .   67
                                                        ──
                                                        94
Nondailies . . . . . . . . . . . . . . . . . . . . . . . .  811
Total number of newspapers published in Greece . . . . . . . .  905 . . . . . . . .  905
Other periodicals . . . . . . . . . . . . . . . . . . . . . . . . . . . . . . . . .  531
Total number of periodicals published in Greece . . . . . . . . . . . . . . . . .1,436
```

Athenian newspapers include five foreign language dailies: two English, two French, and one Turkish. The average circulation of Athenian dailies is about 25,000 with the highest at close to 80,000. Week-end circulations run 50 per cent higher than daily circulations.

strongly-presented political essays balanced with as much world and domestic news as the newspaper is able to gather and print. There is no such thing as a nonpolitical paper in Greece and each one is proud of its political stand. While it is not the policy of Greek

TEN LEADING DAILIES IN ATHENS*

		Daily	Sun.-Mon.
Akropolis	(AM; Conservative)	56,000	160,000
Ta Nea	(PM; Liberal-Center)	76,000	96,000
Kathimerini	(AM; Conservative)	35,000	50,000
Athinaiki	(PM; Liberal)	28,000	34,000
Apogevmatini	(PM; Conservative)	40,000	55,000
Ethnos	(PM; Liberal-Right)	22,000	31,000
To Vima	(AM; Liberal)	25,000	41,000
Eleftheria	(AM; Liberal-Left)	35,000	60,000
Avghi	(AM; Extreme Left)	12,000	18,000
Ethnikos Kyrix	(AM; Extreme Right)	10,000	--

*AMs do not publish on Mondays; PMs do not publish on Sundays; AMs generally have bigger circulations on Sundays, PMs on Mondays.

The main Athens and Salonika dailies circulate as national and regional newspapers and are frequently found in the same homes as copies of the smaller local papers. The bulk of the Greek press, however, is made up of small

newspapers to "sensationalize" news, Greek journalists are exceedingly uninhibited when writing of crimes or sexual misbehavior. There is virtually no enforcement of libel laws to protect personal dignity, and Greek

journalists usually write about an accused
(or even suspected) person as though he were
guilty until proved innocent--the opposite of
the Anglo-Saxon tradition.[3] In libel cases
retraction and publication of an apology are
generally accepted by Greek courts as complete
reparation for damages and for exoneration of
culpability. Moreover, there appears to be
a tendency for all Greek papers to grow more
"popular" in tone. Traditionally, the press
takes seriously its role of public servant and
defender of personal liberties. Greek readers
like a political press, and there is a wide
range of political news and views in the newspapers. Lively editorials, popular in Greece
from earliest days of the press, are still
the most avidly read articles in the paper.
Another essay type called the "chronicle"
(witty satirical articles) is also popular.

Newspapers in Greece, almost alone among
European publications, have great respect for
the authorities, and this is not a "forced
respect" such as one would find in Spain and
certain other countries. Journalists are
generally well-educated and command fair
salaries compared to other professional workers
in the country. Moreover, as in Italy, the
Greek government provides its newspapermen

with identity cards allowing them many
special privileges such as free transportation within the country and special rates
for sea travel.

```
A FEW LEADING PROVINCIAL DAILIES

*Makedonia          (Salonika; AM;
                       33,000)
Ellinikos Vorras    (Salonika; AM;
                       21,000)
Elliniki            (Piraeus; PM)
Nea Ellas           (Larissa; AM)
Tachydromos         (Volos; AM)
Rodiaki             (Rhodes: AM)
Patris              (Pyrgos; AM)
Peloponnesos        (Patras; AM)
Kyrix               (Chania, Crete; AM)
Neos Agon           (Karditsa; AM)
Proini              (Kavalla; AM)


*Greece's foremost provincial daily
(circulation about 33,000); with the
exception of Ellinikos Vorras    all
others have small circulations--
usually around 3,000-8,000.
```

Athens and Salonika are the principal press
cities of Greece. The main Athens papers
circulate throughout the country, and the
Salonika papers (especially the well-edited
daily Makedonia) cover northern Greece. The
largest and most influential dailies in
Athens are the quality Kathimerini and Vima,
and the solid but mass-appeal Akropolis,
Ta Nea, and Athinaiki. The first of these,
Kathimerini (meaning Daily) is a Conservative morning daily running from 10 to 12
pages. Although it has a regular-size eight-
column format like most other Greek papers,
its make up is duller than most and it uses
a minimum of illustrated material. Vima
("Platform"), on the other hand, has a very
lively make up and uses illustrations (many
of them cartoons) liberally. This paper,
a morning daily with a Liberal Center political orientation, usually prints only eight
pages. Probably the most sensational papers
in the country are the small French-language
Messager d'Athènes, and the English-language
Athens News. The leading daily in the
country is Athens' morning Akropolis, with a
circulation of between 60,000 and 75,000.
Also in Athens are published the "Big Two"
among the nation's weeklies; they are Embros
and Tachydromos. They are serious journals
published every Saturday, each having a
circulation of about 60,000.

By far the leading dailies of northern
Greece and among the finest papers in the

whole country are <u>Makedonia</u> and <u>Ellinikos</u>, morning dailies of Salonika. Several of the principal magazines of the country are the literary <u>Nea Histia</u>, the movie <u>Kinimato-graftikos Astir</u>, and the general appeal <u>Eikones</u>, all of Athens. The last-named magazine, a weekly illustrated publication with exceptionally fine photographs, is the only journal of its type in the country. Its popularity is great in Greece and abroad. The magazine publishes an edition in English each month called <u>Pictures From Greece</u> which contains a selection of articles and photographs from the weekly <u>Eikones</u>.

Since all newsprint must be imported and is rationed, most papers suffer from a newsprint shortage.[4] To save space reporters have developed a style of writing which says much in a few words while not sacrificing the color or interest of the report. The editorial cartoon is very popular throughout the Greek press, especially in the dailies of Athens and Salonika. One of the leading contemporary cartoonists is Phokion Demetriadis, whose cartoons are often reprinted in leading newspapers outside Greece. American and British syndicated columnists are popular in Greece and are often published on the front pages of the country's papers. Most newspaper plants are modern and equipment is good. Pre-World War II presses imported from Germany are found in use throughout Greece. American printing equipment of all kinds has become quite popular since the war and is especially well-represented in the bigger papers. Most large papers print from rotary presses, while flat-bed presses are used principally by provincial papers.

PRESS FREEDOM. Article 14 of the Greek Constitution provides freedom of the press "with due adherence to the laws of the state." Among these "laws of the state," certain laws have been enacted which permitted the government to punish newspapers for offending public decency, disclosing significant military information in times of danger, for instigating treasonable acts, and for insulting the Royal Family. In contrast to the general libel law, the provision protecting the Royal Family is strictly enforced. A case in point occurred during the summer of 1962. The failure of the Royal Family to invite the Queen's mother, the dowager Duchess of Brunswick and Lueneburg and Princess of Prussia, to the wedding of a Greek princess, led Greek journalists to imply that the duchess was being neglected by her children. Two editors were promptly jailed, and, despite protests and petitions to King Paul

of Greece for royal pardons, at the end of the year they were still in prison.[5]

To these limitations on press freedom still another was added in 1953 when a law was enacted that gave the government the power to "calm down" opposition papers or to silence them completely. Despite these limitations most observers report that "there is extensive freedom of information in Greece." Sources are easily accessible, and dissemination of information is also free. Restrictions are most apparent in the radio, which is controlled by the government. "No story or comment against the government," reports one observer, "has any chance to reach the air."[6]

In addition to these legal limitations on freedom of the press in Greece, the possibility of the use of economic pressures as instruments of control or weapons of political reprisal are particularly evident in Greece. Already noted has been the fact that all newsprint is imported and subject to allocation. Although there is no evidence that this power has been misused in Greece, in many countries such has been the case. A more serious problem and threat to press freedom is that of government subsidies extended since World War II, first to rehabilitate the damaged plants and later to meet rising costs. As a result of these subsidies and "loans" most of the newspapers of the country are in the debt of the government, and, while many of these newspapers remain critical of the government, it is probable that their number would be greater if their economic dependence were less. Also, in recent years "an arrangement put in the hands of the Premier" the power of approval or disapproval "of bank credits to newspapers, and, although no government so far has used it as a means of threat, in some cases it acts automatically through the fear of consequences...." A strong stand against the government could result in a changed credit standing for the publisher.[7]

The national news agency--Agencia Atenas (Athens News Agency)--depends partially on a government grant for its existence; it gets its other revenues from subscriptions. Its headquarters are in Athens. A smaller agency, called Hellenews, is a privately-owned and operated organization centered in Athens. There are no news and feature syndicates in the country. Most news gets to the Greek papers through Athens News Agency, which has exchange agreements with Reuters, AFP, and various European national agencies. Many Greek papers also subscribe to AP and UPI services.

Holland

The press of the Netherlands, one of the oldest in the world, is primarily an "opinion" press.[1] However, the Dutch people have a great respect for objective reporting, and portions of their press have the characteristics of the "information press" as exemplified by that of the United States. The Dutch press also might be described as principally a "subscription" press with most newspapers being delivered directly to the home and aimed at the entire family. About 150 dailies sell nearly 300 copies each day for every 1,000 inhabitants of Holland. The total circulation of the daily press is three million. Most papers (nearly 75 per cent) in Holland have a political coloring, but only two--Het Vrije Volk ("Free People"), the official organ of the Socialist or Labor party, and the Communist De Waarheid ("Truth")--are official party journals. Het Vrije Volk, publishing some 30 editions from several plants, is the largest Dutch newspaper, with a circulation of nearly 300,000. Four of the others sell from 100,000 to 200,000 copies daily.

About 98 per cent of the total circulation of Dutch newspapers goes by direct delivery to regular subscribers at their homes. Very few single copies are sold at newsstands. Virtually every Dutch family reads at least one paper, with a large percentage of families subscribing to two or more. People who can afford to pay for them usually subscribe to one paper with a nationwide circulation and to one local paper--for the local news and the local advertising columns. Street sales being negligible, there is no need for sensational make up, and most Dutch papers use an extremely dignified and attractive typographical and photographic display style. Probably the neatest and most dignified of the Dutch dailies is the well-edited Nieuwe Rotterdamse Courant (circ. about 70,000) of Rotterdam.

About 40 per cent of the Dutch dailies are independent (neutral) of political party affiliation; however, this does not mean that they are classed as "information" papers or strict "nieuwsbladen." Almost all have definite political biases and show them regularly in their columns. The other 60 per cent of the dailies are considered strongly political and represent the Roman Catholic, Labor (Socialist), Protestant, Liberal, and Communist parties. Roman Catholic papers dominate among the political papers, followed in importance by the representatives of the parties as listed above.

Leading Socialist dailies are Het Vrije Volk (the country's largest daily) of Amsterdam and Het Parool (also of Amsterdam), which calls itself "an independent newspaper" but generally backs socialist opinion. The chief Catholic dailies are De Volkskrant and De Tijd-Maasbode, both of Amsterdam. The outstanding Liberal dailies are Amsterdam's Algemeen Handelsblad and Rotterdam's Nieuwe Rotterdamse Courant.[2] The nonpolitical papers of information are mainly the Amsterdam morning nationals, De Telegraaf and De Courant Nieuws van den Dag, and the Rotterdam PM, Algemeen Dagblad.

The press of Holland is predominantly an evening press with less than a dozen morning papers being published throughout the country. Most Hollanders like to read their papers leisurely at night when their day's work is finished. The papers, which have from 12 to 24 pages (with 40-50 per cent used for advertising), are read thoroughly. No newspapers appear in Holland on Sunday.

THE NATIONAL PAPERS. Twelve national dailies circulate throughout the country. Three of these began as underground papers during the Nazi occupation in World War II. Of these dozen nationals, eight are evening papers. Nine are published in the largest city and capital--Amsterdam, and three in Rotterdam, the second city and most important seaport of Holland. The national dailies account for at least 40 per cent of the total circulation of the Dutch press. These papers have foreign correspondents in several nations, whereas the regional or provincial journals rely almost entirely on the national news agency, Algemeen Nederlandsch Persbureau (ANP) for their news. Most provincial and regional papers have syndicated correspondents abroad in such cities as Washington, New York, London, Paris, Bonn, and Sidney (Australia).[3]

The four largest of the national dailies-- all centered in Amsterdam--are the following:

Het Vrije Volk ("Free People")--circulation about 310,000; official organ of the Socialist (Labor) party; publishes some 30 editions from several locations in the country.

Het Parool ("Watchword")--circulation 160,000; an independent Socialist (Labor party) paper, founded in 1940 as an underground organ.

De <u>Telegraaf</u> ("Telegraph")--circulation
about 210,000; stresses information rather
than opinion; a nonparty paper of mass appeal.

De <u>Volkskrant</u> ("People's Journal")--circula-
tion about 170,000; chief Roman Catholic paper
of Holland. De <u>Tijd-Maasbode</u> (Times-Meuse
messenger), also of Amsterdam, is the oldest
Roman Catholic paper in Holland (f.1846), and
after the amalgamation of De <u>Tijd</u> of Amsterdam
with the former Rotterdam paper <u>Maasbode</u> in
1960 it became one of the larger newspapers
of Holland with a circulation of 113,000.
<u>Trouw</u> ("Loyal") is the most important Protes-
tant daily with a circulation of 115,000.

A few other of the top circulation national
dailies and their approximate circulations
follow: <u>Algemeen</u> <u>Dagblad</u> ("General Daily"),
122,000; <u>Haagsche</u> <u>Courant</u> ("The Hague Journal"),
110,000; <u>De</u> <u>Courant</u> <u>Nieuws</u> <u>van</u> <u>den</u> <u>Dag</u> ("The
Current News of the Day"), 90,000, and <u>De</u>
<u>Waarheid</u> ("Truth")--official Communist organ
whose circulation is never published but
estimated to be not over 45,000. Two highly
influential serious nationals are <u>Algemeen</u>
<u>Handelsblad</u> ("General Commerce Paper") of
Amsterdam with 60,000 circulation, and Rotter-
dam's <u>Nieuwe</u> <u>Rotterdamse</u> <u>Courant</u> ("New Rotterdam Journal") with 52,000.

De <u>Volkskrant</u> of Amsterdam, principal
Catholic paper of Holland and one of the
largest AM dailies, usually runs 12 to 24
pages with 30 to 45 per cent of the space
given to advertising. Its make up is livelier
than most Dutch papers, actually approaching
a mild circus-style. One or two advertisements are commonly found on the front page.
It presents good, solid national and international news, although its news content is
rather limited and highly selective. Founded
in 1906, its circulation today is about
170,000. J. M. Lücker, its editor-in-chief,
is one of Holland's outstanding journalists
who has become well-known throughout the
world press because of his work with the
International Press Institute.

<u>Algemeen</u> <u>Handelsblad</u> of Amsterdam (founded
in 1828; daily, 1830) is the country's oldest
daily paper. It is Liberal politically, its
circulation is about 60,000, and it usually
has 14 to 18 pages with some six to eight of
them filled with advertising. It uses a mild
circus make up with conservative use of red
ink on the front page. Although its specialty
is economic news, it probably provides more
general national and foreign news than any
other Dutch paper. It gives the reader a
rich variety of serious news, lively features,
good coverage of the popular arts, and a
wealth of excellent pictures.

<u>Nieuwe</u> <u>Rotterdamse</u> <u>Courant</u> of Rotterdam,
often considered abroad as Holland's best
daily, has a circulation of only about 52,000.
Founded in 1842, it became a daily the next
year. It usually runs 12 pages (three to
five of them advertising), and uses an extremely dignified, conservative make up with
small headlines. It carries a large proportion of foreign stories originating with its
own correspondents or from Reuters, AFP, and
AP. Maarten Rooy (director) and A. Stempels
(editor) are two of Holland's top journalists.

PRESS SUMMARY. There is a large weekly and
monthly periodical press in Holland, and all
types of magazines--from women's journals to
serious literary journals--are extremely
popular and have a large readership.[4] The
high readership of the newspapers and periodicals is not difficult to understand when one
realizes that Holland's population is almost
99 per cent literate. The Dutch press is
decentralized because there is great interest
in local news; of the total circulation of
nearly three million newspaper copies,
almost 60 per cent come from the local press.
Most provincial papers (regional and local)
are opinion papers, but offer much national
and foreign "hard" news--especially of a
political nature. Dutch newspapers hesitate
to publish political scandals, do not pry
into police records, and very seldom report

juvenile crimes and such incidents as suicides. Foreign news is popular in Holland and the newspapers generally give more space to international events than to national news. Newspapers are primarily opinion papers, with subscribers taking papers which back their religious and political beliefs. As in Britain, journalists receive their training on the job. Universities do not offer "practical" journalism courses dealing with the techniques of writing and editing. According to one outstanding Dutch journalist, the country's press prefers that each paper train its own reporters. He said: "I can look at a story written by almost any Dutch reporter and tell you what newspaper he works on. We like for each of our newspapers to be distinctive."[5]

The Dutch national news agency, Algemeen Nederlandsch Persbureau, was established in 1934 and began actual news dissemination the following year. The agency was a consolidation of four smaller and specialized agencies which existed until 1934. ANP is a cooperative agency of the owners of all newspapers of Holland. Headquarters are at The Hague, and other main offices are in Rotterdam, Amsterdam, Utrecht, and Hilversum. The agency has some 600 correspondents scattered throughout the country; it also maintains a bureau in Brussels, and a few correspondents in the dwindling Dutch possessions. ANP has exchange agreements with Reuters, AFP, TASS, and several European national agencies. AP and UPI also distribute news in Holland, but only a few of the main papers subscribe to them.

JOURNALISM IN HOLLAND. The Constitution of the Netherlands guarantees press freedom within the limitations set by law. "Freedom of information" is occasionally hampered by a rather "unpress-minded" officialdom, but such incidents are becoming less frequent and have

no political background.[6] In tune with the general outlook of the population, the press has little interest in the publication of sensational news; it is highly disciplined, but self-disciplined. Although the Association of Netherlands Newspaper Publishers, a cooperative society, has considered a "code of honor," such a set of rules outlining the press' responsibility was not thought necessary.

Moreover, the association had a Board of Investigation to hear public complaints against the press and also to judge whether the activities or attitude of any newsman is harmful to the dignity of Dutch journalism.[7]

Italy

Until the Association of Italian Advertisers (Utenti Pubblicità Associati) thoroughly investigated the influence of the mass media on Italians in April and May, 1958, no reliable assessment of newspaper readership, broadcast audiences, and magazine circulations existed. The UPA study was the first such ever held in Italy.[1] It was conducted by the nation's two leading public opinion organizations, DOXA or Institute for Statistical Research and Public Opinion Analysis, and SIRM or Italian Institute for Market Research.

At last, foreign correspondents and others concerned with Italian mass media could put leading papers and broadcasts into perspective. Only 40 per cent of the adult population reads a daily newspaper regularly, due partly to Italy's illiteracy rate of 20 per cent of the total population of 51,000,000.[2]

Northern Italy, with less than one-third of the nation's people, has two-thirds of its newspapers, the highest literacy rates, and the biggest purchasing power and corresponding advertising potential. Olivetti typewriters, Necchi sewing machines, Fiat automobiles, and Vespa motorscooters are symbols of Milan and Turin. Unemployment and low farming profits are symbols of southern Italy, especially the island of Sicily.

Journalistically, too, the one national newspaper--and in many ways Italy's leading paper--Corriere della Sera publishes in Milan, through it circulates two morning editions from the Alps to the southernmost towns, in every major European capital, and by airmail in key cities around the world.

Founded in 1876, Corriere della Sera was Italy's first modern reliable paper, with good coverage of top world news and detailed attention to Italian public affairs. Luigi Albertini, who became managing editor in 1898, adapted some British and United States press norms, but was forced from his post by the Fascists in 1925.

With the postwar proclamation of the Italian Republic in 1946, Corriere della Sera began to rebuild its great strength of the pre-Fascist era. This independent, conservative daily began as an evening paper (hence its name, "Evening Courier") but now comes out mornings. Thus the time element works in its favor, as 700 stringers and correspondents throughout the world and 150 newsmen in Milan funnel information into news desks during the night.

News filled, Corriere uses no entertainment space fillers such as puzzles, comics, or gossip columns. Its circulation is estimated at 500,000. Without any equivalent of the U.S. Audit Bureau of Circulations, Italian newspaper circulation figures are verified mainly by the leading advertising agencies, many of whom act as administrators of even local advertising. The TEAM agency represents not only Corriere but also sixteen other leading Italian, French, Swiss, Belgian, Dutch, German, Swedish, Norwegian, and British newspapers with leading European advertisers. TEAM circulation figures for Corriere and other top Italian papers check against those given by Società Internazionale Pubblicità agency.

The country's second largest general daily, La Nuova Stampa of Turin, with a circulation of 300,000, also is a morning paper.

The morning Il Gazzettino of Venice and the afternoon Corriere d'Informazione of Milan, each with a circulation of about 200,000, also rank among the nation's top circulation papers. The Vatican daily L'Osservatore Romano also has a circulation of some 200,000. Il Messaggero, with a daily circulation of about 150,000, is Rome's largest and most influential newspaper. Among the specialized newspapers, Rome's Corriere dello Sport (circ. 300,000) and Milan's Gazzetta dello Sport (circ. 450,000) are the leaders.

Il Giorno of Milan, Italy's newest (founded 1956) daily of importance, has already boosted its circulation to the neighborhood of 200,000, placing it in the top ranks of Italian newspapers. Its great emphasis on serious world and national events, its easy-to-read and racy style, and its attractive typography and make up are giving it mounting popularity and prestige.

THE PRESS--AN OVERVIEW. The influence of the press on Italian public opinion is not very great. Papers of every political tint exist in the country, and the people tend to read the one that best reflects their thinking instead of having their opinions shaped by the press. Most of the papers[3] are politically independent; they are owned by industry, religious groups, banks, and large landowners, and so actually they speak for special interests while theoretically being free politically. In general the Italian press can be divided into three categories: (1) the independent press, (2) the party press, and (3) the specialized press.

Prominent among the Independent newspapers are the aforementioned dailies of Milan and Turin, and three dailies of Rome: Il Messaggero, Giornale d'Italia and Il Tempo. Other leading Independents are Il Resto del Carlino of Bologna; La Nazione Italiana of Florence, and Giornale di Sicilia of Palermo. These papers support to some extent one of the many Center parties of Italy.

LEADING ITALIAN DAILIES

Milan:

Corriere della Sera (AM, 500,000)
Corriere d'Informazione (PM, 200,000)
Il Giorno (AM, 200,000)
L'Unità (AM; Communist; 150,000)
Avanti! (AM; Socialist; 80,000)
Corriere Lombardo (PM, 100,000)

Rome:

Il Messaggero (AM, 150,000)
Il Tempo (AM, 125,000)
Giornale d'Italia (PM, 100,000)
L'Unità (AM; Communist; 100,000)
Momento-Sera (PM, 90,000)
Il Popolo (AM; Christian-Democrat; 50,000)
L'Osservatore Romano (AM; 200,000--
   Official daily of Catholic Church; in
   Vatican City).

Turin:

La Nuova Stampa (AM, 300,000)
Stampa-Sera (PM, 150,000)
Gazzetta del Popolo (AM, 150,000)

Others:

Venice: Gazzettino (AM, 200,000)
Naples: Mattino (AM, 200,000)
Palermo: Giornale di Sicilia (AM, 150,000)
Bologna: Resto del Carlino (AM, 130,000)
Florence: La Nazione Italiana (AM,100,000)

Leading Party papers are L'Unità (Communist) of Rome and Milan, Avanti! (Left Socialist) of Milan, and Il Popolo (Christian Democrat) of Rome. The number of party papers has declined in Italy since World War II, while the overall daily circulation has risen. Party papers still existing tend to be concentrated on the extreme Right or Left.

The weekly press has grown rapidly since

1950 and today is becoming more influential.[4] Weekly newspapers range from very small general journals with some 8,000 circulation to popular picture-weeklies with circulations of several hundred thousand.[5] These "illus-trateds" such as La Tribuna Illustrata were unknown in Italy before World War II. Some of the main weeklies are Tempo, L'Expresso, Il Contemporaneo, La Domenica del Corriere, and Il Candido.

The Italian government goes far in granting privileges to the press in an attempt to keep it vigorous, or "friendly" as some cynics might say. Publications are given such benefits as reductions in taxes, and grants are made to news agencies. Journalists en-joy many privileges and have a high status in the social structure. They generally have access to government buildings and records, and receive many special benefits in their private lives (e.g., a 70 per cent reduction on railroad fares).

Yet, despite good working conditions, news-men are still not universally a professional group because of the Italian system of apprenticeship. The first university courses in journalism were begun by the faculty of statistical science of the University of Rome in 1947. Then followed, in order, a three-year course of journalism at the Uni-versity of Urbino in 1948; a two-year Superior Institute of Public Opinion at the Interna-tional University for Social Studies in Rome in 1950; a four-year Institute of Journalism at the University of Palermo in 1952; and finally, a School of Journalism at the Uni-versity for Foreigners at Messina in 1958. For some time now, Professor Ignazio Weiss of Milan has conducted journalism instruc-tion at the University of Florence, but with-out a formal degree program.

Despite such a varied growth of university-level journalism instruction during the past fifteen years, a majority of Italian repor-ters break into news work by serving an 18-month apprenticeship.[6] At the end of 1962, Italian publishers and editors still were not hiring very many university graduates. And job openings on dailies are shrinking.

In mid-1962, the number of daily newspapers totaled only 90 in 37 cities, down 8 per cent from the total of 1948. This loss,[7] consis-tent with world trends, has been expected because of mergers due to rising costs. Total paid daily newspaper circulation of five million has increased only 2 per cent in the past five years. Thus, the govern-ment decided that rather than allow larger papers to eliminate most of the smaller ones, subsidies would be offered.

The most important governmental aid to the press--the lowered cost of newsprint--allows newspapers to purchase newsprint at two-thirds the regular retail price.

Smaller newspapers are able to remain in business because of the reduced price of newsprint and partly from other subsidies, such as funds from political parties or from promoters of athletic events.[8]

RADIO AND TELEVISION. Despite governmental aid, the number of Italian daily newspapers has declined and may continue to do so, ever so slowly. In addition to competition from the illustrated newsweeklies, dailies now must compete for advertising with television commercials.

Not that Italian television follows the U.S. pattern; to the contrary, advertisers are limited to 12.5 minutes for each 9 hours of telecasting. Rates are standard, sponsors being assigned different times on different days, thereby sharing the favorable viewing periods.[9]

Italy's broadcasting system, RAI or Radiotelevisione Italiana, is a corporation with the government owning 51 per cent of the stock of the television network and all of the branch running the three radio networks. No commercials are aired on the three radio services: the National Program, the Second Program, and the Third Program, each of which is a continuous hookup of transmitters placed in every sector of Italy. There is no Italian equivalent of a U.S. hometown or local radio station. Each radio or television receiver owner pays an annual tax, funds from which finance programming.

Chief criticism of Italian newscasts is governmental pressure.[10] Not until 1960 was the ban on political discussions on Italian radio and television lifted, after having been in effect during the postwar development of broadcasting beginning in 1946. From 1960 through 1962, various political party spokesmen to the right of center have complained that leftwing propaganda has diminished the objectivity of news reports and discussion broadcasts.

Video, both informational and entertainment programming, is popular. In contrast to the 40 per cent of Italian adults who read daily newspapers regularly, 64 per cent watch television at least once a week, more often daily or at least every other day.[11]

The same Association of Italian Advertisers investigation which showed periodical reading habits and televiewing tendencies, in the extensive 1958 survey, found that 80 per cent of Italian adults listen to the radio at least once a week, more often daily.

Better than 640,000 new licenses for television receivers were issued during 1961, showing a more rapid rise in televiewing than in newspaper readership.[12]

Failure of Italian news broadcasts to achieve consistent objectivity in presentation has not lessened their popularity, for Italians know also that only a minority of their newspapers give them an impartial coverage of public affairs. The Italian people are looking forward to improved news service through this medium.

TRUSTWORTHY NEWS AVAILABLE. Leading Italian newspapers do have factual reports of major news events, foreign and domestic. Influenced by Eurovision, the multinational hookup of television stations throughout Western Europe for special programs, RAI does offer some praiseworthy documentaries. And foreign periodicals, ranging from the London Daily Mail to Selezione (Italian-language version of the Reader's Digest) have had their effect upon Italian readers as well as editors, influencing the latter to strive for the presentation of more information about world affairs and human interest activities.

It is common practice for Italian newspapers to print their news with a mixture of editorializing which would be intolerable in the United States. The better Italian papers (e.g., Corriere della Sera, Il Giorno, and Il Messaggero), however, do keep their editorials and news separated. Italian papers are small, seldom more than eight pages. The typical paper is a nine-column, regular size (about 16 by 23 inches) sheet; tabloids have not caught on in Italy as they have in many European countries. Most of the papers are highly departmentalized. The editorial of the day (there is usually only one) generally appears in the left column of page 1. Although make up techniques in Italian papers show marked differences, they all exhibit a quality of care, neatness, and seriousness. Even Milan's Il Giorno with its lively and enticing make up (in many ways resembling London's Daily Express) has a general tone of sobriety and dignity. A typical characteristic of Italian newspaper make up is that of horizontal display.

Usually the only dailies to print more than eight pages are Il Corriere della Sera,

Il *Giorno*, Il *Tempo*, Il *Messaggero*, and
Giornale d'Italia. Very seldom will any
paper run more than 16 pages. Typical are
the six-pagers such as L'Osservatore Romano
and Il *Popolo* (which sometimes print eight
pages) and the eight-pagers such as *Stampa-
Sera* which sometimes print only six pages.

THE THIRD PAGE. A unique characteristic of
the Italian newspapers is the "Terza Pagina"
(Third Page) which is given over to light
articles, features, criticism, reviews,
fiction, and reminiscences. Well-known
personalities (e.g., academicians, literary
figures, artists, and musicians) contribute
to the Third Page.[13] Another typical feature
of Italian papers is the "elzeviro" or
editorial, which has evolved into a special
literary essay form. Most of the newspapers
of Italy rewrite foreign news received from
the wire services paying little attention
to credits on wire stories. In general, the
papers of Italy do not use U.S.-type summary
leads on their stories, but write their
articles chronologically. Although generally
news treatment is serious and dignified,
Italian newspapers often show zeal, originality, and too often, bad taste, in getting
their stories.[14]

ITALY'S COMMUNIST PRESS. The Communist press
of Italy, which rode high in the country in
the early 1950's,[15] has now shrunk to a few
papers with a combined circulation of about
600,000--less than half of what L'Unita's
Sunday edition alone had in 1953. Since
1954 four Communist papers have been forced
to shut down, including the once-powerful
Il *Nuovo* *Corriere* of Florence which stopped
publication in 1956. Only four Red dailies
still exist in Italy.

In 1957 L'Unita ("Unity") did away with its
once-thriving Turin and Genoa editions, leaving only its editions in Rome and Milan. It
had been losing over a million dollars
annually for several years.[16] It is still
the free world's biggest Communist paper,
however, and one which drives its daily fare
of political propaganda at the readers with
great vigor. This paper was founded in 1924.

The Italian government of late has made it
difficult for the Communist papers to continue
by such tactics as ordering state-owned
businesses to cease advertising with the Red
press. Today Communist papers are in serious
financial situations.

PRESS BACKGROUND. Prior to World War I,
Italy was not a center for world news, al-
though some foreign newspapers such as London's
Times kept correspondents there. The war put

Italy in the international limelight and since
then the country has figured prominently in
the world news picture. Between 1922 and 1926
the Italian press was brought under Fascist
political influence; recalcitrant papers were
supressed and critical publishers and editors
left the country for exile in safer locales.
Until after the defeat of the Axis powers at
the end of World War II, the press of Italy
was under the dictatorial hand of the Fascist
party led by Benito Mussolini, and there was
no press freedom. The press, as in Nazi
Germany, was merely a propaganda tool of the
state.

Except for the period of Fascist dictatorship, the Italian press has enjoyed a great
amount of freedom. In 1948 the new Constitution provided for freedom of expression, including press freedom. Article 21 states
that "all are entitled freely to express
their thoughts by word of mouth, in writing
and by all other means of communication" and
that the "press may not be subjected to any
authorization or censorship."[17]

The old (founded 1854) national news agency,
Stefani, was the country's leading news-dis-
seminating organization until after World War
II. It was succeeded in 1945 by the present
Italian agency--Agenzia Nazionale Stampa
Associata (ANSA)--a cooperative organization
of newspaper publishers. Today this agency
has about 400 correspondents in Italy and
about 1,000 subscribers including such varied
groups as publishing houses, government
offices, banks, businesses, and industries.[18]
It has exchange agreements with several
European national news agencies, and with
Reuters. Agency messages inserted in the
Italian papers are very seldom credited. In
general, the papers attempt to give the im-
pression that they have correspondents
scattered everywhere. "Dal Nostro Corris-
pondente" appears as a byline in many papers,
indicating a top story was filed "By Our
Correspondent." Yet at the end of such
stories one finds familiar names such as
Merriman Smith, who actually serves as White
House correspondent for UPI.

There is a long tradition of interest in
politics in Italy and the press has always
mirrored this interest. Most papers give
a large portion of their space to political
reporting and often print full texts of
political speeches. Foreign news gets a big
play in the Italian press, especially in the
big dailies of Milan, Turin, and Rome. Most
of the city papers have their own correspondents abroad or send special "roving" reporters (often well-known literary figures)
on newsgathering junkets. The greater part

of the international news, however, comes to
the Italian press by way of the national news
agency ANSA and the international agencies
Reuters, Associated Press, and United Press
International.

A BRIEF LOOK AT A FEW PAPERS[19]

L'Osservatore Romano,[20] a regular-size newspaper of six columns, is the "official" daily
of Vatican City. Although its circulation
(about 200,000) is not large, its influence
in Catholic Italy (and throughout the world)
is great. It prints general news as well as
Church news, and runs from four to eight pages
daily.

Corriere della Sera of Milan is a nine-
column daily often running to 16 pages. It
gives the reader a serious diet of national
and world news reported in a dignified, comprehensive manner. It is Italy's largest
circulation daily (some 500,000).

Il Tempo of Rome is a well-printed afternoon
paper of 12 pages. Its popular sports section
printed on yellow newsprint attracts readers.
Politically, it supports Monarchists and far-
right Conservatives.

Il Giornale d'Italia (Rome) is another well-
printed, dignified PM paper giving the reader
a variety of reading material from long
foreign stories to lively human interest features aimed at Roman readers. Much of its
foreign news is concentrated on the back page.

Il Popolo (Rome) is the official organ of
the country's Christian Democrat party. As
such, it is preoccupied with political news
and opinion to a greater extent than most
of Italy's metropolitan dailies. However,
this morning daily usually running six pages,
gives a wide variety of news. Foreign news
is mainly on the back page.

Il Giorno of Milan, only seven years old,
is bringing a brisk, new journalism to Italy.
It is filled with world news and interpretive
articles, but also gives a rich diet of
features--local and national. And all is
wrapped in a brightly attractive departmentalized package. Its editions contain more
comic strips than any other Italian newspaper.

Nuova Stampa of Turin, with a daily circulation of some 300,000, is Italy's second largest
paper. Its back page is usually given over to
large pictures.

A TRUER PICTURE. The principal national
association of journalists in Italy is the
"Federazione Nazionale della Stampa Italiana,"
or "National Federation of the Italian Press,"
with headquarters in Rome. Like such associations as the American Society of Newspaper
Editors, it concerns itself with journalistic responsibilities and professional standards.

Since 1961, broader United States influence in Italian press portrayals of
America has been noted. Personnel in the
U.S. Embassy, the U.S. Information Service,
and various American agencies operating in
Italy, before 1961 tended to associate mostly
with the more conservative political elements
of the republic. Since 1961, however, newer
appointees have made special efforts to con-
fer with various political spokesmen, of the
Italian right, left, and center.[21]

As a consequence, Italian newspaper and
broadcast coverage of the United States,
especially editorial commentary, gives as
much emphasis to the U.S. Senate Anti-Trust
Committee as it does to the U.S. Senate
Internal Security Sub-committee. More stress
is now placed on U.S. benefits for rank-and-
file Americans, such as social security and
slum clearance, and less on negative news
values. Thus, the image of the United States
has improved in Italian mass media, except
for the outright Communist press.

FOREIGN CORRESPONDENTS IN ITALY. A foreign
correspondent for a news agency, broadcasting network, newspaper chain, or magazine,
finding himself on assignment in Rome, must
not approach the city and the republic as
a one-nation news source. Rome does not have
the global reverberations of Moscow or Washington, to be sure. But Vatican City obviously is a worldwide news source, not only
during the Ecumenical Conference which began
in 1962 and continued in 1963, but continuously.

In addition, Rome is the crossroads stop-
over from the United States, Britain, and
westernmost Europe to the Middle East and
Asia for tens of thousands of potentially
newsworthy travelers, and conversely, for
countless others journeying from the Orient
westward.

A reporter covering the international scene
from Rome, does not limit himself to key
Italians, Vatican officials, and prominent
visitors. For Rome has three sets of diplo-
mats, those accredited to the Italian government, those accredited to the Vatican, and
those accredited to the FAO, the Food and
Agriculture Organization, a specialized branch
of the United Nations.

Norway

Norway is a country of some 3.5 million people
with an illiteracy rate of only 2 per cent.
The 203 newspapers, including 80 dailies, in
the nation circulate 1,750,000 copies. Prior
to World War II only about 900,000 copies
circulated each day. Norway has one of the
world's highest newspaper readership rates
with more than 500 copies of the dailies published for each 1,000 persons, making Norway
equal with Sweden for second place in world
newspaper readership.[1] In addition to the
daily papers there are some 120 other papers
appearing at longer intervals. Most of these
are triweeklies, all with small circulations,
serving the rural areas of the country. No
newspapers are published on Sunday in Norway
and the big issues of the week are the "special"
editions appearing on Saturday.

LEADING DAILIES		
Oslo:		
Aftenposten (Conser.)	166,000	AM
	141,000	PM
Dagbladet (Liberal)	88,000	
Arbeiderbladet (Labor)	63,000	
Morgenposten (Indep.)	43,000	
VG-Verdens Gang (Indep.)	32,000	
Morgenbladet (Conser.)	23,000	
Nationen (Center Party)	25,000	
Provincials:		
Bergens Tidende (Bergen; Liberal)	65,000	
Adresseavisen (Trondheim; Conser.)	62,000	
Stavanger Aftenblad (Stavanger; Liberal)	37,000	
Drammens Tidende (Drammen; Conser.)	28,000	

NATIONAL NEWS AGENCY

Norsk Telegrambyra (NTB)--main source of
news for Norwegian papers. A cooperative
owned by the newspapers; gets most of its
foreign news through an agreement with
AFP and Reuters; buys a special German service from DPA especially written for Scandinavian readers. Several political parties
own and operate their own news agencies.

The press of Norway is independently owned
and is marked by the fact that there are no
commercial chains and big press groups such
as are found in Britain and other nations.
Most of the big papers are owned by corporations with shares divided among individuals
and political parties. There are a few
"family" newspapers in the country, but
economic pressures are forcing the Norwegian
papers in the direction of corporate ownership and fewer but bigger papers. Oslo, the
capital and major city, is the principal
press center of the country. Papers published
there dominate the press in prestige and circulation and are especially influential in
East Norway. A few of these papers have
national circulation.

Aftenposten, the largest daily in Norway,
combines the best of German-style make
up with the best of United States-sytle
make up. Like many other Scandinavian
papers, the pages are glued together at
the fold.

The country's largest daily is Aftenposten,
a Conservative paper which is excellent in
many respects. It publishes both morning
and evening editions whose combined daily
circulation is more than 300,000. Its larger
weekend edition published every Saturday has
a circulation of some 185,000. Aftenposten
might be compared to the London Times in its
serious treatment of the news and its leadership among the Conservative newspapers of the

country. Aftenposten, however, does not resemble the Times in make up. Although it
does use advertising on its front page, it is
relegated to the bottom portion and does not
detract from the exceptionally pleasing make
up dominated by the skillful use of type and
pictures in the top part of the page. Aftenposten, like many Scandinavian papers, seems
to combine the best of German-style make up
with the best of the United States' style,
and comes up with a very pleasing result.
Like other Scandinavian papers, the pages of
Aftenposten are agglutinated at the fold.
This paper, typical of the carefully-edited
and skillfully made up papers of Scandinavia,
often uses three colors on its front page
(generally yellow, blue, and red in advertisements). Aftenposten, usually printing
18-22 pages during the week and up to 32 on
Saturday, compares favorably with any of the
many excellent dailies published throughout
the Scandinavian countries.

Other leading dailies published in Oslo
which are very influential not only because
of their circulations but because of their
political leadership are the Liberal Dagbladet
(daily: 88,000; Saturday: 127,000), and the
Labor party's Arbeiderbladet (daily: 63,000;
Saturday: 81,000). These papers, like Aftenposten, present well-rounded news presentation
mixed liberally with many excellent photographs and cartoons and offered to the reader
in an attractive, readable format.

The largest dailies (and probably the most
influential) outside Oslo are Bergen's Bergens
Tidende, a Liberal daily with a circulation
of some 65,000; Trondheim's Adresseavisen, a
Conservative paper with about the same circulation, and the Liberal Stavanger Aftenblad of
Stavanger, a highly-literate paper of some
37,000 circulation with much prestige which
is often called "Norway's (Manchester)
Guardian."

GOVERNMENT AND PRESS. The Norwegian press is
one of the freest in the world, and as in the
other Scandinavian countries the press enjoys
a high degree of accessibility to information
of matters of public interest. As in Sweden
certain professions are forbidden by law to
divulge information confided to them. Although Norwegian journalists are not included
among these professions, an Act of June 15,
1951, through the introduction of a special
paragraph in both the Criminal (Section 177)
and Civil (Section 209) Procedure Acts, provides that "the publisher (editor) of a
printed publication may refuse to reveal the
author of an article or notice in the publication or the source of the information contained
therein. The same applies to any other person

who has been informed of the author or of
the source (of information) in the course
of his work for the publishers, editors, news
agency, or printers concerned."

The protection of such confidences is not
absolute, however. Courts may, after weigh-
ing the evidence, require that such information be given, and in cases of a punishable
breach of secrecy, the law says that courts
should require such evidence.

Since the enactment of this law there have
been two cases (one in 1952 and the other in
1959) in which courts made the journalists
subject to three months coercive sentences.
In the first case, after the editor had spent
two weeks in jail the informants gave the
required evidence, and in the second case,
the Court of Appeals reversed (on a techni-
cality) the coercive sentence of the Lower
Court.[2]

A GENERAL PRESS OVERVIEW. The bulk of Norway's total circulation comes from a few
large papers in some five cities. The average
paper has a circulation of about 5,000 and a
readership restricted to a rather small area.

There is a strong political orientation of
the Norwegian press. Readers feel that it
is important to have papers in all parts of
the country representing every shade of
political thought. There are, however, many
so-called "independent" or "nonpolitical"
papers; yet this does not mean that they do
not take sides politically, but rather that
they are independent of party attachments.
Actual ownership by parties is virtually unknown in Norway; the main exception is Oslo's
Arbeiderbladet, the daily organ of the Labor
party. The Communist party's official newspaper is Friheten of Oslo which has a very
small circulation and is not thought to have
much influence.

Conservative party papers dominate the press
picture in Norway; these are not party papers
in the sense that Arbeiderbladet and Friheten
are. They simply support the policies of the
Conservative party. Newspapers representing
the Labor party and the Liberal party are next
in number and importance in the country, followed by the papers of the Agrarian party.
The other parties lag far behind these four
in press support.

There has been no tendency in Norway for
newspapers to form press groups or large
chains as in Britain. However, many of the
smaller papers are having economic troubles
and are feeling the increasing pressure of
competition.[3] The overall trend in the

number of newspapers is down, and a move toward chains and consolidation is not unlikely in the near future.

Norway's first paper was the <u>Norske Intelligenz Seddeler</u> which appeared in Bergen in 1763. Until 1814, when the Constitution granted freedom of expression, the papers were small and cautious and had little effect on national thought. Party newspapers did not make their debut in Norway until the 1880's. Once begun, these political organs grew rapidly and established the pattern of journalism in the country which largely persists today.

During the Nazi occupation of Norway (1940-45) many Norwegian papers were closed and editors were often jailed (and sometimes executed) by the German invaders. Underground newspapers developed and circulated throughout the country. These sheets kept the people informed of developments outside Norway and did much to boost the morale of the freedom-loving Norwegians. Published from secret presses and mimeograph machines, the papers relied mainly on shortwave radio from England as the source of their news.[4]

The Norwegian press today considers education of the people one of its prime purposes. This is undoubtedly one of the reasons for so many cultural and historical articles found in the newspapers. While not neglecting human interest and entertainment features, Norway's newspapers present a steady diet of serious, informative features. This one theme--a unity of serious intent--runs throughout the entire Norwegian press system.

News stories are written in a chronological form in Norway; however, press association style (usually using the U.S.-type summary lead) is slowly making inroads into the country's journalistic writing. Seldom, however, will locally-written news stories have summary leads.

A characteristic feature of the Norwegian paper is the signed and dated "chronicle" ("kronikk") which is spread across the bottom of the editorial page. This "kronikk" is usually an essay of high order, which is ordinarily serious and deals with some national or international problem. The editorial page of a Norwegian paper greatly resembles one in the U.S. with certain modifications (e.g., the tone is more informal, usually there is only one editorial, and the columns used are locally-written and are not syndicated).

The Norwegian editor has about as much decision-making power and authority as any editor in the world. He is usually the "responsible" and key person on the newspaper. However, important editorial and administrative problems are usually dealt with in conference with the publisher.

A few important newspaper characteristics: (a) uses much feature material, especially "personality" sketches, (b) classified advertising is extremely popular, (c) much space is devoted to literature, music, the theater and the arts, (d) comic strips and cartoons are commonly used, (e) photographs used extensively in all sections of the papers, and especially in the popular sports pages.

Magazines are not as popular in Norway as in many European countries. However, there are several widely-read magazines which supplement the newspaper offerings of political, social, and cultural affairs. These magazines circulate throughout the country and enjoy financial success. Typical of such publications is the general illustrated <u>Aktuell</u> which offers the reader a varied diet of first-class photographs mingled with serious cultural articles, news-background pieces, and personality sketches. It is spiced with cartoons, comic strips, and pictures which are generally termed "cheesecake" in the United States.

A few titles translated from several issues of <u>Aktuell</u> during 1958 might serve to indicate the variety of article types contained in these popular Norwegian magazines: "Inventing Things is a Vice of Mine" (story of a Norwegian taxi driver who won medals with his inventions at the Brussels' World's Fair); "Sunshine on White Sails" (story of young boys racing their small boats on a fiord near Oslo); "New Methods in the Cure of Women Alcoholics"; "Underwater Ballet"; "Boldness is Vulnerable" (picture story of European bridge tournament in Oslo); "Great Grandmother on the Go" (story of an eighty-two-year-old woman of Bergen who still swims and rows like a young athlete); "They Dig History" (story of archeological discoveries at Bergen); and "Hunting for Adventures" (story of American author Ernest E. Gann in Norwegian waters).

Portugal

With nine million inhabitants, Portugal has an illiteracy rate of 25 per cent, mostly among the older members of its reading age population. The country's dailies (about 25) have a total circulation of nearly one million. Press centers are the capital, Lisbon, and the other major city, Oporto. Published data and estimates indicate that no newspaper in the country has a circulation[1] in excess of 150,000. With the largest circulation in Portugal and considered by many to be the country's best daily is Diario de Noticias of Lisbon; it was founded in 1864 by two of Portugal's foremost journalistic figures, Eduardo Coelho and Tomas Quintino Antunes. Other leading Portuguese dailies are O Século (f.1880), a morning daily with 90,000 circulation; Diario Popular (c. 80,000); Diario de Lisboa; Diario da Manhã, and Diario de Governo (the official government gazette), all of Lisbon, and Oporto's Primeiro de Janeiro, Diario do Norte, and Jornal de Noticias. The Anglo-Portuguese News, a small British daily is the only non-Portuguese language newspaper in the country. There are 250 weeklies with a circulation of 500,000. The national news agency of Portugal is Agencia de Noticias e de Informaçoes (ANI); it has no exchange agreements with other agencies. Reuters, AFP, UPI, and AP have offices in Lisbon.

Some of the outstanding newspapermen in the country today are Augusto de Castro, Diario de Noticias; A. Avelino Goncalves, Novidades; Barradas de Oliveira, Diario da Manhã; Pedro Correia Marques, A Voz; Luis Marques, Anglo-Protuguese News; J. Pereira da Rosa, O Século; Norberto Lopes, Diario de Lisboa; Antonio Cruz, Diario do Norte; J. Seara Cardoso, O Comércio do Porto; M. Pacheco de Miranda, Jornal de Noticias; and Alberto de Araujo, Diario de Noticias (Madeira Is.).

A BRIEF LOOK AT THE PAPERS.[2] Portuguese daily newspapers are rather gaudy publications compared to those in most parts of Europe. Most are standard-size formats of seven or eight columns to the page. Circus make up is generally used, with color (usually red) used quite liberally with boxes, headlines, and in the case of Diario de Noticias of Lisbon, in the heavy red bars which separate the major stories on the front page. Pages (especially the front pages) have a crowded, confused appearance; it seems that Portuguese editors want to try every make up technique known to modern journalism all in the same issue. It is quite common to find underlined headlines (a common French technique), color headlines (usually in red), bold-face body type, italic body type, and all types of ornamental borders and cutoff rules in a Portuguese daily.

LEADING PORTUGUESE DAILIES	
Lisbon:	
O Século (AM)	90,000
Diario da Manhã (AM)	40,000
Diario de Noticias (AM)	150,000
Novidades (AM)	35,000
Jornal do Comércio (AM)	13,000
A Voz (AM)	10,000
Diario de Lisboa (PM)	40,000
Diario Popular (PM)	80,000
Diario Ilustrado (PM)	50,000
Republica (PM)	45,000
Oporto:	
Primeiro de Janeiro	90,000
Diario do Norte	10,000
Jornal de Noticias	50,000
O Comércio do Porto	60,000
Others:	
Correio do Minho (Braga)	
Noticias dé Evora (Evora)	
Diario do Alentejo (Beja)	
Jornal da Madeira (Madeira Is.)	
Diario de Noticias (Madeira Is.)	
Açores (Azores Is.)	
Correio dos Açores (Azores Is.)	
Correio da Horta (Azores)	
Diario Insular (Azores)	

The use of many pictures (photographs and drawings) and vari-sized headline decks, combined with the extravagant use of color, gives most papers a generally chaotic and gaudy look. Most papers run from six to eight pages, with Diario de Noticias, an eight-column, standard-sized paper, usually printed on about 14 pages. Sunday editions run 20 pages of which 12 to 14 pages are devoted to advertising. Diario da Manhã, a six-pager usually, is rather typical of the Portuguese dailies. It uses color on at least two pages. General news--domestic and some foreign--is found on the front page. Cultural items, reviews and the like appear on the second page. The third page is given over mainly to foreign news and advertising. On page 4 is found government news and more advertising; and page 5 contains "jumps" from the front page and some local news. The last page contains a potpourri of news items and occasionally some advertising. This newspaper is a seven-column paper supporting the National Union party. Probably the most conservative of the Portuguese dailies in content and in appearance is the Catholic daily Novidades, which runs only four to six pages. Although it typically uses circus make up, it is more reserved than most of its fellow dailies and uses no splashes of color. At the other end of the scale from Novidades would probably be Lisbon's Diario de Noticias which fills its pages' eight columns with a conglomeration of typographical and make up techniques.

Diario de Noticias, Lisbon's most liberal newspaper, uses almost every known typographical make up device in one issue. Besides using many pictures and drawings, it underlines heads, uses a red bar between important stories, and uses boxes and cutoff rules in every feasible manner.

GOVERNMENT AND PRESS. For almost 40 years the government of Portugal has exercised close surveillance over the press of that country. Before the military coup of May 28, 1926 the Portuguese press enjoyed unlimited freedom, a freedom that is abused to the point that liberty tended to become license. "Impartial historians," says an International Press Institute survey,[3] "admit that the press must bear a heavy responsibility for the disorders that preceded the advent of the dictatorship."

Among the first acts of the authoritarian regime (established by the coup and based on a single party, the National Union) was to impose press censorship which has been in effect ever since and to place government officials on the editorial staffs of the leading Lisbon newspapers. Moreover, the state in effect took over some of the newspapers such as O Século. It owns about half the shares of Diario de Noticias, Portugal's top daily.

While the government keeps a close watch on the press, it insists in the words of the dictator, Dr. Oliveira Salazar, that ".... the censorship is so benevolent in our country that it (the government) allows itself to be discussed, not just in the mistakes it may make but in its principles and its function. I realize that the censorship inconveniences newspapers, ...(but) its existence has permitted a security of work and even a liberty of action--seemingly contradictory but not really so--that we do not find in other supposedly more liberal regimes. There is no case of seizure of a newspaper, much less of assaults or wrecking newspaper offices as in the past, and it can be said, neither suspension of publication nor crimes to be judged in courts. There are monarchial newspapers and republican ones, Catholic and Protestant, political or simply factual, neutral, favorable or obstinately in opposition, and everyone knows that they can only be what they are because they are not dependent on the government."[4]

While many of the prohibitions which the press must observe are to be found in the laws of traditionally democratic states, vagueness of some of the clauses limiting press freedom, such as "prejudice to the state" and "offense against national honor," deserve special note. Such clauses are subject to broad interpretation by police and administrative officials.

While there is no censorship of incoming or outgoing news and foreign journals or periodicals are seldom seized, no paper appears in Portugal without the censor's official stamp on the first page. All texts including advertisements must be submitted to the board of censors which has headquarters

at Lisbon and branches in all towns. Wield-
ing wide powers the board of censors not only
cancels texts it also alters them; it permits
items to appear in some papers that it sup-
presses in others; it decides on sanctions to
be applied against offending newspapers,
being empowered to suspend them or even to
close them down permanently, and there is no
appeal against its decisions.

The board of censors requires newspapers to
print all notices from the government and the
national information office, especially communiques and official speeches, and thus
serve as propaganda instruments of the state.
Furthermore, the board of censors must approve
the nomination of assistant editors of newspapers. In addition to these controls, there
are other restrictive or discriminatory
measures such as subsidies to government
papers and the inequitable distribution of
newsprint. The government also has the power
to limit the number of pages of newspapers
and to grant exceptions that tend to favor
government organs, since these papers can
claim a special allowance of pages for space
occupied by official texts.[5] Finally, the
state controls the National Union of Journalists, membership in which is obligatory for
all persons in the journalistic profession.

One might think that such restrictions would
have reduced the press to complete subser-
vience, but such is not quite true. There
have always been independent newspapers and,
indeed, there are opposition papers among the
most important ones of the country--the

dailies, Republica, Diario de Lisboa, and
the monthly review, Seara Nova, in Lisbon,
and the dailies Primeiro de Janeiro, Jornal
de Noticias and O Comércio do Porto in
Oporto--to mention a few.

While comment is relatively free as long
as it does not touch on the regime or its
representatives, independent or opposition
papers are closely watched and they have
trouble with the board of censors. Republica
and other papers, especially some in Oporto
and several literary reviews that have published strong views have on occasion been
suspended. Fines and arrests[6] are more
frequent penalties for violations of the
censor's prescriptions.

Opposition to censorship is voiced regularly
by members of the press and occasionally by
persons within the government. During election campaigns some relaxation of the censors
is permitted, but even then in areas where
the government is touchy commentary is sometimes stricken. Finally, it can be said that
in recent years the censorship has become
less rigorous. Matters in which it continues
to operate include comment on international
politics affecting Portugal, news or opinion
tending to lower the regime in the eyes of
the public, and news that is exploited in a
sensational manner. In this last, however,
considerable latitude is permitted in accordance with government policy. For example,
see the front page of Diario de Noticias
(Jan. 5, 1963) for the sensational handling
of the United Nations intervention in Katanga
story.

Spain

Spain's press and broadcasting can be summarized with the alliterative two C's: conformity, censorship.[1] Spaniards almost never have enjoyed a free press, the exception being a few weeks during the five years of the Spanish Republic, from 1931 to 1936. From the fifteenth century, when the first printing presses appeared in the country, until 1931, publications were controlled by officials of the monarchy.

A CONTROLLED PRESS SYSTEM. Francisco Franco's administration, in full effect since 1939 after three years of civil war, has made "guidance" of the mass media a function of government. Therefore, Spaniards have become so conditioned that few indeed openly oppose press restrictions, and no group or individuals have so far opposed it to any lasting effect. Minister of Information Manuel Fraga Iribarne throughout 1962 hinted that in 1963 formal press censorship might end or be curtailed. But even if that should occur,[2] the ranks of practicing newsmen are filled with conformists, though some independent thinking does persist, as was evidenced in the coverage of the miners' strike of 1962.

An individual cannot even enter the profession of press or broadcast journalism without a thorough personal investigation and preparation amounting to indoctrination.

Completion of work in the Official School of Journalism in Madrid[3] or in the branch school in Barcelona or the Catholic journalism school in Madrid is a prerequisite for employment as a newsman at any newspaper, magazine, or radio station. This has been true since promulgation of the executive decree by General Franco on November 17, 1941, requiring all subsequent openings for newsmen in Spain to be filled by selection from among graduates of the "only authorized center for the training of journalists."

The dean and faculties of journalism in Madrid and Barcelona are directly responsible to the Minister of Information and Tourism, a cabinet member of the Franco government and the national director of press censorship.

Weekly reports of all curricular activities are checked at the ministry. Doubt never beclouds the chain of command of the smooth running system which now trains 100 per cent of Spanish news personnel.[4]

To take the journalism school entrance examination, an applicant must hold the Bachiller Superior degree, approximately equivalent to a high school diploma and one year of junior college in the United States. Each would-be newsman must present a 20-page typed autobiography. Anti-Franco tendencies in the data cause rejection of the application. A police certificate must attest that the aspirant to a career in journalism has never been jailed for "subversive" political activities against the government. Nonconformists simply are not trained as journalists.

Graduation after three years of study brings the student automatic inscription in the Official Registry of Journalists, a master list of every working newsman in Spain, updated every six months.

Thus, for example, as of July 1, 1961, one knew for certain that Spain had 3,373 reporters, editors and publishers, and 828 columnists and 326 news photographers active at daily and weekly newspapers and magazines.[5] From other official reports of the Press Directorate in the Ministry of Information building, mid-1961 totals listed 94 daily newspapers and 96 weeklies.

MONDAY EDITIONS. In each city or area with more than one daily newspaper, these dailies pool resources on Mondays to publish an Hoja del Lunes, or Monday Edition, with a skeleton staff. These combined Monday editions for each Spanish region or city with competing dailies assure employees of a shorter work week.

BROADCASTING. Spain's press-radio-television structure is oriented toward entertainment rather than information. Pressured by censorship, newspapers often devote much space to literary essays and fine arts coverage. Broadcasts, too, stress nonnews programming. In 1963, however, the daily ration of radio news was increased from four to eighteen broadcasts a day.

In each population center are both privately-owned commercial and government-owned non-commercial radio stations, often affiliated with national or regional networks.

Only one television channel has been authorized. Though it is government owned and operated, air time sold for commercials helps defray expenses. Madrid studios of the single television network normally originate programs, but on occasion, broadcasts originate in Barcelona. In addition, remote pickups from cameras in a dozen provincial cities can be microwave-relayed back to Madrid for live telecasting or for airing at a later time via videotape recordings. Satellite transmitters in six regions echo Madrid telecasts to every region of Spain.

LOCAL COVERAGE. Regarding local newspaper or radio coverage of news, a distinction should be made between the 50 provinces into which Spain is divided governmentally and the nation's 13 cultural regions. Only in the case of Navarra do province and region coincide in name as well as in area.

The famous region of Andalusia contains eight provinces. A cultural region may have the same name as the smaller governmental province it encompasses along with other provinces. The cultural region of León consists of three provinces: León, Salamanca, and Zamora. Noticias leonesas means news of the cultural region, not just the smaller province of León.

PRESS CONTROLS. Whether local, regional, or national, Spanish news reports are censored. Many topics simply do not receive printed space or air time. By reason of the Press Law of 1938, an entire generation of Spaniards has grown up under a restricted flow of news.[6] Newspapers in Madrid and Barcelona in 1963 were still subjected to tight censorship, but in many other cities galley proofs were no longer required to be shown to censors prior to press time.

Censorship extends not only to secular publications but also to most Catholic periodicals, the principal exception being Ecclesia, official weekly magazine of the Catholic hierarchy of Spain. But even the editors of this magazine in December, 1960 had to yield to censors when they tried to publish a manifesto by 227 Spanish intellectuals against governmental censorship.

The Catholic Church has been gradually disengaging from the Franco government, one of the few open manifestations of a moderate but growing opposition. Catholic Workers Youth groups and the Workers' Brotherhoods of Catholic Action supported the strike of coal miners in northern Spain during May, 1962, even though strikes are illegal. Catholic publications reported on the strike even though priests and conservative writers are sometimes jailed along with other political prisoners, all of them being labeled pro-Communist.[7]

Business leaders tend to chafe at the right-wing socialism or statism which their economy has become. The government's Instituto Nacional de Industria controls 50 per cent of Spain's basic industry and more than 20 per cent of its power supply.[8] Thus governmental thinking gets into most newspaper advertising almost subconsciously.

NEWS AGENCIES. Logos, the Catholic news agency, is the only Spanish wire service permitted besides the official one, Efe--a name derived from Spanish phonetic pronunciation for the letter "F," standing for "Falange," the Fascist political party.

Logos manages to carry stories of social reform in foreign countries which never get on the wires of Efe, whose director must be the Assistant Minister of Information under the bylaws of its charter. Other than Logos, international news received by Spanish newspapers and broadcasting stations carries the logotype "Efe" and the domestic news, the logotype "Cifra," Spanish for "Statistic."

Stations, magazines, and newspapers may also purchase the AP, UPI, Reuters, AFP, or Italian ANSA reports, but they actually may use only Efe dispatches. Televisión Española, the governmental television monopoly, buys UPI newsreels, which are edited to eliminate many spot news stories. The latter usually come from Cifra-Gráfica footage.

LEADING NEWSPAPERS. Spain's leading monarchist newspaper, ABC, a Madrid morning daily,

is feature-filled and has a color photograph for its "cover" or front page on Sundays. On week-days, its front page, printed in rotogravure, has photographs in tan or green. The monarchist lobby, working for a restoration of a king upon the Spanish throne, also publishes another daily with the same name, ABC, in Seville.

If government doling out of newsprint can be considered a political barometer, then Franco's rapport with the monarchists may exist because ABC and other monarchist publications in 1961 and 1962 received increased supplies of newsprint. By contrast, certain Catholic publications displaying a little independent thinking found their supplies delayed through tax computing and other legal red tape. The Ministry of Information determines the quotas for newsprint sales to all Spanish publications. Quota formulas are not explained.

Spain's leading Catholic daily newspaper is the Madrid morning Ya, tabloid-sized and feature-filled. Its Sunday edition displays a slick-paper color front page similar to a magazine cover.

Most Spanish newspapers are tabloids, whether published daily or weekly, in small towns or cities. And like Ya and ABC, most papers run two or three times as many features on literature or entertainment as they do genuine spot news reports.

Chief organ of the Falange, Arriba, is Madrid's third morning daily, and Marca, its fourth in circulation. The national capital also has four afternoon daily newspapers: Alcázar, Informaciones, Madrid, and Pueblo, the first three partly owned by Opus Dei, a Catholic political group.

No Spanish newspaper has a really large circulation, and circulations are neither certified, independently audited, nor listed in any recognized reference. Estimates can be made from figures released by advertising agencies, tempered by data from newsstand dealers, and the press officers of the embassies of the United States, Britain, France, and Switzerland in Madrid.

Based on such estimates, only two newspapers in Spain have more than 100,000 circulation: ABC in Madrid and La Vanguardia, morning daily in Barcelona.

Most Spanish newspapers have less than 10,000 paid circulations, no matter what their circulation and advertising departments claim. Newspaper paid circulation for the entire nation probably does not total more than one million for a Spanish population of 31 million whose adult population is 20 per cent illiterate. However, Spanish publishers claim a total newspaper circulation daily of 2.5 million, an unsubstantiated figure which UNESCO and other worldwide sources have repeated for the past decade. This claimed circulation is more than double actual daily newspaper sales.

The largest publishing company, Pyresa-- an abbreviation for Prensa y Radio Española, S. A., the S.A. meaning "incorporated"-- belongs to the Falange. Pyresa publishes the Madrid dailies Arriba and Marca, thirty-one other morning daily newspapers throughout Spain, five afternoon dailies, five weekly newspapers, four magazines, and several radio stations.

Both privately-owned commercial and government-owned noncommercial radio stations carry censored news. Certain governmental stations broadcast commercials, obtaining 20 per cent of their revenue from advertising and the remainder from the national treasury, from taxes collected annually from owners of radio receivers. There are more than two million licensed radio receivers in daily use.

Falange radio stations, known by the initials REM, which stands for Red de Emisoras del Movimiento, or Network of Stations of The Movement, total sixty-two standard-band transmitters in every key city in Spain, plus two shortwave stations in Madrid.

National Radio Service of Youth Fronts or Servicio Nacional de Radiodifusión del Frente Juventudes, the educational radio network, broadcasts in twenty-five cities.

Spanish National Radio, or Radio Nacional de España, maintains stations in major provincial cities. Its Madrid outlet has a power of 150,000 watts. The three commercial networks are run from Madrid, with affiliates in each sector of Spain.

Next to Madrid, the most influential city in Spain is Barcelona. Its chief daily is a morning paper, La Vanguardia, a five-column tabloid one-third larger than Madrid's ABC. This is Spain's most complete paper, often running to 36 pages. The first page contains photographs, and the second page, advertising. Thus the first news page actually is page 3.

El Correo Catalán, a morning daily, is a standard eight-column paper running 14 pages. The only English paper is a weekly.[9]

Sweden

combined circulation of about 3.8 million are spread through some 95 cities and towns, with Stockholm (the capital and largest city) and Göteborg (the second largest city) the main press centers.

Even though Sweden does not have any single newspaper which might be rated among the "world's best," its whole press system is usually considered as solid, progressive, free, and as prosperous as any in the world. Sweden, a nation of 7.5 million people and a very high rate of literacy (98 per cent), has 186 newspapers, 94 of which appear six or seven days a week. These newspapers, with a

The country's largest dailies are the PM tabloid Expressen (circ. about 420,000) and the qualitative morning Dagens Nyheter (circ. about 360,000), both of Stockholm.[1] Both of the circulation leaders, owned by the same publishing house (headed by Tor Bonnier), support Sweden's Liberal party. Expressen is an extravert among Swedish papers; its formula might be expressed in the words of its editor Carl-Adam Nycop: "Annoy the readers. Stroke them the wrong way. Never

---

PRINCIPAL SWEDISH DAILIES[2]

Stockholm:

Dagens Nyheter (AM; Liberal)	358,000	
	380,000	(Sun.)
Expressen (PM; Liberal)	420,000	
	425,000	(Sun.)
Aftonbladet (PM; neutral)	245,000	
	260,000	(Sun.)
Stockholms-Tidningen (AM; neutral)	148,000	
	180,000	(Sun.)
Svenska Dagbladet (AM; Conservative)	140,000	
	141,000	(Sun.)

Göteborg:

Göteborgs-Posten (AM; Liberal)	230,000	
Göteborgs-Tidningen (PM; Liberal)	64,000	
Göteborgs-Handels-Och Sjofartstidning	50,000	

Malmö:

Sydsvenska Dagbladet Snällposten (AM; Conservative)	86,000	
	140,000	(Sun.)
Arbetet (AM-PM; Social Democrat)	53,000	
Kvällposten (PM; Conservative)	47,000	
	81,000	(Sun.)
Skanska Dagbladet	43,000	

Hälsingborg:

Hälsingborgs Dagblad (AM; Conservative)	31,000	
	45,000	(Sun.)

Lindkoping:

Ostgota Correspondenten (AM; Conservative)	51,000	

Norrkoping:

Norrkopings Tidningar Ostergotlands Dagblad (AM; Conservative; Founded 1758)	25,000	

be servile to King or government."[3] Dagens Nyheter is much calmer; it ranges widely through the fields of culture and news, is readable and reliable. Its salaries are the highest in the Swedish newspaper profession and it draws the top writers to its staff. A British journalist has recently said that its policy might be "to inform and try to point the way."[4]

One of the oldest (f.1858) of the country's leading dailies is Göteborgs-Posten,[5] a morning Liberal paper which is Göteborg's largest and the country's largest outside Stockholm. The majority of the nation's daily papers, publishing from well-equipped modern plants, have circulations below 50,000; only about seven dailies in the country have circulations in excess of 100,000.

Leading Swedish newspapers, while not reaching such journalistic peaks as have the Neue Zürcher Zeitung, Le Monde, the New York Times and London's Times, are technically and editorially very fine. Writing is good; typography is interesting; make up is lively and varied; pictures and cartoons are many and add zest to the pages. Swedish newspapers have their own individuality and are anything but dull.

About 500 copies of daily newspapers are printed in Sweden for every 1,000 inhabitants, indicating that Swedes are a newspaper-reading people. In fact, they rank next to the British in newspaper readership.

Most newspaper copies (about 75 per cent) go to subscribers by mail or home delivery. Distribution is handled mainly by the postal authorities or by "Presbyrån," the Swedish Press Bureau (a distributing organization owned by the press).[6] Newsstands are popular throughout the country; even in the smallest towns it is not unusual to find these stands handling a wide variety of publications--even many from overseas. Presbyrån currently distributes 675 million newspapers and periodicals per annum, or about two million a day.

Most of the Swedish newspapers are journals of opinion, but very few are official party organs and they never overlook their function as "news disseminators."[7] It is impossible to categorize the papers as either "quality" or "popular" as can be done generally in Britain; this is because Swedish papers are multicharacter journals--giving hard news, commentary, strongly-worded opinion, cultural news, and entertainment.[8]

The Swedish press is interested in cultural matters and probably gives more play to serious treatment of the arts and sciences than does the press of any other country. This perhaps helps explain why serious magazines of opinion and intellectual reviews do not flourish in Sweden as they do in many nations. Photographs in the papers are usually large and the copy is not "tightly" edited--two indications that newsprint is plentiful in the country. Pages in the Swedish papers, as is true in Denmark, are agglutinated or glued together at the fold.

There are no significant political weeklies in Sweden such as Britain's Spectator or New Statesman, nor are there any newsmagazines such as the U.S.'s Time or Newsweek or West Germany's Der Spiegel. However, popular picture weeklies of many types are common. There are about 35 general magazines in Sweden with a total circulation of 6.3 million. In addition to these there are 1,700 special interest publications, most with small circulations, although 11 have circulations of 100,000 and ranging upward to 350,000.

The Swedish newspaper reader--especially the reader of one of the "nationals" published in Stockholm--gets a good selection of news, both foreign and domestic. No other newspaper in all Scandinavia (with the exception of Dagens Nyheter) gives its readers as much foreign news as does the PM Expressen, the nation's largest daily. It is common practice in Sweden, however, for the evening papers to give a skeletonized presentation of foreign news and for the AMs to fill in background information and give significance to this news. The entire Swedish press carries a large amount of foreign news, which enjoys wide and thorough readership, a situation which does not exist in most other countries.

Although a few of the larger papers have correspondents abroad, most of the foreign news used in the press comes from the national news agency, Tidningarnas Telegrambyra (TT). This cooperative organization, founded in 1921 and owned by the daily press, is completely free of government control. TT gets its foreign news mainly through exchange agreements with other agencies--particularly Reuters and Agence France-Presse.

News is generally separated from editorial opinion and presented objectively in the American tradition; however, the writing is more lively and frequently more verbose. As one writer has described it:

"...emphasis is placed on giving even straight news reporting a lively twist.

Therefore many wordy frills remain, which at best add a personal touch to the story but often merely impose a rather monotonous coloration of currently fashionable journalistic cliches."[9]

Since 1960, there have been two institutes in journalism (one in Stockholm and one in Göteborg) which train newspapermen for Swedish papers. Except for editors, editorial writers, and foreign correspondents, there are very few Swedish journalists today who have had university training. Most have passed "student's examinations," an achievement which would correspond to about two years of college in the United States. About 95 per cent of all editorial workers in Sweden belong to the Union of Swedish Journalists (f.1901); this union includes executives, writers, and photographers in its membership.

According to British journalist Gerard Fay, "The Swedish reporter is not behind any in the world in getting his exclusive information and using it very often against the will of Government departments and other political or commercial pressure groups who would rather do their work in secrecy. Swedish reporters know what news is and how to get it...(the Swedish press) is an interesting study of voluntary self-discipline, backed by certain constitutional guarantees....Jostling for circulation is not on the same scale (as in Britain) because six out of every ten papers sold in cities and almost nine out of every ten in the provinces go to subscribers, which leaves very little casual sale to be competed for by circulation stunts....At the bottom of the Swedish press structure is a law brought up to date in 1949 whose 123 paragraphs have Constitutional force. It forbids obligatory censorship, even in wartime. It fixes the responsibility for the contents of a newspaper on a single person known as the 'responsible publisher' (usually the editor-in-chief). The publisher and his staff are prohibited by this law from revealing the sources of their information even in Court or to the police...."[10]

Practically speaking there are no newspapers issued less than biweekly in Sweden. Of the provincial papers issued 2 to 4 times weekly there are 31 with circulations of less than 5,000; there are 25 with circulations of 5,000 to 10,000 and 8 with circulations of 10,000 to 20,000. In addition to these there are 4 newspapers with less than 5,000 circulation; 15 with 5,000 to 10,000 circulation; 29 with 10,000 to 20,000 circulation, and 26 with 20,000 to 40,000 circulation that are issued daily except on Sunday.[11]

PRESS FREEDOM. Sweden has perhaps the world's oldest tradition of press freedom. Not only was Sweden the first state in the world to enact a law guaranteeing freedom to publish (with specified exceptions), but it was also by its "King-in-Council Ordinance Concerning Freedom of Writing and Publishing" of 1766 the first state to guarantee freedom of access to information of governmental and public affairs.[12]

Sweden has a great amount of press freedom--probably more than any other nation in the world. Laws of the country specifically grant press freedom and forbid the hampering of news collection and dissemination in any way by any person or group. Legal provisions give the press and public every right to follow in detail the activities of government. There is no state control in Sweden and all important political parties have their newspaper representatives or allies. Political columns are extremely popular and provide some of the liveliest reading in the press. The newspapers, having their constitutional position more clearly defined than most throughout the world, have built up a system of voluntary restraint. A document issued by the Publicistklubben, a professional group of newspapermen, is a code of conduct which is posted in every editorial department throughout the country.

Since 1916 the nation has had a Press Fair Practices Commission, a private group which acts as a buffer between the press and the public and which also settles disputes and problems within the press itself.[13] This group, similar to Britain's Press Council, handles only newspaper cases. The Commission's power is in its publishing of opinion; it is the practice that newspapers involved in disputes publish the findings and recommendations handed down by the "court of honor."[14] The Commission has an independent nonjournalist chairman; otherwise its membership is composed of representatives from three Swedish press groups: the Publicistklubben or "Publicists' Club," the Swedish Publishers Association, and the Union of Swedish Journalists. This group, serving as a court of honor, hears complaints from anybody who believes he has been maltreated by a newspaper; it does not deal with cases in which the newspaper has broken a press law.

Another way the Swedish press indulges in self-regulation is through having its sins pointed out regularly in the Grönköpings Veckoblad. This monthly, somewhat similar to Britain's Punch, parodies and criticizes many Swedish publications, pointing out their weaknesses in handling news events. Editors do not consider it helpful to their reputations to be quoted in this journal which has been blasting away at the Swedish press for more than 50 years.[15]

Consonant with the other protections afforded the press, Swedish law also offers effective protection to the anonymity of a journalist's sources. While the journalist has no legal right to refuse to give information on the <u>contents</u> of information obtained in the practice of his profession, his right to protect his <u>sources</u>, while not absolute, is legally construed as a right to anonymity for the journalist's informant and a corresponding <u>obligation</u> on the part of the journalist to respect that anonymity. The Freedom of the Press Act in its chapter three, with Constitutional force specifies that no journalist "shall reveal the identity of the author or of any person who may have provided information for publication, except with the permission of such author or informant, <u>unless obliged to by law.</u>

More particularly, under this provision, a journalist is legally <u>obligated</u> to refuse to reveal the source of his information either to a private person or to a person in a position of authority if (a) the source has not consented to the disclosure of his identity and, in general practice, if the source has not specifically waived anonymity, and if (b) the journalist is not required by law to reveal the informant's identity, which might occur by reason of the general obligation of the citizen to appear as a witness in court.

Under Swedish Procedure Law, each court itself decides upon the limits of the obligation resting upon each witness, and the court is expected to give careful consideration to the preservation of professional secrets and to the protection of anonymity of sources as specified by the Constitution, so far as such revelation is <u>not vital</u> to a decision in the case. This latter provision is the journalist's basis for the preservation of professional secrets, and protection of sources. Because of this established constitutional and procedural law the right of journalists to keep professional secrets has been protected, and with no cases presenting any sort of threat to that right or privilege, the issue has hardly been discussed in Sweden.[16]

<u>THE PRESS AND LABOR.</u> Freedom of the press, according to the Swedes, confers not only rights but also responsibilities. The most important of these responsibilities is "not only the right but the duty to furnish the public with newspapers." Stoppage of newspaper publication, either by strikes or lockout, therefore, is in effect a violation of the constitution, which also guarantees freedom of the press. To meet this responsibility newspaper management and labor decided:

1. The unions would withdraw from their labor associations (roughly comparable with the AFL-CIO), and publishers would withdraw from employer associations.
2. Unions pledged not to strike, and management guaranteed not to lockout employees.
3. Disputes were to be settled by negotiation and/or arbitration.

The first general agreement for a ten-year period was reached on December 1, 1937 between the Publishers Association and the Swedish Compositors' Union for Typographical Workers. Since then the typographers have been joined in the agreement by the lithographers, distributors and other workers, except for the writers whose guild has traditionally abstained from use of the strike, and the agreement has been renewed every five years.

The result has been that Swedish newspapers have had more than twenty-five years of uninterrupted labor peace, during which conflicts have either been settled by negotiation or arbitration. Today, the arrangement is regarded as a permanent feature of Sweden's newspaper publication.

There are some special conditions in Sweden that make such an arrangement possible. First, printers working for newspapers are separated from job printers and others not working on newspapers. Second, both sides have a highly developed sense of social responsibility. And third, in Sweden the concept of the newspapers as a special kind of public utility which should not be allowed to suspend its service to the people is widely held.[17]

A <u>BRIEF</u> <u>LOOK</u> <u>AT</u> <u>SOME</u> <u>LEADING</u> <u>DAILIES</u>

DAGENS NYHETER: (Stockholm; Liberal AM; f.1864). Sweden's second largest daily with about 358,000 circulation and nearly 380,000 on Sunday. Typical issue runs from 36 to 40 pages. Carries more advertising than any other Swedish paper. Has a regular-size eight-column format; attractive make up; large photographs. Uses color on front page and sometimes inside, especially in advertisements. Carries larger proportion of cultural articles and features than most large Swedish dailies. Good selection of national and foreign news from its own correspondents and much from UPI, AP, AFP, Reuters, and the

Swedish national news agency (TT); many stories run under a combination credit line attributing the story to three, four, or five agencies.

EXPRESSEN: (Stockholm; Liberal; PM tabloid; f.1944). The country's largest daily with a circulation of about 420,000. Published in Dagens Nyheter plant, but with its own editorial staff. Aims at a wide audience made up chiefly of young people--in the "white collar" professions and among high school and university students. It gives liberal space to such subjects as sports and social activities; at the same time it treats seriously literature, music, art, and education. Especially noted for its lively coverage of foreign news; has full-time correspondents in some six major cities throughout the world. Averages four pages of foreign news a day out of its tabloid-size edition of 24 pages. A 28-page paper may contain as many as eight pages of foreign news.

AFTONBLADET: (Stockholm; neutral PM; f.1830). Sweden's first daily newspaper in the modern sense. From the first has had good news coverage and lively editorials; gained national prominence under its first editor, Lars Johan Hierta, who made the paper into one of the country's outstanding liberal organs. Has always given its readers much human interest material, features and cartoons, as well as brisk news stories. In 1956 Aftonbladet was bought by the Swedish Trade Union Confederation, thus actually coming under the control of the country's labor (Social-Democratic) party. However, it calls itself "neutral" politically.

STOCKHOLMS-TIDNINGEN: (Stockholm; neutral AM; f.1889). By 1900 this mass-appeal daily had a circulation of about 100,000--largest in Northern Europe at the time. Politically independent or neutral, and until recent years was especially critical of socialism. Often has supported the Liberal party. In 1956, like Aftonbladet, it was bought by the Swedish Trade Union Confederation, thus ending its often vehement antisocialist policy. Claims now to be politically neutral. Has a regular-size eight-column format; uses a more conservative make up than most of the larger dailies. Usually runs 16 to 20 pages and

gives the reader everything from comic strips to serious literary essays. Relies very heavily on TT, the national agency, for its news.

SVENSKA DAGBLADET: (Stockholm; Conservative AM; f.1884). The main voice of Swedish conservatism; closely allied with the Conservative party, although financially independent. In make up, news treatment and political philosophy, it is much like the Times of London. It was the first Swedish daily to give emphasis to cultural, educational, and scientific topics; its international and its financial and business coverage is considered the most comprehensive and enlightened in Sweden. Its sports coverage is also especially good; usually its largest photographs concern athletic events. It is one of the few European papers still using its front page entirely for advertising--in its case: display advertising. Aims at readers in top business and government positions and intellectual groups in general. Usually runs from 20 to 24 pages.

GÖTEBORGS-POSTEN: (Göteborg; Liberal AM; f.1858). One of Sweden's four largest dailies. Attractively made up, regular-size eight-column daily which often runs a large cartoon on its front page. However, generally its make up is more serious and conservative than any of the large dailies with the exception of Svenska Dagbladet. News coverage is good and its opinion articles are lively and thought-provoking; paper appeals to all classes.

SYDSVENSKA DAGBLADET SNÄLLPOSTEN: (Malmö; Conservative AM; f.1848). Like Svenska Dagbladet of Stockholm its make up is rather dull and its news and commentary are aimed at an intellectual audience. Also like Svenska Dagbladet, its Conservative counterpart in Stockholm, it gives over its front page to display advertising. The leading Conservative paper outside Stockholm.

ARBETET: (Malmö; Social Democrat; f.1887). Largest Social Democratic daily outside Stockholm. Noted for its thorough news coverage and careful editing. Neat and lively typographical presentation and make up. Uses a regular-size format.

Switzerland

Switzerland, a little nation of 5.4 million inhabitants with an illiteracy rate of less than 2 per cent, has about 400 dailies and weeklies.[1] More than half of these appear in towns of fewer than 10,000 residents. Some 120 dailies circulate a total of 1.5 million copies. About 300 copies of newspapers are printed daily for every 1,000 Swiss citizens. More than 80 per cent of the newspapers are "opinion" or "political" journals, with "information" papers taking a subordinate position in the Swiss press structure. All newspapers appear in one of the three official languages--German, French, and Italian. German language newspapers predominate, with French language journals second. The weekly newspapers, forming an important segment of the Swiss press, circulate a total of about 2.5 million copies each week. The well-edited Die Weltwoche of Zurich is undoubtedly the leading Swiss weekly. Another influential weekly was the French language Curieux of Neuchâtel.

Most Swiss daily papers do not have large circulations, the largest printing fewer than 155,000 copies. The press is extremely decentralized due to regionalism and local patriotism, and good newspapers of all types can be found spread throughout the 24 sections of the country. Large circulation dailies appear only in Berne (the capital), Basle, Geneva, Lausanne, and Zurich. While most of the nation's most important and influential papers are "political" (party affiliation or party-bias), some of the general or "neutral" papers have the largest circulations. For example, the country's circulation leader is Zurich's neutral Tagesanzeiger with some 150,000 circulation. Undoubtedly the leading Swiss daily in every respect but circulation, however, is the national "political" Neue Zürcher Zeitung (Radical-Liberal) with a circulation of about 75,000. Although one of small circulation (about 12,000), the Journal de Genève is considered a very fine Swiss daily and one of Europe's best informed.

POLITICAL DAILIES. Leading the Swiss press in terms of prestige and general quality are the national political dailies. Representative, and probably the most influential of these,

are the following: Neue Zürcher Zeitung, Der Bund (Berne, Rad.-Dem.), Berner Tagwacht (Berne, Soc.-Dem.), Journal de Genève (Geneva, Lib.-Conser.) Basler Nachrichten (Lib.-Conser.), National-Zeitung (Basle, Rad.-Lib.) Gazette de Lausanne (Lib.-Dem.), and Il Dovere (Bellinzone, Rad.-Lib.). Political papers developed in Switzerland early in the 1800's, and by 1860 the concept of a political press was a firm part of Swiss society.

GENERAL DAILIES. Outstanding general (or "neutral") newspapers in Switzerland are Tagesanzeiger of Zurich, Feuille d'Avis de Lausanne, La Suisse of Geneva, and Luzerner Neueste Nachrichten of Lucerne, Tribune de Lausanne, and Feuille d'Avis de Neuchâtel. Most of the general newspapers are purely "information" journals, giving news and making no claims to political influence.

OTHER PUBLICATIONS. Besides the "politicals" and the "neutrals," there are several large dailies which are so-called "official" journals. Foremost among them is the Tagblatt der Stadt Zurich, with some 90,000 circulation, and Berne's Anzeiger für die Stadt Bern, with about 60,000. A Communist press hardly exists in Switzerland; La Voix Ouvrière, a daily of about 8,000 circulation is published in Geneva, but it is small, financially weak, and not very influential.

PERIODICALS. Some of the outstanding Swiss magazines and journals are the weeklies Der Nebelspalter (Rorschach), Sie und Er and L'Illustre (Zofingen), and the monthlies Schweizer Rundschau, Schweizer Monatshefte, and the Swiss Review of World Affairs (Zurich), the Politische Rundschau (Rorschach), and the Revue de Suisse (Geneva). The Swiss Review of World Affairs is probably the most popular serious journal. Published by the Neue Zurcher Zeitung (using articles selected from that newspaper and translated into English), this monthly is airmailed to all parts of the world. It may be obtained in the United States from the University of Chicago Press.

PRESS FREEDOM. Switzerland has one of the freest presses in the world. According to Dr. Karl Weber, probably the leading press authority of the nation, freedom of the press means freedom within the and freedom from the state.[2] Editors take orders from nobody, and as in the United States, the state powers are confined to legal penalties for abuse of press freedom. Section 45 of the Federal Constitution, approved in 1848, provides for Swiss press freedom. In exercising this freedom, Swiss journalists realize their responsibility to the people, and recognize that such liberty was not guaranteed in order

"to facilitate the professional work of journalists...but it is an indispensable factor
in the life of a state ruled by the principle
of liberty."[3]

Although Swiss law protects freedom of publication, it has not been extended to protect
newsmen from attempts by courts to force
journalists to divulge sources of information.
While judges are legally forbidden to question
physicians, lawyers, and clergymen to the
point requiring revelation of professional
secrets, journalists in Switzerland have no
right to withhold evidence. In specified instances and circumstances, however, the court
itself may choose to recognize a higher interest in the performance of a service by the
press as, for example, in the discovery of
abuses of the public interest. But in a case
involving disclosure of secret information of
the counter-intelligence section in 1957, an
Associated Press correspondent was imprisoned
and fined with the intent to force him to
disclose the source of his information.

While there is no formulated code of ethics
for professional practice of journalists in
Switzerland, it is the unwritten law that the
Swiss journalist maintains professional
secrecy and does not disclose the sources of
confidential information.[4]

NATIONAL PRESS AGENCY. The national news
agency is the Agence Télégraphique Suisse (ATS),
founded in 1895. A joint stock company independent of the government, ATS is the main
source of domestic news and the chief dis-
tributor of foreign news. It gets its foreign
news mainly from Reuters and AFP. Its main
office is in Berne. The agency has exchange
agreements with a number of national agencies.
All of the big international news agencies
have offices in Switzerland. Much of the
diplomatic news of Europe is channeled to the
world press through Swiss news facilities.

TWO LEADING SWISS DAILIES

NEUE ZÜRCHER ZEITUNG and JOURNAL DE GENÈVE.
These two Liberal Swiss dailies--one in German
and the other in French--are examples of newspapers which consistently blend straight news
and commentary in the best tradition of European journalism. Both are national papers
presenting a large amount of serious news and
opinion on their tabloid pages with a minimum
of illustrative material. They have readers
in government and academic circles throughout the world.

Neue Zürcher Zeitung,[5] the country's leading
daily and one of the best in the world, was
founded in Zurich in 1780. It has always
maintained an independent, courageous policy
and has desired serious news treatment over
a large circulation. Its foreign coverage is
especially good and it maintains correspond-
dents in all the world's important cities.
It publishes both AM and PM editions and has
a circulation of about 75,000, of which about
8,000 are distributed abroad. Statistical
studies made by the International Press Institute from October, 1952 to January, 1953
showed that the Neue Zürcher Zeitung carried
nearly twice as much foreign news as its
nearest competitor among 23 newspapers from
eight countries. The second highest was an
unidentified British paper. Moreover, the
percentage of foreign material to total non-
advertising text was one-third higher than
its nearest (an unidentified French) competitor.[6]

Journal de Genève, founded in 1826 in Geneva,
is usually considered Switzerland's second
best daily in general excellence. It is a
serious and well-informed tabloid like the
Neue Zürcher Zeitung, and is one of the leading newspapers published anywhere in the French
language. A morning paper appearing every day
but Sunday, it has a circulation of about
13,000.

West Germany

West Germany has a population of about 54.5 million and a literacy rate of about 98 per cent. There are some 1,464 daily newspapers in the Federal Republic and West Berlin; of these 690 are main editions and the rest are regional editions or "Kopfblätter" as they are called. The West German press has not recovered its former standing in spite of its recent tremendous growth. In 1932 when the daily press was at its peak there were 4,703 dailies with a total circulation of 25 million. The dailies now boast a total circulation of close to 18 million, by far the largest in continental Europe.[1] Almost 5,000 publications of all types appear in West Germany with a total circulation of slightly more than 75 million. In general, the make up, use of color, writing and production practices of the West German press are superior to those of other European nations.[2]

Nearly all West German publications are privately owned. Very few papers are party organs, although most of them give considerable space to political affairs and evidence political biases. Two newspapers--the daily Welt of Hamburg and the weekly Zeit of the same city--have established themselves as well-written and well-edited newspapers on the Continent which are doing a fine job of presenting domestic and foreign news cast in the interpretive style of London's weekly Economist. Another paper of outstanding editorial and mechanical characteristics is the daily Frankfurter Allgemeine of Frankfurt-am-Main; it is considered by many capable observers as West Germany's best all-around daily and is the nearest thing the country has to a national news daily.

West German papers have no standard format; they range from four and five columns in both regular-size and tabloid varieties, with six columns as the maximum. There is a general tendency in the German papers toward horizontal display with many one-line spread headlines giving the pages a semimagazine appearance. In the country the six-day paper is normal, with a larger weekend edition published on Saturday.

The day of the party press (characteristic of the pre-World War II days) has largely ended in West Germany. Of the 380 dailies listed in Editor & Publisher Yearbook for 1962 only 25 admit any political leanings. Almost 70 per cent of the newspapers published in the Federal Republic and West Berlin are "nonpolitical" while only 10 per cent follow a definite party line.[3] A few powerful political papers still flourish in the country, but the big independent dailies are the ones which are making the greatest advances. Among the party papers of West Germany which exert the most influence are the following: Rheinische Post (Christian Democrat) of Düsseldorf, Westfälische Nachrichten (Christian Democrat) of Münster, Freie Presse (Social Democrat) of Bielefeld, and the Aachener Volkszeitung (Christian Democrat) of Aachen. The largest, by far, of these party papers is Rheinische Post with a daily circulation of about 263,000 in the Catholic Rheinland. The Communist papers are small and relatively impotent in West Germany. Newspapers in West Berlin show more of an anti-Communist attitude than the other West German papers. Among the most vehement anti-Communist dailies of West Berlin are the Morgenpost, Telegraf, Tagesspiegel, Kurier, and Tag.

In the last several years there has been a sharp rise of pictorial papers and magazines in West Germany. While many responsible German journalists deplore this development, others like the well-known publisher Axel Springer, believe that these "illustrated" journals are legitimate adjuncts to a healthy press system and are producing them in addition to other types. The success of such picture publications as the Neue Illustrierte of Cologne with its rather sensational and gaudy photographs and color, and such picture newspapers as Hamburg's Bild-Zeitung with its three million circulation, is an indication that the German people are finding the older type "viewspaper" and the newer British- and American-inspired information-oriented "news" paper unable to satisfy their reading desires.[4]

Most German newspapers still cling to subjective-type stories believed to give the "proper perspective and background" to the news presentation. News, compared to American standards, is often stodgily written and frequently outdated, since even such big, influential dailies as Die Welt of Hamburg and Munich's Süddeutsche Zeitung economize by having correspondents mail in most of their copy.

Daily, weekly, and semiweekly papers of almost every type have grown rapidly in recent years. With the exception of a few leading dailies and the illustrated papers, the individual circulations are not large. The three cities having the largest daily circulation of newspapers are Essen, Hamburg, and Düsseldorf. There are about 350 copies of dailies (exclusive of the illustrateds which can hardly be called newspapers) circulating per 1,000 inhabitants. The largest daily newspapers (other than the picture tabloid Bild-Zeitung) are Essen's Westdeutsche Allgemeine (AM, cir. 427,000) and the after-

LEADING DAILIES
(Circulations over 100,000)

Berlin (West):	BZ	296,000
	Berliner Morgenpost	240,000
	Der Tagesspiegel	100,000
Bielefeld:	Westfalen-Blatt	111,000
Braunschweig:	Braunschweiger Zeitung	133,000
Bremen:	Weser-Kurier	120,000
Cologne:	Kolner Stadt-Anzeiger	179,000
	Kölnische Rundschau	147,000
Dortmund:	Westfälische Rundschau	237,000
	Ruhr-Nachrichten	
	Westfalenpost	113,000
Düsseldorf:	Rheinische Post	263,000
Essen:	Westdeutsche Allgemeine	427,000
	Neue-Rhein-Zeitung	240,000
Frankfurt:	Frankfurter Allgemeine	250,000
	Abendpost	115,000
	Frankfurter Rundschau	105,000
	Frankfurter Neue Presse	101,000
Hamburg:	Bild-Zeitung (photo)	3 million
	Hamburger Abendblatt	320,000
	Die Welt	260,000
	Hamburger Morgenpost	296,000
Hannover:	Hannoversche Presse	148,000
	Allgemeine Zeitung	131,000
Karlsruhe:	Badische Neuste Nachrichten	135,000
Kassel:	Hessische Algemeine	108,000
Koblenz:	Rhein Zeitung	177,000
Ludwigshaten:	Die Rheinpfalz	163,000
Munich:	Süddeutsche Zeitung	202,000
	Münchner Merkur	160,000
Nurenberg:	Nachrichten	190,000
Stuttgart	Stuttgarter Zeitung	140,000

noon daily of Hamburg, the Hamburger Abend-blatt (circ. 320,000). Most of the other circulations of the country's leading dailies range from about 185,000 to 250,000. Although Sunday papers are not as yet common in West Germany, two of them--Bild am Sonntag and Welt am Sonntag--published by Axel Springer, have circulations of close to one million. Usually considered the country's most influential serious newspapers are the Frankfurter Allge-meine, Die Welt of Hamburg, and Munich's Süddeutsche Zeitung. Other good, well-edited dailies are the Kölnische Rundschau of Cologne, the Rheinische Post of Düsseldorf, the Tages-spiegel of Berlin, and the Westdeutsche Allge-meine of Essen. The semiweekly Deutsche Zeitung is generally regarded as the nation's top economic nondaily; Die Zeit of Hamburg and Rheinische Merkur of Cologne are probably the foremost political weeklies of the country.

PRESS WEAKNESSES. Any weaknesses the West German press might have are qualitative, not quantitative. Generally, international press observers think the nation's press is suffer-ing from the extremes of too much editorializ-ing and too much sensationalizing. However, with British and U.S. influence since the war and the maturing of the new journalists since the end of licensing, the German press has

absorbed much of Western journalism ethics and principles. The "information press" concept has a firm foothold in West Germany. Although it has not yet gained a world front rank position, international observers think the nation's press is improving. Its chief handicap is believed to be rooted in the Third Reich, which pretty thoroughly dis-pelled qualitative journalism as it was ex-emplified by the world-famous Frankfurter Zeitung. Today there are only six or eight papers of national reputation, and none of the international reputation of the old Berliner Tageblatt and the historic Frankfurt daily mentioned above. In pre-Nazi days these two papers enjoyed about the same kind of journalistic prestige as did London's Times, France's Le Temps (Le Monde today), and Argentina's La Prensa. The only two papers today which come close to the quality of these earlier dailies are Hamburg's Die Welt and Frankfurt's Frankfurter Allgemeine.

Objective reporting in the U.S. sense never has been (and to a large degree is not yet) the vogue in German press circles. The German press, however, is showing improve-ment each year--both in attempting to be more objective in its news presentation and interpretation, and more effective in its typography and make up.

THE GERMAN PRESS: A BRIEF BACKGROUND. During

the Weimar Republic, before Hitler took over
the country, a thriving press respected
throughout the world typified the cultural
achievement of the German people. Large publishing houses like Ullstein, Mosse, and
Hugenberg published not only popular dailies
like the Vössische Zeitung, Lokal-Anzeiger and
Berliner Tageblatt, but an immense and wide
assortment of intellectual fare. Graphic arts
in the country achieved a foremost place in
the world. The courageous and influential
Frankfurter Zeitung achieved a place with
London's Times and Zurich's Neue Zürcher
Zeitung as one of the best newspapers in
Europe. This period ended in 1933 when the
Nazis thrust themselves into power. Press
freedom, enjoyed during the Weimar Republic
and to some extent before that time, ended in
Germany with the coming of Hitler into power.

Under Hitler it was not possible for editors
to express opinions freely. The press, as
well as all other media of mass communication,
soon became instruments of the state. Hitler
generally hated the press; he was suspicious
of the publishers; he was afraid of their
power. The only newspapers which received
any cooperation from his regime were papers
like the Volkischer Beobachter ("People's
Observer") and Der Angriff ("The Attack")
which he could use as personal instruments of
propaganda and power. He always visualized
the press as a potent weapon and possible
danger to his regime.

Hitler was convinced that most papers were
owned by Jews; consequently, he believed them
to be "anti-German." After taking over the
government, Hitler considered the press as an
"arm of the revolution" and as "an instrument
of education," and put his good friend Max
Amman in charge of the Reichspressekammer,
which actually ran the press as an educational
instrument. Through this organization, and particularly through the Ministry of Propaganda
directed by Joseph Goebbels, the Nazis controlled the thinking of the German masses and
disseminated propaganda to almost every country. The old and respected Wolff news agency
was soon renamed the Deutsches Nachrichten-
Büro (DNB) under the Nazis and became the
official propaganda disseminating agency.

During the war the number of papers and newspaper readers declined constantly, until at the
end of hostilities in Europe there were fewer
than 1,000 papers in Germany with a total circulation of between 10 and 15 million. At the
end of the war and only four days after the
armistice (May 12, 1945) the occupying forces
began requiring that all newspaper publishers
be licensed. So from 1945 until 1949 the German press went through a period of Allied

licensing and controls.[5] During this time
the press was marked by a shortage of qualified personnel, a lamentable condition of
facilities, and a shortage of newsprint.
There was no competition among the newspapers.
Die Welt in the British zone and Die Neue
Zeitung in the American zone where the leaders
among the papers during the licensing period
and served as textbooks for German editors
on how to edit a good newspaper. The Americans, British, and French licensed about 150
papers in their zones during this period.

After licensing ended in 1949 new papers
appeared everywhere. In one month 150 new
journals sprang up in the British zone alone.
After a short period of circulation drops on
many papers, circulations began to grow, and
they have been growing constantly ever since.[6]

TYPES OF PAPERS IN WEST GERMANY. There are
various ways German newspapers can be categorized. For example there are the local and
provincial ("boiler plate") editions of metropolitan papers, the "generalanzeiger"
papers which are politically indifferent and
try to please everybody (best example: Hamburger Abendblatt), the "boulevard" papers
which are the entertainment-picture journals
(best example: Bild-Zeitung of Hamburg), the
party papers such as the Rheinische Post,
and the independent papers such as the pro-
U.S. Welt of Hamburg and the Frankfurter
Allgemeine.

Three types of provincial papers are (a)
the "Kopfblatter" which are local papers
using material bought from mat services; the
mat news and features comprise most of the
papers' contents, (b) the "Ring" papers
which correspond to chain papers in Britain
and the U.S.; however, they are generally
printed in a central place, with the front
page made over for each community; a local
nameplate is used for each separate edition,
(c) the "Gemeinschaft" or community papers
usually published in a centrally-located
plant to save money; they are individually
owned, however, and are not controlled by a
company as in the "Ring" setup.

Typical of the vast majority of German
newspapers is the Rhein-Neckar-Zeitung of
Heidelberg. Founded in 1945, it has 72,000
circulation with a main edition and eight
subsidiary editions. Its front page and
about two-thirds of its editorial page are
devoted to national and international news.
About the same amount of space is devoted to
local news, from one to three pages to sports,
a half to three-quarters of a page to economic,
financial, and market news and about two pages
to features and entertainment (theater, opera,

music, books, and radio). Four and a half to
five pages of advertising complete the 12 page
average of its main edition. Advertising and
circulation pay its costs.

(more like magazines) with large circulations
(between 500,000 and 1.5 million). Biggest
of these are Stern of Hamburg, Quick and
Revue of Munich, Neue Illustrierte of Cologne,
Frankfurter Illustrierte of Frankfurt, Con-
stanze of Hamburg, Weltbild of Munich, and
Kristall of Hamburg.[7]

Some of the big weekly illustrateds.
Quick and Weltbild offer the same type
news and features as newspapers, but
can give more background information
because there is no pressure of a time
limit. Tele and Kicker are television
and sports specialties respectively.

Most of the daily papers in West Germany
are morning editions. Afternoon papers are
extremely scarce, with the Hamburger Abendblatt
the only PM paper having a substantial circulation. The two main Sunday papers are Bild am
Sonntag and Welt am Sonntag, both published by
Axel Springer & Sohn and circulated in Hamburg,
Berlin, Frankfurt, Essen and Munich.

The big weeklies generally contain the same
type of information and features as the daily
newspapers; however, they tend to place news
developments in their proper perspective and
give more background since they do not work
under the pressure of time. Their circulations
are not large (usually from 10,000 to 75,000)
but they have considerable influence in the
country. Among the outstanding weeklies of
various types are Die Zeit of Hamburg, Christ
Und Welt of Stuttgart, Rheinische Merkur of
Cologne, and the Protestant Sonntagsblatt of
Hamburg. There are also ten illustrated papers

West Germans read many foreign newspapers.
The Swiss papers (especially Neue Zürcher
Zeitung, Die Tat and Die Weltwoche) are the
most popular foreign journals. Le Monde is
preferred among the French papers; the Times
and Manchester Guardian among the British
papers, and the New York Times, the Christian
Science Monitor and the New York Herald
Tribune among the American papers.

DPA: THE CHIEF NEWS AGENCY. The West German
national press association or news agency
is Deutsche Presse Agentur (DPA) which was
founded in 1949.[8] It is a limited liability
company owned by newspaper publishers and
the broadcasting corporations. DPA, independent of the government and political parties,

is the country's principal information agency
and one of the largest in Europe. The agency,
with headquarters in Hamburg, has about 30
offices in the Federal Republic and some 25
bureaus abroad. It employs a staff of nearly
1,500 correspondents. DPA has exchange agreements with several foreign news agencies, but
receives most of its foreign news from Reuters.
The agency sends its news to West German newspapers by voice radio, teletype and Hells-
chreiber printer. DPA competes mainly with
the American AP and UPI, which have special
news files for German papers. The large
dailies of West Germany regularly use stories
supplied by the American agencies as well as
those supplied by Reuters and DPA.

PRESS FREEDOM. In the Federal Republic and
West Berlin the long absent freedom of the
press is anchored in the Federal Constitution
as well as in the Laender constitutions.
Article No. 5 of the Republic's Basic Law
provides, however, that "everyone has the
right freely to express and to publish his
opinion by speech, writing, and pictures and
to freely inform himself from generally accessible sources," and that "freedom of the press
and freedom of reporting by radio and motion
pictures are guaranteed."[9] The government
tried to get a press law passed in 1952 which
would have banned anything which might have
hurt the nation's reputation; it would have
also stipulated that the press "must publish
only what would correspond to the truth."
The proposed bill was withdrawn owing to
strong protest from the press. A law passed
in 1953 forbids the sale of literature of an
obscene or indecent nature to young people.
It is called the "Schmutz-und-Schundgesetz"
(dirt-and-trash) law. A control commission,
made up of members of the government, the
press, the teaching profession, and the clergy,
decides whether a publication is "indecent."
Generally, it would be safe to say that the
press of West Germany enjoys the same freedom
as is the case in Britain and the U.S. Moreover, journalists' right of professional
secrecy has gained some recognition in German
law.[10]

    Although West Germany has no long tradition
of freedom of the press, West German journalists are jealous of their freedom (viz.,
their response to the "Spiegel Affair" in
1962) and are profoundly aware that freedom
must not be confused with license. "Press
freedom guarantees," remarked Dr. Hermann
Knorr, editor of the Rhein-Neckar-Zeitung,
"are only as good as the will of the public
to make them good. If the press publishes
material that causes its readers to say, 'The
press goes too far and should be controlled,'
it will be controlled."[11]

THE GERMAN PRESS COUNCIL. A bill offered in
1952 by the Federal Ministry of the Interior
providing for legal control of the press by
"supervisory authorities" alerted newsmen to
the need to forestall government attempts to
restrict the recently regained press freedom.
During the next few years the idea of "self-
discipline" spread, and in November, 1956
ten leading proprietors and journalists met
to found the German Press Council.

    The Council set for itself four main tasks:[12]
1. Safeguarding the freedom of the press and
    ensuring unrestricted access to the sources
    of news.
2. Pinpointing and eliminating abuses within
    the press itself.
3. Keeping an eye on the development of the
    press structure and guarding against the
    growth of combines and monopolies that
    would jeopardize freedom.
4. Representing the press vis-à-vis the
    government, Parliament, and the public.

    With respect to freedom of the press, during
its first three years the Council expressed
its views in fifteen rulings. Among the
matters involved were police methods of
seizure, the right of editors to refuse to
testify, discrimination against press photographers, and a much-discussed law "concerning the protection of personal honor" (libel
law).

    An example of one of these actions occurred
when a bill, widely known under the name,
"Lex Soraya," was proposed that would amend
the law in order to provide greater "protection for the honor" of foreign Heads of State.
Complaints had been made concerning reports
published about the private life of Princess
Soraya, the former Queen of Iran, and the
Federal government tried to put a stop to
such "abuses " and "disturbances of international relations" by law. The German Press
Council supported by the entire press, inter-
vened, and the proposed amendment of penal
law was dropped.

    The Press Council would not carry the
weight it does with the public as well as
the government if it failed to point out and
express disapproval of abuses occurring as
a result of sensational journalism. The
best-known example of this was the decision
(made at the behest of the Press Council) of
the illustrated weekly, Quick, to discontinue
publication (already begun) of a lurid series
about the murder of a prostitute in Frankfurt.

    The German press and particularly the Press
Council realizes that the problem of press
freedom cannot be met merely by resisting

administrative and legislative measures. It
must include also a fight against abuses of
press freedom.

SOME ADDITIONAL INFORMATION

NEWS MAGAZINE. The country's outstanding
news magazine is Der Spiegel ("the Mirror"),
a lively weekly journal patterned after Time
magazine of the U.S. Published in Hamburg by
Rudolf Augstein, this magazine uses the "cover
story" technique and typical Time-style de-
partmentalization. Founded in 1947, it grew
rapidly, and now has a circulation of 500,000.

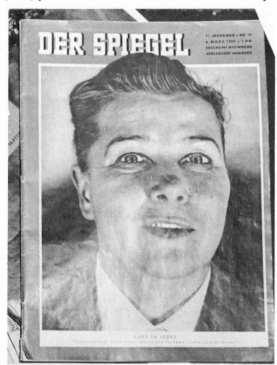

The magazine devotes a great amount of space
to news from the U.S. and often has its cover
story about an American personality. Der
Spiegel contains sharp writing and has become
successful on a formula of critical attack
and fight-picking articles. Its policy is
"deliberately aggressive," said Chief Editor
Hans Detlev Becker in 1958.[13] In October,
1962, a series of exposé articles involving
Defense Minister Franz Josef Strauss were
climaxed by one disclosing "secret" informa-
tion--that, despite all the money spent on
defense, the armed forces were poor and would
crumble under Communist attack. During the
night of October 27, the first of five members
of the magazine's staff were arrested. Public
response to this apparent reversion to Gestapo
techniques was widespread and immediate with
the result that Chancellor Adenauer was forced
to accept the resignation of Strauss who had
arranged the arrests.[14] Magazines in West

Germany range from the weekly Das Neue Blatt,
a sexy gossip sheet, to Westermanns Monat-
sheft--a high-quality magazine of the arts.
The largest magazine is Hör zu! ("Listen")
a Springer publication dealing with radio
and television (circ. about three million
weekly).

NEWSPAPERS. Many old Nazi publishers are
back in business again. But there are numerous publishers who were anti-Nazi now
exerting great influence on the German press
(e.g., Axel C. Springer who is now Europe's
biggest newspaper publisher, and Rudolph
Ullstein of the well-known Ullstein prewar
publishing family.)

Bild-Zeitung (circulation about three
million) is the largest daily on the European
continent (with the exception of Russia's
Pravda). Published simultaneously in Hamburg
(headquarters), Essen, West Berlin, Frankfurt, and Munich, this Springer publication
is a picture-filled tabloid paying little
attention to news. It uses big black heads--
and often vivid red heads and rules--on its
circus make up pages. Actually the paper
should not be classed as a "newspaper." The
sensational "news" features of Bild-Zeitung
are, however, not of the sexy type found in
some London papers. It publishes an edition
on Sundays called Bild am Sonntag.

Most of the serious papers in West Germany
carry few light features and no comic strips.
The afternoon Hamburger Abendblatt (West Germany's largest PM daily) is the exception;
it uses a full page of comics and all types
of features; it even runs fiction illustrated
with pastel colors. Practically all papers,
however, carry cultural type feature sections
called "Feuilleton" which run everything from
poetry and personal essays to American-style
factual features.

Newspapers are not nearly so thick as in
the United States but contain more pages
generally than their counterparts in the
rest of Europe. For example, a copy of the
Frankfurter Allgemeine usually runs about
20 pages, with the special weekend edition
often exceeding 60 pages. Most of the major
papers now use Roman type for their heads and
body type. Notable exception: Frankfurter
Allgemeine which clings to the old German
gothic (text) type in its heads although now
using Roman body type.

Usually considered the two best general
dailies in the nation are the Frankfurter
Allgemeine of Frankfurt-am-Main, and Die
Welt of Hamburg (with simultaneous editions
in Essen and West Berlin).[15] The former is

an independent paper following the line of democratic Liberalism; the latter is independent Conservative. Both present a well-balanced diet of serious news and commentary. Die Welt is a daily with a bright, modern appearance (typical of all Springer publications), whereas the Frankfurter Allgemeine with its old German text headlines and "grey" look is probably the most conservative in its make up of all West German newspapers. Both papers are well-edited and reliable and come close to being "national" dailies. The Frankfurt daily probably holds a slight edge on Die Welt in prestige within Germany; it is modern Germany's newspaper which comes nearest to being like the famed old Frankfurter Zeitung of pre-Hitler days.

The regional editions ("Kopfblatter") of the big city papers are presenting strong competition for the small independent local journals. These small papers have joined cooperative organizations called "Zeitungsringe" (Ring Papers), so that technical facilities may be pooled and shared. Mats of papers are distributed to the member papers from a central editorial office and each local editor then adds his local advertising and news. This has proved a great financial aid to the smaller papers.

JOURNALISM TRAINING. The study of journalism has a definite place in the academic structure of West Germany. There are many departments and courses in journalism or press science ("Publizistik") in the universities. Among the universities which give most emphasis to "Publizistik" are the University of Münster, Free University of Berlin, Leipzig University, the Universities of Erlangen, Hamburg, and Nuremburg, Ludwig Maximilian University (Munich), University of Cologne, and the Ruprecht Karl University of Heidelberg.

PRESS PERSONALITIES. Among the influential West German press personalities should be named Axel C. Springer, publisher of Bild-Zeitung, Die Welt, Hamburger Abendblat, and five magazines (with a total circulation exceeding 5,000,000) including Das Neue Blatt and Hör Zu!; Rudolf Augstein, publisher of Der Spiegel; Rudolf Pechal, publisher of Die Deutsche Rundschau; Benno Reifenberg, publisher of Die Gegenwart, and Herbert von Borch, editor of the small but influential weekly, Aussenpolitik. They are Germany's opinion leaders.[16]

U.S.S.R. and European Communist Nations

Great changes have taken place in the press systems of the countries behind the Iron Curtain since the days when they operated in freedom and had enterprising, sometimes highly-influential, papers which were respected throughout the world. With Communist domination came another type of press.[1] Today the press must walk a narrow line. An editor can be dismissed for nothing more than an embarrassing typographical error.

Today the important papers of the area are published either by the Communist party itself, or by trade-union councils, departments of the government, by "national front" groups, and youth organizations. All publications are state controlled; they are colorless, dull, and might be best characterized as propaganda sheets.

Newspapers in the Communist nations report the speeches of the Party leaders, extol the virtues of Socialism, praise national "progress," and print letters and reports from "correspondents" (spy-informants) scattered about in farm, mine, and factory. In most of the Communist nations censorship (deleting unfavorable material) is actually not practiced; there is no need for it since editors are members of the Communist party. They well know what would happen to them if they overstepped the Party line.

With the exception of Yugoslavia, the Communist nations of Eastern Europe have newspapers and other periodicals patterned after those of the Soviet Union and they reflect the basic Kremlin press philosophy. Communist newspapers dominate the press picture throughout the U.S.S.R. and the Soviet satellite nations of Eastern Europe, and also in the nationalistic Red nation of Yugoslavia. Throughout the area only the most devout Communists are allowed to be journalists, and each must surrender his individuality and conform to the Party line. In all these Communist nations the press is looked on as an arm of the government and the Party, an instrument with which to control the social system, to educate the masses, to agitate for progress, and to "self-criticize."

There are corresponding papers and journals published in each of the Soviet satellite nations representing different groups such as the Party, trade unions, government, youth, writers, teachers, etc. The average-size paper of the area is four pages (Yugoslav papers are thicker) dealing mainly with party news, Soviet bloc, and national items, all heavily loaded with anti-West propaganda.

Advertising is rather prominent in the East European press, although certainly it is not nearly so important as in a commercial press. An increasing emphasis on advertising has been noted since 1960. Theoretically there should be no need for advertising in the Communist press where there is no competition within private enterprise. Why, then, do the Communists advertise?

Some of the advertising is simply publicity for the state--pushing programs and projects. Most of it, however, seems designed to move surplus items that cannot be found everywhere (e.g., tennis racquets and automobiles). Practically all advertising is limited to state enterprises; once in a while, however, indications of the existence of private industry appear in the classified sections of certain publications. Weeklies and monthlies in the Communist countries carry very few advertisements; with the exception of foreign trade journals, high quality art work and color is lacking.[2]

The idea that advertising is wasteful and adds unnecessarily to consumer costs has not been borne out by experience in Communist countries. Communist prejudice if not hostility toward advertising is rooted in Marxian ideology, a tenet which has held that advertising and other competitive market techniques are wasteful.

The need for advertising is seen by many publications in the Communist bloc, exemplified by _Izvestia_ of the U.S.S.R. which recently said that managers of film studios and TV centers should "turn their gaze towards advertising," and by _Trud_, the trade union paper, which said that "advertising is becoming more sensible and useful." _Trud_ went on to say: "The function of state advertising agencies is not only to deal with surplus stocks, but to educate the public on the variety of new goods being made available."[3]

Red economists have come to recognize the usefulness of advertising as a "device for broadening the knowledge of the consumer in regard to quality as well as new and more economical products" and thus to reduce the need for and costs of grading and inspection of many items which is necessary when several plants manufacture undifferentiated products.

Professor Stefan Varga, a Hungarian economist, states that socialist advertising can help in achieving the economic plan through informative and educational advertising. Informative advertising, such as posters and announcements in theaters, he says is as necessary in socialist countries as anywhere else. He states that educational advertising is directed at influencing the consumer attitudes of the older generation, and its main purpose is to incite the use of new products.

Greatest circulation gains in the Communist nations of Eastern Europe outside the Soviet Union have been made in Yugoslavia, Bulgaria, and Hungary since World War II, although cir-

culations have risen throughout the entire region. _Pravda_ of the Soviet Union is the largest and most influential daily in the Communist nations. In most respects it sets the tone for its equivalent (the official Party paper) in each of the Soviet-bloc nations of Eastern Europe. Usually, the main Communist party daily in each of the countries is that country's paper with the largest circulation and the most prestige. Following are the main Party dailies in nine Communist nations of Eastern Europe with their approximate circulations as of 1962:

Albania: _Zeri i Poppulit_ ("People's Voice"), 58,000, AM published in Tirana; _Bashkimi_ ("Unity"), 30,000, AM published in Tirana.

Bulgaria: _Rabotnichesko Delo_ ("Workers' Cause"), 560,000, AM published in Sofia; _Narodna Mladezh_ ("People's Youth"), 280,000, AM published in Sofia.

Czechoslovakia: _Rude Pravo_ ("Red Justice"), one million, AM published in Prague; _Pravda_ ("Truth"), 250,000, AM published in Bratislava.

East Germany: _Neues Deutschland_ ("New Germany"), 800,000, AM published in the Eastern Sector of Berlin; _Berliner Zeitung_ ("Berlin Times"), 500,000, AM published in East Berlin.

Hungary: _Nepszabadsag_ ("People's Freedom"), 620,000, AM published in Budapest; _Esti Hirlap_ ("Evening Journal"), 125,000, PM published in Budapest.

Poland: _Trybuna Ludu_ ("People's Tribune"), 250,000, AM published in Warsaw; _Express Wieczorny_ ("Evening Express"), 550,000, PM published in Warsaw.

Rumania: _Scinteia_ ("Spark"), one million, AM published in Bucharest; _Munca_ ("Labor"), 500,000, AM published in Bucharest.

Soviet Union: _Pravda_ ("Truth"), 6.5 million, AM published in Moscow; _Izvestia_ ("News"), 4 million, PM published in Moscow.

Yugoslavia: _Borba_ ("Struggle"), 350,000, AM published in Belgrade; _Politika_ ("Policy"), 300,000, AM published in Belgrade.

Soviet Union

The Soviet press today is the world's prime example of a "captive" press. As a branch of the government, its one main purpose is to see that the U.S.S.R. is praised internally and externally as an example of what Communism can do for a nation and a people. With this overall aim there is obviously no place for the "free press" theory as understood in the Western nations. The press basically is looked upon as an educational institution, a carefully-controlled indoctrination instrument which the government claims is "a powerful means of raising the cultural and political level of the people."[1]

About 8,000 newspapers are published in the Soviet Union, with a total circulation of some 55 to 60 million. Only about 150 of these are dailies. By far the largest circulation held by any daily is that of Pravda, which claims to print between six and seven million copies every day.[2] Although Russian is the "lingua franca" of the Soviet Union, newspapers of all types are published in nearly 100 languages throughout the 16 republics. Dailies are printed in about 60 languages. More than 2,000 periodicals other than newspapers also exist in the U.S.S.R. (total circulation about 360 million); these are published in nearly as many languages as are the newspapers.

The entire press is under tight government control; editors are carefully selected and watched, and the government news agency TASS is closely supervised. Editors are so thoroughly indoctrinated that there is really little need for explicit censorship on Soviet newspapers. All papers are government-controlled, transmission facilities are owned by the state, and the entire domestic press is an instrument of propaganda in the hands of the high officials of the Communist party who rule the country. The fact that some papers are issued by clubs, trade unions, factories, and other groups does not mean that the government does not carefully control them.

Soviet readers, regardless of what newspaper or magazine they read, are constantly exposed to these repetitive themes[3] which state that:

a. Western nations are depraved and degenerate;
b. the U.S. and Britain seek to dominate the world;

c. a few wealthy plutocrats in the U.S. and Britain enjoy almost total power while the masses of common people suffer great privation;
d. the West is surrounding the Soviet Union with missile bases and military sites, obviously planning a war against "peace-loving" Soviet citizens;
e. the Soviet Union won World War II almost single-handed;
f. the Soviet Union is progressing rapidly in every sphere--especially in science, education, medicine and general cultural pursuits.

Soviet readers, although their fare of press material is almost entirely a product of their own government, read avidly and carefully. Kent Cooper, writing of the Russian reading habits, reports that there

"...is a thirst to read the news that they are permitted to have, even though the reading is a dreary process. They (the Russians) do buy the Soviet newspapers. There are several reasons for this. One is when there is nothing else to read one just buys what he can get.... Another reason is that those who can and do read the big newspapers...feel secure when seen reading Pravda and Izvestia...."[4]

The press of the Soviet Union is centered in Moscow. The real press leader in the U.S.S.R. is Pravda ("Truth"), the organ of the all-Union Communist party. This paper, the only one which publishes 365 days a year, sets the pace for the entire Soviet press not only in ideological matters but also in general editorial and mechanical matters.

Pravda scatters its more than six million copies daily over the sprawling U.S.S.R. from printing plants in 16 cities. Its editorials are commonly found reprinted verbatim in all parts of the Soviet press. Soviet newspapers are probably influenced most by Pravda; but to a slightly less extent they are what they are because of TASS, the official Soviet news agency; Sovetskaya Pechat ("Soviet Press"), the trade magazine of the press, and Izvestia ("News"), the organ of the Presidium of the Supreme Soviet (the principal government newspaper).[5]

TYPES OF SOVIET NEWSPAPERS. The press in the U.S.S.R. can be classified in three main divisions according to the scope of its newspapers. These newspaper categories are (1) the national or "All-Union" papers, (2) the provincial or "territorial" papers, and (3) the local papers.

Such big dailies as Pravda, Izvestia, and Trud, with headquarters in Moscow, are representative of the "national" papers. The "provincial" papers are much smaller in circulation than the "nationals" but in most respects resemble the bigger papers. They usually serve a province or even a republic. Typical of the larger of such provincials are Radyanska Ukraina of Kiev and Kommunist of Erevan. Such provincials as these have the responsibility of sifting the official news and policies down to the readers in their respective areas.

At the bottom of the Soviet press structure are the many and varied "local" papers which range from well-edited dailies like Leningradskaya Pravda (a Leningrad morning "city" paper) and Vechernaya Moskva (a Moscow afternoon "city" paper) to the hundreds of thousands of small irregularly-published "wall"[6] newspapers (or "bulletin-board sheets") which flourish in the rural areas. Most of the "local" papers in the U.S.S.R. are either district, city, or "wall" publications and leave the discussion of major issues and handling of national and world news items to the provincials and the nationals. They content themselves generally with local affairs and the filtering of Party directives down to the "grass roots" reader.

Front page for Pravda for July 18, 1962, spotlighting Khrushchev's interview with American newspaper editors. The banner reads: "N. S. Khrushchev interviewed by group of American journalists on July 13, 1962."

PRINCIPAL MOSCOW DAILIES[7]

Pravda ("Truth"): AM daily published in 16 cities; main office in Moscow. Official organ of the Communist party of the Soviet Union. Sets tone of the Soviet press. Circulation about 6.5 million. Only paper published 365 days a year.

Izvestia ("News"): AM daily (except Monday) organ of the Presidium of the Supreme Soviet; official government newspaper; published in six major cities, with headquarters in Moscow; circulation about 4 million.

Trud ("Labor"): AM daily organ of the Central Council of Trade Unions; specializes in union affairs, but contains some general news; circulation about 1.4 million.

Komsomolskaya Pravda ("Young Communist League Truth"): Official paper of the Young Communist League of the U.S.S.R.; a morning paper published from main Pravda plant, but by a different editorial staff; circulation about 3.5 million.

Sovetskaya Rossiya ("Soviet Russia"): A popular general AM daily begun in 1956; printed in seven other cities; like Pravda, it is an all-Union Party paper; circulation about two million.

Krasnaya Zvezda ("Red Star"): AM daily published by the Ministry of Defense in Moscow; Army news stressed, although contains general news.

Sovetsky Flot ("Soviet Fleet"): Navy daily; similar to "Red Star".

Vechernaya Moskva ("Evening Moscow"): PM local Moscow daily; has many U.S. characteristics--cartoons, human interest stories, advertisements; circulation about 250,000.

Gudok ("Whistle"): Daily mainly for railroad workers; carries general news and commentary; published by the Ministry of Transportation.

Sovetsky Sport ("Soviet Sport"): Popular sports tabloid.

Syelskoye Khozyaestvo ("Agriculture"): Published by the Ministry of Agriculture principally for a farm audience; circulation about 700,000.

Moskovskaya Pravda ("Moscow Truth"): Local Moscow daily; separate from main Pravda; circulation about 500,000.

OTHER LEADING MOSCOW NEWSPAPERS

Pionerskaya Pravda ("Pioneer Truth"): Semiweekly tabloid in two colors for children; circulation about three million.

Moscow News (in English); Semiweekly paper published mainly for tourists by the Society of Cultural Relations with Foreign Countries.

Neues Leben ("New Life" in German): Tri-weekly of same nature as Moscow News.

Les Nouvelles de Moscou ("Moscow News" in French): Semiweekly newspaper of same nature as English-language Moscow News.

Sovetskaya Kultura ("Soviet Culture"): Published triweekly; deals with radio, TV, morals, the arts, lectures, concerts, etc.; circulation about 190,000.

Literaturnaya Gazeta ("Literary Gazette"): Published triweekly; vigorous literary critic-ism; cultural articles; organ of the Union of Soviet Writers; circulation about 900,000.

Uchityelskaya Gazeta ("Teachers Gazette"): Published triweekly by the Ministry of Edu-cation; foremost Soviet newspaper devoted to pedagogical matters; circulation about 800,000.

SOME LEADING MOSCOW MAGAZINES

Krokodil ("Crocodile"): Published three times a month by the newspaper Pravda; U.S.S.R.'s leading political "humor" maga-zine; satirical articles and cartoons, highly anti-West in content; circulation nearly 2 million.

Sovetskaya Pechat ("Soviet Press"): Monthly trade journal for journalists; serves as a guide and instructor for Soviet periodicals; begun in 1955; runs 60-70 pages on glossy paper; illustrated; no advertising; few car-toons.

Novy Mir ("New World"): Monthly literary journal; probably the best known in Soviet Union; very influential; circulation about 200,000.

Soviet Union: Monthly propaganda magazine published in 11 non-Soviet languages (separ-ate editions in each language); languages include Chinese, English, French, German, Spanish, Korean, Japanese, Finnish, Hindi, Urdu, and Arabic.

Znamya ("Banner"): Monthly influential literary magazine.

Moskva ("Moscow"): Monthly influential literary magazine.

Oktyabr ("October"): Monthly influential literary magazine.

LEADING PROVINCIAL DAILIES

(All publish 300 issues every year)

KIEV (UKRAINIAN S.S.R.): Pravda Ukrainy ("Ukraine Truth"). In Russian. Radyanska Ukraina ("Soviet Ukraine"). In Ukrainian; Circulation about 500,000; one of the largest dailies outside Moscow.

LENINGRAD (RUSSIAN S.S.R.): Leningradskaya Pravda ("Leningrad Truth"). A.M. Vecherny Leningrad ("Evening Leningrad"). PM.

MINSK (BYELORUSSIAN S.S.R.): Zvazda ("Star"). in Byelorussian. Sovetskaya Bedorussiya ("Soviet Byelorussia"). In Russian.

TIFLIS (GEORGIAN S.S.R.): Kommunisti ("Com-munist"). In Georgian. Zarya Vostoka ("Dawn of the East"). In Russian.

EREVAN (ARMENIAN S.S.R.): Kommunist ("Com-munist"). In Russian. Sovetakan Ayastan ("Soviet Armenia"). In Armenian.

RIGA (LATVIAN S.S.R.); Sovetskaya Latvia ("Soviet Latvia"). In Russian. Cinya ("Struggle"). In Latvian.

VILNIUS (LITHUANIAN S.S.R.): Sovetskaya Litva ("Soviet Lithuania"). In Russian. Tiesa ("Truth"). In Lithuanian.

TALLINN (ESTONIAN S.S.R.): Sovetskaya Estoniya ("Soviet Estonia"). In Russian. Rahva Haady ("People's Voice"). In Estonian.

ALMA-ATA (KAZAKH S.S.R.): Kazakhstanskaya Pravda ("Kazakhstan Truth"). In Russian. Sociadistik Kazakhstan ("Socialist Kazakhstan"). In Kazakh.

BAKU (AZERBAIJAN S.S.R.): Kommunist ("Com-munist"). In Azerbeijan.

KISHINEV (MOLDAVIAN S.S.R.): Sovetskaya Moldavia ("Soviet Moldavia"). In Russian.

Usually referred to as a "humor" or "satiri-cal" magazine, Krokodil is the most zestful (and propagandistic) of the Soviet Union's publications. Its avowed basic task: to struggle against capitalism, expose the "negative aspects of living, bureaucratism, pride, officiousness, and the trivial." Published by Pravda, this magazine appears three times a month and has a circulation of close to one million. Krokodil began in 1922 as an illustrated supplement to the newspaper Rabochy ("Worker"). Today it runs from 14 to 18 pages splattered with colored type and cartoons. The best-known cartoonist

for this magazine is Vitaly Goriaev, who consistently depicts capitalist warmongers ex-
ploiting the common man.   John Gunther in his
book Inside Russia Today (1958) said that on
most subjects Krokodil "is outspoken, even
daring, and both its artwork and humor are on
a fairly sophisticated level...."   One thing
is certain: Krokodil is one of the most blatant
and violent anti-Western journals in the
U.S.S.R., and like all of the others (but more
colorfully) creates and perpetuates a vil-
lainous stereotyped image of the capitalistic
West.

SAMPLE CARTOONS:

"Democratic Capitalist"

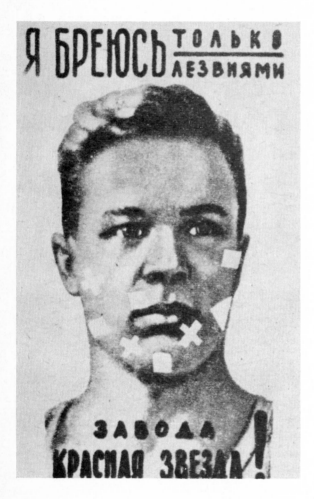

Krokodil seems to have the freedom to lam-
poon the shortage and quality of consumer
goods in the U.S.S.R.   The caption says:
"I shave only with blades made by Red
Star."

This cartoon shows a worker of the U.S.
hopelessly entangled in the cog-wheels
of capitalism representing medical costs,
war tax, and the like.   The leering face
of the fat, cigar-smoking "exploiter"
looks on with pleasure.

A BRIEF LOOK AT THE "BIG TWO" NEWSPAPERS

PRAVDA. Pravda ("Truth") is the largest and most influential daily in the Soviet Union. Its circulation is estimated at between 6.5 and 7 million, which if true, would give it the greatest circulation of any daily newspaper in the world. Pravda usually runs four or eight pages, but sometimes publishes 16-page editions. The leading All-Union daily, it is printed in 15 cities other than Moscow. It rushes page mats to the more distant of its printing sites each night by jet planes. Actually, Pravda is the only truly "national" paper, circulating even in the far eastern provinces. A subscriber may receive the

PRAVDA (Truth) is shown in upper right and KOMSOMOLSKAYA PRAVDA (Young Communist League Truth) in lower insert. Both are leading Communist party dailies in the Soviet Union. The "youth" Pravda is published in the main Pravda plant in Moscow, but has a separate staff. Pravda is the leading newspaper of the Soviet Union and sets policy for the entire press. As can be seen from the front pages shown above, both dailies indicate conservative make up and a careful concern with good typographical techniques. Pravda was founded as a clandestine journal in St. Petersburg in 1912. Men high in the Communist party always edit these two newspapers. Stalin, Beria, and Molotov were once Pravda editors.

paper for a year for the equivalent of about $3.

Most of Pravda's foreign news comes from TASS (the official Soviet news agency); however, the paper has some 60 correspondents abroad. Within the U.S.S.R. Pravda has about 40,000 correspondents scattered throughout all the republics, not only to channel any important news back to Moscow, but to keep a check on the daily and weekly operations of the newspapers. The newspaper, the spokesman of the Communist Party of the Soviet Union, has some 150 writing editors of whom about 30 handle foreign news. The foreign news staff in Pravda's editorial department is divided into four sections--Asia, Africa, Europe, and America--each with journalists who are specialists in the region concerned. About 300 editorial workers, excluding correspondents, are employed by Pravda.[8]

Pravda sets a high journalistic tone; it does not write down to its readers; it deals mainly with education, science, and politics. Neither does it sensationalize to make a play for readership. These facts are often noted as praiseworthy by Western journalists, and indeed out of context they do seem so; but it should be remembered that Pravda is a "captive" medium of communication in a very real sense, and it is quite obvious that government or "subsidized" journals can maintain stricter standards and a more serious demeanor than free-enterprise journals which must compete in the marketplace for readers. Also it must be remembered that Pravda is required reading for Soviet Communists.

This central Party organ was founded as a clandestine paper in St. Petersburg in 1912. It succeeded Iskra ("Spark")[9] which had been established by Lenin as the first Bolshevik paper 12 years before. Pravda was often closed down by Czarist police and from time to time was forced to publish from hidden presses. When the Communists took over the government after the Revolution in late 1917, Pravda remained their chief spokesman; it has always been edited by men high in the party (e.g., Stalin, Beria and Molotov have been editors).

Pravda stresses Party news and foreign news mainly as it relates to internal matters in the countries concerned.[10] The newspaper's policy is set by an Editorial Board made up of Party members; however, the newspaper does have non-Party members on its staff. Pravda is very profitable; in its plant are printed some 25 other periodicals, among them several outstanding magazines (e.g., Krokodil). It owns apartment houses, several schools,

and a Palace of Culture, as well as other assets.

Editorials in Pravda are always prominently played; most often they are in the left-hand column (or two) of the front page. Sometimes the whole front page is one long editorial. These articles are reprinted throughout the Soviet press, usually being sent by TASS via voice radio to be copied down simultaneously in the various newspaper offices.[11]

Most Pravda editorials deal with Party matters, and internal developments in science, general culture, and education. An editorial, published by Pravda on April 8, 1955, and dealing with Soviet education is typical of such editorials and part of it is quoted below:

"Soviet higher education is solving the noble task of raising young men and women in the spirit of the all-conquering ideas of Marxism-Leninism, in the spirit of ardent Soviet patriotism and proletarian internationalism. Our higher education institutions are justifiably proud of their graduates--bold honest persons of lofty ideas and profound principles, persons embodying the best traits of the Soviet people.[12]

Headlines in Pravda (reflected in similar wording in other Soviet newspapers) are usually of the short label variety conveying some ideological, political, or propagandistic note. Following are a few typical headlines gleaned from several issues of the newspaper; it can be noted that the basic Soviet propaganda "line" can be seen in these headlines:

"Heroic Little Cuba Threatened by Warmongering U.S.A."
"A Great Victory in the Peaceful Competition with Capitalism"
"For Peace and Friendship Between USSR and Germany"
"New Threats by American Aggressors"
"USSR Wants to Ban Atomic Weapons"
"Capitalist Nations Show Lack of Culture"
"Soviet Science Marches On!"
"Higher Education and the Public Schools"
"Western Minds Lag Behind Economic Position"
"U.S. Atomaniacs Seek to Destroy Civilization"

Pravda has a regular-size page of six columns. Its make up is neat and serious in tone. Headlines are mostly of the one-line spread variety. A common practice is that of using type (larger than the body type) beside the short "Pravda" nameplate in order to emphasize some important announcement or tell some brief party story. Although the contents of the paper may be extremely dull to Western readers,[13] the use of type, pictures, and cartoons is such as to give the paper a dignified and pleasing overall physical appearance. Probably the one main weakness in general make up (of this and all Soviet papers) is the use of long stories stretching down and across several columns,[14] this tends to give a gray look to portions of the paper. Using U.S. terminology, one might classify the kind of front page make up used by _Pravda_ as "contrast and balance." Heavy elements (usually pictures) generally appear in the top right and bottom left corners.

IZVESTIA. Next to _Pravda_ in size and importance among the All-Union newspapers of the U.S.S.R. is _Izvestia_ (full name: _Izvestia Deputatov Trudyashchikaya SSR_--"News of the Soviets of the Workers' Deputies of the U.S.S.R."). This paper, the official organ of the Presidium of the Supreme Soviet, appears six times a week from six printing centers in the Soviet Union. _Izvestia_ is the voice of the Soviets throughout the Union (a "Soviet" compares roughly to a state legislature in the U.S.). In most respects _Izvestia_ looks about like _Pravda_, having a dignified, rather monotonous make up, and generally running 4, 8 or 16 pages. This newspaper, like all Soviet papers, could hardly be called "lively," either in its contents or in its make up. Since 1960, however, the paper has become increasingly lively. For instance, in March, 1960, _Izvestia_ started carrying a western-style Sunday supplement called _Nedelia_ (The Week), a thirty-two page tabloid-pictorial, complete with comic page, and a potpourri of short articles satirizing life in the West.

About half of the stories found in _Izvestia_ are also carried by _Pravda_; however, _Izvestia_ stresses relations of the U.S.S.R. with other governments, while _Pravda_ prefers to emphasize internal matters within the foreign countries themselves. _Izvestia_ prints as much news as possible about government machinery elections, and the like (both in the Supreme Soviet and in the various Soviets of the Union), whereas _Pravda_ concerns itself with Party news in the U.S.S.R. and abroad.

Izvestia publishes some 4,000,000 copies every day but Monday, with about half coming off its modern presses housed in its 30-year-old building in Moscow. The other half, carrying basically the same material, are printed from presses located in five other major cities of the U.S.S.R. Mats are flown from Moscow to the regional printing plants as is the case with _Pravda_; these mats make up the biggest part of the regional editions but are supplemented by local news written by _Izvestia_ writers in the five "branch" areas.

Most of the work in the production of _Izvestia_ is done in the paper's own building; stories are written usually in each writer's private office and handed to the immediate superior for checking. Then they are passed along to higher editors who check them again before sending them to the composing room. There is no large newsroom (and this is true of most Soviet papers) in the _Izvestia_ building as is typically found in the U.S. and British newspaper plants; the _Izvestia_ editorial plant is divided into many small offices.

The names of these two important Soviet papers--_Pravda_ (meaning "truth") and _Izvestia_ (meaning "news")--are the triggers which set off many jokes from non-Communist journalists. The most common, probably, is stated in the leading Spanish journalism textbook and plays on the two words: "En _Pravda_ no se encuentra nunca una _Izvestia_ y en _Izvestia_ es imposible tropezar ni una sola vez a _Pravda_."[15] ("In _Pravda_ there is never any "news" and in _Izvestia_ there is never any "truth"). What makes this even more interesting is that a Spanish journalist should make such a quip.

THE SOVIET CONCEPT OF THE PRESS. In the U.S.S.R. the press is considered an arm of government, an instrument to organize and educate the masses, and a social force treated to help the communistic society reach its desired goals. The main characteristics of the Soviet concept are:

1. The press is considered a social and political instrument;
2. Every citizen has access to the press;
3. News is considered chiefly as social processes, and not as incidents and "personality sketches";
4. The idea that news can be "objective" is rejected by Soviet journalists;
5. The press is looked upon as a "house organ of government" and this is held to be highly desirable;
6. The idea of "self-criticism" is considered of great importance;
7. The press must constantly struggle against Capitalism and all enemies of the working people.

According to the _Large Soviet Encyclopedia_, the basic tasks of the press are (a) to educate the masses, (b) to explain party and government policies, (c) to mobilize the masses in the construction of communism, (d) to develop criticism and self-criticism, and (e) to expose war mongers.[16]

Newspapers are supposed to raise the cultural level of the Soviet people by withholding anything the government considers harmful, degrading or purely entertaining. For example, such subjects as crime, romance, social events, and human interest features are absent from the papers. The press furnishes a steady diet of cultural and political items, all slanted to the propagandistic and ideological purposes of the national leadership. The idea of unbiased news is alien to the Soviet press concept; Communism is the big story, and government and Party pronouncements take precedence over all other news.[17]

Lenin once characterized the press as "not only a collective propagandist and collective agitator," but also "a collective organizer."[18] And Lenin, contrasting the Communist press with the Western press, declared that "capitalism has made the newspaper...a tool for the profit of the rich, for the information and amusement of them, an instrument to deceive and fool the mass of workers."[19]

Stalin later expressed his ideas on the importance of the press in the U.S.S.R. in these words:

"The press is a prime instrument through which the Party speaks daily, hourly, with the working class in its own indispensable language. No other means such as this for weaving spiritual ties between Party and class, no tool so flexible, is to be found in nature."[20]

And in 1957 Nikita Krushchev added these words pertaining to the press concept in the Soviet Union:

"...the press is our chief ideological weapon. Its duty is to strike down the enemies of the working class, the foes of the working people. Just as an army cannot fight without arms, so the party cannot do ideological work successfully without such a sharp and militant weapon as the press. We cannot put the press in unreliable hands. It must be in the hands of the most faithful, most trustworthy, most politically steadfast people devoted to our cause."[21]

The press of the U.S.S.R. has the responsibility of stressing the superiority of Communism and encouraging unanimous praise of the Soviet leaders and their policies.[22] A Pravda editorial has defined the Soviet press' main purpose as "intensifying the propaganda" of Communistic ideology and "inculcating in the people a feeling of Soviet national pride, unbending strength of spirit, and firm,

unshaking faith in the triumph of our great cause."[23]

Soviet editors claim that they have press freedom. This "freedom" is quite different from "freedom" as understood in the United States. Actually, it is simply freedom to publish what the government will allow to be published; it is freedom to comment--up to a certain point. In one sense of the word, it is freedom, but it is freedom only within the confines of strict Party discipline and the press' own social and political order.

Soviet press freedom is thus really a matter of defining terms. Article 125 of the Soviet Constitution (adopted in 1936) states that all citizens are granted "freedom of the press" and that "these civil rights are ensured by placing at the disposal of the working people and their organizations printing presses, stocks of paper...and other material requisites."[24] So, as Alex Inkeles interprets it, "freedom of the press" to the Russian means:

"...access to the means of expression, not the right to say things. The American usually means the freedom to express or the right to print certain things. The Soviet journalist maintains that the access to the means of expression is denied to most in the Western nation."[25]

To Soviet journalists, the U.S. idea of press freedom is meaningless; they see American newspapers as "capitalistic pawns" in the hands of the few wealthy enough to decide if and when material will be printed. They see U.S. newspapers as journals dictated to by economic interests. The American press, to them, is one in which the people really have no freedom of expression and no protection against propaganda distributed by the capitalists.

Disregarding the semantic difficulties in a discussion of this "freedom" concept, it can definitely be said that the U.S.S.R. has censorship. No publications are allowed which contain items which might cause agitation against the government or the Party, which are of a pornographic nature, which arouse nationalistic or religious "fanaticism," or which reveal state secrets. The state censorship agency is known as Glavit; its influence is pervasive, reaching into all the media of public communication and entertainment.

It is obvious to any student of the world press that the U.S.S.R. serves as the classic example of a country in which a controlled

press exists, a press that is practically in-
separable from government and its propaganda.
Obvious also is the fact that the newspapers
are outstanding in their lack of individuality;
one has only to examine a few copies of various
publications to realize how great this "same-
ness" really is. Although Soviet journalists
claim they are not told what stories to use
and how to play them, a study of the Soviet
press will show that at least all "big" stories
(those affecting the Party Line or prominent
Communist personalities) are not only used by
all the newspapers, but in general appear on
the same pages in the respective papers and
receive the same treatment.[26]

In the U.S.S.R. every agency is dedicated
to furthering the goals of Party and government,
and it is not surprising that papers would have
little individuality. A "stereotyping" press
is needed, one dedicated to welding every person into one great machine, to regulating mass
thinking and action. Newspapers must act as
one to "educate" the people to devotion to the
country, to Communist ideology, to hard work,
to a willingness to fight for the Soviet Mother-
land, and to a belief that the Western "capitalistic nations" are preparing to make war
against the "peace-loving" Soviet Union.

The concept of what a newspaper is supposed
to be in the Soviet Union naturally determines
the type of journalism training. Such training
is centered in the publications themselves and
in the School of Journalism at the State University of Moscow. At this university the
student enrolls in a five-year program after
he has passed entrance examinations in Russian
language and literature, U.S.S.R. history,
geography, and foreign language.

Most of the faculty members of the University's journalism school are workers on Soviet
newspapers or magazines, and the student's
five-year course includes what might be termed
a "liberal arts" education as well as a rather
thorough "practical journalism" education.
Students must learn the "trade" by serving as
"interns" in various news offices and working
on the University's training newspaper,
Journalist. This is usually done in the first
two years, while taking such courses as political economy, history of the Communist party,
Russian literature, history of foreign literature, foreign language, law, economics, and
physical culture. The last two years are
mainly spent by the student in special semi-
nars (i.e., "Press Criticism" and "Press
Theory") in advanced writing classes, and in
the writing of long "research" papers (e.g.,
all seniors must compare the New York Times
with Pravda). When the journalism students
are graduated, they are assigned jobs in the

communications media by the faculty of the
University.[27]

Although most of the academically-trained
journalists are produced by the State University of Moscow, journalism courses are
available to students at about a dozen other
universities in the Soviet Union. Journalism
training in the U.S.S.R. has never become
widespread and is carefully controlled and
standardized.

SOVIET ELECTRONIC MEDIA. Radio. In the
U.S.S.R. at least 200,000,000 people are
reached by the Soviet radio, which has as its
chief mission the indoctrination and control
of the masses. Of course, the Soviet radio
provides sugar-coated overlay of culture and
education. It was estimated that in 1960
there were some 450 radio stations in the
U.S.S.R. and nearly 9,000,000 individual
receiving sets. In addition, there were some
30,000,000 wired receivers within the Soviet
Union, with most of the growth having taken
place in the rural areas. Radio in the
U.S.S.R. has proved especially valuable in
filtering Party directives to the masses and
in transmitting TASS news reports throughout
the day to all parts of the sprawling nation.

Television. The Soviet TV system is just
as busy selling state policy and Communism
as is radio. Incessantly it sells the Soviet
system. TV, stressing serious discussions,
lectures and documentaries, is extremely drab
compared to U.S. television. There is very
little entertainment on Soviet TV. Some
50,000,000 Soviet citizens (about one out of
every four) live in the range of TV stations.
There are about 4,000,000 television sets in
the U.S.S.R. Owners must pay a monthly
license fee for the privilege of viewing.
Expansion of TV is very rapid in the U.S.S.R.
and probably the vast majority of Soviet
citizens can be reached by 1965. Since
television is considered not a luxury, but a
vital propaganda instrument, by the authorities,
there is no doubt but that its expansion is
being pushed. The chairman of the State Committee of Broadcasting and Television of the
U.S.S.R. has summed up the main purpose of
radio and TV in these words: "It must promote
the building up of a Communist society in the
U.S.S.R."

PRESS CHARACTERISTICS. About 75 per cent to
85 per cent of the daily newspapers of the
U.S.S.R. are published outside Moscow in line
with the Soviet emphasis on decentralization
of resources. About two-thirds of all newspapers are printed in Russian; however important regional or provincial papers appear in
about 80 languages.

Newspapers generally are almost void of general news; they are "functional" rather than "reportorial," being composed of articles devoted to particular group interests (e.g., Krasnaya Zvezda or "Red Star" is the Army's daily, and Trud or "Labor" is the trade union daily). Papers contain very little news of personalities, especially those outside the government. They ignore such things as comic strips and household hints, reports of accidents, and sex. There is practically no entertainment featured in the papers. The papers serve mainly as government and Party bulletin boards and ideological textbooks.

Until very recently there were practically no photographs and cartoons in the papers; although their number is growing, illustrations still are not used widely. There are no opposition political views expressed in the Soviet newspapers, but the papers are quite critical of themselves.

Two important Russian-language dailies are a little different from the others in that their content is lighter than most Soviet journals; they are Vechernaya Moskva ("Evening Moscow"), which in many ways resembles a U.S. paper, and Komsomolskaya Pravda ("Young Communist League Truth"), one of the leading All-Union dailies.

Also rather light in make up and content is the English-language Moscow News, published three times weekly, mainly for English-speaking tourists. It has a department called "Our Guests," which is probably the nearest thing to a society column in the Soviet press.[28]

Most newspaper staffs are small; this is not because there is a shortage of professionally-trained newsmen but hinges on the fact that at least half of the contents of the papers come from non-journalists. The Communist party desires the participation of the largest number of citizens in press activities and encourages articles and letters from those outside the newspapers. Many of the writers for the papers are scientists, educators, economic specialists, and Party and government leaders.

Editors of the big newspapers are all men who are high in the Communist party; they are capable newspapermen and at the same time specialists in Communist ideology. They are also technical experts, organizers, teachers, and politicians. An editor, then, is a multi-sided personality, who even though he is well qualified for his position, is subject to almost constant supervision from above. The senior editors in the Soviet Union are well paid, however. According to a recent statement, they receive the equivalent of from

$1,250 to $2,500 a month.[29]

Soviet editors hew to the line of the Party and make few ideological errors mainly because (1) most of them are leading Party members, (2) they are under constant observation by the political police (M.V.D.) and are well aware of what goes on in the periodic "purges." (In 1951 hundreds of publishers and editors were "expelled" from their positions because of "negligence" and for "reasons of style." Many of these former editors have not reappeared on the journalistic scene.)

Most Soviet dailies use "amateur" journalistic contributions regularly. Even Pravda runs newsy items written by factory workers, members of the armed forces, and collective farmers. This "press participation" is supposed to stimulate an intense loyalty to the press by the masses.

The Western news agencies are not used by Soviet newspapers; all foreign news comes from TASS or from the few correspondents of the big papers like Pravda, Izvestia, and Trud.

Most papers have four pages (sometimes running to eight and sixteen pages) and use the same make up techniques with only slight variations. The same stories are displayed each day in about the same way by all papers; often several papers will use identical stories in identical positions, often under identical headlines and accompanied by identical pictures.

A typical Soviet newspaper is arranged in this way: page 1 carries government notices, official bulletins, and usually a long editorial; the next two pages generally contain national news, letters and special articles and sometimes a "feuilleton" (semi-fiction feature story with a political moral), and the back page is usually given over to foreign news provided by TASS, athletic events and a potpourri of items. If the paper runs eight pages, this arrangement is simply expanded.[30] Advertising found in a paper is government advertising or that concerning sports events, theater offerings and the like. Besides this, there are "personal advertisements" about such things as marriages, divorces, and deaths--items required by law to be published.[31]

TASS: THE SOVIET NEWS AGENCY. Telegrafnoie Agentsvo Sovetskavo Soiuza, or TASS as it is known throughout the world, arose in 1925, taking the place of an agency called ROSTA which operated from 1919 to 1925. Prior to 1935 there were five internal wire agencies in the Soviet Union; in 1935 they consolidated and took the name of TASS.

Today the agency maintains "feeder" services in 15 republics, and averages over 1,500,000 words daily from its nearly 60 foreign correspondents. Some 5,000 Soviet newspapers receive its service; they pay according to their circulation, and the agency operates on these fees. Most of the subscribers are small papers (nearly 4,000 of them) which get the TASS service by radio instead of telegraph as is used by the larger subscribers. TASS has its own transmitter in Moscow and sends at a rate of about 20 words a minute so journalists at the small papers can take stories in longhand.

TASS denies that it tells papers what they should use;[32] it sends no columns or editorials (except the daily _Pravda_ editorials which are relayed simultaneously by all Soviet radio stations). The news agency has about 800 domestic and some 50 full-time correspondents abroad; in addition it maintains some 250 overseas "stringers."

CONCLUSION. In the Soviet Union, Big Brother is talking to everyone in a steady, droning voice. Be loyal! Work hard! Produce more! Beware the Western nations which will try to destroy you! Merge your interests, your thoughts, your activities! Be ready to protect yourselves against the war-mongering capitalists! Praise Soviet advances!

From the multifaceted press system and the ever-talking electronic media the Soviet citizens get a constant barrage of directives, "correctives," and propaganda, interspersed with "culture" and "art."

The Message in the U.S.S.R. is the same, whether it is printed in a poorly-designed "wall" paper or whether it appears in a slick "culture" monthly magazine. It may be translated into a dozen or so dialects scattered through the republics, but it is the same. This is a total monopolistic Message. It is the only Message the Soviet people are allowed to hear.

Do the Soviet people believe this Message?

This question is a difficult one to answer, of course, because of a lack of surveys and because of the many exceptions one might encounter. But most careful observers would say that in general the Soviets do believe what the press and electronic media feed them. They get practically nothing else which refutes the "line" given them by Big Brother. They hear and read the same thing everywhere they go; they have no alternative other than to believe.

In the Soviet Union is found the world's best example of "total" propagandistic journalism. Saturation is complete. Organization of the mass messages is foolproof (deviation is dangerous!) and seldom do wrong impressions find their way into the mass mind. A giant machine is the Soviet mass communications system, peopled by identical little Communist robots who all fit neatly into the Party Purpose. There is no doubt but that the Soviet mass media form a gigantic war machine, which because of its monolithic structure, is devastatingly effective in the battle for men's minds.

Bulgaria

When the Communists took over this country in 1944 and transformed it into a Soviet puppet state, the press, which had been virile and largely independent, was cast in the image of the Russian press.[1] After seizing power in Bulgaria, the Communists quickly took over the dissemination of information via the printed word; most of the editors and journalists were discharged; not only were they discharged, but many of the leading newspapermen were executed because they were felt to be dangerous to the "new order." In December, 1947, the new Constitution was proclaimed, and beginning in 1948 all media of mass communication were brought officially under government control. Until 1948 the Communists had throttled the press illegally; since, they have throttled it legally, and as in the U.S.S.R. have considered it an arm of the government and a part of the education system.

The whole press of Bulgaria is so closely modeled after that of the Soviet Union that except for local items, the papers of the two nations are almost indistinguishable. Daily newspapers are published in the capital, Sofia, and in four other cities; however, the big papers are all located in the capital. Newspapers today have four pages on the average as compared to from 8-24 prior to 1944.

In 1962 there were eight central daily papers in Bulgaria, four district dailies, and some 50 others of assorted types. Magazines in the country are many, varied, and popular. Some 300 have more than two million readers; about 50 magazines are published in foreign languages--French, German, English, Arabic, Russian, and Spanish. These are designed mainly for use in other countries. The main propaganda magazine, making use of politically-satirical cartoons, is the weekly Sturshel ("Hornet") whose counterpart in the U.S.S.R. is the trimonthly Krokodil. Drujinka ("Small Battalion"), largest of the general children's magazines, is a monthly with a circulation of about 55,000.

As the most important propaganda tool in Bulgaria, the press is dominated by the Communist party.[2] The newspapers receive service from the Soviet Union's news agency, TASS, and from Red China's Hsin Hua ("New China") news service. Newspapers occasionally run cartoons, most of them highly propagandistic and critical of the West.

The leading newspaper of Bulgaria is Rabotnichesko Delo ("Worker's Cause"), the daily mouthpiece of the national Communist party. This daily, corresponding to the U.S.S.R.'s Pravda, is published in Sofia and has a circulation of about 600,000. Founded in 1927, it has grown steadily and now is one of the leading dailies in Eastern Europe.

Bulgarski Telegrafitscheka Agentzia (BTA) or "Bulgarian Telegraph Agency" is the country's national agency. It was founded in 1918 in Sofia. It is a state agency with a news monopoly in the country; however, in 1950 its news disseminating activities became co-ordinated with those of TASS (Soviet Union's news agency). Today BTA receives most of its foreign news from TASS and channels it to every Bulgarian newspaper.

Five broadcasting stations were transmitting about 20 radio programs in 1962. The National Broadcasting Station has two programs which are broadcast 24 hours a day. A dozen languages are used in broadcasts. Television began in 1960 and has been growing in popularity since. Plans in 1962 called for Bulgarian TV to hook up with other Iron Curtain nations-- U.S.S.R., Hungary, Czechoslovakia, East Germany, and Poland.[3]

Bulgarian magazines are numerous and extremely popular. At least three million readers are exposed to the more than 300 magazines published in the country; there appears to be a magazine designed for most every taste. Magazines in addition to those printed in Bulgarian, appear in German, French, English, Russian, and Spanish. They are designed for export. The principal magazine for distribution in the Soviet Union and other Communist nations is the pictorial Nasha Rodina ("Our Homeland").

LEADING PUBLICATIONS. A wide variety of newspapers and periodicals exist in Bulgaria. In addition to the numerous types of magazines, there are three main classes of newspapers-- central, district, and city. The most influential, of course, are the central dailies which set the tone for the rest of the press. A few of the leading dailies[4] of Bulgaria follow:

Rabotnichesko Delo ("Worker's Cause")-- official journal of the Central Committee of the Communist party; an AM paper founded in 1927; circulation nearly 600,000.

Narodna Mladezh ("People's Youth")--Party youth paper begun in 1947; an AM with a

116

circulation of about 280,000.

Otechestven Front ("Fatherland Front")--
Journal of the Presidium of the People's
Assembly; AM founded in 1942 as an underground
paper; circulation today about 200,000.

Zemedelsko Zname ("Agrarian Banner")--Spokes-
man for the Bulgarian National Agrarian Union;
AM founded in 1902; circulation about 180,000.

Vecherni Novini ("Evening News")--Sofia local
general PM paper; founded 1951; circulation
about 150,000.

Trud ("Labor")--Labor union paper; AM founded

1948; circulation about 150,000.

Narodna Armia ("People's Army")--Journal
of the Defense Ministry; AM founded in 1944;
circulation about 90,000.

A few of the leading periodicals in the
country are Bulgaro-Suvetsko Edinstvo ("Bul-
garian-Soviet Unity"), a weekly with a circulation of about 100,000; Septemvriiche
("September Child"), a semiweekly magazine for
children under 13 having a circulation of some
275,000; Sturshel ("Hornet"), a weekly political satire journal with a circulation of about
275,000, and Novo Vreme ("New Times"), a monthly
aimed mainly at the intellectuals with a circulation of about 75,000.

Czechoslovakia

Since the end of World War II and the absorption of Czechoslovakia by the Communists, the press of this country has been generally a miniature pattern of the press of the Soviet Union. After the customary "purging" of the reactionary editors and publishers by the Communist party, the Czech press settled down to being simply an arm of the government and an instrument of the Party for the socialization and stabilization of the society.

Here briefly is the purpose of the Czech press as stated in material sent the authors by Ladislav Derka of the Czech Embassy in Washington (December, 1962):

"It is the mission of the Czechoslovak press to further and assist the Czechoslovak people in their endeavor for economic development and for peace and to play an important role in the education of the people for socialism. News publishing cannot be conducted by private enterprise."

There are some two dozen daily papers published in the country today. In addition there are about 475 weeklies, 225 fortnightlies, 330 monthlies, and 170 other publications. Besides the very influential daily press, an important role is played in the country by the large magazines, most of which are weeklies.

Another important group of Czechoslovak papers are those published in the factories, farms, and other social organizations. These deal mainly with work and problems of the organizations concerned. In 1962 there were nearly 450 such papers in the country with a total circulation of nearly 60 million.

The main center of mass communication in the country is Prague, the capital and largest city. Here is published the influential Rude Pravo (Red Justice), the nation's largest daily. This morning paper, with a circulation close to a million, is the Central Organ of the Communist party, and the counterpart of the U.S.S.R.'s Pravda. Other important Prague dailies are Prace (Labor), with a circulation of some 255,000; Mlada Fronta (Youth Front),

circulation about 175,000; Svobodne Slovo (Free Word), circulation about 125,000, and Lidova Demokracie (People's Democracy), circulation about 122,000. The leading local or city paper of Prague, an afternoon journal, is Vecerni Praha (Evening Prague), with a circulation of about 85,000.

In Bratislava, the country's second city, are published five important dailies. The largest is Pravda (Truth), representing the Communist party of Slovakia, with a circulation of some 250,000. Praca (Labor), with 110,000 circulation, is the organ of the Trade Union Council. Uj Szo (New World), published in the Hungarian language, is the journal of the Revolutionary Trade Union Movement. It has a circulation of some 50,000. Obrana L'udu (People's Defense), with a circulation of about 30,000, is published by the Ministry of National Defense.

Probably the most important newspaper published outside Prague and Bratislava is Nova Svoboda (New Freedom) published in Ostrava. This is a regional Communist party journal published six mornings a week with a circulation of about 75,000.

BRIEF HISTORY. The first Czech newspaper to appear in the Czech language was the Saturday Prague Post published in 1719 by Karel Frantisek Rosenmuller. Slovakia's first paper was the Latin Mercurius Hungaricus later appearing under the title Mercurius Veridicus ex Hungaria published in the years 1705-21 by Frantisek Rakoscy. Nova Posoniensia, published in 1721 by the Slovak scholar Matej Bel, was the first Slovak newspaper with a Slovak national background, although it was not published in Slovak. It was followed almost a half century later by the first paper to be published in Slovak: the Pressburg News which Daniel Tallyai started in 1783.

The Czech and Slovak press developed in relative freedom, and it was not until World War I that the press was subjected to harsh censorship by the Austro-Hungarian authorities. Many papers were forced to close down. However, in 1917, spurred on by the October Revolution in Russia, the Czechoslovak papers became more vocal for self-determination.

The country's press grew rapidly until 1940 when Nazi Germany largely dictated press policy under the so-called "Protectorate." From nearly 2,000 newspapers and magazines published prior to 1940, the number dropped during the course of World War II to 500 by 1944. It was during the German occupation that the leading Communist party daily of today, Rude Pravo, gained its important status.

East Germany

There are some 40 dailies, 35 weeklies, and about 400 magazines published in East Germany. Since the editors are careful to keep their circulations secret, it is difficult to estimate the total circulation of the country's newspapers. All the papers are under the strict control of the government's official Press Office, and as is true in the Soviet Union, most of them are filled with a heavy diet of "party line" material, and it is not believed that readership is high even though about 99 per cent of the East Germans are literate. Indications are that most of the citizens of East Germany rely heavily on radio broadcasts from the West for their news. Few people outside the Communist party and the young people of the Red youth groups seem to have any loyalty to the East German press. The papers do not appear to exhibit much competitive spirit.

The East German press is dominated by the Communist party and most publications are either owned by the Party, receive subsidies from it, or are basically in sympathy with it. However, in theory there are newspapers which present the views of minority political groups. The big papers, however, are Red-dominated and are published in Berlin's eastern sector; they are the morning papers Neues Deutschland (circulation about 800,000; the largest in the country) and the Berliner Zeitung (circulation about 500,000), and the PMs BZ am Abend and Tribüne (circulations about 200,000). Also in East Berlin are found these leading dailies: Der Morgen (representing the Liberal Democrats-- the "bourgeois" element in the country); Neue Zeit (Christian Democrats); National-Zeitung (National Democrats--composed mainly of former Nazis); Junge Welt (newspaper of the Communist "Free German Youth" movement), and Tägliche Rundschau (official Russian-run paper).[1]

The only newspapers in East Germany attempting to imitate Western journals in their make up are the two East Berlin PMs--BZ am Abend and Tribüne, but even though they splash their two-color banner headlines across Page One and do attain an interesting and eye-catching effect with their use of typography and pictures, this hardly compensates for their dull contents. All but about two or three dailies in the country are controlled by or affiliated with some political faction, and the main body of news presented daily tends to be composed of dull political items and polemics.

Although newspapers from East Germany have easy access to West Germany, the reverse is not true. The only way for West German papers to get to readers of the Soviet section of the country is by illegal means; several semiunderground groups undertake the dissemination of West German papers in East Berlin and East Germany. Outside the Soviet sector of East Berlin, the papers are in the main small organs of relatively little impact. The largest and most influential outside Berlin are the Leipziger Volkszeitung (360,000), Das Volk of Erfurt, and Dresden's two dailies Die Union and Sächsische Zeitung.[2]

The broad tasks of the East German press follow: (1) to stress the permanence of the DDR, (2) to promote German-Soviet friendship, (3) to offer explanations which will head off discontent, (4) to create hatred and suspicion of the West, and (5) to create and perpetuate internal fear of and obedience to the state.[3]

A few summary facts about the East German newspapers: they are often late (up to three days) printing news events (must be "cleared"); a news item is important only as it relates to Communist programs and progress; local stories of wrecks, divorces, and crime are few and played down; social progress is the main story; the papers are generally dull by Western standards; all papers are Communist party (SED) or front organization journals; there is little income from advertising; the Communist party (SED) controls East German papers and the national news agency; the SED operates journalism education (at the University of Leipzig) and clears all practicing journalists in the country.

The only East German publication with influence and a following outside East Germany was the literary magazine Sinn und Form. Founded in 1949 by a group of Marxist intellectuals including Johannes R. Becher, Ludwig Renn, and Anna Seghers, more than one-third of its 10,000 subscribers were in West Germany, Switzerland, and Austria.

For thirteen years Sinn und Form avoided the nets of officialdom and created for itself a sphere of relative freedom. It was the first magazine in the Communist world to print writings by such "heretics" as Jean-Paul Sartre, Franz Kafka, and Hemingway, whose books are banned in East Germany.

In 1960, following a number of violent attacks by Neues Deutschland, the central organ of the Communist party, the magazine's paper quota was cut in half and it was forced to reduce the number of copies printed. Because of its continued refusal to "hew to the Party line" and of its influence, particularly among East German students, Sinn und Form was liquidated late in 1962.[4]

The national news agency of East Germany is the Allgemeine Deutsche Nachrichtendienst (ADN). This "General German News Service" is a state-controlled agency founded in Berlin in 1946. It serves both press and radio, having information offices throughout East Germany. It is controlled and financed by the government, and is closely linked with the U.S.S.R.'s TASS from which it gets its foreign news file. It has exchange agreements with all the Soviet-bloc news services. It probably has some 1,000 staff members.

Hungary

Today there are about 20 daily newspapers in Hungary circulating a total of some million copies each day. Since World War II the overall circulation has increased considerably. The press of the country (under Communist domination since Soviet occupation in 1944) is centered in Budapest, the capital. Serving national minority groups in Hungary are about half a dozen foreign language papers. All papers are controlled by the Communists, whose party in Hungary is called the Hungarian Workers' party. Although the Party, through various pressures and censorship, controls the press, individual papers are often operated by certain groups--such as trade unions and social organizations.

Recurrent themes in the press might be summed up as these: homage to the U.S.S.R., optimistic reports of the nation's economic and social progress, Western degeneracy and U.S. decadence in particular, and the superiority of Communism as a way of life. Non-Communist nations are regularly pictured by the press in the most unfavorable way.

Hungary's principal newspaper is the daily Nepszabadsag ("People's Freedom"), formerly called Szabad Nep ("Free People"). This morning paper, founded in 1956 under its present name, is the organ of the Communist party of Hungary and as such sets the tone for the rest of the country's papers. Its circulation is about 620,000. In its contents and format it is modeled after Pravda of the Soviet Union, and like the big Soviet daily it is required reading for all Party members. It is read aloud in schools, factories, army camps, and on farms. In addition, it is read daily over the radio.[1]

In addition to the publications listed which exert influence all through the country, there are several religious papers of considerable prestige. They are A Kereszt ("The Cross") and Uj Ember ("New Man"), Catholic publications published fortnightly and weekly respectively; a Calvinist weekly Az Ut ("The Way"); a Lutheran weekly Evagelikus Elet ("Evangelical Life"), and a Jewish monthly Uj Elet ("New Man").

The national news agency is Magyar Tavirati Iroda (MTI) or "Hungarian Telegraph Office," which is under the government's Central Information Office. Its central office is in Budapest, and it has about 20 regional offices throughout the country. MTI gets most of its foreign news from TASS, but has a few exchange agreements with other national agencies. As is true in all Communist-dominated countries, this news agency is an arm of the government and is the chief instrument by which the state stereotypes the newspapers. The MTI is patterned after the Soviet Union's TASS, just as the various Hungarian newspapers are patterned after their equivalents in the U.S.S.R.

```
PRINCIPAL PUBLICATIONS*

  (Newspapers):

Nepszabadsag ("People's Freedom");
  AM, f.1956 . . . . . . . . . . .620,000
Esti Hirlap ("Evening Journal");
  PM, f.1956 . . . . . . . . . . .125,000
Magyar Nemzet ("Hungarian Nation");
  AM, f.1942 . . . . . . . . . . . 80,000
Uj Vilag ("New World");
  Weekly, f.1948 . . . . . . . . .200,000
Magyar Ifjusag ("Hungarian Youth");
  Weekly, f.1957 . . . . . . . . .180,000

  (Other Periodicals):

Ludas Matyi ("Matyi the Gooseboy");
  Weekly satirical journal.
Muvelt Nep ("Cultured People"); Weekly
  journal of the arts.
Irodalmi Ujsag ("Literary Gazette");
  Weekly literary paper.

*All of these publications are published
 in Budapest.
```

BRIEF BACKGROUND. Soon after the Nazi army left Hungary in 1945 and before the Reds gained political control of the country, the Hungarian press was basically free. Each party had its own journal. By 1948 the Communists had completely taken over and all non-Party papers had vanished. There was one so-called "non-party" paper published mainly for the intellectuals who did exist, but actually it too was subject to Communist control. This paper was called Magyar Nemzet ("Hungarian Nation") and had been founded in 1942. A new liberalism began to develop in the press in 1955 when Krushchev denounced Stalin and the so-called "new era" of Communism began in the satellite nations. This liberalism reached its high point in the bloody revolution in Hungary in late 1956.

A nationalistic spirit among the Hungarians, fanned into revolt by coalition party papers

in October, 1956, lasted only a short time
before it subsided before the guns and tanks
of the Soviet Union. But this spirit indicated that the Hungarian people yearn for
basic civil liberties--among them a free press.
For a few days during the short-lived upris-
ing in Hungary against the Moscow-dominated
Communist party, the press had enjoyed a
brief period of uncensored bliss. However,
after the masters from the Kremlin squelched
the revolt, the press again fell under the
strict control and domination of the Party,
where it is today.

Therefore, after the revolt of 1956, the
press was returned to a position it had occupied since 1948: all publications exist only
to serve the Communist cause and are free to
do nothing but obey. Today all the publications reflect the Moscow ideology. Many
observers say that although the press is returned to its 1948 status, the journalists
of the country are becoming ever bolder and
are not likely soon to forget their brief
free press of 1956.

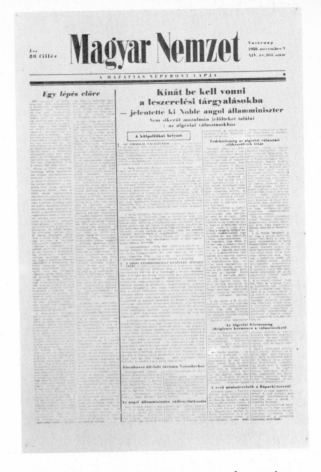

Magyar Nemzet prior to Hungary's coming
under the domination of the Soviet Union,
was the main independent paper of the
country. It had high standards and was
especially noted for its sociological,
financial and historical articles. It
was suspended for nearly a year after
the unsuccessful Revolution of the
Winter of 1956.

Poland

In 1962 some 50 dailies in Poland were circulating nearly 5.5 million copies. About 125 weeklies were published, at least 350 monthlies, and some 50 fortnightlies. Radio subscribers numbered close to six million. Television had eight broadcasting and fifteen relay stations, reaching nearly half the country. Probably more than half a million TV sets were in use. The electronic media were advancing rapidly. Both the printed media and the electronic media in Poland are patterned after those in the Soviet Union, and the aims are practically identical.

In recent years, however, Polish newspapers have shown certain signs of individuality-- not much, but some. At times they have even been bold, and have taken on a "Western" flavor. This does not mean that they are really freer than their counterparts in neighboring Communist nations; it simply indicates that they are developing a sort of journalistic character that looks to the West and to the Soviet Union for leadership while remaining within the Communist order. At times some of the more courageous of the Polish papers attack the Communist party for the miseries of postwar life, but this has happened far less often since 1961. While still basically a spreader of Party concepts and notices to the people, the Polish press does try to go beyond this narrowest of Communist press precepts; it appears to visualize its role as more than simply "education and agitation." The idea that the press has another task-- reflecting public opinion and relaying it to the Party--is quite strong. This concept makes for "two-way" traffic in information within the Party framework; such a concept does, of course, include the relaying of critical public opinion to the Party. And it is probably in this respect that the Polish press is more "liberal" than its Communist neighbors.

The Western concept which stresses information dissemination and entertainment has not developed very far in Poland, although there is apparently a trend in that direction. Many Polish papers are beginning to look like Western papers; a few are even running comic strips and crossword puzzles. Trybuna Ludu, the official daily of the Party's Central Committee, began running display advertisements in 1957 and since then display advertising has become quite common in the Polish

press. In many of the larger papers, advertisements consume as much as 30 per cent of the total space; of all the Communist press systems, the Polish is probably the most advertising conscious. Circulation is also pushed by Western-type promotion contests and beauty pageants.[1]

POLAND'S NATIONAL NEWS AGENCY. Polska Ajencja Prasowa (Polish Press Agency), usually referred to by its logotype--PAP--is the official government news disseminating organization founded in 1944. Its headquarters are in Warsaw, having been moved from Moscow in 1945 where the agency was organized the year before. It has branch offices in all the larger Polish municipalities. PAP is headed by a director, a deputy director, and two chief editors (for domestic and foreign news). It publishes about 15 press bulletins daily in four languages. PAP has foreign offices in several important cities, among them New York, London, Moscow, Paris, and Peiping. Although it receives most of its foreign news from the Soviet's TASS, it has exchange agreements with Reuters, AFP, and several national agencies (among them: Hsin Hua of Red China, Agerpress of Rumania, TT of Sweden, and ADN of East Germany).

A significant aspect of the country's press today is its desire to be more literate and "culturally-oriented"[2] and to augment its

Communist-line articles with more objective versions of world news. The Poles in increasing numbers are evidencing an inquiring spirit and a distaste for the more blatant trappings of dictatorship, and the press is going as far as possible in satisfying this thirst for information.

and it is dangerous for newspapers to disregard them. Questions of foreign policy which seem openly critical of the Soviet Union must be avoided; open opposition to the Communistic philosophy (although suggestions for reform can be made) is forbidden; and direct military information related to

```
POLAND'S PRINCIPAL NEWSPAPERS

Warsaw:     Trybuna Ludu (People's Tribune). . . . . . . . . . . . . . AM; 250,000
            Sztandar Mlodych (Youth Banner). . . . . . . . . . . . . . AM; 100,000
            Express Wieczorny (Evening Express). . . . . . . . . . . . PM; 550,000
            Zycie Warszawy (Warsaw Life) . . . . . . . . . . . . . . . AM; 220,000
            Glos Pracy (Labor's Voice) . . . . . . . . . . . . . . . . AM; 120,000

            Chlopska Droga (Peasant's Way) . . . . . .    twice weekly; 300,000
            Szpilki (Needles) . . . satirical . . . . . . . . . . weekly; 200,000
            Po Prostu (Simply Speaking). . . . . . . . . . . . . weekly; 150,000
            Zielony Sztandar (Green Banner). . . . . . . . . . . weekly; 120,000
            Politika (Policy) . . . . . . . . . . . . . . . . . . weekly;  30,000

Katowice:   Trybuna Robotnicza (Workers Tribune) . . . . . . . . . . AM; 450,000

Breslau:    Gazeta Robotnicza (Workers Gazette). . . . . . . . . . . AM; 150,000

Krakow:     Gazeta Krakowska (Crakow Gazette) . . . . . . . . . . . . AM;  60,000

Lodz:       Glos Robotniczy (Labor's Voice) . . . . . . . . . . . . . AM; 130,000
```

Another important aspect of the press is a growing concern with press freedom. Said the editor of the weekly Po Prostu ("Speaking Frankly") in 1957: "There is no place for censorship in a democracy. Without democracy, there is no socialism."[3]

All papers are publicly owned and controlled by the government in Poland; this has been the case since the Nationalization Act of 1946 placed all media of mass communication in the hands of the state. There is one paper, Warsaw's weekly Nowa Kultura (founded in 1957), which in theory (Communist theory) is an independent paper; its editor and staff are elected by secret ballot and the editor is responsible to the staff. Other such cooperatives are being planned within the Polish press. However, this is far from being free since most of the staff members (this is the publication of the Polish Writers Union) are under its discipline. But it may be a step toward a kind of freedom within the Communist order and does give more chance for the interplay of personalities. It should be remembered, however, as Mitchell Stanley said in 1957, that the "basic fact remains...that the guiding role is still in the hands of the Polish United (Communist) Workers party."[4]

There are in Poland three main press taboos

troop locations, new weapons, etc. must not be printed.

The first real sign that the Polish press was becoming restless and desirous of more freedom under the Communist power structure was in 1954. Previously, it had been docile and uncritical. Slowly since 1954 a spirit of criticism has developed among the people and in the press. The publishers have become more "unpredictable," and in general the nationalistic trend of the country has been reflected in the newspapers and other journals. During the intra-Communist party differences of 1956 (between the "Stalinist" faction and the non-Stalinists) the press gained considerable freedom and prestige, and in 1957 a desire for more independence-- a situation totally new in an Iron Curtain state--developed ever further and with it a feeling of responsibility to the readers.

Polish papers began to point out dangers and shortcomings of a Communist society. This type of press offering obviously found (and is finding, even with increased censorship) a ready and growing audience in the country--especially among Polish young people and intellectuals.[5] In 1957, for example, the weekly Swiat ("World"), patterned after the U.S. magazine Life, ran excerpts from

George Orwell's book, Nineteen Eighty-Four, which depicted the empty life in a conformist and totalitarian society. Another publication carried a long review of ex-Communist Arthur Koestler's Darkness at Noon, exposing Communist terrorism. Some papers have printed highly favorable stories about the U.S. and Western prosperity and have even called the Western nations "truly democratic."

In spite of all this, it should be remembered that censorship in Poland can still control material of all types appearing in the press, and one must suspect that when "anti-Communist" stories do appear they have some sort of propagandistic value to the Communists and are not to be taken at face value. Also, it would be a mistake to believe that Moscow's power in Poland has deteriorated to the point that such press "escapades" as those mentioned above could occur without the Kremlin's sanction.

In summary, it might be safely said that the Polish press is still firmly under control of the Communist party, but like that particular party in Poland, it has been indicating a certain amount of "restlessness" and nationalistic spirit. It should also be noted that the Poles seem to have the feeling that they have been cut off from the main stream of contemporary thought by their close association with the Soviet Union; they appear extremely anxious to catch up. Both the main Catholic and Communist elements in the country are showing certain signs of divergence from the strict Soviet pattern in their art, music, discussions--and in their publications. This is especially true among the young people and the intellectuals.

There seems a definite "national awareness" in the country despite fourteen years of allegiance to the Kremlin, and Polish publications are evidencing this awareness in many ways. The press of the country, like the people in general, has certain close affinities with the West--especially Western Europe; and Polish newspapers are taking on more and more characteristics of the Western press. The newspapers are often quite critical even since Gomulka tightened censorship in 1957 and warned that the press should find some favorable things to say or "we'll self-criticize ourselves into self-liquidation." Some observers

have mentioned that even the state-owned news agency, Polska Ajencja Prasowa, is becoming as much like Reuters and AFP as like TASS.

It may simply be that as Poland tends to become more nationalistic, its press is automatically veering in the same direction. Whether or not the Polish press is showing certain signs of "rebellion" against the U.S.S.R., however, is really not too important in the overall press situation. For the fact is that, as in Yugoslavia, the Communist party still calls the tune to which the press dances. A nationalistic press is not the same thing as a free press, or for that matter, a pro-Western press. At any rate, the Polish press in recent years has evidenced some ideological (or "propagandistic?") changes, and at least in the physical appearance of its publications, has become more "Westernized."

Polish newspapers and other media, although showing certain signs of individualism, are nevertheless instruments in the Communist system. The papers are not allowed to print material that might hurt Polish relations with other Communist nations, and criticism of foreign policy must be ever so mild. In other words, as is true in the Soviet Union, the journalists must operate in the framework of the social and political context of the Communist system.

The newspapers of Poland are of two types: the party papers and the nonparty papers. Both types are controlled by the Central Committee of the Party directly or indirectly, of course. The nonparty papers simply deal with general problems more than do the party papers, which emphasize party matters.

Polish editors are influenced greatly by the Soviet press. Copies of Pravda reach Warsaw the middle of the afternoon and the editors of the main newspapers check the Moscow paper carefully. They also read Izvestia. Radio Moscow is also a source of information and ideas for the Polish editors. The press also gets an official daily translation from the PAP--Polish Press Agency--the main source of information. Western newspapers can be found on the newsstands of Warsaw, a situation not existing in all the Iron Curtain nations.

Yugoslavia

This Communist nation, independent of Soviet domination but with a press just as firmly under government control, has a population of some 17 million and a literacy rate of about 80 per cent. All publications in the country are controlled by the Union of Communists of Yugoslavia; they serve as an arm of the government and Party and exist to carry forth the Communist system. In other words, the press of Yugoslavia is just as much an instrument of government as is the press of U.S.S.R. even though in theory the people of the country have freedom of expression.[1] More important, however, than Constitutional guarantees is the fact that since World War II all private publishing enterprises (and other communications media) have been nationalized. Newspapers and other publications are in the hands of the state and various social and political units of the state to be used to further the interests of the government.

There are some 20 daily newspapers in Yugoslavia with a combined circulation of nearly a million and a half. Two Belgrade morning dailies--Borba ("Struggle") and Politika ("Policy")--with some 350,000 and 300,000 circulation respectively, account for about half of the country's circulation.[2] Borba leads the Yugoslav press as does Pravda in the U.S.S.R.; local Communist papers all over the country usually reprint Borba editorials according to instructions sent them by the country's national news agency.

Publication centers are evenly distributed throughout Yugoslavia in 10 of the largest cities. Outside the capital, Belgrade, the largest daily (and certainly one of the nation's gaudiest) is Vjesnik ("Messenger") of Zagreb with a circulation of some 120,000.

PRINCIPAL NEWS AGENCY. Yugoslavia's national news agency, founded in 1943, is Telegrafska Agencija Nova Jugoslavija and is generally referred to as TANJUG. Its central office is in Belgrade and it has branch offices in the capitals of each of the six republics. All news must pass through this agency to which all the nation's papers look for their domestic and foreign material. An independent agency, it subsists on subscription fees, received not only from the papers, but from radio and TV stations and other government and nongovernment groups. The agency, though independent financially, is an arm of the government, and as such tells the editors what (and often where and when) they can publish. Heading TANJUG is a director and 10-man board appointed by the chairman of the government's Council of Science and Culture. The agency's permanent correspondents are stationed in about 14 of the world's main cities, and it maintains part-time "stringers" in several others. TANJUG has exchange agreements with Reuters, Agence France-Presse, United Press International, TASS, and three European national agencies.

```
          PRINCIPAL NEWSPAPERS

Belgrade:

Borba ("Struggle") . . . . . AM; 350,000
Politika ("Policy"). . . . . AM; 300,000
Vecernji Novosti ("Evening
    News") . . . . . . . . PM; 155,000

Komunist ("Communist") . weekly; 80,000

Zagreb:

Vjesnik ("Messenger") . . . AM; 120,000
Vecernji List ("People's
    Newspaper") . . . . . . PM;  80,000

Sarajevo:

Oslobodjenje ('Liberation"). AM;  60,000
```

Yugoslav newspapers are printed in six languages: Serbian, Croatian, Macedonian, Slovenian, Italian, and Hungarian. Papers in both the Cyrillic and Latin alphabets are found in the country. There are about 100 weekly newspapers published in the country; the largest and most influential of these is Komunist (f.1957) which already has a circulation of nearly 80,000. It publishes editions in three languages.[3]

Newspapers in the country are lively in content and format compared to Communist newspapers elsewhere. Many Western techniques (e.g., comic strips, crossword puzzles, and elaborately-illustrated feature articles) are found in most of them. Especially "Westernized" in appearance are Borda,[4] Politika, and Vjesnik. However, like all Communist publications, the Yugoslav newspapers slant everything to further the Communist cause. It is obvious to the reader of the papers that, in spite of the unexpected vitality of make up and a hodgepodge of entertainment features, they are basically like the Soviet papers.[5] They are

also notably stereotyped in appearance, with
all papers of the country obviously receiving
careful instructions. It is interesting to
note that Tito's picture or accounts of his
speeches appear only on the front page of
Yugoslav papers.

Among the principal magazines of Yugoslavia
are four published in Belgrade: Duga (an illustrated weekly), Jez (weekly humor and satire),
Stvaranje (literary monthly), and Omladina
(youth weekly). Most Yugoslav periodical
publications of major importance are printed
in the Cyrillic alphabet, as is true in most
parts of the Balkans and in Russia. The
Slovenes and the Serbs, and especially the
former, comprise an important portion of
Yugoslavia's population and are considered
among the most cultured people in all the
Balkans. They exert great influence in the
country and this probably accounts for the
large amount of "cultural" and "international
affairs" material found in Yugoslav newspapers.

A BRIEF LOOK AT THREE PAPERS. Borba
("Struggle"). 8-col., regular size paper;
f.1922; total circulation--close to a million
each morning; uses color sparingly (in name
"Borba" on front page and a touch of same
color in cartoons on back page); neat make up
and good printing; many feature stories of
historical, cultural nature; on last four
pages (normal edition: 16 pages) are comic
strips, classified and display ads, and crossword puzzles.

Politika ("Policy"). 5 col. tabloid in
Cyrillic type; normally runs editions of two
sections of 12 pages each; lively make up,
especially in second section which contains
cartoons, comic strips, features and cultural
articles and some fiction; also carries puzzles and Walt Disney's "Mickey Mouse"; back
page given over to State advertising.

Vjesnik ("Messenger") of Zagreb. Pages
with varying number of columns (usually five)
on its regular-size sheet (about 15 x 22
inches); probably the gaudiest of all Yugoslav
papers; uses large nameplate with background
in green (usually) ink; often uses large
cartoons on front page with big story played
in upper left; printed in Latin alphabet in
Croatian language; two sections of 8 pages
each, with second section mainly entertainment and elaborately illustrated features
and fiction articles; full page of comics;
back page is a picture page with brief cut-
lines stressing photographs from all over the
world.

BROADCASTING. Yugoslavia's first permanent
radio station was begun in Zagreb in 1926--
the first radio station in the Balkans. By
1939 there were only four stations in the
country. In 1946, with the advent of Communism in the country, there were 12 stations; in 1953 there were 18, and in 1961,
30. Embassy representatives in Washington
predict that by 1970 there will probably be
twice that many, or 60.

As in the Soviet Union and other Communist
nations, radio is vital for reinforcing
Party and state directions which are fun-
neled to the masses by the printed media.
Not only does the Yugoslav constantly read
the Word, but he has it drummed into his
ears as well.

There are only about a million radio receiving sets in the country, but through use
of loudspeakers attached to radio outlets
and wired distribution systems in the rural
areas, the number of persons reached is
tremendous. Television is just beginning
in Yugoslavia and in 1963 was having little
effect as a medium of mass communication.

However, it is expected that in a very
short time television will be developed for
use as a major arm of propaganda, especially
in urban areas.

Latin America: Overview

It is difficult to generalize in a few words about the press and broadcasting systems of Latin America. First of all, we are speaking of twenty separate republics, not one unified country. These nations range from the one-third of an island called Haiti (French-speaking) to the half-continent called Brazil (Portuguese-speaking).

Even emphasizing the obvious common elements of the Latin American republics--such as predominant use of the Spanish language--must be tempered with exceptions. Out of 210 million Latin Americans, one-third of them--74 million Brazilians--speak Portuguese, not Spanish. In Peru, Bolivia, Ecuador, and Guatemala, millions of Latin Americans speak their native Indian languages, not Spanish.

Number one problem in Latin America can be stated in one phrase: overpopulation. Not Asia, but Latin America is now the world's fastest growing area, increasing 2.6 per cent annually, with a few spots in Latin America increasing 3 per cent each year. Despite the Alliance for Progress and Latin American efforts to push economic growth, the best efforts are failing to keep up with the boom in babies. Neither a small-family pattern nor political stability protect much of Latin America. As a consequence, more than half of the adults in Latin America still cannot read. That is, they cannot read well enough to scan a newspaper headline, though some of them are classified as "literate" because they can read and write their own names--bureaucratic juggling of statistics to put one's best political foot forward.

Therefore, Latin America does not enjoy the wide newspaper and magazine readerships found in the United States, Western Europe, and Japan. Latin America's capital cities--among the largest and most modern looking metropolitan centers in the world--are showcases, with big dailies, slick-paper magazines, competing television stations, and radio networks. But the hinterlands tell a different story.

The "average" Latin American still lives in a town or village of less than 2,500, has six years of schooling at best or more often one year or none. If his town has a newspaper, it is a weekly or small daily with a few thousand circulation, poorly-printed, without much world news, and not enough advertising revenue to improve.

One thing the rural or semiurban Latin American does have, however, is a cheap radio receiver, often a portable model not requiring any cord or wall plug, for his town may not have electrical service to private dwellings anyway.

Radio broadcasting, therefore, in the many semi-isolated parts of Latin America becomes one of the few links with the outside world.

By contrast, in the largest Latin American cities, huge daily newspapers, nationally-circulated magazines, and television stations compete with radio not only for the advertising budgets available but for the audiences for news and views.

Two of Latin America's cities each have six million population: Mexico City and Buenos Aires. Brazil's two giants are São Paulo with four million residents and Rio de Janeiro with 3.25 million. Lima, Santiago, Bogotá, Caracas--each has more than one million population.

These large cities boast several outstanding dailies: La Prensa and La Nación in Buenos Aires, Excelsior and Novedades in Mexico City, O Estado in São Paulo, El Tiempo in Bogotá, and El Mercurio in Santiago rank with the other major newspapers of the world in style of writing, devotion to extensive coverage of world news, and similar journalistic criteria.

The School of Journalism of Pennsylvania State University, in a study of leading United States and Latin American newspapers for the period January-March, 1959, found that O Estado, El Nacional of Caracas, El Mercurio, El Dia of Montevideo, and La Prensa each carried more column inches of foreign news each day than did the Washington (D. C.) Star, the Chicago Daily News, St. Louis Post-Dispatch, Los Angeles Times, Philadelphia Bulletin, Denver Post, or Louisville Courier-Journal. Only the encyclopedic New York Times carried more column inches of foreign news per day during the period studied than five of the seven largest Latin American dailies.[1]

PRESS PRESSURES. With an average per capita annual income of less than $300, obviously Latin Americans feel a strong economic pinch. Many low-salaried reporters take two or more jobs, compromising their objectivity. Squeezed by inflation, publishers and station owners delay replacing worn out presses and radio-TV transmitting equipment.

Where political instability has spawned military authoritarianism, press freedom has vanished or diminished. The Inter-American Press Association and the Inter-American Broadcasters Association help keep hope alive among freedom-striving editors, writers, and broadcasters throughout Latin America. But in one country, Cuba, a totalitarian regime has ended any semblance of journalistic freedom. In Haiti, Nicaragua, and Paraguay the press must praise the government in power. With periodic attacks by Communists, the Venezuelan regime, though disposed to democracy and freedom, has been forced to curtail information from time to time. Guatemala has been suffering in a

similar fashion.

Because of continuous exchange difficulties and lack of dollar reserves for their inflation-ridden economies, most Latin American republics have had to cut back some in importing newsprint from Canada, seeking instead to barter coffee, sugar, and similar crops to the Scandinavians.

There is a bright spot in the newsprint picture. Mexico has a growing paper industry in its state of Oaxaca. And in central Chile, a mill turns out tons of newsprint each day.[2] Even crisis-ridden Argentina now produces a small amount of its paper needs. And a new paper industry in Colombia is growing rapidly.[3]

Also on the positive side, in the last decade newspaper advertising has grown up considerably. There has been a general improvement in the quality of newspaper, magazine, and broadcast advertising, with a rise in volume, but because of the problem of inflation, payments from advertisers or agencies to the media often are delayed.[4]

TANGIBLE PROGRESS: SUPPLEMENTS, PRIVATE NETWORKS. In addition to the general growth of advertising, other tangible elements of progress for the Latin American mass media include: (1) Reporting of family living: oldtime Latin American periodicals had women's society features, the doings of the wealthy class. But the new emphasis centers in family living, including homemaking hints, problems of education, and similar features once segregated to fillers on women's pages but not written for the entire family. Such modern, adult reporting is evidenced in the Sunday magazine supplements carried with the larger newspapers.

For example, Hablemos, a Sunday supplement which resembles in appearance This Week, is published and edited in New York by Casey Hirshfield, and distributed in nine of the twenty republics.[5] In Mexico, the supplement Nosotras Decimos (founded in 1953) distributes with twenty-one dailies in every sector of the republic. The influence of the U.S. publications Life En Español (circulation in Latin America 407,000)[6] and Selecciones del Reader's Digest can be evidenced in both newspaper and magazine editing and writing. (2) Growth of journalism schools and professional newsmen's groups: In 1946, there were only six schools of journalism in Latin America, each small and somewhat isolated from potential publisher-employers. In 1963, there are more than fifty full schools of journalism, plus a dozen or more smaller trade-school institutions offering newspaper and broadcasting training.

In recent years, bravely in the face of governmental pressures and threats, more and more Latin American working newsmen have demanded basic freedoms and professional working conditions.

In addition to such established groups as the Inter-American Press Association (Sociedad Interamericana de Prensa or SIP) and the Inter-American Broadcasters Association (Asociación Interamericana de Radiodifusores or AIR), primarily for publishers and station owners, the working newsmen now have their Inter-American Federation of Working Newspapermen's Organizations and the Inter-American Association of Announcers.

As a result of more trained reporters entering journalism and then joining professional groups, one finds more reporting in depth in the leading papers. For example, Elsa Arana Freire of La Prensa of Lima won an IAPA award in 1962 for a graphic, firsthand report of the life and plight of shanty-town dwellers in Peru.[7] If enough such candid reporting continues, Latin American leadership may yet awaken to its basic needs before any more Castro-type tyrannies can entwine themselves.

Special conferences help too. The first Pan American Press Seminar, held in New Orleans during April 15-18, 1962, sponsored by the International Trade Mart of New Orleans (International House), found North, Central, and South American editors candidly appraising each other's strengths and weaknesses.[8]

Within each of the Latin American republics are now found organizations for reporters, for editors, for publishers, for broadcasters, for news photographers, for advertising executives, and in some of these countries, for public relations executives.

In Mexico especially has the professionalization of public relations work taken place in recent years. Mexican PR executives not only serve their own domestic clients, but like U.S. agency executives, serve other Latin American clients too. For example, Relaciones Públicas Mundiales of Mexico City holds the 1962-63 contract to handle public relations for the mining industry of Peru.[9] This same Mexican firm handles all public relations in Central America for the Japanese (government-sponsored) Trade Promotion Organization.

BETTER MEDIA STATISTICS. Publishers and broadcasters, advertising and public relations executives, social scientists and general observers--all now have better measuring devices for ascertaining the true mass media picture in Latin America.

The Inter-American Press Association maintains an Office of Certified Circulation (Oficina de Circulación Certificada or OCC), serving the leading newspapers all over Latin America.[10]

Broadcasting audience surveys in at least a few of the Latin American republics--Mexico, Brazil, Chile, Peru, Argentina, and Uruguay--now give a truer picture of the impact of various stations and networks.

Also, airmail deliveries of foreign periodicals are as prompt as the jet plane schedules, contrasted with the delays of only a few years ago.[11]

And the recently-created Technical Center of the Inter-American Press Association now concerns itself not only with printing-plant and editing problems, but also with distributing, circulating, and readership measurements.[12]

Thus we see several positive factors to balance against the longtime evils besetting Latin American journalism: subsidies given to "progovernment" newspapers, outright bribes to unethical reporters, regulation by the government of newsprint or broadcast transmitter distribution, and in some cases, outright censorship.

NEWS FROM LATIN AMERICA. United States reporters sent to cover Latin America as foreign correspondents have no trouble filing stories to home offices from most Latin American cities. Cuba, of course, is an exception. But they do sometimes experience difficulties in obtaining information sufficient enough to file anything. The problem centers in basic news sources, governmental officials, reluctant to give out anything but the most favorable aspects of their stewardships of office.

Through the years, complaints that insufficient news from Latin America appears in U.S. publications and on the air were answered by the wire services and network news services with the reply that great quantities of stories are filed, but that few of these stories get chosen for exposure by stateside editors, who must think in terms of reader-listener interests. The seriousness of the Castro crises on our doorstep in Cuba should have ended the myth that Americans are not hungry for important news from Latin America.

But what do editors select? By and large, still the overt violence stories, the spot news, not the reports of social trends of long-range significance, with some notable exceptions.

As for the reports actually filed from Latin America, one can find more praise for the quantity than the quality. In certain unstable quarters, stringers who happen to be natives of the republic in question still file guarded reports. To be more candid would be to forfeit their own domestic status.

An example: in August, 1960, the Associated Press stringer in Managua filed a story, an official denial from General Anastasio Somoza Jr. that any fighting was going on near the Honduran-Nicaraguan border at the town of Jícaro. The AP solemnly moved the dispatch: no fighting; rumors to the contrary were just that. But an American newsman, Marvin Alisky, happened to be in Nicaragua at the time, interviewed some of the wounded brought back from Jícaro, and was able to telephone a story to NBC in New York, giving the details of the battle at Jícaro. The AP correspondent, a Nicaraguan under pressure from the government, then managed to stick his neck out long enough to file a second-day story that rebel resistance had been mopped up by General Somoza's forces. How many Jícaros do we suffer each year?

To look into such matters in detail, the Center for the Study of Democratic Institutions in 1962 had several key veteran Latin American correspondents report on news files for the month of February, 1962.

Hal Hendrix, Latin American editor of the Miami News, found the AP reports for the month far from representative in the light of what actually was erupting. A similar verdict was pronounced for UPI reports by Al Marlens, news editor of Newsday (Garden City, N.Y.). By contrast, Joseph P. Lyford of the Fund for the Republic found the New York Times file from Latin America for February, 1962 extensive, meaningful. Latin American leaders and editors have commented about this study by pleading for more correspondents to cover their vital area of the world.[13]

More and more U.S. schools of journalism are now offering a course in which the foreign press, news agencies, broadcasting systems, and Cold War propaganda pressures are considered. This book itself is a response to teachers of such courses, looking for appropriate guides. Perhaps we are at last about to send into the mass media fields young graduates, eager to serve as correspondents, and--more important--trained to some extent to understand the complexities of the foreign area being covered than too often has been the case. Experience without training or orientation can be as unsound as training without subsequent field experience. Both are needed, especially by newsmen trying to cover changing, complicated, volatile Latin America.

Mexico

The one key word which characterizes the Mexican press since 1945 is "growth." Like the United States, Mexico actually has fewer daily newspapers in 1963 than in 1945 but a larger total circulation. But unlike the U.S., Mexico has more cities with competing dailies than in former years, whereas in the U.S., the monopoly pattern of cities without competing dailies holds true for 90 per cent of our cities.

In 1956, Mexico had 155 dailies.[1] By 1960, this figure had shrunk to 141 dailies, 18 of them in Mexico City and 123 of them provincial.[2] During 1960-62, 19 new dailies were successfully launched, but 9 older, weaker ones folded, giving Mexico a gain of 10 daily papers. Thus, at the beginning of 1963, Mexico had 151 dailies (18 in Mexico City and 133 in the 29 states and two territories of the Mexican republic).[3]

Significant is the factor of competition. During the past decade, the number of competing dailies in Mexico City has remained approximately the same, though four or five dominate, both in political influence and in circulation. But as for the provincial press, in 1960 there were 29 cities with two or more competing dailies, and 22 cities with only one daily.[4]

Less than three years later, late in 1962, Mexico had 68 cities with daily newspapers, 39 of them with competing papers and 29 cities with noncompeting dailies.

In Peru, a foreign correspondent can cover the republic from Lima, backstopped by the six Lima dailies. In any of the Central American capitals, or in Uruguay, Bolivia, Paraguay, or the Dominican Republic, this same situation holds. But a newsman no longer covers the Republic of Mexico backstopped only by the four or five leading dailies of Mexico City. The provincial press has grown in quality and quantity. Regional news has become significant nationally.

Despite the spread of television and radio stations and receivers throughout the republic, both Mexico City and provincial newspapers have gained or held their own in circulation. Smaller newspaper circulations than in former years center in the tiny dailies and in some of the weekly papers.

PROVINCIAL LEADERS. For example, in 1951 El Norte of Monterrey had 45,000 daily circulation; in 1963 it has 65,000. Diario de Yucatán in Mérida in 1951 had 33,000 circulation; by late 1962, it had 45,000 certified Sunday circulation and 41,000 weekdays.

But whether holding their own or increasing in circulation from 2 per cent or more in recent years, Mexican newspapers show vigor.

Other provincial leaders include the three Healy papers of the state of Sonora: El Imparcial, PM daily in Hermosillo with 12,000 circulation weekdays and 20,000 Sundays. José Healy also publishes an Hermosillo AM El Regional, and an AM in Navojoa, El Informador.

Guadalajara, Mexico's second largest city with 800,000 population, has three dailies: El Occidental (AM, circulation 70,000), El Sol (PM, circulation 60,000), and El Informador (AM, circulation 43,000). Even though it has the smallest circulation of the three, Informador retains prestige in general as the leading daily not only of the city of Guadalajara but also of the surrounding state of Jalisco, in terms of news coverage and traditional standing with the general public.

Similarly, the relatively small circulation for the Healy papers in the state of Sonora, does not accurately indicate their influence as well-edited papers read by opinion leaders, key people in all walks of public life.

Monterrey, third largest city in Mexico with 700,000 population, supports four daily newspapers. The aforementioned El Norte (AM with 65,000 circulation) also publishes a PM daily, El Sol (circulation 45,000). Norte-Sol publisher Rodolfo Junco de la Vega has two competitors: El Tiempo, a daily with a 15,000-circulation early morning edition and a 20,000-circulation midday edition; El Porvenir, an AM with 41,500 circulation weekdays and 44,000 Sundays.

Several other provincial cities, in addition to Guadalajara and Monterrey, not only have lively newspaper competition, but also competing television and radio stations.

POPULATION PROBLEM. Mexico's land area of 750,000 square miles makes it one-fourth the size of the United States or approximately as large as Western Europe, with a population of 36 million. Mexico's population now increases almost one million each year, the highest rate of growth in the world, with two or three small-nation exceptions. The fertility of Mexican women, the absence of widespread birth control means, and expansion of modern medical facilities combine to boost the total population faster than the campaign to eradicate illiteracy can advance. Obviously the Mexican press serves a national need, for newspaper circulations--provincial and in Mexico City--are growing.

If the percentage of the total population truly literate actually has decreased while the total newspaper circulation has increased, obviously more literate Mexicans are buying newspapers than ever before. Their press seems to be providing them with the kind of information they seek.

In 1953, Mexico's literacy rate rose to 65 per cent, its highest level in history.[5] But then the population explosion began to overtake the valiant efforts at building adult literacy centers, the national program of rural school construction, and the praiseworthy efforts of the Cultural Missions of the Ministry of Education, traveling normal schools and welfare agencies.[6] A decade later, by 1963, the Mexican literacy rate had slipped to 55 per cent, even as village peasants were building their own schools, even as more and more young Normal School graduates went into the field to teach reading.

PRESS FREEDOM. One cannot consider Mexican mass media nor public life very deeply without analyzing the "Revolution," a program of specific improvements to raise the standard of living and to step up national integration of the impoverished, the illiterate, the physically isolated, the Indians, and any Mexicans not participating fully in the national life.[7]

This Revolution, a strictly non-Communist phenomenon, antedates the Soviet rise to power in Russia and has no connection with any such idea of revolution. There have been many Mexican military revolts, mostly in the nineteenth century, but only one real social Revolution. It began in 1910 and is still going on, aided by the mass media.

The military phase of the Revolution, during 1910-20, ended the long-time dictatorship of Porfirio Díaz. For thirty-five years, Díaz ruled with cruelty and force, permitting only a weak press which would praise him. Since 1920, the social phase of the Revolution has accented a series of governmental administrations pledged to carry out programs of reform, including more land and rural schools for peasants, effective suffrage, and freedom of speech and of press throughout the republic.

Countless Cold War editorials in Mexican papers criticize the Communists of the world while exalting the Mexican brand of revolutionary reform.

In the late 1920's, a few newspapers suffered direct governmental pressures for trying to undermine the Revolution. Then came a serious threat to press freedom. In 1937, the governor of Jalisco began a road building program. Guadalajara's great daily El Informador editorially attacked the seemingly high cost of the program. Thereupon the paper was prevented by one means or another from publishing regularly for one year. However, other newspapers came to Informador's support and it finally won its case in a court of law.

In general, Mexican papers traditionally do not criticize the President of the Republic. But they may criticize his cabinet and they do. Similarly, a provincial paper usually does not attack the governor of a state but rather officials at lower levels.

Yet in 1958, El Sol de San Luis and El Heraldo, dailies in the state capital of San Luis Potosí, vigorously attacked editorially Manuel Alvarez, governor of the state of San Luis Potosí, paving the way for his political opponents to succeed him.

But very often, newspaper reporters must begin interviews with "con todo respeto," ("with all respect") before asking a governor, a federal official, or any high-ranking person in public or private life questions which might be irritating or less than complimentary or flattering.

Existing side by side in Mexico are daily examples of professional, probing reporting to the level of genuine significance and shallow publicity gushiness disguised as news writing. Though much progress has been evidenced during the past fifty years, Mexico has not yet rid itself of bribe-taking reporters and columnists. These unethical "newsmen" operate most frequently in the smallest cities and towns as weekly newspaper reporters while blackmailing prominent persons; for a fee, the subject of an unflattering story is not included in the published version or perhaps the story never even gets written.

Even in Mexico City, underpaid reporters have from time to time written favorably about personalities in the news for a fee. In 1959, Novedades printed a letter lifted from the Cuban embassy after Castro had replaced Batista. Batista's ambassador to Mexico had written that Aldo Baroni, columnist for the otherwise ethical daily Excélsior, had received substantial sums to write favorably about Batista.

This scandal prompted Excélsior, generally Mexico's best paper, to double check its reportorial ranks for any other bribe takers. Mexico's President Adolfo López Mateos personally endorsed a campaign by the Reporters Union to stamp out payoffs.

In Mexico City today, chief remaining pocket of such corruption centers in the ranks of bullfight critics.

Bullfighters often reserve up to one-third of a season's profits for magazine, newspaper, radio, and television critics and commentators. For pesos, some newsmen have made lackluster toreros appear to be skilled bullfighters of the first rank.

In the smaller towns and cities, a festering journalistic sore remains in police news reporting. A motorist who neglects to pay off a police-beat reporter after an accident may find that the story in print turns an otherwise innocent driver into a reckless, drunken speedster.

THE ROLE OF "PIPSA." No official or direct press censorship or control would be tolerated within the idealistic framework of the Revolution of more than fifty years or under the reformist, libertarian Constitution of 1917. Yet the government has a subtle instrumentality of control through PIPSA or Productora e Importadora de Papel, S. A. (Producer and Importer of Paper, Inc.), sole Mexican agency for importing and distributing newsprint throughout the republic and for manufacturing paper in Mexico. PIPSA is a combination governmental-private enterprise corporation, headed by Homero Barrenechea, who serves as general manager. On PIPSA's board of directors are both a few governmental officials and several publishers of leading newspapers and magazines, including Rómulo O'Fárrill, Jr. of Novedades and Martín Luis Guzmán, publisher of the leading weekly news magazine Tiempo.

PIPSA has invested in a newsprint-producing plant in Tuxtepec, Oaxaca.[8] Paper from the state of Oaxaca and from Canada and Finland gets distributed from PIPSA headquarters in the Mexico City suburb of Industrial Vallejo, D. F.

Despite governmental partnership in PIPSA, and despite some subsidizing by key governmental ministries to certain newspapers, the basic libertarian philosophy of the press has continued to grow.

Mexican newswriting has become more like that of the United States, with the essential data stressed first. Yet many leads can be found which are involved and many news stories still appear with editorializing woven into the body of the report.

Some of the best writing in the country appears on editorial pages of the larger dailies, supplemented by political cartoons and essays which caricature people and events in the national and foreign news.

GROWTH OF ADVERTISING. In recent decades, Mexico has led the remainder of Latin America in its developing of advertising, both as to quality and quantity.

Dailies in the larger cities give more than half their space to advertising. Even the smaller dailies carry a page of classified ads and large display movie ads are common. In radio and television, advertising has made Mexican broadcasting the most profitable among the twenty Latin American republics.[9]

The Barbachano Ponce company, producer of sixty-second and longer commercials for motion picture theaters, contracts to exhibit advertising in movie theaters throughout Mexico through Cine-Sistema, S. A.[10] In even the remotest villages in Mexico, where neither newspaper nor magazine nor television advertising regularly reaches and where even almost-universal radio commercials have relatively weak impact due to a locally poor distribution of receivers, one always finds a movie theater. It may be open-air and function weekends only in the most isolated villages, but it does exhibit, including filmed advertisements.

MEXICO CITY'S LEADING DAILIES. Leading newspaper of Mexico, Excélsior, an AM with 122,000 circulation weekdays and 129,000 Sundays, approximately 40,000 of which is sold in every major city of the republic.

Excélsior's publishing company is owned by key employees. In 1934, the board of directors of these stockholders selected Gilberto Figueroa as executive publisher and general manager, a post he held successfully until he died of a heart attack November 12, 1962.[11]

Excélsior publishes two afternoon "extras" to its regular morning edition: Ultimas Noticias de Excélsior, whose first edition circulates 99,300 and whose second edition circulates 64,700. This newspaper company also publishes the well-known weekly magazine Jueves de Excélsior and Revista de Revistas.

Carefully edited, packed with national and world news, Excélsior also serves as a sounding board for those seeking to influence key Mexican officials, most of whom read it regularly. Its letters-to-the-editor column, "Foro," often consumes an entire page and is very popular.

Excélsior's Editorial Page

Founded in 1917, Excélsior truly can call itself the "Newspaper of National Life," the slogan appearing under its flag and masthead.

Second most prominent national newspaper of the republic is the Mexico City daily Novedades, an AM with 98,000 circulation weekdays and 119,000 Sundays. Founded in 1936, Novedades' publisher Rómulo O'Fárrill, Sr. also publishes an English-language tabloid AM, The News (circulation 19,000), edited by William Shanahan. Executive publisher of Novedades is the owner's son, Rómulo O'Fárrill, Jr., president of the Inter-American Press Association for 1962-63.

The other Mexico City daily of "The Big Three," El Universal, an AM with an Audit Bureau of Circulation weekday total of 131,000 and a Sunday circulation of 148,300, was founded in 1916 by Félix F. Palavicini (1881-1952), the "father of modern Mexican journalism" who did much to bring dignity to the Mexican press and to give emphasis to news over views.

El Universal in the 1940's and 1950's prospered under Miguel Lanz Duret. Since his death, his widow, Dolores Valdés de Lanz Duret, as publisher, has retained a good editorial

staff. She is one of the two women publishers active in the Inter-American Press Association, the other being Diana Julio of Bahía Blanca, Argentina.

This paper publishes an afternoon satellite, El Universal Gráfico, with a circulation of 74,300.

La Prensa, AM tabloid, cooperatively owned by its employees, is Mexico City's leading leftwing paper, with a certified circulation of 119,000. Often critical of the United States, Prensa in 1962 became critical of Cuba's Castro and the Soviet Union, but retains its somewhat neutral position in the Cold War in many of its editorials. In this respect, it contrasts with the pro-United States editorials of the big three, Excélsior, Novedades, and Universal.

A study of ten leading Mexican dailies, including Excélsior and Novedades and eight provincial papers, showed a generally negative image of the United States in the news and views from and about the United States published in January, 1960.[12] The pattern likely did not alter much until the Cuban crisis of October, 1962, when Castro was revealed as a puppet of Krushchev, even in the editorial pages of La Prensa.

Ovaciones, Mexico City AM founded in 1947, in 1962 became one of the two major Mexican dailies to be printed offset, the other one being Correo, an AM in Ciudad Juárez (across the border from El Paso, Texas). In 1963, the Healy papers of Sonora also plan to convert to offset.

Ovaciones circulates 87,000 mornings, plus a small afternoon edition devoted to sports for an additional estimated 20,000 copies.

Among the less influential and less news-filled dailies of Mexico City are ABC (AM), Atisbos (midday, rightwing), Diario de México (AM, generally ignored), El Nacional (AM, formerly the voice of the government but now more specifically the voice of the PRI political party), and Diario de la Tarde (PM satellite of Novedades, with a circulation of 40,000, largest of the also-rans).

Another daily in the capital is Esto, sports-news centered tabloid of 80,000 circulation, headquarters paper of the García Valseca chain.

GARCÍA VALSECA CHAIN. Mexico has Latin America's largest newspaper chain, the thirty-two newspapers owned by Colonel José García Valseca. In 1960, the group reached its peak with thrity-six papers, but since then the

colonel has closed his four smallest ones.
In addition, a thirty-third García Valseca
publication, _Paquita_, a newspaper-type magazine supplement, goes on sale all over the
republic every Monday, devoting itself to
women's features.

Esto in the federal capital emphasizes sports.
But most of the provincial GV papers stress
public affairs. Nineteen of the GV dailies
are called _El Sol de_, followed by the name of
the city or region being served: Durango,
Pacífico (Mazatlán), Sinaloa (Culiacán),
Fuerte (Los Mochis), San Luis, Guadalajara,
Parral, Norte (Saltillo), Zacatecas, Centro
(Aguascalientes), Tampico, Tarde, (Tampico),
León, Toluca, Tlaxcala, Bajío (Celaya),
Guanajuato, Hidalgo, and Puebla.

Most of the García Valseca papers are standard-size morning dailies publishing some
world news, some national news from Mexico
City (carrying the logotype of CGV, standing
for _Cadena_ García Valseca), and much local
news reported in an objective manner.

The GV papers plus the large independent
dailies, such as _El Norte_ of Monterrey and
Informador of Guadalajara, set examples of
good reporting from the hinterland, constrast-
ing with many of the small-town crusading
weeklies.[13]

WEEKLY PAPERS. During the past decade, some
of the better small-town weeklies have become
either dailies, triweeklies, or semiweeklies.

The smaller weeklies crusade against locally-
administered governmental policies, sometimes
becoming so violent in their denunciations of
locally-prominent persons that shots are fired
at the editor or the columnist.

In 1956, 1957, and in 1960, weekly editors
were killed in the states of Baja California
and Mexico (the state adjacent to the Federal
District). Also in 1960, another weekly
editor in Veracruz was beaten severely for
editorially attacking certain local politicians.[14]

Typographically, the weeklies are the weakest
link in the Mexican journalistic spectrum. In
terms of news, they often simply do not offer
much competition to dailies, to radio, or to
magazines, even for their own regions.

MAGAZINES. Mexico's leading weekly news magazine, _Tiempo_, has a format similar to _Newsweek_
or _Time_. Because its name means "Time" in
Spanish, _Tiempo_ distributes inside the United
States as _Hispano Americano_ at the legal insistence of Henry Luce's Time Inc.

Founded in 1942 by Martín Luis Guzmán, who
still serves as publisher, _Tiempo_ in twenty
years has become of genuine influence not
only throughout Mexico but also in key cities
of Central and South America.

Although _Tiempo_ sells only 17,421 to the
Mexican public, every major Mexican library
and institution of learning subscribes. Among
its readers are key opinion leaders of public
and private life. In addition, every city of
the five Central American republics south of
Mexico has subscribers among its top intellectuals and writers. And several South American
editors and columnists frequently quote
Tiempo, giving it an impact far out of proportion to its 20,000 circulation.

Visión, the New York-owned news magazine
issued every other week, circulates 200,000
copies throughout Latin America (including
its Portuguese-language edition, _Visão_, in
Brazil), of which 46,000 copies are sold in
Mexico, as certified by the Inter-American
Press office of certified circulation.

Both _Tiempo_ and _Visión_ use the _Time_-type
categories for news: hemispheric affairs,
business and finance, sports, fine arts, etc.

Utilizing a _Look_ or _Life_-like format are
the Mexican magazines _Hoy_ (twice-monthly,
15,000 circulation), _Impacto_ (weekly, 37,000
circulation), _Mañana_ (weekly, 26,000 circulation), _Nosotros_ (weekly, 17,000 circulation),
Siempre (weekly, 60,000 circulation), and
Todo (twice-monthly, 21,000 circulation).

A magazine writer so prolific that almost
no major Mexican periodical has not carried
one of his articles, Nemesio García Naranjo,
died at age 79 on December 21, 1962.[15]
García Naranjo, a moderate liberal or middle-
of-the-road political commentator with some
conservative tendencies, sometimes had his
byline in conservative _Hoy_ and liberal _Siempre_
at the same time.

As elsewhere in Latin America, in Mexico
the Spanish-language editions of _Life_ and
Reader's Digest number among the most popular
magazines.

BROADCASTING. Radio broadcasting began in
Mexico in 1923,[16] and television in 1950.
Mexico City's XHTV Channel 4 went on the air
on August 31, 1950, the first regularly
licensed television station in Latin America
with daily service.

Though industrialization grows rapidly, as
does urbanization, Mexico is still a nation
of rural life. The typical Mexican lives in

a town of 2,500 or less, in a nation plagued
with adverse terrain. More than half of the
total land area rises more than 3,200 feet
above sea level. Of the land that is not
mountainous, much is desert or tropical swamp.
Mexican geography and geology, combined with
climate, have worked against road building.
Modern highways run north and south, from the
United States to Central America. But east
and west, Mexico still lacks enough farm-to-
market roads.

A growing middle class in cities and larger
towns buys more newspapers and magazines each
year. But in the rural areas, a population
boom negates any lowering of illiteracy,
whereas adverse terrain still nestles dozens
and dozens of semi-isolated settlements. But
cheap, transistor radio receivers are sold
where seemingly no other modern conveniences
are. Radio stations are linking the semi-
isolated homes to the urban portions of Mexico.
More than four million Mexican homes use their
radios daily.

XEW'S IMPACT. Through the years, the station
drawing the largest radio audiences before
and since the advent of television[17] is XEW,
with 200,000 watts of power. Its spot at 900
kilocycles on the dial is familiar to millions
of Mexicans, and to tens of thousands of Central Americans as far away as Costa Rica, plus
thousands of Spanish-speaking Americans along
our own side of the United States-Mexican
border.

XEW's programs are echoed across Mexico not
only directly with its powerful 200 kilowatt
transmitter, but also with its own network of
satellites or repeater transmitters: XEWA in
San Luis Potosí, XEWK in Guadalajara, XEWB in
Veracruz, and XEWM in Monterrey.

In addition, its programs are duplicated on
shortwave from XEWW in Mexico City and on the
frequency-modulation band via XEW-FM.

XEW's news roundups are well edited and professionally announced. Its documentaries on
world affairs help Mexicans understand Cold
War news.

RADIO NETWORKS. Despite XEW's power and popularity, 29 other standard-band radio stations
vie for listeners in Mexico City, and throughout Mexico there are 385 standard-band (550
to 1600 kc.) stations, as compared with only
215 radio stations in 1953. In addition there
are several shortwave and FM transmitters. A
majority of the provincial stations are independent but 50 are fulltime affiliates of the
Radio Cadena Nacional or RCN network, and
several others carry a few RCN programs under

contract. The other large network, RPM or
Radio Programas de México, has more than 70
affiliates, plus several part-time associated
stations.

In television, Mexico City's "Big Three,"
XEW-TV Channel 2, XHTV Channel 4, and XHGC
Channel 5 dominate commercially. One edu-
cational noncommercial TV station, XEIPN
Channel 11, is owned and operated by the
National Polytechnical Institute (Instituto
Politécnico Nacional). Begun from spacious
studios at the IPN campus on March 2, 1959,
XEIPN-TV is Latin America's first full-time
educational television station.

Two of Mexico City's three commercial
channels have satellite repeater channels
in the surrounding states. XEW-TV, which
broadcasts on Channel 2 in the Federal District, repeats on Channel 4 in the state of
Jalisco, Channel 13 in Aguascalientes, and
Channels 3 and 9 at a high pass in the mountains south of Mexico City, echoing the
signal to several states, and as far away as
the Veracruz coast.

Away from the Federal District, 17 other
TV stations telecast from 13 provincial cities
in almost every sector of the republic,
giving Mexico a total of 26 channels (counting XEW-TV's and XHTV's repeaters).

TRAINING NEWSMEN. Mexico's growing press and
broadcasting industries have demanded trained
newsmen, a factor prompting the National
University of Mexico to initiate in 1951 its
School of Social and Political Sciences, one
of whose four degree programs leads to the
Licentiate in Journalism after five years of
study. Newspaper, magazine, radio, and television writing, reporting, and editing are
included in the required course work.

Similarly, the Women's University in Mexico
City for several years has offered a three-
year course leading to a certificate in
journalism. The University of Veracruz maintains a school of journalism. In addition,
in Mexico City there are three trade schools
for mass media students. But in general, a
majority of the newsmen in Mexico, whether
secondary school or university graduates in a
traditional discipline, still begin their
careers by apprenticing to veteran reporters
or editors.

UPGRADING THE NEWS. The professional organizations of editors, of news photographers,
of broadcasters, of announcers, of advertising executives, and of public relations
executives have all stressed the need to
raise standards of daily practice in the mass

media. To some extent, this goal is being
accomplished, though the picture for Mexico
as a whole is uneven.

As for free flow of information, both for
foreign correspondents and for Mexican newsmen, there is official freedom of the press.
The pressures--for they do exist--are covert,
indirect, and often at the source. That is,
no governmental instrumentality prevents the
printing or airing of news. But sometimes
the source of major news, governmental officials, will tell little or nothing of a negative nature regarding their stewardships of
office.

Mexico's federal government, in its zealous-
ness to encourage the growth of its domestic
periodicals, went so far as to introduce a
10 per cent tax on foreign publications coming
into the country, early in 1962.[18] But soon
even Mexican magazine publishers joined their
U.S. counterparts in protesting, and the tax
was repealed.

Thus, in a world pressured by the Cold War,
Mexico remains a good neighbor, with news
from and to the United States flowing in
healthy quantity and quality.

Despite 50 years of political, economic,
and social progress, Mexico still struggles
against a too rapidly rising population, large
pockets of illiteracy, poverty, and isolation.
The republic's mass media have helped integrate, stimulate, and incorporate the lowest
economic sectors into the national way of
life. Most important of all, from a journalistically point of view, these media do inform
Mexico each day of what is happening in the
nation and the world.

Central America

Central America is comprised, politically, of five republics (geographically, a sixth, Panama, sometimes is added).

Three of the five countries south of Mexico--Guatemala, Honduras, and Nicaragua--are rich in anthropological and agricultural treasure. But in terms of mass media development, the other two--Costa Rica and El Salvador--stand out.

COSTA RICA. Costa Rica enjoys the highest proportion of newspaper readers and radio listeners in Central America; not surprising for the republic which leads the area in literacy, with a rate of 85 per cent. Costa Ricans are almost all Spanish-speaking, contrasted with Guatemala, where two-thirds of the people are Maya Indians.

Costa Rica's total population in 1962 was one million, 150,000 of whom live in the capital city of San José. A democratic republic of small-farm landowners with a tradition of press freedom, Costa Rica contrasts sharply with its neighbor to the north, Nicaragua, in such matters.[1]

Six San José dailies dominate the nation journalistically: Diario de Costa Rica (AM, circulation 22,000); La Hora (PM, circulation 14,000), owned by former President of Costa Rica Otilio Ulate, who also publishes Diario de Costa Rica; La Nación (AM, circulation 36,000), edited by Ricardo Castro Beeche, former president of the Inter-American Press Association; La Prensa Libre (PM, circulation 20,000); La República (AM, circulation 17,000); and Ultimas Noticias (PM, circulation 12,000), published by the same company which operates República.[2]

In broadcasting, station TIW represents Costa Rica's most popular radio outlet, and the key station of the republic's only network, the CRC or Circuito Radio City, with affiliates in three cities away from San José (in Puntarenas, Ciudad Quezada, and Golfito).[3] TIW newscasts are well edited, frequently aired, and contain a balanced summary of national and world news.

Television centers in San José though provincial towns are served through booster transmitters throughout the central portion of the republic.

San José offers the widest choice of foreign and domestic magazines of any Central American city.

EL SALVADOR. El Salvador is in second place in Central America in terms of literacy and in terms of newspaper sales and radio receiver distribution. Through an intensive adult literacy campaign since 1949, Salvador is now 50 per cent literate. Its capital, San Salvador, boasts what may be Central America's best edited newspaper, La Prensa Gráfica (AM, circulation weekdays 45,000 and Sundays 64,000). José Dutriz, publisher, in 1960 arranged for Howard Taylor of the Copley Newspaper Chain of California and Illinois to modernize the typography and make up of this daily.[4]

Though not as influential as La Prensa Gráfica, another Salvadoran daily, Diario Latino (AM, circulation 17,500) circulates in most of the tiny republic's towns as well as the capital city.

The only Salvadoran radio network, RCY or Radio Cadena YSU, uses station YSU in San Salvador as key outlet, with affiliates in San Miguel and Santa Ana. YSU-TV Channel 4 reaches the entire republic with its video signals.

GUATEMALA. Guatemala was the home of the first newspaper in Central America, the Gazeta de Goathemala, which appeared in 1729, only seven years after newspapers originated in Mexico City, a vital seat of Spanish empire.

Guatemala City's leading daily, El Imparcial (PM, circulation 31,000), during the pro-Communist regime of President Jacobo Arbenz, ousted in 1954, struggled for press freedom. Currently under President Miguel Ydígoras, Imparcial has published as much information as governmental censorship will allow. The Ydígoras regime has been under various attacks by Castro agents from Cuba and leftwing Guatemalans. Anti-Red Imparcial has maintained its nation's security interests plus its journalistic mission to inform its readers as conditions allow.

Radio looms large as an information medium in Guatemalan cities and larger towns, but in the villages--backbone of the republic--it has not reached its potential because tens of thousands of Indians speak their own dialects instead of Spanish, language of the broadcasts. Two commercial and one government television stations compete in Guatemala City.

HONDURAS. Honduras suffers from widespread illiteracy and poverty. Hondurans also suffer from lack of much factual information about the events of the world. The press is entirely political. According to Dr. Mary Gardner of the University of Texas,[5] who taught journalism in Honduras during the summer of 1962, not a paper in this republic has a paid circulation of more than 10,000.

There are only five dailies, four in Tegucigalpa and one in San Pedro Sula. None of them truly can be termed a first-class newspaper. Foreign correspondents consider El Día (AM, circulation 10,000), somewhat independent, the most reliable of the five. El Cronista (circulation 9,000) subscribes to the Cuban press service, Prensa Latina, and runs pro-Communist news and views. It has the republic's only rotary press.

President Villeda Morales has maintained press freedom, despite the attacks and tensions of the pro-Castro and anti-U.S. elements. Two radio networks, Cadena HRN and Cadena Radio Centro, program news simultaneously and separately to Tegucigalpa and San Pedro Sula, Honduran urban centers.[6]

PANAMA. Though historically and politically Panama was the northwestern province of the South American republic of Colombia until its independence in 1903, geographically Panama is the tail of Central America. Its economy, culture, and political life center in the Canal Zone which bisects the Isthmus. And because the United States operates the canal, Panama City, adjacent to the Canal Zone and capital of the republic, is generally bilingual. Radio broadcasts are in Spanish but newspapers in English rival the Spanish-language dailies: the Star-Herald Company publishes both La Estrella and the Star & Herald. A rival company publishes both El Panama-América and The Panama American.

Television station RPC-TV Channel 4, operates in Panama City and Colón, with its booster station, Channel 12, repeating the programs in provincial cities.

NICARAGUA. Historically tragic is the press censorship and dictatorship of President Luis Somoza and his brother, General Anastasio Somoza, Jr., following the footsteps of their father, the late General Anastasio Somoza, Sr. The tragedy centers in the fact that beginning in 1912, for more than two decades, Nicaragua virtually was a protectorate of the United States. Our Marines occupied and ran the country until they were withdrawn in 1933.

With that legacy, it had been hoped that Nicaragua would maintain civil liberties, including press freedom, once the republic got on its own feet. But in 1937, General Somoza converted Nicaragua into a dictatorship, and press freedom vanished. Today his sons maintain a showcase for foreigners, allowing one opposition paper, La Prensa of Managua,[7] to operate, but whenever reports get severely critical of the Somoza regime, Prensa editors return to jail.

Five other Nicaraguan dailies exist, but only La Prensa can be considered newsworthy or reliable for foreign correspondents, Nicaraguans, or even officials in Managua who tire of their own governmental propaganda.

One glimmer of hope came in 1960, when the Somoza regime decided to allow Marvin Alisky to organize a School of Journalism. Early in 1963, that school was still open, helped by visiting Professor Fred Marbut of Pennsylvania State University, under a Fulbright grant.[8]

In broadcasting, the Somozas control the only television station, housed with their radio station in the building of their chief newspaper, Novedades. Newscasts are strictly censored. If a free election's results in 1963 are really honored, a thaw in the mass media frozen controls may yet take place.

The Caribbean

Crossroads Caribbean includes the big negative factor of Castro's Communist regime in Cuba. (Cuban mass media will be covered in a separate section.) But the area also contains the journalistically positive factor of Puerto Rico.

PUERTO RICO. Since 1952, the former U.S. territory has been the Commonwealth of Puerto Rico, semiautonomous entity--neither a state nor a territory--whose residents are U.S. citizens.

Puerto Rican radio and television stations are licensed by the Federal Communications Commission in Washington and must maintain the same standards as stations of mainland United States.

Similarly, Puerto Rican newspapers utilize the Audit Bureau of Circulation, New York advertising agencies, and the U.S. postal service.

But Puerto Rico is not only part of the United States, but also part of Latin America. Though somewhat bilingual, Puerto Ricans mainly speak Spanish. Capital city San Juan does boast of an English-language tabloid daily, the San Juan Star (founded in 1959, circulation 12,000). But its two "national" (island-wide) dailies are in Spanish: El Imparcial (AM with 68,000 circulation but 80,000 on Tuesdays), and El Mundo (AM with 70,000 circulation but 84,000 on Tuesdays). For Puerto Rico, the Tuesday edition resembles the larger mainland Sunday issue.

Mundo also operates radio station WKAQ, founded in 1922, key outlet for a four-station network. Mundo's television station, WKAQ-TV, serves as key outlet for an island-wide three-station video network. With a literacy rate of better than 80 per cent, Puerto Rico has good readership of its few good newspapers, its magazines, plus the many mainland U.S. periodicals. Its radio and television receiver distribution is high, with most Puerto Rican homes listening to daily newscasts.

Of the three island republics of the Caribbean--Cuba, Haiti, and the Dominican Republic--Cuba has lost its republican status, and Haiti has the barest semblance of mass media develop-

ment or normal governmental machinery. A French-speaking, Negro nation, Haiti is better than 90 per cent illiterate, has Latin America's poorest distribution of radio receivers, and suffers under the dictatorship of President François Duvalier. Haiti apparently cannot hope for either press freedom or a press which merits much mention.

DOMINICAN REPUBLIC. But its neighbor, the Dominican Republic, after three decades of the dictatorship of General Rafael Trujillo, during 1962 regained many of its freedoms and some of its self-confidence. The December, 1962 election of President Juan Bosch was the first free balloting Dominicans have enjoyed in thirty-nine years. Genuine freedom of the press has come to this nation for the first time. El Caribe, AM daily with 34,000 circulation, published and edited by Germán Ornes, exiled by dictator Trujillo but now back in Santo Domingo, is the republic's leading newspaper.

JAMAICA. The Dominion of Jamaica, part of the British Commonwealth, lies south of Cuba, and serves as a listening post in the Caribbean for news correspondents, similar to those in Key West, Florida, and in Puerto Rico. Jamaica's influential daily, The Daily Gleaner, circulates 60,000 mornings and 65,000 Saturdays.

Cuba

Cuba's seven million population on an island 800 miles long but only 25 to 100 miles wide would seem to rate more news coverage in the United States and Europe than even gigantic nations such as Brazil. The reason: a Communist regime in Havana, only 90 miles south of Key West, Florida; Cuba has become the branch office in the Western Hemisphere for expansive, aggresive Communism.

But Cuba's lack of a truly independent press did not begin with the harsh controls of Fidel Castro. During almost all of its existence as a republic, Cuba has had a bribed and corrupted press, perhaps the most bribe-ridden press in Latin American history.[1]

UNHAPPY PRESS HISTORY. During four centuries of rule by Spain as a colony, Cuba never knew a free press, nor much of any kind of political freedom. In the Spanish-American War of 1898, the United States freed Cuba from Spain, then occupied the island to clean up disease and put the Cubans on their feet financially and politically. During 1899-1901 Cuba was run by American generals. In 1902, U.S. Governor-General Leonard Wood turned the island over to the first elected Cuban president, Tomás Estrada Palma, as the island became an independent nation.

But by 1906, chaos had returned, Estrada Palma was censoring the press, and Cuban soldiers held back street rioters. The United States returned a caretaker government through 1908. Again in 1909 Cuba shakily began its second adventure in self-government. By 1919, it had become accepted practice for the governmental ministries to pay reporters to withhold the most unfavorable reports of these agencies.[2]

In the 1920's, 1930's, and 1940's, bribery alternated with overt press censorship, as various regimes tried first the carrot, then the whip; first, the lure dangled in front to make the mule trot, then the lash to speed him up by inflicting pain.

When Fulgencio Batista grabbed power in 1952, he promised to end the widespread corruption of the Carlos Prío regime. But before long, dozens of newspaper, magazine, and radio "reporters" came around to ministries on Saturdays to receive their checks as "public relations consultants." The botella (bottle)

system of handouts returned in full, the subsidies being in money, not liquor, despite the slang name for it.

In 1956, Havana, with a population of one million, actually had 21 daily newspapers, 5 television stations, and 32 standard-band commercial radio stations, the most competitive mass media city in the world. Not even the London or New York areas--whose greater metropolitan areas each totaled nine times as many inhabitants--could support that many dailies and stations, with a higher level of industrialization and much higher advertising rates.

Havana did it with undercover subsidies to many of the media or to their working newsmen.

When Fidel Castro came to power January 1, 1959, he promised to end such prostituted journalism. But within a few months, his own intolerance proved to be worse.

Hoy, the official Communist party organ, is the ideological style sheet for the other papers in Cuba.

In 1959, Castro's voice for his revolutionary movement, Revolución, created when he came to power, engaged in polemic arguments with the Communist daily, Hoy. But by 1960, the non-Reds and the anti-Reds were being forced out of Cuban public life and into jails.[3]

In 1956, Havana had 21 dailies, including a Chinese-language and two English-language papers. When Castro came to power in 1959, Havana had 16 dailies. In 1960, Prime Minister Castro supressed any semblance of independence remaining among Cuban papers. In November, 1961, Castro closed two more dailies, Prensa Libre and Combate, leaving only three dailies which antedate the Castro regime plus the two which he encouraged to begin in 1959.

Prensa Libre and Combate were suspended to "conserve paper, ink, machinery, and manpower to turn out more books," the official announcement stated. These books and pamphlets were to be distributed anywhere in Latin America Castro agents could spread their propaganda.

In 1963, Havana has five dailies:

Hoy--Communist party daily. It has become the official organ of the Cuban government.

Revolución--original voice of Castro's revolutionary movement. During 1961 and 1962 this daily gradually lost its leading position to Hoy. In 1960, Revolución's non-Communists, already in a minority on the staff, were replaced with Communist newsmen. In 1962, the former official organ of Castro dropped the line in its masthead proclaiming it to be the "Newspaper of the 26th of July Movement." Today it takes its editorial clues from Hoy.

El Mundo--in the early 1950's, Mundo had been one of the handful of Cuban dailies journalistically respectable, free of the stigma of bribery. But in 1955, a few Mundo reporters began to accept fees from governmental ministries, tarnishing the otherwise good paper's reputation among those in the know. In February, 1960, the Castro dictatorship seized this daily. Today Mundo echoes Hoy though it does carry classified ads--the only private-enterprise advertising in Cuba. Governmental agencies and businesses, however, do use ads.

La Tarde and La Calle--two inconsequential evening dailies, following the Hoy line. Late in 1962, the latter missed a few issues.[4]

Of the famous Cuban magazines of the pre-Castro era, such as Carteles, all have gone out of existence except Bohemia, seized and now published as a pro-Castro magazine. A

rival Bohemia Libre, published in exile by anti-Castro staffers of the original magazine, has distributed in the Caribbean from Caracas, Venezuela, and from Miami, Florida.

Castro's news agency, Prensa Latina, disseminates Cuban propaganda and news where it can. PL serves a Communist paper in Mexico, another in Chile, a pro-Castro paper in Honduras, and gives its copy away free to a few radio stations outside Cuba. Prensa Latina offices have been closed in Argentina, Brazil, Venezuela, Peru, El Salvador, Costa Rica, and Panama. In the United States, Prensa Latina and its chief correspondent, Francisco Portela, were fined $2,000 on federal indictments for failure to register as agents of a foreign power.[5]

PAPERS IN EXILE. In June, 1962 the Cuban press in exile lost a leader when the Miami, Florida, edition of Avance ceased publication after two years of existence. Jorge Zayas, editor of Avance, had his Havana edition suspended in January, 1960 when he refused to publish the footnotes or "coletillas" added by pro-Castro printers, labeling as "untrue" news and editorials critical of Castro.[6]

Also ceasing operations in Miami in 1962 were two other Havana dailies in exile, El Mundo and Diario de la Marina. The plant of the former continues to run a Castro paper in Havana. The latter was considered Cuba's leading daily before 1959.[7] The former English-language Times of Havana late in 1962 resumed publishing in exile in Florida.

PERSECUTED FOREIGN CORRESPONDENTS. Almost all of the foreign correspondents who were in Havana prior to 1959 have been forced out of Cuba, many of them first being jailed and harassed. Not only American correspondents for Time, Newsweek, the New York Times, the NBC network, the AP, and UPI, but also British correspondents, such as John Bland of Reuters, have been jailed, then expelled from Cuba, for writing candid reports.[8]

GOVERNMENT BY TELEVISION. Before Castro came to power, Cuba had radio and television receivers and transmitters in every sector of the island. In many respects, Cuba was underdeveloped, the showcase of Havana not being typical of the remainder of the republic. Despite one of the higher per capita incomes among Latin American republics, the good standing was relative. A majority of the homes outside of those in Havana did not have running water, and in the typical small town, a Cuban house had a dirt floor and unscreened windows. But Cubans did possess radios. And every public gathering place had its TV set.

The Castro regime has made good use of television and radio to issue orders, to inflame the population, and to project the charismatic personality of Castro. The bearded dictator's four-hour telecasts in a loose sense gave Latin America its first government-by-video.

Many of the former radio and TV properties were dismantled. But the leading networks for television and radio, CMQ and CMQ-TV, have become almost literally the voices of Castro. With monitoring stations in Key West, Florida, videotape of these Havana telecasts have become familiar to U.S. viewers watching NBC, CBS, or ABC in the United States.

In radio, U. S. freedom broadcasters from Swan Island in the Caribbean and from Florida beam anti-Castro attacks into Cuba. And conversely, a powerful Cuban transmitter--the 50,000-watt CMQ--airs programs 24 hours a day not only to Cubans but to listeners elsewhere in the Caribbean.[9]

NEWS FROM CUBA. Havana's radio version of the late show blares into Key West, Florida, to the listening posts operated by the Associated Press and United Press International, where excerpts are soon on their way via teletypes to newspaper and station clients all across the United States.

As for correspondents inside Cuba, the United States must rely mostly on British, Canadian, French, Swiss, and other newsmen. The seriousness of the problem was underlined on the night of December 2, 1961, when Castro "unmasked." According to UPI, Castro said he had been a dedicated Communist since his college days but that he concealed his views to seize power. This UPI report was seized upon by all those in the U.S. who criticized any earlier United States relations with Castro.

Lost in the uproar was the report from the Associated Press for the same evening, which said:

Fidel Castro, proclaiming "I believe absolutely in Marxism," admitted publicly today he was leading Cuba down the road to Communism. "I am a Marxist-Leninist and will be one until the day I die," the Cuban Prime Minister declared in a midnight television speech...Castro said last night that until a few years ago he was "biased against communism because of imperialist propaganda." He said the change

in his political thinking began after he seized power.

Thus the AP report contradicted the UPI report. Later research demonstrated that the AP report, based on an actual transcript of the Castro speech, was the correct version. The garbled UPI version was never corrected and still is being cited by many in the United States as "proof" of the way Castro grabbed power.[10]

Castro's newspaper Revolución also carried this speech on December 2, including this sentence:

Cuando ya nosotros salimos de la Universidad, en el caso particular mío, ya realmente yo estaba grandemente influido-- no voy a decir que era un marxista-leninista--ni mucho menos.

(Translation: When we left the university (in 1950), in my own particular case I had been greatly influenced. But I will not say I was a Marxist-Leninist, not by a long shot.)

Elsewhere in this same text, also monitored and checked by the U.S. Department of State, Castro said:

Can I call myself a full-fledged revolutionary at the time of the 26th of July? No, I cannot call myself a full-fledged revolutionary. Could I call myself a full-fledged revolutionary the first of January 1959 (when he took power)? No, I could call myself almost a full-fledged revolutionary.

Thus American readers, listeners, televiewers, commentators, and political leaders had a "choice" between the correct AP report and the incorrect UPI report. Americans have been quoting one or the other ever since, depending on what they know, what they are trying to prove, or what version they happen to have seen.

All of which underscores the vital need for accurate reporting from Latin America, which censorship--in the case of the Cuban dictatorship--can impede.

Cubans inside their island nation do not get much accurate news of the outside world. But people away from Cuba apparently do not get enough news about what is happening in Cuba, either. The political tragedy of Cuba has been compounded by the journalistic obstacles.

South America

During the past decade newspapers throughout South America have greatly increased their offerings and now appeal to a much broader base of the population. Newspaper reading has been gaining popularity meanwhile, and circulations have grown--rather slowly--but steadily.

Argentina

Agitated Argentina is the alliterative description of this once-great nation, now reduced to tragic, uncertain day-to-day expectations that civil peace and press freedom will prevail.

Before 1943, Argentina led the remainder of Latin America in standard of living, in the excellence of its periodicals and schools, and similar indices. In June, 1943, a rightwing military group of colonels grabbed power, with Juan Perón manipulating as part of the junta. In 1945, he had himself "elected" President with force and gave Latin America its first genuine totalitarian regime. (Castro has given Cuba the second totalitarian government). Dictators have been numerous in Latin America; they traditionally have censored the press into remaining uncritical, while they looted the treasury of the countries concerned. But totalitarianism goes beyond; as the name implies--as Stalin, Hitler, and Mussolini perfected it--total control obtains. Certain music must not be played on the radio; certain jokes must not be printed; specific clothes fashions are prohibited--total cultural control.

When Perón was ousted in 1955, Argentines hoped that after a caretaker government brought back constitutional norms, press and other freedoms would restore this republic of one million square miles to its place as a Latin American leader.

Argentina has salvaged a few items meriting pride. With a literacy rate of better than 90 per cent, it still leads other Latin America republics in terms of potential readership. Capital city Buenos Aires still boasts two of the best edited dailies in the world, La Prensa and La Nación. And the Argentine news agency, Saporiti, founded in 1900, is the oldest national or regional wire service in Latin America. (Another agency, Telenoticiosa Americana, also serves Argentine mass media.)

But the feeling of stability in everyday life which Argentina enjoyed for most of this century before 1943 has not returned. The 1963 Argentine mood is panic.[1] Disorder mounts: economic, political, social. There are street riots in front of factories whose machinery is falling apart. Argentina is the only nation in the civilized world with a poorer ratio of automobiles per 1000 population today than in 1929.

Inflation cripples broadcasting quality. Newsprint costs have forced smaller papers, such as Rosario's Crónica and La Tribuna, to cut their daily editions to six pages.[2]

In the first flush of optimism in the post-Perón era of 1958, Argentine leadership assumed that the 150 dailies, circulating two million copies, would prosper. But neither newspaperdom nor the Argentine economy in general has recovered from the Perón looting.

Buenos Aires maintains six journalism schools, not just for the six million residents of Buenos Aires but for the entire republic of 22 million. Yet the quality of reporting in Argentina is steadily declining. With the exception of a few great papers, such as La Prensa, Argentine dailies need to train anew most of their newsmen. The editorial workers in the 30-40 year age group worked or were schooled (indoctrinated) during the 1943-55 Perón dictatorship.

Journalism under Perón attracted political extremists and opportunists who exploited the press for personal gain. Some newsmen became messengers, not reporters, carrying governmental propagandic releases from ministries to editors' desks for copy processing.

Many professional newspapermen of the pre-Perón era have now retired and their replacements are not journalists in the oldtime Argentine tradition. In the 1930's Argentine newsmen would shake their heads sadly when they learned that certain stringers in Central America and Cuba received money for not reporting unfavorable governmental news. Such a debasement of journalism could not occur in Argentina! Today it does.

As in many parts of Latin America beset by ruinous inflation--such as Brazil, Bolivia, and Chile--in Argentina too, newsmen are forced to "moonlight," that is, take two or three jobs.[3]

Before the Perón era, a professional Argentine newsman would never consider taking an extra job on a rival paper, or at a magazine, radio, or television station whose editorial policies contradict the parent medium's principles. Yet in 1963 there are Argentine reporters working for rival morning and evening dailies, or other combinations with just as obvious a conflict of interests.

BUENOS AIRES DAILIES. The capital city of Buenos Aires, with more than 6 million of the republic's 22 million citizens, has 12 Spanish-language dailies plus 8 foreign-language dailies, more than one-sixth of all the daily papers in the republic.

Cosmopolitan Buenos Aires has dailies in German, French, Italian, Yiddish, Polish, and combination Arabic-Spanish for its Lebanese groups. The English-language Buenos Aires Herald (circulation 15,000) has been publishing since 1876. There are rival German-language dailies but only one in Italian, yet one-third of all residents of Buenos Aires are Italian in origin; they are better integrated and more hispanicized than are those of German origin.

Argentine circulation leader, La Razón (PM and Sunday daily with 438,000 circulation) carries no editorial page.

Clarín (AM, circulation 328,000 weekdays and 345,000 Sundays) tries to maintain political independence, but unlike Razón does carry an editorial page.

When the government disposed of Perón-seized papers, Democracia (AM, circulation 155,000) was purchased by private interests, as was Crítica (PM, circulation 113,000). Another Buenos Aires daily in the same category, when salvaged from the Peronistas, was purchased by its employees. Thus Noticias Gráficas (PM, circulation 100,000) became a cooperative. Once again Peronist, Democracia closed down in August, 1962.

La Nación (AM, weekly circulation 235,000 and 300,000 Sundays), founded in 1870--only one year later than the more famous La Prensa-- is edited by the able Juan Valmaggio.

LA PRENSA

ITS STORY IN BRIEF. This well-known Argentine daily, since its founding in 1869 by Dr. José Clemente Paz, has been recognized throughout the world as the greatest Spanish-language newspaper and one of the best in any language. Its first issue summarized the newspaper's ideals with these five words: "Verdad, Honor, Libertad, Progreso, Civilización."

Briefly, here is the story of La Prensa: founded 1869 in Buenos Aires; published continuously until finally taken over by Perón's government; became a "Peronista" organ and was so published until Perón was ousted and the newspaper was returned to the Paz family on Dec. 21, 1955; it resumed publication in its old tradition on Feb. 3, 1956. (This Feb. 3 issue of the paper has already become a collector's item.)

In 1898 the founder's son, Ezequial P. Paz, took over at the age of 27. For 45 years as publisher and chief editor of La Prensa, he was not absent a single day from his office. He retired in 1943, and was succeeded by Alberto Gainza Paz, the son of the founder's daughter.

After Juan Perón took over the Argentine government in the mid-1940's, a campaign to silence La Prensa and other anti-government papers began.

Between Jan. 26, 1951 when La Prensa's free voice was silenced and Dec. 21, 1955 when the paper was restored to its old owners, it had published under the direction of the Peronista regime. This paper which before its captivity by Perón had circulated some 400,000 copies daily, sank to less than 200,000 under its Peronist management; and probably a third to a half of this circulation was forced sub-scriptions to government offices.

With news replacing the traditional classi-fied advertisements on its front page, La Prensa reappeared on Feb. 3, 1956 under the direction of Alberto Gainza Paz.

La Prensa is still a great morning daily of 300,000 circulation, but no longer runs the thorough, hard-hitting editorials of yester-year. The generally chaotic political situa-tion seems to have confused even Argentina's most respected observers.

MAGAZINES. Argentina's most important magazines are published in Buenos Aires. The weekly news magazine Veritas, published and edited by Francisco Rizzuto, Jr., stresses business re-ports and hemispheric events, with little attention given to stories from outside North or South America. Veritas' format resembles U.S. News & World Report.

Vea y Lea, another news weekly magazine, stresses sports and recreation and utilizes a full-page cover photograph. Hogar is another news magazine, among the 800 weekly magazines and newspapers of Argentina. All but fifty of these periodicals have small circulations.[4]

BROADCASTING. Like the press, Argentine radio and television stations have suffered first under Peronist censorship, then under post-Perón austerity and inflation.

Newsreel cameras and microphones have become shop worn but are being patched rather than replaced. The high level of professional polish to Argentine broadcast productions has suffered in the face of rising prices for equipment and curtailed net profits.[5]

The Radio Splendid network, formerly oper-ated by the Razón newspaper corporation, now as an independent corporation operates Station LS4 in Buenos Aires, plus provincial affili-ates (usually using the word "Splendid" in their title) in 14 cities and towns.

Radio Mitre in Buenos Aires is key station for a network of radio stations in 14 provin-cial cities, including Rosario, Córdoba, and Mendoza.

Radio Rivadavia in Buenos Aires heads a network of stations in 15 provincial cities. It has joint ownership with Radio Belgrano of Buenos Aires, which often feeds the same network. The hookup itself is called the Belgrano Network.

In television, four Buenos Aires commercial channels--7, 9, 11, and 13--vie vigorously for good audience ratings. Channel 8 in the provincial city of Mar del Playa can be picked up by some residents of the southern portions of Buenos Aires. An outstanding provincial television station is Channel 10 in Córdoba.

HOPES AND FEARS. Looking back on its proud pre-Perón history, Argentina hopes to main-tain its few quality mass media and expand as the economic and political pressures will allow. But in 1963, fears outweigh hopes in Buenos Aires, as inflation, unemployment, and political extremists combine to threaten the free institutions, including press and broadcasting, of this literate, modern nation.

One can imagine that in the not too distant future La Prensa, the paper which once had the hardest hitting editorials in South America, will become completely subordinated to pressures as so many other organs have.

Brazil

Big Brazil merits far more extensive news coverage in the United States and in other major nations than it usually gets. With a population estimated at the beginning of 1963 at 74 million, Brazil is the eighth largest[1] nation on earth, ranking right after China, India, U.S.S.R., the United States, Japan, Pakistan, and Indonesia.

In land area, Brazil looms as an even bigger world power, fifth among all the countries of the world. Only the Soviet Union, Canada, China, and the Unites States--in that order--have a larger area. The U.S. surpassed the South American giant only by making Alaska a state. Brazil is still larger than continental United States, or Australia, or mainland China without Tibet. With one-sixth the population, Brazil has two million more square miles than India. It occupies nearly half the surface of South America with a coastline 4,600 miles long.

One of the twenty-two states of the federal republic of Brazil, Amazonas, is larger than Alaska. Three other Brazilian states are bigger than Texas and six are larger than California. Bahia, only the sixth largest of the twenty-one Brazilian states, equals France in size.

Fortunately for foreign news correspondents, most Brazilians live on or near the Atlantic Ocean from Fortaleza in the north to Porto Alegre in the far south. Neither the bulk of the people nor their mass media have moved deep inland, though the central portions of the nation are beginning to open up. For almost 200 years, from 1762 into 1960, Rio de Janeiro had been the national capital. In April, 1960, Brasília, 650 miles northwest of Rio, became the new federal capital, a move designed to help develop the interior of Brazil.[2]

THE NEWS CENTERS: RIO AND SÃO PAULO. Brasília soon acquired a newspaper, magazine, radio and television station, and cable and telegraph offices. But almost three years later, it is still a part-time capital.[3] Rio de Janeiro remains Brazil's news capital, followed closely by the republic's largest city, São Paulo.

With more than four million population, São Paulo prides itself on being one of the fastest-growing cities on earth. It overtook Rio several years ago, not only in inhabitants but also in industrial tempo. Capital city of the state of the same name, São Paulo's mayors and governors figure prominently in national politics and several of them have been presidents of the republic or cabinet members over a period of decades.

Leading newspaper of São Paulo, and often cited as Brazil's top paper, O Estado de São Paulo, a morning daily, circulates 130,000 weekdays and 180,000 Sundays. Thorough in its national news coverage, Estado is found in Brazilian university and school libraries and the offices of clipping services. Its publisher, Júlio de Mesquita, active in the Inter-American Press Association, keeps a large, energetic staff busy.[4] Founded in 1875, Estado has long enjoyed a good journalistic reputation, despite governmental pressures on the press during the crises of recent years.

Folha da Manhã, a morning daily of 96,000 circulation, Folha da Tarde, an afternoon daily of 160,000 circulation, and Folha da Noite, an evening daily of 80,000 are owned by the same publishing corporation, but are operated as three separate São Paulo dailies, rather than as merely three editions of the same paper.

Other prominent paulista dailies are A Gazeta, afternoon paper, and Diário de São Paulo, morning paper, each with a circulation of 100,000. A Gazeta Esportiva, a daily devoted to sports news, circulates 180,000. São Paulo also has six other Portuguese-language dailies, Portuguese being the national language, plus a daily in German, one in Italian, and one in Japanese. The state of São Paulo has the largest number of residents of Japanese origin in Latin America.

Rio de Janeiro, still the cultural capital of Brazil, with a population of 3,225,000, supports sixteen Portuguese-language dailies, plus the English-language Brazil Herald, a 12-page morning tabloid, with 10,000 circulation. Most of the other dailies range in circulation from 10,000 to 100,000. Largest Rio daily and largest newspaper in Brazil is O Globo, with a circulation of 277,000. Globo's treasurer and assistant publisher, Herbert Moses, for more than three decades has been an active leader in the Brazilian Press Association (Asociação Brasileira de Imprensa).[5]

Two Rio dailies, Diário da Noite, a late-afternoon-early evening paper with 90,000 circulation, and O Jornal, which circulates 50,000 mornings, are members of the Diários Associados newspaper chain, headed by Francisco de Assis Chateaubriand.[6]

Until 1959, Assis Chateaubriand single-handedly remained Brazil's top Press Lord, directing a mass media empire of 31 newspapers, 12 television stations, 22 radio stations, four magazines, and a news agency. But in 1959, he set up a Board of Directors to control 49 per cent of the stock now, and who will control the other 51 per cent after his death. Through 1962, his sons, Gilberto and Fernando, and his two top executives, Edmundo Monteiro and João Calmon, have been locked in legal battle over the arrangements. Assis Chateaubriand, born in 1891, no longer directs his publishing-broadcasting chain personally.

Luta Democrática ("Democratic Struggle"), a Communist daily in Rio, fills its front page with five to eight pictures. Its chief antagonist, Tribuna da Imprensa, rightwing anti-Communist daily, whose 30,000 circulation almost matches the Communist paper, was published and edited by Carlos Lacerda until he became governor of the state of Guanabara (former Federal District surrounding Rio de Janeiro until the federal capital and its surrounding district were moved to Brasília in 1960).

Correio da Manhã, an AM Rio daily with 60,000 circulation, is a quality paper with serious news coverage. Two other Rio AM dailies, Diário de Noticias (80,000 circulation) and Jornal do Brasil (54,000 circulation) heretofore left of center and neutralist in the Cold War, in 1962 became critical of Castro's Cuba and the U.S.S.R. and editorially sympathetic to the U.S.[7]

JOURNALISM EDUCATION. Diário Carioca, Rio AM with 60,000, has for one of its editors and columnists Danton Jobim, a poineer in journalism education in Brazil. A professor of journalism at the University of Brazil, Jobim has been a visiting professor of journalism at the University of Texas and the University of Paris, and the author of the standard history of Brazilian journalism.[8]

Dr. Fernando Tude de Souza, professor of journalism at both the University of Brazil and Catholic University, has also been director of the Rio office of the Fulbright Commission, bringing U.S. journalism professors to Brazil as visiting lecturers. Dr. Tude de Souza pioneered in the offering of course work in radio news in Brazil.[9]

At the Casper Libero School of Journalism of the Catholic University of São Paulo (Escola de Journalismo Casper Libero), graduating seniors are sought by publishers and broadcasters. In all, eight full schools of journalism now train Brazilians for mass media work.

BROADCASTING. Brazil has 500 radio stations compared with 300 daily newspapers. With 48 per cent of Brazilian adults illiterate, radio newscasts take on special importance in the dissemination of information.

Edmundo Monteiro, executive of the Assis Chateaubriand publishing-broadcasting chain, operates 12 TV stations and 22 radio stations as Emisoras Associadas.

The Rio daily O Globo operates one of the most news-prone radio stations in Brazil, Rádio Globo, often monitored by foreign correspondents for news tips.

Rádio Nacional, operated by the Ministry of the Interior and Justice, produces a half-hour daily of governmental news which all of Brazil's privately-owned, commercial radio stations must carry, under federal law. The idea behind this Hora do Brasil news roundup is to combat tendencies towards lack of information on the part of illiterate adults.

Television audiences have grown in the half dozen largest cities in recent years. By late 1962, TV-Tupi, a popular channel in Rio, had larger audiences than any of the radio stations at night.

In São Paulo, better than 94 per cent of the homes have radios and more than half have TV receivers.[10] Channel 5 has the largest audiences.

In Belo Horizonte, capital city of the state of Minas Gerais, except for the national capital of Brasília the most important inland city, as early as 1956 became a strong television center. Its TV-Itacolomi, popularly known simply as Channel 4, began to outdraw any radio station in the state, being topped in audience circulation only by the traditionally influential provincial paper, Estado de Minas.[11] In 1962, Channel 4 had a larger nightly audience than all of Belo Horizonte's radio stations combined.

Radiodifusora do Amazonas in the city of Manaus on the Amazon River, A Voz do Oeste in Cuiaba in the state of Mato Grosso, and stations in Recife, capital of the northeastern state of Pernambuco help diminish otherwise isolated communities from the news tempo of the nation.

MAGAZINES. O Cruzeiro, weekly news magazine
in the picture format of Life or Look in the
U.S., is not only Brazil's largest magazine
but the largest single magazine in Latin
America, with a circulation of 850,000. Of
that total, 600,000 copies in Portuguese are
sold weekly inside Brazil and 250,000 copies
in Spanish are sold biweekly in 16 other
Latin America republics.

When Life magazine in 1961 did a picture
feature on the slums or favelas of Rio, O
Cruzeiro retaliated by sending a reporter-
photographer team to New York to do a feature
on a Puerto Rican immigrant family in a slum
neighborhood.[12]

Another large-format pictorial weekly,
Manchete, also has Brazilian-wide popularity,
as does Selecções, the Portuguese-language
edition of The Reader's Digest.

Visão, a news magazine similar to Newsweek,
published biweekly in São Paulo, is part of
a hemispheric-wide Spanish-language magazine,
Visión, edited in New York and Mexico City.
Visão's editor, Hernane Tavares de Sa, is one
of Brazil's leading writers and intellectuals.

A Noite Ilustrada is a popular general interest weekly magazine.

Some Brazilian newspapers have Sunday-
supplement type magazines, but not necessarily
on Sunday. For example, Sincra, a magazine
section distributed with various papers all
over Brazil, appears with the Friday issue
of the Rio daily Correio da Manhã.

PRESS CENSORSHIP. Brazil enjoyed periods of
press freedom until the era of Getúlio Vargas,
whose dictatorship--mild by most standards--
began with the great economic depression of
1930 to 1945. During the term of President
Eurico Gaspar Dutra, 1945-50 (Brazilian presidential terms run five years), press freedom returned. A reformed Getúlio Vargas got
himself elected president again in 1950 for
the 1950-55 term but scandal involving his
administration drove him to suicide in 1954,
giving the republic a caretaker government
until the election of Juscelino Kubitschek
in 1955. Upon taking office in 1956, Kubitschek ended the press censorship which the
insecure interim government had imposed.[13]

In 1961 Jânio Quadros was inaugurated in
January and resigned in August, putting the
government in the hands of the vice-president,
João Goulart. The new liberal president and
a predominantly conservative Congress were
at odds, resulting in the creation by Congress
of the post of prime minister to divide the
executive powers.

During the turmoil of August and September,
1961, press censorship returned. Federal
authorities put a ban on outgoing dispatches
during four days at the end of August, in Rio
de Janeiro and the state of Guanabara which
surrounds it. The Inter-American Press
Association protested, pointing out that
Guanabara Governor Carlos Lacerda publicly
admitted that he cooperated in establishing
the news blackout.[14] During 1962 the press
remained free but pressured.

In August, 1962, foreign correspondents
were warned officially that they are subject
to expulsion from the country if they trans-
gress the Brazilian concept of unfair criticism
of the government in their reports. The warning was issued by the Chief of the Political
Police as the result of an article published
in the Paris daily Le Figaro about Brazil
playing in the soccer World Series in Chile.
The article stated that "seventy million
Brazilians prayed in voodoo temples that
Brazil would win the championship."[15]

Brazilian governmental officials are sensi-
tive to news dispatches referring to the
large number of Brazilians of Negro origin.
The republic prides itself on being free of
racial prejudice and references to voodoo
are considered derogatory.

Except for the staff of the Brazil Herald,
Brazilian newspaper, magazine, radio, and
television reporters and editors are all
Brazilians. Under the Brazilian Constitution,
promulgated in 1946, only a native-born
Brazilian can be employed as a journalist.
A federal decree in August, 1962 tightened
the interpretation of the law,[16] to eliminate
persons registering as newsmen but actually
engaged in other professions or trades and
merely trying to enjoy privileges accorded
bona fide newsmen. Brazilian journalists are
exempted from paying income tax and receive
a 50 per cent discount on Brazilian airlines.

Another bit of nationalism that made foreign
news correspondents nervous was the decision
in June, 1962 of the Chamber of Deputies,
lower house of the federal Congress, to require that foreign news agencies employ
Brazilian reporters to cover congressional
sessions.[17]

GENERAL OBSERVATIONS. Journalism Professor
and Diário Carioca editor Danton Jobim has
observed that Brazilian newspapermen often
feel a prominent person deserves respect,
that it becomes rude or showing a lack of
consideration to write about the physical

size, age, or other personal details of
certain public figures, even if these personalities are of marked interest to the
public.[18]

Of course, personal data are reported when
the newsworthy individual is a criminal or
in an accident. And little by little a
North Americanization of Brazilian journalism
is taking place, with more such details now
in evidence than formerly.

Brazilian journalism schools have helped

diminish the personalized, subjective,
literary reporting in favor of more objective
news coverage.

Brazil's economy during 1962 and into 1963
suffered the pressures of inflation, sharp
rises in the cost of living, and the various
tensions--political and social--such a situation provokes. So far, the traditional
Brazilian respect for individualism has pre-
vailed over governmental tendencies to restrict the flow of news.[19]

Chile

Chile is long and thin, shaped like a thermometer, and its climate acts accordingly. The farther south one goes to its tip, near the Antarctic, the colder the weather. The farther north, towards the equator, the warmer.

Chile stretches along the Pacific 2,600 miles, almost the distance from New York to San Francisco. Yet its average width is less than 100 miles. Five million of the 7,800,000 estimated 1963 population live in the Central Valley, less than 600 miles long.

Within this central region lie the major cities, the principal newspapers, radio and television stations, the industrial, commercial, and cultural leadership.

The rights of the press in Latin America often depend less on the laws than on the President's interpretation of these laws. Chile has a long tradition of freedom of the press. But the President's authority can bring subtle press restrictions if he chooses. President Jorge Alessandri, elected in 1958 for a six-year term ending in 1964, has been friendlier to the press than was his predecessor Carlos Ibáñez (president during 1952-58).

During the height of the Ibáñez regime, in 1956, under presidential prodding for "responsibility" in reporting, Congress passed the legal framework for a Colegio de Periodistas (Council of Journalists).[1] In August, 1958, this Council went into effect, with all reporters, writers, news photographers, and radio-TV newsmen being required to join. The Council is separate from regular professional newsmen's and publishers' associations.

PRESS COUNCIL. This Colegio has an elected National Council of ten newsmen, with headquarters in Santiago, maintaining a Register of Journalists and serving as a court of appeal for the regional councils in Antofagasta, Valparaiso, Santiago, and Concepción. These regional councils, after examining complaints for valid evidence, may admonish or even suspend for six months from the practice of journalism a newsman guilty of unethical conduct.

As the federal statute, giving the Council its power, does not spell out in detail what

constitutes unethical practice, a great responsibility has been placed upon the Regional Councils in policing their own members.[2] Defendants can appeal to the Supreme Court of Chile if they feel the Regional or National Councils have been unfair or arbitrary. The National Council may, by a two-thirds vote, remove the name of a newsman found guilty of unethical conduct, from the Register of Journalists, thereby barring him from holding a journalistic job.

To be eligible for the Journalists Register, an applicant must be 18 years of age or older and must not have a criminal record, must have completed his third year of humanities study beyond secondary school, and must be either a graduate of a recognized school of journalism or must have been a practicing newsman during three of the past ten years prior to the date of application.

A LITERATE NATION. Chile's population is almost 80 per cent literate. Therefore, even with a population of only 7.8 million, the 45 daily newspapers of the republic sell one million copies.

Although Chileans are a good reading public, attuned to world and national affairs, some of their officials are reluctant to hold news conferences. Often reporters write stories from government press releases handed out at the various ministries.

All but one of the eight dailies in the capital city of Santiago have known political orientation. Its most respected paper, the leading newspaper in Chile, is El Mercurio, an AM with 125,000 circulation weekdays and 175,000 Sundays. The publisher, Agustín Edwards, also publishes two afternoon tabloids in Santiago, an afternoon tabloid in Valparaiso, and a moring daily in Valparaiso-- five newsworthy papers.

Edwards' El Mercurio of Valparaiso, linked by name and appearance to the more prominent Mercurio in Santiago, has only 19,000 circulation daily but 31,000 Sundays. Steeped in prestige, the Valparaiso Mercurio was founded in 1827 and is the world's oldest daily newspaper in the Spanish language.

The Edwards Santiago afternoon tabloids are Ultimas Noticias, with a circulation of 50,000 and 65,000 Saturdays, and La Seguna with 45,000 circulation and 50,000 Saturday.

Edwards' PM tabloid in Valparaiso, La Estrella, circulates 17,000.

In 1961, Howard B. Taylor, an editor for

the Copley Newspapers of California and Illinois, went to Santiago and Valparaiso as a technical consultant, encouraging the editors of the Edwards chain to modernize their make up with more white space, more horizontal make up. The editorial excellence of the content he left alone.[3]

PRO-GOVERNMENT PAPERS. Although President Alessandri campaigned as an independent, he was supported by the political parties to the right of center. Therefore, he got and kept the support of these Santiago dailies: El Diario Illustrado (37,000 circulation), owned by Conservatives; the Edwards papers, El Mercurio, Ultimas Noticias, and La Segunda; the newspaper of the middle-of-the-road Radical party, La Tercera de la Hora (85,000 circulation); and La Nación (circulation claimed is several times the paid circulation of 15,000 independent advertising agencies attest to).

La Nación is one newspaper that always supports the Administration in power, regardless of political affiliation. After every presidential election, it gets a new staff of editors and reporters.

El Mercurio, La Nación, and El Diario Illustrado are called the serious press. They give little space to sensational news, but furnish a well-balanced roundup of world and domestic news, making good use of the wires of the Associated Press, the United Press International, Agence-France Presse, and Reuters.

ANTI-GOVERNMENT PAPERS. Chief respectable opposition newspaper since 1958 has been La Ultima Hora (35,000 circulation), organ of the Socialist party, whose candidates came within 33,000 votes in 1958 of defeating the Alessandri candidates.

In opposition not only to the current Alessandri regime but to the moderate centrists and anti-Communist leftists is El Siglo (circulation 5,000), the Communist daily.[4]

Another Communist paper, Clarín-Noche, comes out at midnight and is sold by street urchins to late theater goers. This tabloid is filled with crime news.

It has no connection with Clarín, daytime daily, Santiago's only nonpolitical paper, which ignores public affairs in favor of crime stories and other sensational news, with a circulation of 25,000.

MAGAZINES. A number of Chilean magazines are edited for women, featuring household, beauty, and dietary hints. Among the general-interest magazines, Ercilla (circulation 29,000), a weekly news magazine, carries an objective analysis of the week's political events in Chile.

Zig-Zag (circulation 10,000), a weekly magazine that carries a variety of feature articles, is well edited and quoted in professional circles.

Topaze (circulation 7,000), a weekly magazine with superb cartoons, pokes fun at the government and almost anyone in the news.[5]

NEWS SERVICES. In addition to the worldwide news wires of AP, UPI, Agence-France Presse, and Reuters, Chilean publications and broadcasting stations make use of the two national news agencies of Chile: Agencia Noticiosa Corporación de Periodistas (Journalists' News Agency Corporation), serving both newspapers and radio, and Agencia Noticiosa Prensa (Press News Agency), serving television and movie-theater newsreels.

BROADCASTING. For many years a popular radio program three times each week was "Topaze," a series of satirical sketches and commentaries based on the lampooning in the aforementioned magazine Topaze. Through the 1950's, Avelino Uruzúa, publisher of the magazine, became a radio personality by producing and narrating the "Topaze" radio series.[6]

Even after publishing duties curtailed Uruzúa's radio time, other lighthearted commentators remained. In general, Chilean straight newscasts have been well-written, well-edited.

The republic's television and radio stations, privately-owned and commercial, are organized into a strong, private group, the Asociación de Radiodifusoras de Chile, whose 1962-63 president, Jorge Quinteros Tricot, is quick to speak up when some station feels it has not received sufficient information from a governmental agency.

Copper mining has always played a big part in the Chilean economy, and the mining industry maintains a radio station, Radio Sociedad Nacional de Minería.

JOURNALISM TRAINING. University-level journalism training got its start in Chile[7] with the enactment of a 1952 national law authorizing the establishment of a journalism school at the national university. Classes began in 1953, with Ernesto Montenegro as school director. After a few years, he was succeeded by

Ramón Cortez, former director of the Santiago daily La Nación, who remained active with the school until his death in 1962.

With the promulgation of the 1958 Press Council law, enrollment in Chilean university journalism classes increased. Most Chilean editors have supported university training in journalism. Top publishers, editors, and reporters have volunteered to serve as part-time faculty members.

FILING NEWS. Chile has a long tradition as a nation producing good writers.[8] There is a national pride in the leading well-written periodicals and broadcasts.

And although the government does not interfere with foreign correspondents filing dispatches to their home offices, foreign newsmen, especially from the United States and northern Europe, feel a sense of isolation in Chile. Like Australia, Chile faces the South Pacific, far from the hub of the Western World, the North Atlantic community. Even in a jet age, Santiago doesn't seem the crossroads that Mexico City, Rome, London and Paris do.

Stories about Chile proper do not frequently circle the globe. Yet Santiago from time to time is a good listening post for broadcasts and travelers from crisis-ridden neighboring Argentina, Bolivia, and Peru; a good relay point for certain stories.

Colombia

Cultured Colombia is the alliterative reference often made to describe this South American republic. But the adjective should be applied to the capital city of Bogotá, not to the entire nation. The 1.2 million Bogotanos are separated by both culture and terrain from most of the 13 million other Colombians.

Geography has influenced the journalistic, political, and economic life of Colombia. A land divided by mountains and jungle, its transportation has been difficult in most areas, impossible in a few regions. The result: a high degree of regionalism.

Bogotá is the commercial, cultural, and political center; Medellin, the industrial stronghold; Cali, the chief agricultural center; and Barranquilla, the Caribbean port for its coffee, 80 per cent of Colombia's export trade.

Politically, Colombia has been divided right down the middle by knife-edge ferocity between the two traditional parties, the Conservatives and the Liberals. Neither the twentieth century history of the republic in general nor of its press in particular can be told without using the Conservative-Liberal impasse as the focal point.

The republic's Constitution of 1866 was amended in 1957 to require a fifty-fifty sharing of all governmental offices between Liberals and Conservatives. Even the presidency must alternate between a Liberal and a Conservative. Thus years of on-again, off-again bloody civil war in the hinterlands has ended.

After the 1953-57 dictatorship of Gustavo Rojas Pinilla, Colombia's greatest newspaper, the liberal Bogotá daily El Tiempo, began operating freely again. Rojas Pinilla had used arson and jail sentences to try to bring Tiempo editors into line, but when such tactics failed, the dictator closed the paper. Since 1958 this daily has re-established its prominent place among leading newspapers of Latin America.

PRESS FREEDOM. During 1958-62, the Liberal party's Alberto Lleras Camargo, as President of Colombia, upheld fully the provision of the Constitution guaranteeing a free press. His successor, who took office in the summer of 1962, Conservative party leader, Guillermo León Valencia, has also observed the democratic tradition of not interfering with a free press.

Some of Colombia's leading publications have shown their own sense of public responsibility by reporting with accuracy, fairness, and with an alertness to genuine dangers to the republic. During 1961, El Tiempo warned of the threat to Colombian freedom by Communists using "underdog" sympathy for Castro in Cuba as a shield to promote anti-U.S. feeling. In October, 1962, when Castro's missile deal with the U.S.S.R. was fully understood in Colombia, the impact of such reporting was brought home to Colombian readers.

LEGACY OF GÓMEZ. Colombian newspapers are primarily party organs. It has not been accidental that the publisher of the leading dailies, El Tiempo's Eduardo Santos and El Siglo's Laureano Gómez, have been presidents of the republic and leaders of the two major political parties.

When Santos took office after being elected in 1938 for a term ending in 1942, he stated that he wanted to better the position of the working man. This angered Gómez, who, through clever propaganda techniques, welded Conservatives and the nonaligned into a militant political action group, somewhat pro-Axis. His conservative morning daily, El Siglo, even openly supported the Fascist Camisas Negras (Black Shirts), praised Spain's Franco and Italy's Mussolini, and denounced the United States.

During 1940 and 1941, Siglo became the Colombian voice of the Hitler-Mussolini Axis. Six conservative dailies in the provinces echoed Siglo's views. A sample editorial excerpt from El Siglo in 1941:

We were born Spanish. The twenty cowardly governments of Latin America have put themselves into the hands of masonic, atheistic democracy. Each day the yoke of Anglo-Saxon Americana is drawn tighter around our throats. ...But all is not lost. There is still heard the voice of Laureano Gómez to direct us...back to Spain.

A new president was to be chosen to take office in 1942. Liberal Alfonso López succeeded Dr. Santos as president, re-enforcing Gómez' fury. When in October, 1943, President López had Colombia declare war on the Axis, Laureano Gómez became violent, running

editorials in _Siglo_ that Colombia had been
sold to the U.S., the "rapist of Panama,"
referring to our acquiring the Panama Canal
Zone in 1903 from the former Colombian province which became the Republic of Panama.
Such editorials lost López popularity.

In 1943 a prizefighter was knifed to death
in Bogotá. He had published a small radical
newspaper, _Voz_. _El Siglo_ saw its chance,
changed the murdered fighter from a leftwinger
to a conservative martyr. Attempts at revolution began to crop up.

In 1946, Conservative candidate Mariano
Ospina Pérez became president and the editorial
thunder from the far right subsided.

But two years later, in the spring of 1948,
the Organization of American States was holding
its inter-American conference in Bogotá. A
leader of the Liberal party, Jorge Gaitán, was
assassinated as he walked down the street.
Rumors spread widely. Rioting went on, as Communist agents encouraged the plunder of stores
and offices. By the next day, $171 million
damage had been wrought. This frightful wreck-
age of Bogotá also helped wreck the Ospina
regime, paving the way for the Gómez dictatorship. The fighting spread to the hinterlands,
with thousands of Liberal and Conservative
Colombians killing one another.

By June, 1949, the situation had split provinces and cities into warring camps. Laureano
Gómez, having been in Spain for a few years,
came home to take charge. He was quickly
elected president. But the rioting and fighting late in 1949 got worse, though his newspaper _El Siglo_ proclaimed that it had stopped.
Mobs attacked the liberal _El Tiempo_.

By June, 1953, the chaos was such that
another dictator, General Rojas Pinilla, replaced Gómez. But instead of ending press
persecution, Rojas continued it. Not until
1957 did the Colombian press regain the press
freedom it had before 1949, a period of more
than eight years.[1]

OUTSTANDING NEWSPAPERS. As mentioned, the
morning Bogotá daily, _El Tiempo_, Colombia's
leading newspaper, is for the Liberal party
on its editorial page. Its news columns are
objective, trustworthy, impartial. With a
daily circulation of 157,000, it zooms to
305,000 Sundays. Roberto García Peña is
editor. _El Tiempo_ was founded in 1911.

El Espectador, a morning Bogotá daily, with
circulation of 109,000 was founded in 1887.
Its circulation total includes its afternoon
satellite edition. Like _Tiempo_, it is a
Liberal party paper.

Bogotá's chief Conservative party dailies
are _El Siglo_, an AM of dwindling circulation,
not as fiery as in its days of prominence,
and _La República_, another AM with 70,000 circulation. The latter was founded in 1953
and does not suffer from _Siglo's_ demagogic
reputation.

The most important dailies outside the
capital city are _El Colombiano_ of Medellin,
an AM with 55,000 circulation, and _El Heraldo_
of Barranquilla, an AM with 33,000 circulation.
The Medellin paper is an organ of the Conservative party, but impartial in its news columns.
The Barranquilla paper is politically independent.

El Colombiano, an organ of the Conservative party, is one of the most important
dailies outside the capital city of
Bogotá.

MAGAZINES. Unlike most of the newspapers
and magazines, the Bogotá weekly news magazine,
which resembled _Newsweek_ and _Time_ in appearance, was reasonably politically independent.
Called _Semana_, which means "Week," it has
suspended publication but hopes to resume
soon. _Semana_ had readers throughout Colombia,

and in neighboring Latin American republics.

Another prominent weekly news magazine of general interest is Cromos, also published in Bogotá.

BROADCASTING. Although Bogotá has a reputation as the "Athens of South America" with its many book shops, poets, novelists, and outstanding newspapers and magazines, the hinterland of Colombia, isolated by lack of good roads, accounts for most of the 43 per cent of the adult population who are illiterate.[2]

Radio broadcasts thus become especially important as links to the outside world. La Voz del Cauca, Voz de Tolima, Voz de Antioquia, and similar radio stations called "The Voice of" in various towns, reach millions of Colombians who never see a newspaper and could not read one if they could buy one.

A radio network, Radio Cadena Nacional, has supplied its affiliates with numerous informational programs in recent years, such as the 1962 series on the U.S. Peace Corps units in Colombia. Such stations as Radio Pacífico in Cali carry most of these RCN documentaries and newscasts.

Of special note has been Radio Sutatenza, the educational radio station in Sutatenza operated by Father Jose Joaquín Salcedo, in the province of Boyaca. This priest began

his School of the Air in 1947 with a 100-watt transmitter. Since 1950, the national government has contributed more than 30 million pesos to this project (8.30 pesos to the dollar). The small radio station has become a network, with a broadcasting corporation, Acción Cultural Popular (Popular Cultural Action), with a 25,000-watt transmitter and four 10,000-watt transmitters.[3] More than 500,000 listeners study reading, hygiene, trades, and history.

There are 40 daily newspapers in Colombia, but 100 radio stations, or more than twice as many broadcasting outlets as papers.

Television programs have centered mainly in Bogotá, though several provincial cities are now ready to begin receiving telecasts from their own stations or from micro-wave relay stations.

JOURNALISM TRAINING. Principal training center for newsmen in Colombia is the School of Journalism and Broadcasting of Javiarana University in Bogotá. Reacting to the success of Javiarana's program, three other Colombian universities now have projected courses of study in journalism, waiting to be implemented.

Given the Bogotá tradition as the home of writers, and peaceful coexistence between Liberal and Conservative politicians, Colombia now seems ready to flourish in mass media development.

Ecuador

Journalism, like politics and other important facets of public life in Ecuador, is a "Tale of Two Cities." Guayaquil is the largest city in this republic fronting the northern South American Pacific coast, but Quito is the national capital, the traditional cultural center, and in many ways the news center. Yet as the chief port, Guayaquil now rivals inland Quito as a commercial center and hence as a news source for stories of business and economics.

MAJOR NEWSPAPERS. Only eleven cities in Ecuador publish the 24 dailies of the nation. Aside from the papers of Quito and Guayaquil, none are very large in circulation, nor influential as newspapers. Most of the provincial newspapers have 2,000 to 5,000 circulations.

In Quito, El Comercio, AM daily with 32,000 circulation weekdays and 37,000 Sundays, is influential far out of proportion to its paid circulation. Since its founding in 1906, it has tried to maintain a news-centered position, running major domestic and world news rather than sensational stories. News reports receive far more space than opinion columns in El Comercio.

Its afternoon satellite, Ultimas Noticias, with a circulation of 11,400 carries late-breaking followups to Comercio's top national and local stories.

Quito's two other AM's Diario del Ecuador and La Tierra, with small circulations, are overshadowed by El Comercio, and by the leading papers of Guayaquil.

Ecuador's oldest daily, El Telégrafo, founded in 1884, an independent AM in Guayaquil, has much hard news packed into its 16 pages thanks to its co-publishers, Manuel Eduardo Castillo and Abel Romeo Castillo, both of whom are active as executive editors.

El Universo, largest daily in Ecuador, is a Guayaquil AM paper (f.1921), with a circulation of 60,000 daily and 65,000 Sundays. It is the only paper in Ecuador receiving the full service of the Inter-American Press Association's Office of Certified Circulation.

MAGAZINES. One of the most popular magazines,

Embassy, is a picture magazine with a format somewhat similar to Look or Life. Quito is the publishing center for the literary and scholarly journals of the republic, through the Casa de la Cultura Ecuatoriana, or Ecuadoran Cultural Center. Foreign correspondents and writers are welcomed at this center and aided by a staff of professional bibliographical librarians. It is located in the heart of Quito, a few miles from the commercial center, not too far from the Central University.

CIESPAL. With funds from UNESCO, from the Ecuadoran government, and from the Central University in Quito, in 1958 a plan was drawn up for the International Center of Graduate Studies in Journalism for Latin America, commonly called by its initials in Spanish, CIESPAL or Centro Internacional de Estudios Superiores de Periodismo para América Latina.

One of the planners was Dr. Raymond B. Nixon, editor of the Journalism Quarterly and professor of journalism at the University of Minnesota. In March, 1960, UNESCO called a conference in Quito to draw up the curriculum. Various Latin American journalism school directors participated. The U.S. delegate was Dr. Marvin Alisky of Arizona State University.[1]

Jorge Fernández, one of the editors of El Comercio, was chosen as executive director of the Center. CIESPAL offers two-month courses to Latin Americans who already hold university degrees in journalism or who have professional experience in newspaper work. Many of its students so far have been men who teach journalism at one of the more than fifty Latin American journalism schools, editors and reporters from key dailies, writers for news magazines, and broadcast newsmen.

CIESPAL occupies rooms at the Central University in Quito, near the university's regular undergraduate journalism school but completely separate from it.

Among the outstanding professors of journalism teaching short courses at CIESPAL have been Danton Jobim, one of Brazil's leading newspaper editors and journalism professors (see section on Brazil), and Jacques Kayser, director of the Press Institute of the University of Paris.

BROADCASTING. At the journalism schools of both the Central University in Quito and at the University of Guayaquil, radio news courses are offered, with the more extensive training in newscasting being at the latter. As a result, in recent years, Ecuador enjoys a professional level of writing and announcing broadcast news in its two major cities.

Radio Católica in Quito carries considerable news of the political activities of the Catholic Church in Ecuador. Station HCJB, more popularly known as La Voz de los Andes, owned and operated by the World Missionary Fellowship, broadcasts in both Spanish and English, and in shortwave overseas broadcasts in Portuguese to neighboring Brazil, and in Quechua (language of the Incas) to Indians in neighboring Peru. HCJB enjoys a popularity among good music lovers of Quito with its daily concerts, as does Radio Quito, another station with nightly recorded concerts.

In Guayaquil, Radio Cenit has especially well-edited newscasts because its news editor, Hugo Delgado-Cepeda, also serves as professor of broadcast journalism at the university.

Other Guayaquil stations with full news reports include Radio Bolívar, La Voz Liberal, Radio Universal, and Radio América. Another Guayaquil station, Ondas del Pacífico has the advantage of local and national news from the newspaper El Universo as the basis for its newscasts.

PRESS FREEDOM. A free flow of information inside Ecuador has always been uncertain. For example, in December, 1953, the Quito daily El Comercio, its evening affiliate Ultimas Noticias, and its broadcasting station Radio Quito, were permitted to resume operations. These media

had been shut down by the government for 44 days because Comercio editor Jorge Mantilla refused to publish an insulting communique from the Ministers of the Interior and of Defense. The communique stated that these ministers would not tolerate severe newspaper criticism. Finally the government printed the communique at its own plant and the newspapers distributed it with their comic section, ending the period of suspension.

The President of Ecuador serves a four-year term. During 1949-52, President Galo Plaza allowed press freedom. During 1953-56, President Velasco Ibarra pressured papers and bullied a few editors. During 1957-60, President Camillo Ponce returned Ecuador to a period of press freedom. Then rabble rouser Velasco Ibarra was re-elected in 1960 for the 1961-64 term, but he was forced from office in November, 1961, after having censored the press, instigated pro-Castro crowds to riot against his political opponents, and in general substituted chaotic emotionalism for public administration.

Succeeding to the presidency was Vice-President Carlos Arosemena, who came into power with the support of almost the entire political spectrum, including the Communists, whose party is legal in Ecuador. Walking a political highwire, Arosemena during 1962 was careful not to censor or pressure the press.[2] Thus, as 1963 began, the mass media of Ecuador had shaky freedom, on their own for the time being but no guarantee of any long range security.

Peru

Peru's land area is almost the size of Alaska or twice the size of Texas. Yet its 11 million population clusters on the coast and in a few dozen cities and towns in the Andes. The northeastern jungle contains only a relatively few Indians.

Like ancient Gaul, Peru is divided into three parts: the narrow sea coast, the Andes mountains, and the eastern jungle. Mass media development away from the coast centers in a handful of cities. Approximately 60 per cent of the population or 6.6 million speak Spanish, 40 per cent or 4.4 million speak chiefly two Indian languages, Quechua and Aymará, with the handful of jungle Indians speaking two dozen other Indian dialects.[1]

Not even all of the two-thirds who understand Spanish count journalistically because only half of the population 14 years of age and over can read. More than half of all Peruvians live at slightly above the subsistence level. Peru does not enjoy the wide distribution of radio receivers found in Mexican, Argentine, Chilean, Uruguayan, or Brazilian homes.

Lima's population totals almost 1,350,000 including adjacent suburbs. No other Peruvian city is even one-sixth as large. Arequipa, second city of the republic, totals 250,000 population. Only four other Peruvian cities exceed 50,000 population. In newspaper, magazine, radio, television, political, economic, and cultural influence, Lima dominates Peru.

PRESS FREEDOM. During most of the period of its existence as a republic, Peru has not enjoyed much more press freedom than it did during the almost four centuries, after the coming of the Spanish Conquistadores when it was a colony of Spain. Not until 1945, in the closing months of the first six-year term of President Manuel Prado were all traces of censorship lifted.[2]

The outlawed left-of-center, anti-Communist reform political party, APRA,[3] was legalized after having been outlawed and persecuted. But in October, 1948, political chaos returned to Peru, and General Manuel Odría headed a military junta which took over the government. APRA was again outlawed and press censorship returned. Then in 1956, Manuel Prado was elected President again for the 1956-62 term.

With his inauguration press freedom returned and flourished.

Neither strikes, personal criticism of the Chief Executive by some papers, nor any other crisis during the six years from July, 1956 to July, 1962 brought any censorship. Peru's press was free.

But on July 19, 1962, a military junta took over the government just nine days before Prado could end his second six-year constitutional term. The 1962 election had been a three-way tie, with Victor Haya de la Torre of APRA, General Odría, and Fernando Belaúnde each receiving approximately one-third of the popular vote; no candidate had a majority. In the resulting confusion, General Pérez Godoy and a military junta assumed power. On the streets of Lima, police clashed with Aprista demonstrators. The APRA daily newspaper, La Tribuna, was prevented from circulating by police, while troops occupied its editorial offices.

After a couple of days, the military regime apologized for damage done to the Tribuna press equipment, returned the newspaper to its rightful publisher and editors, and allowed it to circulate freely. For the remainder of 1962, Peruvian papers were free of open, direct pressure or censorship. As 1963 began, papers remained independent of governmental control but pressures could be found just below the surface.[4]

LIMA'S DAILIES. The six daily newspapers of Lima dominate Peru. No provincial paper even begins to approach their influence.

Oldest extant newspaper in Peru, El Comercio, is also one of the oldest existing newspapers in all Latin America, having been founded in 1839.[5] Only El Mercurio of Valparaiso, Chile, founded in 1827, antedates it.

Its first issue proclaimed that Comercio would be dedicated to "order, liberty, knowledge."[6] This morning daily has kept faith with that promise, supporting public order when opposed by sudden or violent change, representing nineteenth century liberalism of the rugged individual type, and presenting news of sciences, fine arts, and world affairs.

As its name "Commerce" implies, financial news always receives extensive coverage in Comercio. Editorially, it supports the exporters, the landowning families who still control the wealth of Peru.

Comercio puts out an afternoon satellite edition of only eight pages, but devotes its main reportorial efforts to its morning edition of 24 to 30 pages. Until 1960, Comercio's morning front page was devoted to advertising but now features a U.S.-style make up of top news, similar to its afternoon edition.

Peru's leading newspaper, in terms of national and world news coverage, is another Lima AM, La Prensa. Using a modified brace make up, often a front-page map to orient readers to far-away events, and clear reporting, Prensa has a circulation of 58,000 daily and 77,000 Sundays, certified by the Inter-American Press Association office of circulation.

If Comercio, with a circulation of 80,000, is the voice of the exporters, Prensa is the voice of the importers. Whereas the former champions the mining, agricultural, and banking barons, the latter favors the newer strata of the upper class, rising merchants and captains of fledgling industry. The aristocratic Miró Quesada family owns and directs Comercio. Pedro Beltrán, chief cabinet member under President Prado until 1962, publishes Prensa.

With these two dailies in a general sense speaking for management, a third Lima AM, La Tribuna, speaks for labor. This organ of the APRA political party, circulates 40,000 daily. It is the only major Peruvian daily directly owned by a political party. Very often Tribuna's reporters dig deeper than most other Peruvian newsmen. But its editors omit those items which run counter to the Aprista party's political platform. For example, some anti-labor stories are dropped.

An afternoon tabloid, Ultima Hora, has an Inter-American certified circulation of 89,000. It stresses crime news, cheesecake photographs and sports.

A rival Lima tabloid, La Crónica, leads Peruvian papers in circulation with its three-edition daily total being 186,000. Crónica's first edition sells 73,000 mornings. Its two afternoon editions account for the remainder of the circulation total. Its news emphasis parallels Ultima Hora.

Crónica has the most modern newspaper plant in Peru, a nine-floor building which also houses its radio station, Radio La Crónica. Former President Prado has invested money in these media.

Lima's sixth daily, Expreso, also a tabloid, politically supported left-of-center Fernando Belaúnde for president, but has been much more critical of Castro's Communist regime in Cuba than the Belaúnde group, some of whom combine anti-U.S. feelings with pro-Castro sentiments. Begun in 1961, Expreso has never had a certification of its circulation. An AM paper, Expreso uses many sensational news items and photographs, but does not skimp in running short versions of much major world news. It subscribes to United Press International, Agence-France Presse, and the Italian agency ANSA.

WEEKLY PAPERS. Lima's six dailies and Arequipa's three dailies, the chief newspapers of the nation, all subscribe to UPI. Comercio also belongs to the AP and serves as its Peruvian headquarters.

Some Peruvian towns have weeklies but the only ones with marked impact on public opinion in the realm of national affairs are found in Lima. Non-Lima weeklies have no readership outside their own small communities and relatively tiny circulations there.

By contrast, three leftwing weekly newspapers in Lima circulate among labor union membership, among university students, and among minor politicians in the four largest provincial cities as well as in every low-income neighborhood in Lima.

All three are anti-United States. Perú Popular, openly an organ of the Communists, is edited by Gustavo Valcárcel, who led the 1958 riots against visiting Vice-President Richard Nixon.

Voz Obrera (Worker's Voice) proclaims itself the official organ of the Workers Revolutionary party, a Trotskyite movement loyal to the late anti-Stalin Red leader.

Lea calls itself "Voice of the Workers in the Service of Collectivism" on its masthead. It too has had praise for Castro, for Communism, and for anti-U.S. politicians.

By contrast, the six Lima dailies have been reasonably responsible in their news columns and in their editorial interpretations of world events.

MAGAZINES. Most of the magazines published in Peru originate in Lima. Caretas, appearing twice a month, has topnotch color photographs of Peruvian life in a Look magazine format.

Vanguardia, edited by Eudocio Ravines, former Communist and now rightwing extremist, devotes itself to its own brand of anti-Communist journalism.

Rochabus, weekly news magazine, stresses cartoons which poke fun at leading politicians.

BROADCASTING. Competing for the advertising dollar with Peru's 39 dailies (most of them tiny in circulation except for Lima and Arequipa), its two dozen magazines and twenty weekly papers, are 48 radio (550-1600 kc.) stations and five television stations.

Lima has 20 of the 48 radio stations of the republic.[7] Radio news in some Peruvian regions has greater impact than newspapers because radio receiver distribution has grown faster than literacy. But most radios in Peru are found in cities and towns supporting newspapers.

There are also 42 shortwave transmitters in the republic, 22 of them in Lima, attempting to meet the challenge of widely-spaced semi-isolated communities. Most of the shortwave transmitters duplicate a companion standard-band station. Thus all but eight of the 48 standard-band stations have shortwave transmitters duplicating their broadcasts simultaneously.

The government operates Radio Nacional in the largest radio studios in the nation. In Lima, it broadcasts at two places on the dial, 850 and 1120 kilocycles, attempting to capture a standard-frequency audience at two spots on the dial with the same program. It also beams the same program via shortwave from Lima and from four satellite transmitters in the provinces.

Remaining stations are privately-owned commercial outlets. They range in power from 250 to 10,000 watts. Only Radio Nacional has a 50,000-watt transmitter.

Few audience rating surveys are statistically reliable in Peru, but those of the Grant Advertising Agency of Lima are. These surveys show Radio La Crónica, owned by the daily newspaper La Crónica, consistently leading other Lima stations, due partly to serialized dramas (soap operas).

Popular music keeps Radio Central often in second place. Several small Lima stations fail to total even a 1.0 rating (calculated by multiplying the percentage of sets in use during a quarter-hour period by the percentage tuned to one station).

Radio Sport obviously emphasizes sports news, whereas Radio Reloj's chief audience lure is the correct time, the weather report, and a news headline. A similar station programming time signals, weather reports, and headlines can be found in Mexico City.

In 1958, Peru's first television station, OAD-TV or Channel 7, was launched by UNESCO as a noncommercial education outlet. It is now operated by the Ministry of Education. Literacy, health, and vocational lessons are stressed.

Also in 1958, prominent radio station Radio América began its television affiliate, Channel 4. Lima also has two other commercial stations, Sol-TV or Channel 9 and Panamericana-TV or Channel 13. Away from Lima, only Arequipa has a television station, Channel 2.

PERU'S NEWSMEN. In 1945, the first School of Journalism was established at Catholic University in Lima. Its director, Matilde Pérez Palacio, through visiting Fulbright lecturers from the United States, brought Peru its first instruction in public relations and in radio writing. In 1947, the University of San Marcos, the republic's national university, began its own journalism school in Lima.

Encouraging journalism education at the university level are the professional newspaper and broadcasters groups. The Federación Nacional de Periodistas (National Federation of Journalists), the Asociación Peruana de Periodistas (Peruvian Association of Journalists), and the Asociación Nacional de Radiodifusoras del Perú (National Association of Broadcasters of Peru) strive for professional upgrading within their ranks and among apprentice newsmen.

If the present military junta ruling Peru maintains its hands off policy towards the press, Peruvian mass media may continue to edge slowly upward in achievement.

Uruguay

Uruguay has a large head on a small body. Almost 40 per cent of its population resides in or near the capital city of Montevideo. This democratic South American republic's land area covers only 72,000 square miles, comfortable for its population of almost 3 million.

A highly literate nation, better than 90 per cent of Uruguayans can read and certainly do. Montevideo's many bookstores and magazine stands give a clue. The city has 14 dailies (two of them foreign language), whereas the remainder of the nation has only ten dailies. All of the provincial papers have small circulations.

MONTEVIDEO'S DAILIES. As for the dozen Montevideo Spanish-language dailies, eight of them are nationally influential. Uruguayan newspapers are political, supporting either the Colorado (Liberal) party or the Blanco (Conservative) party. Since 1836 these two parties have struggled politically and journalistically, but unlike many other Latin Americans, the Colorados and the Blancos rely on ballots, not bullets.

For ninety years, from 1868 into 1958, the Colorados were the majority party, whereas since 1958 (and again in the 1962 elections), the Blancos have been the majority party. Not only are both parties in Congress but they even share the presidency. In place of the typical strong-man Latin American president, Uruguay has the Swiss system of a plural executive, a nine-member Executive Council, with the majority party having six seats and the minority party, three. Each year the Council chooses a President to be chairman of the plural executive and ceremonial head of state.

A prominent daily, El Día, an AM with a circulation of 120,000 daily and 160,000 Sundays, represents the political views of the dominant wing of the longtime majority party (1868-1958), the Colorados.

El Día was founded by José Batlle y Ordóñez in 1886. From then until his death in 1929, Batlle used it to publicize his political and social reforms, such as the plural executive Uruguay adopted. The paper has been antitotalitarian, antagonistic towards both communism and rightwing dictatorships.

The largest Uruguayan daily is the Montevideo PM El Diario, with a circulation of 170,000. Its editorial political persuasion officially is Colorado, but it is of an independent, conservative variety.

La Mañana is the morning counterpart of El Diario. That is, on social matters editorially it supports the Colorados but on economic matters it often is more conservative than the liberal party with which it is associated. With considerable financial news, Mañana (circulation 37,000 daily but 95,000 Sundays) draws many businessmen readers. Its Sunday business reviews circulate throughout the republic.

Another Colorado daily, Acción is relativly a newcomer among Montevideo papers, dating only from 1948. Most of its rivals are two, three, or more decades older. Acción's publisher, Luis Batlle, is a nephew of the late Batlle y Ordóñez and a cousin of the sons and daughters of the reformer president. But this close relationship does not prevent the two Colorado papers, Acción and El Día, from differing sharply on various issues. Acción's circulation is 65,000.

La Tribuna Popular, a late-morning daily, seems opportunistic and editorially inconsistent. Sometimes it supports Blanco candidates and at other times Colorados. Some of its popularity stems from its emphasis on sensational local news and its sports coverage. Founded in 1879, Tribuna is the oldest major Uruguayan paper, with a circulation of 75,000.

El Debate (f.1931), important Blanco AM daily, staunchly conservative, for years reflected the views of the late, long-time leader of the Blanco party, Luis Alberto de Herrera. In the 1940's it was pro-Franco and pro-Perón, the only major Uruguayan paper consistently friendly to the former Argentine dictator. With the ouster of Perón from neighboring Argentina in 1955, Debate began to change its attitude toward the United States from hostility to milder skepticism. With the rise of Castro's Red regime in Cuba, Debate has felt the Cold War pressures of being more understanding of the United States.

Two Blanco dailies, El País (AM with 60,000 circulation) and El Plata (PM with 90,000 circulation), share the same press, plant, and to some extent, the same key personnel although each is incorporated as a legally distinct publishing company. Eduardo Rodríguez Larreta, former foreign minister and a prominent Blanco Senator in the Congress, is titular publisher of El País but merely a large stockholder in the Plata corporation. In economic matters, both papers are moderately conservative. In political affairs, both are staunchly pro-United Nations and global in viewpoint.

Oldest Montevideo daily but no longer a major journalistic force, El Bien Público, founded in 1878, tried to speak for the Catholic Church. Politically, it supported the far rightwing. A morning daily except Mondays, it circulated 20,000, until it suspended publication Dec. 31, 1962, after a printers' strike.

PROVINCIAL PAPERS. Even though the Montevideo dailies circulate nationally in this small republic with good roads and modern transportation facilities, there are 190 weekly newspapers away from the capital. Uruguayans are a literate, newspaper-reading nation.

The second city, Paysandú, is not even one fourteenth as large as Montevideo. Its only daily, an AM with 10,000 circulation is the most important provincial paper. El Telégrafo does not circulate away from Paysandu.

Total daily and weekly newspaper circulation of Uruguay, almost a half-million, approximately equals the number of radio receivers in daily use.

BROADCASTING. Of the 60 radio stations in Uruguay, twenty-two of them are in Montevideo. Newcasts are generally well-edited and better presented than in many other Latin American republics. The government operates one station, but the others are privately owned and financed by commercial announcements.[1]

The leading television station in Montevideo, Channel 10, is popularly known as Saeta, after the initials of the parent broadcasting corporation, Sociedad Anónima Emisoras de Televisión y Anexos.

MAGAZINES. Marcha, lively political and literary journal, vies for magazine readership with Selecciones del Reader's Digest and Life en Español. The Spanish-language twice-a-month edition of Brazil's weekly Portuguese-language O Cruzeiro is a popular magazine in Uruguay, especially in areas nearest the Brazilian border.

WIRE SERVICE. The national news agency is Agencia Nacional de Informaciones or ANI, founded in 1945. It has seventy correspondents throughout the country.

Montevideo long has proved to be a good listening post for foreign correspondents from AP, UPI, AFP, Reuters, NBC, BBC, and other organizations. Whenever there are crises in neighboring Argentina or Brazil, especially, Montevideo, with a tradition of freedom of information, becomes especially useful to correspondents.

Even the Communist weekly Justicia sometimes reports more openly than Communist periodicals elsewhere in Latin America, influenced by the traditional open-society liberty-loving Uruguayans. It prints items other Red publications suppress. For example, Justicia broke the news of the split in Brazilian Communist ranks between those favoring the Soviet Union's gradualism and Red China's warlike demands for bloody action everywhere in the world possible, at once. Months later, the same material finally found its way into print in the two respective Brazilian Communist publications.

On occasion in South America, Montevideo serves news correspondents as a composite Geneva and West Berlin.

Venezuela

Political stresses on the press of this nation might be summed up with the alliterative Volatile Venezuela. With 350,000 square miles, its land area approximates that of Texas and Oregon combined, with more open spaces, for its 7.1 million population.[1]

Venezuela's annual per capita income of $700--the highest in Latin America--does not reveal accurately the widespread substandard living conditions away from the showcase cities of Caracas and Maracaibo. Thus, although three-quarters of Venezuela's dwellings are owner-occupied, more than one-half have thatched roofs and mud floors, less than one-third have running water, and the average size of a home is under three rooms.[2]

Therefore, even with its oil-rich economy, Venezuela still suffers from 38 per cent illiteracy. Politically, the republic's history has been cursed with dictatorships complete with press censorship. After a series of nineteenth century strong men, in 1899 Venezuela got still another military master, General Cipriano Castro, who ruled until 1908, when Juan Vicente Gómez began his twenty-seven-year dictatorship. It lasted until December 17, 1935, when the old tyrant died of natural causes. For decades, the press had been under wraps.

The aftermath naturally found the unshackled press running wild with its newly found freedom to criticize the caretaker government. From the mid-1930's into the 1940's, press restraints were rare. Then Venezuela's participation in World War II against the Axis brought security restrictions to the flow of information.

The October, 1945 revolution was the most fundamental in Venezuelan history, the upshot of deep-seated class conflicts. It brought into prominence the Democratic Action (AD) party of Rómulo Betancourt. Earlier, in 1941, AD had founded the newspaper El País, which later faded from view.

In 1948, a counter-revolution replaced representative government with a military junta, which organized a dictatorship lasting ten years. With the fall of dictator Marcos Pérez Jiménez in 1958, the freed press began to enjoy to the fullest its right to publish almost anything.

COMMUNIST INFLUENCE. Taking advantage of the pent up feelings bred by a decade of right-wing dictatorship, the Communists were ready to exploit the heady feeling of complete freedom once civil liberties returned. Venezuela showed once again that rightwing dictatorships do not stop Communism but in the longrun help it. The legacy of Perón in Argentina, Batista in Cuba, and similar examples were well understood by Venezuelan Reds. Only the democratic, liberal anti-Communist reform program of Rómulo Betancourt's AD party prevented Communists from capturing the imagination of the Venezuelan masses.

In the person of Hector Mújica, director of the School of Journalism of Central University in Caracas, the Communists have had an agent in a key position. Since Castro came to power in Cuba in 1959, Mújica's classes have been the headquarters for selling Venezuelan youth on the Latin American "need" for Cuban Communism.

CARACAS DAILIES. Fortunately, the major Caracas dailies have refused to hire the Communist-oriented products of the republic's principal journalism school. Even so, some Castro sympathizers are reporting for the smaller papers.

Largest Venezuelan daily is the PM tabloid Ultimas Noticias, with a circulation of 96,000. Largest regular-size daily, El Nacional, an AM, circulates 80,000 weekdays and 98,000 Sundays.

El Universal, an AM with 72,000 weekdays and 97,000 Sundays, features excellent run of the press color, and a cautious, conservative editorial policy.

La Esfera, with a weekday circulation of 36,000 and a Sunday circulation of 50,000, subscribes to UPI, Agence-France Presse, and the Italian service ANSA. In addition, it sometimes translates significant reports from the New York Times, the London Times, and other major papers of the Western nations of the Cold War. Aware of the danger of Communist propaganda, Esfera promotes democratic social reforms while fighting leftwing and rightwing extremism.

La Religión, daily of the Catholic political groups, circulates 16,000.

Away from Caracas, the only large daily, Panorama (AM with circulation of 62,000) serves the country's second largest city, Maracaibo, whose population of 450,000 is less than half of Caracas' 1,200,000.

In all, Venezuela has thirty dailies, two dozen weeklies, and several magazines, in addition to a large broadcasting system.

BROADCASTING. For a decade, Caracas has had three highly competitive television stations. In 1952, the government put its noncommercial Channel 5, Televisora Nacional on the air. In 1953, two commercial, privately-owned competitors took to the air: Channel 4, partly owned by the American Broadcasting Company of the U.S. in partnership with Venezuelan broadcasters, and Channel 2, operated by Radio Caracas, an established radio broadcasting company.

Radio Caracas, with spacious studios in its own Radio Center Building, and the other Venezuelan radio stations are privately-owned and commercial except for the governmental Radio Nacional. It too provides several news broadcasts daily.

FLOW OF NEWS. Venezuelan newsmen have numbered among themselves the republic's top writers and novelists through the years. Even the less-developed provincial press has produced a few such top writers.[3] The hindrance to professional upgrading in Venezuela has not been talent nor reportorial drive, but political crises.

In recent years, pro-Communist terrorists have bombed and fired upon the democratic, anti-Communist, liberal moderate governmental officials of the administration of Rómulo Betancourt. Normally, the freedom-loving Democratic Action majority party would reject press censorship, but faced with insurrection threats by extremists, late in 1962, it petitioned the government to act. The Betancourt regime's attorney general brought to trial the editor of the newspaper Clarín for urging in print that people overthrow the government by force.

Even in the midst of such tensions, Venezuelan editors have been striving to train more technical journalists, competent to report on the oil industry, the basis of the Venezuelan economy. The dailies El Nacional and La Esfera have been especially outstanding in covering the developments in this vital, technical field.

The "Other Two" Republics

The continent of South America contains ten of the twenty Latin American republics. We have treated in detail eight of these ten. The other two, Bolivia and Paraguay, are not as highly developed in the mass media. The press has a daily impact chiefly in the capital cities of these two republics, and even the wider influence of radio is curtailed somewhat by lack of receivers in impoverished rural Paraguay and by the language factor in Bolivia.

BOLIVIA. Bolivia's large land area of 400,000 square miles makes it almost the same size as the eastern seaboard of the United States, from Maine to Florida. But its 4 million population hardly makes it a major power. Two-thirds of the Bolivians are Indians, speaking Aymará, though some of them are bilingual in a limited sense. Even among those speaking Spanish, illiteracy is the rule. Four dailies in the national capital of La Paz, two dailies in Cochabamba, and two dailies in Sucre and Oruro make up the Bolivian press, except for a few weekly newspapers of small circulation.

The three newspapers of any significance in Bolivia are El Diario, an AM with 36,000 circulation; Ultima Hora, a PM of 20,000 circulation; and La Nación, a midday daily of 20,000 circulation. All three are published in La Paz, with a few copies circulated in Sucre and Cochabamba. La Nación speaks for the National Revolutionary Movement party, which has dominated the government since 1952, and which has waged somewhat of a social reform program.

Another La Paz daily, Presencia, speaks unofficially for the Catholic Church but does not seem to have any widespread influence or readership.

There are more than a dozen privately-owned, commercial radio stations in Bolivia, but the most influential station is the governmental station, Radio Illimani.

PARAGUAY. Journalistically, economically, politically we can describe these two countries alliteratively as Bleak Bolivia and Primitive Paraguay.

If Bolivia is not as highly developed as her South American neighbors in the mass media, this republic is still not at the bottom of our list, for at least in Bolivia, press censorship has been inconsistent and even absent at times in recent years. But in Paraguay, press censorship has been ever-present. Since 1954, General Alfredo Stroessner has been dictator, and late in 1962 he had himself nominated as the only candidate for president for the February, 1963 election. Unless assassinated, he seemed likely to serve a third five-year term as chief executive, which would mean a censored press.

A high degree of illiteracy robs Paraguayan papers of much impact. In the capital city of Asunción, four of the nation's eight dailies publish, each with a small circulation. With a large percentage of its population Spanish-speaking, Paraguay can utilize radio more easily than can Bolivia.

All Paraguayan stations are privately-owned, commercial outlets except Radio Nacional, voice of the government, but all are censored and controlled as to news and information as if they were governmental.

Neither Bolivia nor Paraguay are easy countries from which foreign news correspondents can file accurate, candid dispatches back to home offices. UPI copy comes into these countries but not much of it gets published or aired. Of the two, Bolivia has a more genuine flow of news than does Paraguay.

Middle East: Overview

The press of the Middle East (including what is often referred to as the "Near East") is young and still developing. There is no tradition of freedom in the Western sense; in fact, the press of the region is accustomed to being dependent on political subsidies for its livelihood. Even today, although this situation is improving, the dependence on outside financial aid is there, and only about half the Middle East papers have reached the point where they are not losing money. In most instances throughout this region the newspaper costs too much for the laborer or peasant, and in general the press is an institution of the upper classes. Another factor which accounts for the low circulations in the Middle East is the large number of illiterates--about half the population.

According to a British observer of the Middle Eastern press in 1958, it might be compared to the British eighteenth century press (with the exception of the Israeli press which greatly resembles the British press of the second half of the nineteenth century).[1]

On the whole circulations in the region have risen in the last decade. In many parts of the Middle East (especially in the United Arab Republic) circulations are reported rising rapidly as literacy drives are adding large new segments to the reading public.[2] Egypt, Syria, Iraq, Iran, Lebanon, and Isreal each has at least 20 dailies, and Turkey has about 100. Cities in the Middle East with the greatest number of newspapers are Ankara, Istanbul, Cairo, Beirut, Damascus, Aleppo, Baghdad, and Jerusalem. Among the most influential of the Arab dailies in the predominantly Arab region are those published in Cairo, the chief city of Egypt and now the capital of the UAR. Especially influential are the Cairo dailies Al Gomhouria, Al Akhbar and Al Ahram. By Middle East standards, these Egyptian dailies are big businesses.[3] Also in this category would be the Turkish dailies Hurriyet, Yeni Sabah, Cumhuriyet, and Milliyet. Turkey, of all the nations located at the eastern end of the Mediterranean, has the greatest number of newspapers.

State subsidization of progovernment papers is common in the Middle East, but this is slowly changing. Throughout the region journalists often take bribes from government officials and act as "press agents" for political figures. The usual reasons given for this practice are that the journalists are grossly underpaid and the moral standards of the Middle East are flexible and varied.

There are usually provisions for governmental prepublication censorship in the Middle East press systems. Although not used to any great extent, they are available in "times of emergency," and the governments decide when such emergencies exist. Lebanon, with one of the most progressive press systems in the Middle East, also is said to have the freest press.

Most Middle East governments, in spite of occasional restrictive practices, generally give considerable aid to the press. Government help usually takes one or more of these forms: (1) direct payments, (2) secret support, (3) discounts on communication transmission costs, and (4) free passes on railways for journalists. Long considered a deterrent to the development of the press in this region is the lack of an economy which can support a press free of government and party subsidies.

In the last few years representatives of numerous Western newspapers and news agencies have complained that news is very difficult to obtain in most Middle Eastern nations. The International Press Institute has noted this fact many times in its publications. Inadequate communication facilities are one handicap. But the main one seems to be that most Middle East governments are reluctant to impart information to the press. Mainly the philosophy seems to exist among the governments of this region that the press' main purpose is to act as publicity agents and propaganda mouthpieces for the national leadership. Certainly, evidence has piled up in recent years to indicate that the governments of the Middle East are very careful what they release to the press and what they keep secret.

Three main characteristics of the press of the Middle East, if any generalizations can be made, are: (1) molding opinion is considered the primary purpose, (2) the press is mainly political and highly partisan, (3) newspapers appear almost constantly while others are fading away throughout the region, and (4) circulations are usually small. Except for the bigger papers of Egypt and Turkey, the Middle East papers seldom have more than 6,000 circulation. Outside these two states, the largest daily in the region is Ma'ariv (circulation about 75,000) of Tel Aviv, Israel. Professional standards in the regional press are almost non-existent; however, reform is taking place and papers are becoming more conscious of criticisms hurled at them from press groups throughout the world. Advertising is still not very important in the newspaper financial picture, a fact which accounts largely for the serious economic troubles which have existed in recent years throughout the region's press.

Newspaper staffs are usually small and poorly-trained. Egypt is the only part of the region where journalism has a significant place in the academic structure of formal education, although Turkey is reported to be making some headway in this respect. Distribution of newspaper copies is handled chiefly by commercial street sale agents, with only a small number of copies going to regular subscribers. News received by the region's newspapers from Middle East sources is almost all obtained from stringers and contributors, and is received by mail.

Most of the newspaper plants in the Middle East are small and poorly equipped, although the UAR (Egypt), Lebanon and Turkey have newspapers with very modern buildings and facilities. Large numbers of hand-fed presses are used to print the papers of the region, and folding is often done by hand. Newspaper format most often is comparable to the standard-size U.S. journal, but there are many variations on this general size. Tabloids among the dailies can be found, but they are rare.

A large number of Middle East papers are printed from hand-set type in Greek, Armenian, and Arabic, although mechanical composing machines of various kinds are being introduced rapidly into certain countries of the region. In most of the Arab press, which makes up the majority of the Middle East newspapers outside Turkey, the stories run on the page from right to left, and the back page to an American reader would be the front page to an Arab reader. Since World War II there has been a great reduction in the number of pages in Middle East newspapers; most of them today have from four to eight pages. This reduction began during the war, when newsprint imports were reduced to save shipping space and newsprint was rationed by the governments. Although this situation is getting a little better, Middle East papers still have difficulty getting enough newsprint. In the UAR, however, there is plenty if publishers can pay the price. And throughout the Middle East in general the price is high, and rising every year.

On the following pages three Middle East countries--the United Arab Republic, Israel, and Turkey--are taken up separately and in some

length in an attempt to show different types of press systems existing in the region. One of these countries--the UAR--represents a stable and well-established press with a rather large circulation; the second--Israel--represents the smaller nations of the region which have a multilingual press with a small circulation and considerable freedom, and the third--Turkey--represents a nation with a large number of highly nationalistic newspapers which are theoretically free but bound by a number of restrictive press laws.

Before getting to these three countries, however, it might be well to round out this overview of the press of the Middle East by looking briefly at the situation in the following nations:

IRAN--The press of Iran is centered in the capital, Tehran, a city of more than one million inhabitants. Most of the Iranian daily papers (some 20) are small, having circulations of only 2,000 to 10,000. However, two dailies have circulations of more than 50,000--Etella'at with 70,000 and Kayhan with some 65,000. Illiteracy in the country is high--about 80 per cent of the 20 million population. There are about 80 papers published in Iran. Persian is the main press language; papers are also published in Armenian, Hebrew, French, and English.

Objective reporting is not highly considered in Iran. Many reporters are on the government payroll. It is understood in Iran that papers do not print anything "derogatory" about the government; the Shah (king) may not be criticized. The government has on several instances in the last few years snatched papers off newsstands because they contained very brief items thought "detrimental" to the government.

About half the Iranian papers are owned by political parties or rich politicians. Magazines are published by the larger publications. No Communist publications are allowed in the country. Government advertising is essential for continued publication in Iran; this in itself helps keep the press friendly to the government. Newsprint in Iran is very costly; it is obtained from Russia exclusively.

The national news agency is PARS, a branch of the government's Press and Propaganda department. TASS, from its Moscow office, supplies foreign news free to the Iranian press. This nation is developing a comprehensive program of journalism education, which got off to a good start with the help of Dr. Quintus Wilson of the University of

Utah (now at West Virginia) in 1957. Dr. Burton W. Marvin of the University of Kansas was in Iran as a professor in 1960-61.

IRAQ--This country appears to be caught in a strange political situation; there are strong nationalistic tendencies (meaning Arab nationalism) pulling the nation toward some type of union with other Arab nations, and there is also an ever-increasing leaning toward Communism and the giant Soviet neighbor to the north. Recent reports seem to indicate that the press has fallen under the domination of the Communists or other groups to the Far Left. The Manchester Guardian Weekly reported as far back as 1958 that the Communists were in control of the Iraqi press and electronic media of communication, and that all these media carried "open and insistent Communist propaganda."4

The largest daily in Iraq is Al Akhbar (circulation about 15,000) published in Baghdad, the capital, a city with the majority of the country's dailies. All the papers are small, and with the exception of Al Akhbar, have circulations under 8,000. Editors must be very careful of what they print, and must not show editorial tendencies which are against the national interest. Censorship in Iraq is the strictest of any in the Middle East.

Cities other than the capital which have dailies are Basrah and Mosul. About 85 per cent of Iraq's five million people are illiterate. The nation's press is Arabic and receives news mainly from Cairo's Middle East News agency. The English-language daily of Baghdad is the Times, with a circulation of from 4,000 to 5,000.

JORDAN--In this little country (about three-fourths the size of Florida) there are about a half dozen newspapers with any important circulation or influence. Three of the leading papers (dailies) are Al Difaa and Al Jihad of Jerusalem (Old City) and Al Urdon of Amman. These three account for more than three-fourths of the country's total circulation. All papers are printed in Arabic. They are of standard size, usually seven columns in width. The dailies are issued six days a week, and have conservative and balanced make up. Total circulation is only about 30,000, making the Jordanian press almost invisible in the Middle East press picture.

The press is centered in the old city of Jerusalem. The papers are government-oriented. And as elsewhere in the Middle East, broadcasting is under the tight control and supervision of the government. In Jordan there are several communities with populations of as much as 20,000 which are without a newspaper. The Jerusalem Times is the only English-language paper in the country.

LEBANON--The press of Lebanon is centered in the capital and cultural and intellectual city of Beirut. In the country there are about 40 dailies with a total circulation of some 200,000. The country probably has the freest press in the Middle East;5 however, by no stretch of the imagination could it be called free. A few "independent" papers like L'Orient, Al Jaridah, and Al Hayat are struggling to continue in the free press tradition. Economically the press is suffering, and has been forced to search for subsidies. This means that most of the editors find it necessary to reflect the policies of the pro-Nasser Lebanese government.

The only openly Communist paper in Lebanon is Al-Akhbar, published weekly in Beirut. There are about 100 weeklies in the country, most of which are printed in Arabic or French. By far the largest daily is Al-Hayat, with a circulation of some 18,000. The others have circulations ranging from 1,000 (Al-Hoda) to about 10,000 (Al-Jaridah). All are in Beirut, a city accounting for about a third of Lebanon's 1,500,000 people.

SYRIA-- Most of the more than 20 daily papers of Syria are in Damascus, but there are several in the city of Aleppo, the second largest city. Only one daily of Damascus-- Al-Ayyam, the most prosperous and the largest with some 18,000 circulation--publishes as many as eight pages in an edition. Other dailies produce editions of four pages. In Damascus other leading dailies are Al-Nasr, Al-Alam, and Al Nour (Communist). Outside Damascus the leading dailies are Al-Shabab and Barq Al-Shemal, of Aleppo. There are some 20 weekly papers in Syria, all circulating to very small readerships. In 1963 the economic outlook for the Syrian press, long bad, was not any more promising. The Syrian press gets much of its foreign news from London (Reuters) and from Cairo (Middle East News), and is increasingly relying on the latter source.

Even before Syria united with Egypt to form the UAR in early 1958, its press was small and was generally subsidized by the political parties; today the situation seems even worse. President Nasser of the UAR cut off the subsidies when he banned some of the Syrian parties. In addition, several of the larger Cairo dailies are beginning to circulate widely in Syria, providing stiff competition for the small and struggling Syrian papers.

Israel

The press of Israel is as varied as its multi-racial and polyglot population. Twenty daily newspapers together circulate about 150 copies for every 1,000 inhabitants of this little nation of nearly two million people. Some 330 other publications (60 weeklies, 150 fort-nightlies and monthlies among them) are published in Israel. Most of the dailies are printed in Hebrew; however, there are some in five other languages--Arabic, English, French, Hungarian, and German. The dailies average from four to eight pages, but publish up to 12 and 14 in weekend issues which feature cultural, religious, political, and literary articles. A majority of literate Israelis (about 95 per cent of the population) read several papers each day, and although the in-dividual circulations are not large, the amount of material read in the country is very great.

Every shade of political opinion is covered by the Israeli press. The papers are free of governmental censorship in theory, but tight control is exercised over military news and information vital to national security. This "control," imposed by the Government Press Division, has become especially rigid since 1957 when the Cold War in the Middle East began to get hotter.[1]

Of the nation's 20 daily newspapers, 18 are morning and two are afternoon journals. The press centers of Israel are Tel Aviv, the largest city (population about 370,000); Haifa, the chief seaport, and Jerusalem, the national capital. Unlike the United States, Israel has no locally-owned home town weekly papers. Production costs plus a very small advertising potential makes small town publishing extremely risky. The newsprint situation in Israel, very serious until 1956, now seems to be much better.

Among the more than 300 periodicals published in the country are about 50 government news-papers and reviews, ranging from weeklies to yearly publications. Periodicals appear in Hebrew (about two-thirds of them), Arabic, French, English, Yiddish, Bulgarian, Rumanian, Hungarian, Polish, German, and Persian. They include picture magazines, technical journals, literary reviews, and political, art, religious, and general magazines.

THE DAILIES. Largest of Israel's daily papers

is the independent evening Ma'ariv (f.1949) of Tel Aviv with a circulation of about 75,000. Other influential Hebrew language dailies (all AMs) are Jerusalem's Hakol (f.1949), and Tel Aviv's trade union Davar (f.1925), and the independent Ha'aretz (f.1918). · At each end of the political scale are two Hebrew dailies: Herut ("Freedom") of the rightist Herut party, and the Communist party's Kol Ha'am ("People's Voice") which takes its cues from Moscow. About in the middle would be Haboker ("Morning"), represent-ing the conservative, pro-West General Zionist party.

The principal dailies (all AMs) in other languages are the English Jerusalem Post (f.1932), the German Yediot Hadashot (f.1936), the Arabic El Yom (f.1948), the French Information d'Israel (f.1948), and the Hungarian Uj Kelet (f.1948).

NEWSPAPER CHARACTERISTICS.[2] Dailies average four to eight pages, with larger editions on the Sabbath or other special days. There is an obvious paucity of photographs in the papers, which are generally marked by their conservative and dignified appearance. In general, advertising is of a local nature, and consumes a little less than one-third of the total newspaper space. Most progressive of the dailies seems to be the lively PM circulation leader Ma'ariv ("Evening"), which fills its seven-column tabloid format with colorful features and spot news. It is the closest thing in Israel to a sensational paper.

The Jerusalem Post is a carefully edited daily usually running eight pages. With a very conservative make up, this English language newspaper is amazingly informative. Its small headlines, concise articles, scar-city of advertising, and nine-column format enable it to present a wealth of national and international news. Many national articles are staff-written; others come from Israel's national news agency, ITIM (f.1950). The bulk of the Post's international news is supplied by Reuters and United Press Inter-national. In 1962 its circulation was about 16,500.

Ha'aretz ("Land") of Tel Aviv, a politically independent Hebrew language daily, is the country's largest morning newspaper (circula-tion about 40,000). As is typical of the Israeli newspapers, it uses photographs very sparingly. Its usual six pages seldom contain more than one cut and it is normally only one column wide. About a third of the front page is given over to display advertisements, many containing drawings. Like The Jerusalem Post, its pages have nine columns.

Another important Hebrew daily is <u>Davar</u>
("The Word") of Tel Aviv. This nine-column
morning newspaper is the organ of the General
Federation of Labor. It usually runs eight
pages, and as is typical of the papers in
Hebrew, it uses about one third of its front
page for display advertising. Although it
averages only about three photographs an issue
(a few as large as two columns), the number of
illustrations is increased by the frequent use
of editorial cartoons (in the German style)
on its attractive commentary pages. Its news
coverage is less thorough than that of its
morning competitor <u>Ha'aretz</u>; nevertheless, its
opinion essays are probably the best published
in the press. Almost every issue of <u>Davar</u> includes at least one article by some important
government figure.

Francis Williams, back from a tour of observation in 1958, wrote in a British journal that
the Israeli press is in a poor economic condition (for example, he says that only three
papers are independent financially). He referred to the press of the country as a "tied
party press" which was "not a national" press
at all. According to this British press
specialist, the least political and probably
the most influential of the dailies is the
evening <u>Ma'ariv</u> (the largest with about 75,000
circulation). Of the AMs, says Williams,
<u>Ha'aretz</u> is the only one independent of a
political party. He points out that <u>Ma'ariv</u>
is considered "sensational" in Israel, but
would not fall into that classification if
judged by British or American standards.[3]

Israel's national news agency is ITIM, with
headquarters in Tel Aviv.[4] It was founded in
early 1950 by a group of Israeli newspapermen
under the name of Itonout Israel Meouguedet
(Israeli Associated Press). Its purpose was
to collect and distribute national news to the
press of the country, and furnish news to
radio stations. The agency is controlled by
a board of managers representing the share-
holding member dailies. ITIM's second most-
important bureau is in Jerusalem. An exchange
agreement exists with Reuters of the United
Kingdom.

BROADCASTING. Kol Israel ("The Voice of
Israel") is the government broadcasting service and is under the Prime Minister. Kol
Israel transmits from its Jerusalem and Tel
Aviv studios for about 20 hours daily. Daily
news bulletins are broadcast in Hebrew, Arabic,
French, and English; also special newscasts
go out to new immigrants each day in at least
seven other languages. An Arabic station
broadcasting to Arabs in Israel was founded
in 1958.

Turkey

There are some 300 newspapers published daily in Turkey, with a combined circulation of more than three million. During 1962, however, it appeared that many of the dailies were losing circulation quite rapidly; this was due mainly to continuing governmental interference in press matters.[1] The average daily circulation of the leading papers is between 20,000 and 50,000, with a few papers reaching the 100,000 mark from time to time. Istanbul and Ankara are the country's principal press centers. Dailies are also published, but with much smaller circulations, in such provincial cities as Adana, Samsun, Trabzon, and Izmir. Most newspaper plants in Turkey are spacious and modern and equipment is good. Besides the dailies, there are about 300 other papers-- weeklies, biweeklies and monthlies--published in Turkey. There are more than 50 weekly, and some 300 other, magazines in the country. The magazine press is healthy and journals of all types abound--all well-edited and attractively printed.

Three characteristics stand out in the Turkish press picture today: (1) the nationalistic tone of the entire press, (2) the great amount of editorial space given to foreign news (about one-half to domestic news; about one-fourth to foreign news, and about one-fourth to features), and (3) the harsh government measures--apparently still substantial-- used against the press.

AUTHORITARIAN BACKGROUND. There is still the tendency of the government to follow the practices of former Premier Adnan Menderes' authoritarian government. Before his fall in 1960, Menderes made a practice of jailing journalists who opposed him, padlocking hostile Turkish papers. Since the harsh Menderes regime was deposed in 1960, Turkish editors have fought fiercely for a more liberal government press policy, but it has been a tough fight and the situation is still far from good.

In 1963 the Turkish government, headed by Premier Ismet Inonu, was still reflecting the old Menderes philosophy of press suppression. The managing editor of Istanbul's influential Cumhuriyet was jailed for "disturbing the established order." And the editor of Atac, a cultural magazine, was also put into prison for publishing material not to the liking of the Inonu government.

Although there is some evidence of anti-press practices, it would hardly be fair to say that the situation is exactly the same as under the Menderes regime. Imprisonment, fines, threats, and censorship constantly plagued Turkish journalists while Menderes was in power. Newsprint was strictly controlled; all types of restrictive press laws were rigorously used. For example in 1958 press laws were limiting the dailies to eight pages; in addition, a government decree was passed that year which forbade publications to buy newsprint from any source other than the government which owned and operated the paper mills. All advertising under Menderes' government had to go through a governmental agency which decided where it would be placed. Newspapers which opposed the government received small amounts of newsprint as well as reductions in advertising.

One of the antigovernment newspapers in 1958 was forced to cut circulation from about 95,000 daily to less than 75,000. The big antigovernment daily Ulus of Ankara was ordered to suspend publication for several months during 1958 for printing cartoons critical of the government.[2] This same paper also found its circulation dropping drastically (from about 100,000 to some 20,000) in 1958 due to the government's reducing newsprint allocations to it by one-fifth. Publisher Kasim Gulek of Ulus said at the time: "They'd cut me off entirely, but it would be difficult to explain why they want to ruin the newspaper founded by Ataturk."

The editor of the Turkish weekly counterpart of Time magazine--Akis ("Reflection") of Ankara--was jailed at about the same time that Ulus was having its newsprint troubles. Reason: Akis criticized a government official. Four of Turkey's leading dailies--Milliyet, Ulus, Hurriyet, and Aksam--were cited in 1958 with court actions for publishing items which were termed "provocative." Probably the most vocal and influential of the press' critics of the Menderes' government was Ahmet Emin Valman, the publisher of Vatan ("Nation") and the "dean of Turkish journalists." Another formidable foe of the government's restrictions was Sahap Balcioglu, editor of Kim of Istanbul, a weekly news magazine.

Things looked much better in the winter of 1960 when Turkey's revolutionary government wiped out restrictions imposed by Menderes. A new law lifted the ban on criticism of public officials, and prison terms for publishers who criticized. Under the new law an official who felt he was libelled could sue.[3] Today publishers have representatives on a board that allocates newsprint, printing equipment, and most advertising.

NEWSPAPERS TODAY. The Turkish press, although
Menderes is gone, still has many problems.
Government officials still fear and distrust
the independent publisher. Newspapers still
struggle under the weight of excessive taxation. A multitude of regulations continue to
strangle the freedom-seeking press. Newspaper offices and facilities are generally old
and outmoded, and most always drab. There is
a shortage of equipment--even such basics as
typewriters. However, it should be said that
compared with the authoritarianism of the
Menderes regime, the Turkish press is well off
and faces a hopeful future.

The two principal daily newspapers in Ankara
are Zafer and Ulus, with some 45,000 and 30,000
circulation respectively. About a dozen others
publish in Ankara. There are about 45 popular
papers in Istanbul, each running from six to
eight pages. The three largest (all "popular"
papers) are Hurriyet (190,000), Milliyet
(100,000) and Yeni Sabah (90,000), each having
large readership in the provinces. Also in
Istanbul, Cumhuriyet (90,000) and Vatan
(30,000)--independents--and Dunya (45,000)
and Aksam (20,000)--party papers--have great
influence. All these papers use colored ink
extensively on their front pages, in nameplates, in cartoons, or in boxes.

NEWS AGENCY. The leading national news agency
in Turkey is the semiofficial Anatolian News
Agency with headquarters in Ankara. This
agency is subsidized by the government. There
are several domestic news services and feature
syndicates which also service Turkish periodicals. Most foreign news comes into the country through Reuters, the Associated Press, and
Agence France-Presse which have a pool arrangement with the Anatolian News Agency.

BRIEF PRESS HISTORY. The first Turkish newspaper was founded in 1831 as an official journal and was called Takvimi Vekayi ("Calendar
of Events"). The first independent paper was
Tercumani Ahval ("Interpretation of the Situation"), founded in 1859 by Agah Efendi and
Ibrahim Sinasi, who are usually recognized as
the "fathers of Turkish journalism." Only a

Cumhuriyet's front page during the era of
censorship under Menderes. The blank
spaces on the page were quite common in
many newspapers in Turkey from 1958 to
1960 when the regime fell.

little more than 50 years ago the press of the
old Ottoman Empire (part of which is now Turkey)
was merely a daily record of praises to the
Sultan, couched in a language filled with
Persian and Arabic expressions. In 1908 the
Young Turks's revolution brought about a rise
in nationalistic feeling and the Turkish language became increasingly predominant in the
press. Persian and Arabic-rooted words faded
away slowly. Turkey's defeat in World War I
shrank her boundaries, and the press adapted
itself to the resulting homogeneous Turkish
Republic which was created by Ataturk in 1923.[4]

United Arab Republic-- Egypt

Only about 20 per cent of the 21 million inhabitants of the U.A.R. (Egypt) are literate. There are some 20 dailies in the country, with a total circulation of about 500,000. The capital, Cairo, is not only the press center of the U.A.R. but is the biggest publishing center in the Middle East. The Cairo press had its beginnings at the end of the eighteenth century when Napoleon brought in the first printing press with his expedition. An official gazette was begun, of which the Official Gazette of the United Arab Republic is the descendant. After the British occupation of Egypt, the press participated in the nationalist struggle, and after independence was gained, the press became mainly partisan-- political parties owning some papers and others being owned independently. Today the Cairo press (and magazines) is thriving; pay for journalists is good, and technically the publications are examples for others throughout the Middle East.[1] There are ten dailies published in Cairo today which circulate all over the Arab world. The country's government has gained a firm hold over most newspapers in the country through planting its own people in editorial positions. There are no party papers in the nation since political parties are not legal in Egypt. All papers are government-oriented due to censorship and press regulations.[2]

In theory the independent papers are free, but in fact they follow the government line closely. Strict measures can be taken against any journalist guilty of writing a story or an editorial against his "patriotic convictions," which is a polite way of saying that he may not write anything "disagreeable" to the regime. A very strict censorship is imposed on all military and government news. This was true even before Egypt and Syria formed the U.A.R. in February, 1958 (Syria withdrew and proclaimed her independence, September 29, 1961). From all indications in 1963, government control of the press is as tight as ever; some observers believe it is even tightening.

The independent press, as is true throughout the Middle East, has many economic difficulties, while the government papers have ample money and newsprint. Slowly the independent press of Egypt is being strangled. The largest Egyptian daily is Al Gomhouria of Cairo, the official government paper. It has a daily press run of about 180,000 and gives about half the copies to government offices and the military. The paper is printed in Arabic. The next largest daily, also published in Cairo, is Al Akhbar (circulation about 160,000). It is followed by Al Ahram, with 140,000.

The Egyptian press is a street-sale press, and many of the papers reflect the influence of the London popular press in their rather gaudy display, and the U.S. press in their writing style. Until very recently most big dailies carried only about three stories on Page One (the "back page" to a U.S. reader), but now they carry from 10 to 30. Egyptian newspapers recruit part-time or full-time beginners with no experience, and usually start the neophyte journalists in the library. Most of the editorial workers on Egyptian newspapers are recruited from journalism schools and classes of the educational institutions in the larger cities. Most Egyptian papers have eight pages. Newsprint cost and scarcity is the big production problem of the Egyptian editors.

The Big Three of Cairo--Al Gomhouria, Al Akhbar, and Al Ahram--have separate circulations of 100,000 or more, and one in Alexandria printed in Greek--Imerissia Nea--has a circulation of about 40,000. These are the largest papers of the nation. The best of the dailies are generally small and have circulations ranging from 5,000 to 30,000. Several foreign-language newspapers of Cairo which have considerable local and regional prestige are: Le Journal d'Egypte (48,000), and La Bourse Egyptienne (30,000), and Egyptian Gazette (English), with 20,000. Popular magazines published in Cairo are Al Hilal (pocket monthly read throughout the Middle East), Al Kawakeb (weekly aimed at women), and Al Mussawar, an illustrated color weekly publication which is the largest Arabic weekly in the world.

The political cartoon is highly developed in Egypt. Reproductions of these cartoons are often carried by the New York Times in its Sunday editorial supplement. Cairo papers whose cartoons are especially well-known are Al Akhbar and Al Gomhouria. When the tone of the cartoon is complimentary, it will use folklore or proverbs as the theme; when the tone is critical, the cartoon is usually sharply and cynically humorous. Cartoonists are well paid and have much prestige among journalists. Besides the cartoons, most of which are political and deal with international subjects, the dailies of Egypt (especially in Cairo) emphasize foreign news and analysis. They devote about as much space proportionately to international affairs as do any papers in the world.

NEWS SERVICE. With headquarters in Cairo, the Egyptian agency, Middle East News, in 1963 had correspondents in 30 countries. By the end of 1963, it is estimated that it will be operating in at least twice that many countries. The agency was founded in 1955, but until 1962 it concentrated its operations within the Arab world. In 1961 it was re-organized and began focusing its attention on more distant horizons. In 1963 the agency's general manager, Zein Nagati, described his organization as "a private company within the framework of a public organization." This "public organization" comprises the National Publications House and the National Distribu-tion Company. Middle East News also gets revenue from its television, photo, and feature services. Already the agency has bureaus in several African nations, and in early 1963 was planning to make Rome the center of its European news system. From all indications the agency aspires to become a news organization of truly international scope-- even linking such distant spots as South America and Indonesia.

Far East and Southeast Asia: Overview

Since World War II newspapers in Asia, and particularly in Southeast Asia, have multiplied rapidly. Although outside Japan the papers are generally small, they are making great impact in their respective countries and have done much to instill a spirit of nationalism.[1] In Southeast Asia the press constantly attacks anything that smacks of European colonialism; meanwhile, on the other hand, portions of it are making no secret of their pro-Communist and pro-Soviet Union feelings.

Japan, in the Far East, has for many years had a highly developed press system, which in the last decade has provided the nation with a tremendous circulation. In Japan, too, is found one of the world's most advanced broadcasting and telecasting systems. One of the largest dailies in Asia (and for that matter, in the world) is published in Japan. There are some 175 dailies in Japan, and circulation per 1,000 persons is above 400--a readership rate double that of any other Asiatic nation and among the highest in the world.

In Communist China the press has expanded greatly in recent years; today some 800 dailies appear in many editions and untold numbers of small "wall" newspapers circulate within the cities and the mass collective settlements called "people's communes." People's Daily, or Jen Min Jih Pao as the Chinese call it, is the principal newspaper of the country. As the chief Communist party national paper, it has tremendous influence throughout continental China and in Southeast Asia among the Chinese "outlanders." It is widely quoted throughout the world press. The New China News Agency, one of the most powerful in Asia (with headquarters in Peiping), is the sole supplier of foreign news to the Chinese Communist press.

Generally, the press of Asia (and especially Southeast Asia) is still in its childhood, with the low literacy rate still the controlling factor in its development. In Southeast Asia there is a very large Chinese press with

nearly one-fourth of the total circulation of Indonesia, Thailand, Malaya, and Burma closely linked to China--either Communist or Nationalist.

With the exception of the northern and central parts of Asia there seems to be little political stability; consequently, in the sprawling Southeast Asian nations there are many (most are small) struggling journals either of a revolutionary character or existing only on subsidies from the governments. Also the whole of Southeast Asia might be termed the world's greatest melting pot of peoples, philosophies, and religions; nations are torn by civil wars--either between local nationalism and Communism or between colonial rule and Communism. The press is molded to a great extent by all these factors. It is understandable that newspapers are having a difficult time in this unstable and explosive situation.

All kinds of problems face the press of the Far East. One of them is the great number of languages. For example, in Malaya publications appear in seven different languages and dialects; Chinese, English, Malay, Tamil, Punjabi, Jawi, and Rumi. This sort of situation is not uncommon throughout the region. Another problem is a shortage of equipment and personnel. Printing is usually with hand-set type on outmoded presses, and journalists generally have had little or no formal journalistic training.

Another problem is illiteracy. All the Asiatic nations of the continent, and even the island state of Indonesia, have low literacy rates, and this coupled with the fact that literacy is spread over so many languages, helps explain the underdeveloped state of the press. Generally speaking, the press of Asia (again excluding Japan) is about where the U.S. press was almost a century ago. One of the least-developed press systems of Asia is that of Burma. Since World War II the press of this nation has barely been able to stay in existence. Many of the larger towns of the country have no newspaper, and in this nation of nearly 20 million people the circulation of the largest newspaper is only some 15- to 20,000. The total Burmese circulation is probably no larger than 200,000.

Omitting Japan and the Philippines (with press systems much like that of the U.S.), and Communist China (with a press system patterned after that of the Soviet Union), here are a few characteristics which in a general way may help describe the press of the Far East:

Printing is crude;

Advertisements are small and few or non-
existent;

Papers often accept subsidies from individuals or political parties;

There is little regard for objective reporting;

Papers are small--seldom more than four to
eight pages;

Papers are small--seldom circulating more
than 10,000 to 20,000 copies;

There are many small mimeographed and handwritten sheets;

Papers are passed on from person to person,
posted in public places and read aloud by
literate citizens;

There is a general shortage of equipment--
type-casting machines and presses;

There is a general shortage of trained personnel;

Many "featurized" articles and semifictional
stories are used;

Stories are usually written in a chronological style;

Chinese-language papers tend to dominate in
most parts of Asia--especially in Southeast Asia;

Dailies concentrate in the bigger cities of
Asia, with very few published in smaller
provincial towns.

A few of the leading daily newspapers of the
Far East and Southeast Asia are People's Daily
(Red China); Asahi, Mainichi and Yomiuri
(Japan), Central Daily News (Nationalist China),
The Times of India, The Hindu and The Statesman (India), and Dawn (Pakistan). These are
all mentioned in more detail on the following
pages. Three weekly newspapers, all published
in Southeast Asia and certainly among the best
of the weeklies of this region, are the Standard of Bangkok (Thailand), the Nation of
Rangoon (Burma), and the Times of Viet-Nam of
Saigon.

A few of the more prominent newspapers published daily in the Far East and Southeast
Asia which are not covered on the following
pages, but which should be mentioned are these:

Straits Times of Singapore (f.1845; circulation about 100,000; largest and most influential in Malaya); Malay Mail of Kuala Lumpur
and the Malay-language Majlis of the same city
are two other important Malayan dailies. A
weekly, the Sunday Times (circulation about
120,000) is also quite influential; it is
published in Singapore.

Wah Kiu Yat Pao (AM; circulation about
70,000) and Wah Kiu Man Pao (PM; circulation
about 50,000) of the British colony of Hong
Kong.

Dinamina (75,000) the dominant vernacular
(Sinhalese) daily of Colombo, Ceylon, and
Ceylon Daily News (55,000) the leading English-
language paper of the island.

Okinawa Times (AM circulation about 65,000;
PM circulation about the same), and Ryukyu
Shimpo (AM and PM circulations each about
50,000), both published in Naha, capital of
Okinawa.

Two of the leading papers of Viet Nam,
published in Saigon, are Cach Mang Quoc Gia
(National Revolution), 35,000, and Saigon
Moi (New Saigon), 30,000.

Afghanistan's two leading newspapers, both
published in Kabul, are Anis (Friend) with a
circulation of 25,000 and Islah (Reform)
with a circulation of 20,000.

One indication of increasing cooperation
among some of the countries of Asia was the
formation in early 1962 of the Organization
of Asian News Agencies to promote regional
cooperation in professional and technical
matters. Countries whose news agencies form
this organization are India, the Philippines,
Japan, Indonesia, Afghanistan, Nationalist
China, South Korea, Pakistan, and South Viet
Nam.

Burma

Burma, a southeast Asian nation of some 19 million people, has about 20 daily newspapers circulating a total of perhaps 150,000 to 200,000 copies each day. When it is considered that the illiteracy rate of the country is approximately 50 per cent, it is not difficult to understand the small total circulation figure. Newspapers in Burma are privately owned with no subsidies provided by the government. The press in Burma is as free as any in Southeast Asia. Most of the newspaper revenue comes from advertising. Besides the dailies, there are some eight weeklies in the country with a combined circulation of about 50,000. The most influential of these weeklies is generally considered to be The Nation, a serious and news-filled paper which in 1962 circulated about 12,000 copies. Most of the newspapers are printed in Burmese; however there are some in Chinese, English, Tamil, and Telugu.

As can be seen by looking at the total number of papers and the combined circulation, the individual papers are mainly small journals reaching a limited readership. Most of the papers are published in Rangoon, the nation's capital and chief city. About a half dozen papers are published in Mandalay, Burma's second city. The largest of these is Bahosi, which in 1963 had a circulation of some 11,000.

There are many regions of Burma without newspapers of any kind. Although circulations are not large, the people of Burma who can read (and many who cannot read but who like being read to) are extremely newspaper-conscious. Editors and other newspapermen in Burma are fairly well educated and are rapidly becoming better educated as journalism training is beginning to catch on; however, on many of the smaller papers there is an obvious lack of training among the staff members.[1]

Journalism education so far has mainly been limited to courses taught in the Burma Translation Society's School of Journalism in Rangoon. A few trial classes had been offered prior to 1957 (the year the BTS's program began) in the University of Rangoon, but had died out. Journalism is considered a dignified profession among the Burmese and a rather large number--including some women--of energetic and intelligent persons have entered the field in the last decade. There was really no organized system

of training persons entering the profession until with the initiative of former Prime Minister U Nu the Burma Translation Society began its journalism program.

Most of the Burmese dailies are printed on rather old and outmoded equipment and generally with undersized staffs; however, the workmanship (at least in comparison with many other Southeast Asian nations) is very good. A few of the leading dailies of Burma, all in Rangoon, are the Bamakhit (Burmese), Burma Express (English), Burma Nedu (Tamil), Daily Herald (Burmese), New China Pao (Chinese), and the New Times of Burma (English). Two outstanding weeklies among the nation's magazines are the Burmese Review and Monday Times (English), and the Hindi-language Navajivan, both of Rangoon.

The national press agency of Burma is the Burma Press Syndicate, Ltd., founded in 1947. Its headquarters are in Rangoon. The BPS is a cooperative of several leading newspapers of the country, with the director being the owner of a Rangoon daily. The agency has only the Rangoon bureau which serves all its subscribers very easily since they are all located in Rangoon. BPS's service includes foreign, economic, political, and sports material. News is sent by messenger or mail, or in the case of urgent news, telephone. It plans to begin providing news to the provincial press by telephone in the near future. The agency has distributed the Reuter news file since 1950. As yet, the news agency has little equipment and few staff members.

One paper should probably be dealt with a little more thoroughly before leaving this survey of the Burmese press. This is the English-language weekly Nation published in Rangoon. This paper, using seven columns and 10-point body type throughout its regularly eight-page editions, is a dignified journal showing many characteristics of traditional British serious journalism. Although a weekly, appearing each Monday, the paper shows many characteristics of a daily--in content and make up. It is noted for the great amount of space given to international events and serious national affairs (e.g., a typical issue of eight pages will contain at least five full pages of foreign news). A few local stories of a light nature do appear, and usually on the front page. For example, on the front page of the November 3, 1958, issue among such heavy headlines as "Propaganda and the Uncommitted Nations" were stories from the provinces carrying these headlines--"Police Trace Fish Robbers" and "Thefts Traced to Pet Crow."

Communist China

Communist China (or the Chinese People's Republic), a vast nation of some 700 million people, has a press system patterned very closely after that of the Soviet Union.[1] This resemblance is marked by the propaganda function of the Chinese press, the strict control of the newspapers by the Communist party, the exclusion of commercial advertising from most publications, and the importance of the press in sifting government policy down through every element of the social system. Some few of the country's newspapers may be occasionally referred to as "non-Party" (these are rapidly being eliminated), but all obey the dictates of the Party's Department of Propaganda.

The Red Chinese press functions, not to satisfy people's needs for information or interpretation, but to make the thoughts of the masses conform to official Party policy. As in the Soviet Union, the press is supposed to kindle and keep burning national pride and loyalty, aid in developing all phases of the Communist system, organize and develop Party units, and promote social and cultural progress. In this "propagandistic press system"[2] of Red China, little use is made of TV and radio mainly because at present the Chinese are too poor to buy receiving sets. Newspapers are by far the chief media of mass communication. Chief among these newspapers is the Jen Min Jih Pao or "People's Daily" of Peiping, an eight-page daily with a circulation of nearly one million. Serving as a Pravda and Izvestia wrapped in one package, this paper is the pace-setter of the Chinese press, and its influence filters down into the most remote Chinese village or factory.

In this nation of some 300,000,000 illiterates (about half of the population) are about 800 daily newspapers with a total circulation of some 15,000,000. An additional 5,000,000 copies are published weekly. Although these figures are rather crude estimates, they do indicate something of the newspaper reading being done in Red China today. This readership is certainly not impressive for a modern nation of some 600,000,000 inhabitants; however it should be realized that the Communists see to it that publications reach readers in every farm, factory, village, and mine, even if these publications are nothing more than crude handwritten or mimeographed "notices" or "wall" newspapers.

THE AIM OF THE PRESS. Four main functions characterize the Red Chinese press: (1) education (propaganda) work for the Communist government, (2) agitation or stimulation to progress, (3) forming and directing public opinion, and (4) serving as an instrument by which the government can control society.[3] The chief organ of the Communist party and the most influential "national" paper is Jen Min Jih Pao ("People's Daily"), the largest and most powerful Communist paper outside the Soviet Union. The larger cities of Red China have papers which might be called "national" publications; they circulate to some extent throughout the country among Party leaders and help set policy for the smaller provincial and district papers which are so important in the Communist press system.

Probably the leading "national" papers are Jen Min Jih Pao, Kwangming Jih Pao, Ta Kung Pao, Chung Kuo Shao Nien Pao, and Kung Jen Jih Pao.[4] Below these national papers are the regionals and provincials serving to filter Party policy and information downward in the press hierarchy. And beneath these are the thousands of scattered district or "local" papers (many are "wall" papers) which concentrate on more local and practical problems while bringing certain announcements pertaining to the "official line" to the "grass roots" Chinese society.

Peiping (Peking), the Red Chinese capital city, is the main press center. The newspapers are pretty well distributed throughout the larger towns and cities of Communist China. Next to Peiping, Shanghai is the most important press city. Two other prominent publishing centers are Tientsin and Nanking. Newspaper promotion, handling, and circulation are almost entirely carried on under the jurisdiction of the country's postal authorities.

Peiping's chief newspapers are the following dailies: Jen Min Jih Pao, Chung Kuo Shao Nien Pao (a youth paper), Kung Jen Jih Pao (trade unions paper), Kwangming Jih Pao, and Ta Kung Pao (business-economic paper). Leading provincials are Chieh Fang Jih-Pao ("Liberation Daily") and Wen Hui Jih Pao of Shanghai, Ta Kung Pao of Tientsin, Kiangsu Nung Min Pao of Nanking, Nan Fang Jih Pao ("Southern Daily") of Canton, Hsin Hua Jih Pao ("New China Daily") of Chungking, Hupeh Jih Pao of Hupeh, and Anhwei Jih Pao of Anhwei.

Jen Min Jih Pao of Peiping, with its approximately one million daily circulation, is by

far the largest paper in the country. Only a
few other dailies have circulations of as
much as 200,000; they are <u>Kung Jen Jih Pao</u>
("Daily Worker") <u>Chung Kuo Shao Mien Pao</u>
("Young People's Paper") and <u>Kwangming Jih
Pao</u> ("Kwangming Daily") of Peiping, and <u>Ta
Kung Pao</u> ("Commercial Paper") of Tientsin,
and the two Shanghai dailies <u>Chieh Fang Jih
Pao</u> ("Liberation Daily") and <u>Wen Hui Jih Pao</u>.

RED CHINA'S LEADING DAILY. <u>Jen Min Jih Pao</u>
or "People's Daily" as it is generally known
in the U.S. is a powerful and pervasive instrument whose influence reaches into all
levels of society. Published in the capital
city of Peiping, its one million daily copies
circulate throughout the Chinese People's
Republic, setting policy for the regular press
and sifting government information down through
the "wall" and "blackboard" papers to the
lowest units of social and political life.
Directly or indirectly this newspaper feeds a
daily diet of pure Marxist jargon to almost
everyone in the country. Like <u>Pravda</u> in the
U.S.S.R., it contains no gossip columns,
comics, or sports and leaves the printing of
"local" news to the more than 170 provincial
dailies and the thousands of smaller journals.
It is the official newspaper for both the
Party and the government, and its eight packed
pages (no advertisements) reflect this dual
role in their stories and pictures.

<u>Jen Min Jih Pao</u> was founded in 1948 in Yenan
where the Communists grouped their forces for
the subjugation of the country. Today it
publishes from a modernistic, well-equipped
plant in Peiping; its editor is Wu Leng-Hsi,
who is also director of the government-controlled news agency. The paper was referred
to in 1958 as "a colossal bore" whose "turgid
editorials crawl on, column after column" and
whose "leaden propaganda handouts in the form
of 'news' stories weigh down the front page."[5]

The tremendous impact of this leading Chinese
Communist daily is indicated by the following
quotation from French correspondent Robert
Guillain's book, <u>600 Million Chinese</u>:

"I have seen the pedicab boy, the street
sweeper, the mother of a family, stop in
front of the famous paper in the public
places where it is hung, and try labori-
ously to decipher its difficult texts.
I have heard it read in public, for the
benefit of college students; it comes
over loud-speakers for train travelers.
More often still a lecturer reads it to
the illiterates who still abound among
the adult population....Can this extraordinary attention to the texts of the
<u>People's Daily</u> be explained by the desire

for knowledge which has suddenly seized
the Chinese? I do not think so....The
reason why the reading of the <u>People's
Daily</u> is so wide-spread is that it is...
demanded by the authorities...."[6]

NATIONAL NEWS AGENCY. Working hand-in-hand
with the <u>People's Daily</u> is the official Red
Chinese news agency--Hsin-Hua (New China News
Agency), which like the leading Party daily
was founded in Yenan. It has grown into a
giant propaganda machine, with a radio-tele-
type network throughout Europe, Africa, the
Middle East, Asia, and Latin America. Regular
transmissions are sent throughout the world
from headquarters in Peiping. The news agency
has about 30 bureaus in Red China and has
staffs in most European capitals as well as
in Moscow, New Delhi, Baghdad, Cairo, Damascus,
and Havana. As a propaganda organization,
Hsin-Hua presently is concentrating its effort
among the noncommitted nations--those wavering
between the East and West.

Among its many activities, it does not neglect
its internal responsibilities. It furnishes,
for instance, news and instructions to the
"keepers" of the "wall" newspapers throughout
the country. In organization and purpose, it
is practically identical to the Soviet Union's
TASS. Headquarters are in Peiping and some 30
foreign offices are maintained throughout the
world (none in the U.S.). It reportedly has
more than 1,500 sub-offices and about 50,000
"stringers" in all parts of Red China and in
the armed forces. A branch of the government's
Information Department, Hsin-Hua sends its news
by short wave radio throughout the country,
where it is monitored every day by the Chinese
papers. Most of the agency's foreign stories
are merely translations of TASS reports. News
from Red China to the outside world is scarce.
No Asiatic or Western newspapers have permanent
correspondents in Peiping, and only AFP and
Reuters have staffers there.

"WALL" NEWSPAPERS. Printed papers are supplemented by the many mimeographed and handwritten
sheets (often called "wall" newspapers), without which information could never reach the
more remote Chinese communities. These "wall"
newspapers are quite common everywhere in China
as they are in most parts of the Far East.
They are often printed on paper and tacked to
buildings, trees, and fences or placed on
regular bulletin boards at strategic spots along
the streets. A variety of these papers, often
referred to as "blackboard papers" are chalked
on blackboards set up in prominent places. Hundreds of schoolroom blackboards covered with
long texts often written in colored chalk can
be found in the streets, railway stations and
in most public places.

The French journalist, Robert Guillain, wrote in 1957 after observing this phase of Chinese journalism: "Each school, each institution has its board, often illustrated with simple chalk drawings. This is, in fact, a very important means of indoctrination; it is simultaneously a poster and a wall newspaper, passing on to the masses, economically and in small doses, the orders of the leaders and the collective thought."[7]

PRINTING QUALITY. The real newspapers, especially the big "nationals," are generally well-written and well-printed. It is the general opinion that among all the larger publications (newspapers and magazines) the workmanship is of high quality. For example, Dr. Raymond B. Nixon, writing in the Journalism Quarterly which he edits, points to the quality of Red Chinese publications. He states: "Anyone who thinks of the Chinese Communists as crude and illiterate would do well to examine some of their printed propaganda....As for the printing, much of it is of as fine quality as the best Western presses can produce."[8]

MAGAZINES. Controlled by the state and Party, Chinese magazines serve the same basic purpose as newspapers--to disseminate government propaganda and control the thoughts and ideas of the people. The post office not only handles the distribution of the magazines, but also the subscriptions. Probably the most influential magazine in Red China is a semi-monthly journal called Red Flag. Started in 1958 by the Communist party, it is the main theoretical journal of the Regime, dealing with subjects such as politics, economics, science, literature, art, and philosophy. All articles are written by Party members.

Other leading magazines of Communist China are Chinese Youth, Chinese Women, Chinese Workers, Literary Gazette, Fine Arts, People's Music. All the major magazines are published in the communications center and capital, Peiping.

ELECTRONIC MEDIA. Radio broadcasting by the Reds in China began in 1945, and by 1949, when the Communists took over the country, there were 16 radio stations operated by Mao's forces. Private stations were taken over by the state. Some were shut down. Today the broadcasting network, like the press, is considered an arm of the government. Receiving sets are distributed to various parts of the country by the government and all owners are carefully registered. There are three main types of programs offered by the radio stations:

political propaganda (news and commentaries), education (technological and scientific progress), and entertainment (music and dramatic productions mainly). People's Daily, like Pravda in the U.S.S.R., uses radio to distribute editorials and other important announcements to regional papers. Today there are about 100 radio stations in Communist China.

Television got started in Red China in 1960, although an experimental station had been set up in Shanghai two years earlier. Television today is mainly used for educational purposes, with courses in the sciences on the secondary level getting the greatest attention. However, the fare of the three main stations in Shanghai, Peking, and Harbin include daily diets of sports, opera, popular science and children's programs. Very few private TV sets are in use; the approximately 15,000 receiving sets available in 1962 were for public use--set up in hotels, railway stations, and parks.

BRIEF BACKGROUND.[9] When the Communists took over the country in October, 1949, they ordered the re-registration of all newspapers; those publications considered "politically unacceptable" were denied registration permits. Several hundred prominent Chinese newspapers thereby went out of business immediately. In the remaining newspapers, the Communists allowed the old staffs to continue, but new editors--all prominent in the Communist party-- were placed in charge.

Actually the Communists had begun publishing newspapers four years before they "liberated" the country, as they put it, from Chiang Kai-shek's government. In 1945 the Communists had established a journal in Yenan called Chieh Fang Jih Pao ("Liberation Daily"), which still exists in Shanghai. A little later in Chungking they opened a sister newspaper to Chieh Fang Jih Pao called Hsin-Hua Pao ("New China Newspaper"), which also still publishes.

Today, the only newspaper in continental China surviving the Communist coup and publishing under its old pre-Communist name is Tientsin's Ta Kung Pao, one of the newspapers most often quoted outside China today. It is one of the few allowed to be exported from Communist China. Ta Kung Pao contains general news (or what the Communists consider "news"), but mainly it specializes in business, economic and financial reports. Its circulation is estimated at about 125,000.

Nationalist China

The "free" Chinese (about 11 million of them) living on the island of Taiwan (Formosa) off the Chinese mainland have a press which is generally considered free in most respects, but which is operating under an authoritarian government which restricts the press' activities.[1] If this seems a vague and rather evasive opening sentence, it is because the press situation on Formosa is rather hazy. In most instances President Chiang Kai-shek's Kuomintang party does not interfere with the Republic's newspaper operations and the island's editors have little to complain about. This, however, is not always the case, and the government can apply many types of pressure-- from force to censorship and economic sanctions--to keep the editors "in line."

There are some 30 daily newspapers published on Formosa, and although the circulations are not made public, they are known to be very small. About half of the dailies are published in Taipeh, the island Republic's capital. In addition to the daily press, there are about 250 periodicals published on the island. In general, the press of Free China is much like that of the United States. For example, the program of journalism study at the National Chengchi University in Taipeh, and the great amount of mass communications research being carried on in Formosa, reflect a strong U.S. influence. There are some 25 radio stations on the island and one government-owned TV station.

The press, up until a quite restrictive press law was passed in 1958, enjoyed a great amount of freedom. Newspapers often attacked persons in high and low positions and dug about for human interest material (the more personal and scandalous the better) with great vitality. This situation is changing, however, and the newspapers conduct themselves with more restraint and with much more "respect" toward government officials. Still occasionally a newspaper--usually one of the two English-language dailies--will blast away at a government policy or official.[2] Actually the only person who is spared criticism is President Chiang himself, although his programs and policies do sometimes receive editorial jolts from a few of the papers.

Even though the new Constitution of 1947 grants the people freedom of expression,[3] many observers feel that there is no real sense of freedom on the island. "If you doubt it," says a recent British visitor, "you have only to go hunting for opinions in Formosa. A few people will talk freely to you, in the privacy of friendship, but nobody at all will be rash enough to express a divergent view into a television camera or a newspaper column."[4]

This British journalist goes on to call Chiang's government "a semitotalitarian machine primarily concerned with its own survival and mastery...for all the pious pretence at democratic forms."

There are other observers who maintain that the government is little concerned about throttling the press. Typical of the views which take this more optimistic position is the following:

"...newspaper editorials and stories, the relaxed, usually cheerful attitude of the people, the boldness of reporters and photographers...do not suggest the rigors of a police state which uses terror as the chief instrument of control."[5]

It should be noted, however, that of the more than 30 island dailies, only about one third are privately operated, and even among the publishers and officials of some of these can be found members of the powerful Kuomintang party (the party dominated by President Chiang). The government itself is in the publishing business, having its own "official" organs. Chief among these is the Republic's largest daily, Central Daily News,[6] which represents the Kuomintang and expresses party and government views. Two other large dailies, also published in Taipeh and representing the government, are Hsin Sheng Pao and Chung Hua Jih Pao.[7]

President Chiang has made it clear many times since his government moved to Formosa from the mainland that he considers Free China at war with the Communists. This more or less perpetual "state of emergency" or "time of crisis" understandably leads to tighter controls on the press, and a realization of the rather difficult position of Chiang's government should help explain the occasional cases of press control which do arise.[8] It is certainly not difficult to understand why the restrictive Press Law of 1958 putting a number of limitations on the newspapers' activities would be necessary in such a period of crisis. One might wonder why such restrictions were so late in coming.

After all, the Free Chinese press is the
major non-Communist voice in Southeast Asia
and is believed to exert great influence on
public opinion--not only on Formosa--but
throughout a wide area where millions of "overseas Chinese" look to Chiang's government for
guidance and hope.

There are four national agencies on Formosa,
the largest of which is the Central News
Agency. It has seven overseas offices, and
provides news in both English and Chinese to
every paper on the island. Central News
Agency has exchange agreements with Japan's
Kyodo agency, with the American UPI and the
French AFP. Other agencies serving Formosan
newspapers are China News & Publication Service, China Union Press, and Military Information Service.

Dailies of Nationalist China, other than
those published in the capital city, are found
in Keelung, Hualien, Kaohsiung, Penghu, Matsu,
Taitung, Taichung, and Tainan. The leading
Taipeh dailies are Central Daily News (Chung
Yang Jih Pao), Hsin Sheng Pao, China News,
China Post, Hua Pao, Chen Hsin Hsin Wen
(economic paper) Kung Lun Pao, and Min Tsu

Evening News. About half the dailies of
Nationalist China are published in Taipeh.

On Taiwan there is little reliance on advertising; there seems to be a deep-rooted distaste and distrust of advertising. This suspicion is one reason that newspapers of
Nationalist China are so slim. Morning editions carry eight pages and afternoon editions
have only four. This is true only in the
capital dailies; seldom does a provincial paper
exceed four pages. All papers publish seven
days a week--one edition each day. Although
the Chinese reader gets a rather poor and
spotty view of national and local news, he
finds that his papers provide him with a liberal supply of foreign news. In this respect,
the Chinese papers are similar to those of
Japan. The dailies of Taiwan rely completely
on subscribers and copies are delivered to
the homes.

The leading newsmagazines published on the
island are Chung-kuo I-chou ("China Newsweek"),
Taiwan Pictorial, the pictorial weekly Sinica,
published by China News Press, and the popular
fortnightly Free China. These are all published in the capital.

India

In 1962 there were about 8,000 newspapers and periodicals being published in India, at least 2,000 more than in 1957. Some 300 dailies of significant size (about 450 in all) circulate three million copies in this vast country, the world's second most populous (about 400 million people). One third of the dailies are English-language publications. The rate of Indian literacy is rising rapidly; however, probably no more than 20 per cent of the population can read or write.

Printed and electronic journalism has not advanced rapidly in India for many reasons, but chief among them are these: (1) there are many languages and dialects in the country,[1] (2) there are five principal religions, and (3) there are more than 100 castes. These basic considerations, all keeping the country divided, may be supplemented by these: there is great poverty among the potential audiences of the mass media; publication and broadcasting costs are increasing rapidly; about 75 per cent of the population live in small isolated villages, and there is the tendency of the government to use authoritarian pressures on the press from time to time. These basic facts are the root of many problems--educational, economic and political--and it is difficult for a healthy press to thrive in such a situation.

There is very little "light" or human interest news in the Indian newspapers. Features are hard to find except in some weeklies. Official speeches, government proclamations, and official handouts get the big play. Considerable stress, however, is given to international affairs. Government advertising in the papers is increasing. India has been called a "semisocialist" nation, and state advertising forms about one-third of the space in many of the papers of the larger cities. This practice of placing government ads in papers, of course, opens the way for abuses and pressures. India's press is in a strange position in the world's press--finding itself working in a basically British journalistic tradition with overtones of libertarianism but finding itself flirting with many practices of authoritarianism. Perhaps the press is merely relecting the philosophy of the government itself, seeking a "neutralist" path to the socialism of the U.S.S.R. and the capitalism of the USA.[2]

The Indian press is a product of British journalism with an overlay of U.S. journalism introduced since India's independence. The press is strong in such aspects as editorial writing and analysis, the lack of sensational material, and in speech reporting, but relatively weak in straight news reporting and editing. This statement is a generalization, of course, and does not apply to excellent dailies such as The Hindu, The Statesman, and The Times of India. A striking feature of the Indian press is the high proportion of foreign news stories (about 15 per cent of the editorial space in the vernacular press and nearly 25 per cent in the English-language press). Indian newspapers lean heavily on news agencies for their foreign news. Only the larger dailies have foreign correspondents; most of these correspondents are in London, a few in the Middle East (usually in Cairo), and most of the others in nations adjacent to India.

The English-language press is the most influential in the country. All Indians who have any wide influence or prestige in the country know English. About a dozen English-language papers are extremely important in that they reach, and presumably help mold opinion among, the nation's intellectuals or opinion-leaders. The ultranationalist Indians bemoan the lingering importance of English, but it remains the main language of the nation's economic and political leaders.

Bombay's Indian Express, with a circulation of about 210,000, is the largest English-language daily in the country. However, usually considered the three most influential English-language dailies of India are The Statesman of Calcutta, The Hindu of Madras, and The Times of India in Bombay. They might be considered "national" newspapers in that they have readers scattered throughout the country. The Hindu has been compared to Britain's Guardian of Manchester by British press critic Francis Williams.[3] The Statesman generally represents British progressive opinion, and The Times of India is a well-balanced and serious journal which is the leading daily of West India. Actually it is published in New Delhi as well as in Bombay and has a circulation of some 160,000.

Very few of the smaller Indian newspapers are prosperous. Most are forced to publish from inadequate plants, using untrained staff members and inferior equipment. The smaller papers are unable to get their share of advertising, most of which is published in the more than 60 English-language dailies. The English-language papers generally (a) resemble national papers since English is the language of the educated India, (b) are the most accurate of the nation's papers, and (c) cover a wider range of news stories than do the other papers.

Ananda Bazar Patrika of Calcutta is the largest Indian-language daily with a circulation of about 90,000 copies in the Bengali dialect; this paper is published also in Allahabad and is the oldest daily in the country published by Indians. The vast majority of Indian newspapers have small circulations—under 10,000. There are about 800 weeklies—newspapers and magazines—in the country. More than half of these are magazines. Periodicals are printed in 14 languages.

According to Dr. Roland Wolseley of Syracuse University, who has studied the Indian press in recent years, the newspapers of the country face a multitude of problems; some of these are (1) badly organized communities from the newsgathering aspect, (2) small, untrained, badly-paid staffs, (3) too few stringers and correspondents in the rural areas, (4) poor facilities for work, (5) too few pages in the papers, (6) too little literacy, (7) too many distribution problems, and (8) too many languages and dialects.[4] Another serious problem confronting newspapers of the country is the scarcity and high cost of newsprint. As one

Indian journalist put it in 1957: "The single largest problem facing the newspaper business in India, as in other parts of Asia, is the availability of newsprint at reasonable prices."[5]

About half of the country's daily newspaper sales are made in four cities—Madras, Bombay, New Delhi, and Calcutta—and in these cities perhaps one family in two buys a paper. In the rural provincial areas, only one man in a village may buy a paper; however, papers are always passed on among friends and relatives, and it is common for the school teacher or some other professional to read the paper aloud to large audiences.

SOME LEADING INDIAN NEWSPAPERS

Calcutta:

Ananda Bazar Patrika (Bengali)
Amrita Bazar Patrika (English)
The Statesman (English)
Vishwamitra (Hindi)
Jugantar (Bengali)

Bombay:

Times of India (English)
Bombay Chronicle (English)
Hindustan (Urdu)
Vishwamitra (Hindi)

Madras:

Hindu (English)
Andhra Patrika (Telugu)
Thanthi (Tamil)
Indian Express (English)

New Delhi:

Hindustan Times (English)
Milap (Urdu)
Hindustan (Hindi)
Nav Bharat (Hindi)

PRESS FREEDOM IN INDIA. Although the press in general might be considered free, an "Objectionable Matter" Press Law of 1951 forbids newspapers to publish anything which might be indecent, scurrilous, or intended to blackmail. This law also forces the publisher to deposit a sum which is forfeited if anything objectionable is printed. The government can also keep the press in line by withdrawing its advertising from a critical newspaper.[6] This type of government pressure is not often used in India, but there have been cases of its use in the last few years. For example, The Times of India, and the weekly

Madras paper Swatantra have been among recent victims of this type of government pressure. The Indian press in general--and especially the bigger daily papers--enjoys a great amount of freedom, and all types of criticism are found in the papers. It should be noted, however, that many of the smaller papers are principally government spokesmen and propaganda organs, and are naturally satisfied with the status quo.

In 1957 "The Newspaper Price and Page Law" was passed in India and was a further indication of the government's interference in press matters. This law in effect regulates the size of Indian newspapers, for if an editor increases the number of pages in his newspaper he must raise the sales price accordingly. In other words, every paper's price is in relation to the number of pages. Another aspect of the law is that the government decides how much advertising there will be in the newspapers.

An editorial in the Saturday Evening Post harshly criticized the law in 1957 and opined that leaders in Indian government desire to keep the newspaper circulations small because "tiny, impoverished newspapers influence few people."[7] The law, according to the American magazine, would force Indian editors to keep their papers small; they could not hold their price down while offering a better product in order to increase their circulations. The editorial called the law a "step in the direction of dictatorship," and said that "where the press is weak, dictatorship becomes easy."

According to Dr. B. V. Keskar, Minister of Information and Broadcasting in 1957, the law was intended to "give some protection to the regional language press." He said he didn't see how the price-page law could harm press freedom because "the most venomous criticism could be made in a four-page paper."[8] The Saturday Evening Post editorial answered this by saying that four-pagers cannot give much information about the modern world; about all they can do is "print government announcements." And concluded the magazine's editorial: "This is why every city in the Soviet Union has a standard four-page newspaper. That is a dangerous example for India to follow."

THE WEEKLY PRESS. In spite of its many glaring weaknesses, eccentricities, the weekly papers of India make a real contribution to the journalism of India. They exist throughout the country in a multitide of forms and reflect the many-faceted society. The history of Indian journalism began with weekly papers; in 1780 the Bengal Gazette was begun in Calcutta, and it is considered India's first

newspaper. Indian weeklies began as opinion journals aimed mainly at intellectuals of the upper classes; however, under Gandhi the weekly press changed greatly in that the papers began to have great impact on the masses. Especially was this true in the political realm. The weeklies became more popular in nature, although a certain literary air still clung to them. Since 1950 illustrated weeklies have grown in quantity and quality. Most Indian languages have at least one picture-weekly.

These weeklies are supplemented by the special Sunday supplements of the dailies. These Sunday sections (or magazines) provide the reader with a potpourri of items--from poems to astrological forecasts. Some of the English dailies carry comics in color in their Sunday supplements. There were 1,881 weeklies in India in 1962.[9]

INDIA'S NATIONAL NEWS AGENCY. The Press Trust of India (PTI) was founded in 1905. In 1948 it became a cooperative nonprofit news trust governed by the Indian press. PTI service is received by all the larger papers and by many government offices by teleprinter. PTI is a partner in Britain's Reuters Trust; however, it is free to make contracts with any agency and to develop its own foreign service. News is transmitted in English only. This makes it necessary for all vernacular papers to translate the news, with much loss of time, money, and effort--as well as accuracy.

BROADCASTING. The government controls and conducts All India Radio, the sole broadcasting organization of the country. About thirty stations today compared with only six in 1947 indicate that although radio is growing in the country, it is still in its infancy. Music is the main fare on radio, but news is important. Programs are presented in all the major languages of India and in 48 dialects. About 100 newscasts a day are provided for Indian listeners (during 24 hours). Television was still new in 1962 and operated from Delhi twice a week on Tuesdays and Fridays for one hour. TV sets are increasing rapidly, however, but they are mainly being used in the schools.

There are slightly more than 1.5 million radio sets in use--most of them in four principal cities. The government has more than a half-million subsidized community radios in the villages. But this is a mere dent, amounting to about one such set per village. Lack of electricity in many regions, lack of repair facilities, and too many languages have hampered the growth of the electronic media in India. All India Radio, government-owned radio network, broadcasts mainly in Hindi, the official

language, but there are only a handful of
Indians who can understand newscasts on AIR.
In some parts of India, however, AIR newscasts
are given in five languages and in as many as
15 dialects.[10]

INDIAN PRESS SUMMARY. India is exhibiting
increasing interest in journalism education
and is attempting to improve its press system.

Literacy is increasing faster than are news-
    paper circulations.

Hindi (official Indian language) papers
    appear to have the brightest future in
    the country. Currently Vishwamitra,
    published in three of the largest cities,
    is the foremost Hindi-language newspaper.

The majority of small provincial papers
    have little prestige as "news" media,
    but are in combination the main link
    between the government and the rural
    peoples.

There is little possibility of any paper's
    circulation soaring up suddenly in India.

The seriousness and lack of sensationalism
    in Indian newspapers is impressive;
    editorial writing is on a high level in
    all the bigger papers.

Much space is devoted to domestic and foreign
    politics.

The press generally shows no tendency to
    pry into private lives, nor does it ex-
    ploit personal tragedies.

Until recently there was no emphasis on sex,
    and still there is very little.

Layout is varied in the Indian newspapers.
    The Statesman has one of the brightest
    make up patterns among Indian papers.

Until early in 1958 when it "went modern,"
The Hindu of Madras had run only classified advertising on its front page.

Most of the small papers have similar con-
    tents, due to their tight budgets.
    Specialization is rare among Indian jour-
    nalists and the papers indicate this in
    their news columns.

Sports news and commercial reporting is
    extremely drab in the Indian newspapers,
    judged by U.S. standards.

Of the weeklies, Anandavikatan (a Tamil
language paper) with a circulation of about
150,000, is the leader. It is followed by
another Tamil weekly, Kalki, with a circulation of about 100,000.

Blitz, with a circulation of about 85,000
has the highest circulation of the English-
language weeklies. It is followed by Screen,
a movie magazine. In third place is the
Illustrated Weekly of India.

Generally considered the leading news magazine of India is Link of New Delhi, which
presents its wares in a format quite similar
to that of Time of the U.S.

The government says that no paper may use
more than 40 per cent space for advertising,
in an attempt to help small, struggling papers
get a start and continue.

Most Indian papers rely almost entirely on
press agencies for their foreign news.

New Age (published in Madras and Delhi,
f.1953) is a monthly theoretical journal of
the Communist party of India.[11] It was suspended during World War II.

The principal wire services transmit news
only in English. Most reporters on the major
papers must know English.

Indonesia

and editorials (usually one) and columns on the second page, more news and some advertisements on the third page, and advertisements (mostly display; very few classified advertisements) on the back page. The few cuts which

Indonesia, a nation composed of about 3,000 islands stretching down from the southeastern tip of Asia, has nearly 100 daily newspapers with a total circulation of some 600,000. Of the 85 million inhabitants of the Republic, only about half can read and write. But great strides are being made in combating illiteracy; for example, as late as 1940 only seven persons out of every 100 were literate. The press is concentrated in the capital city of Djakarta (formerly called Batavia) which is on Java, the Republic's most populous island. Nearly half of the Indonesian newspapers are published in the capital. There are about 30 weekly newspapers in Indonesia, circulating about 250,000 each week. Newspapers are published in the Indonesian language (called Bahasa Indonesia) and in Dutch, Chinese, and English. Indonesian language papers are the most numerous and the most influential in the nation.[1]

Djakarta, the capital, is the main press center, but other prominent cities such as Surabeja, Medan, Bandung, and Jogjakarta have important national newspapers. Probably the most influential of the Indonesian language dailies (all in Djakarta) are Merdeka (independent; widely quoted), the violently anti-Communist Kengpo and Indonesia Raya, the Masjumi (Moslem) party Abadi, and the Socialist Pedoman. The English language dailies Indonesian Observer and the Times of Indonesia, although small and poorly printed, exert considerable influence and serve many of the 80,000 Europeans and Americans living in Indonesia. Java Bode is usually considered the leading Dutch newspaper in the country. Principal dailies which serve the nearly three million Chinese in Indonesia are the well-edited and printed Kengpo (one of the nation's largest with a circulation of about 40,000), and the leftist Sin Po. Pedoman, with some 55,000 circulation, is the country's largest newspaper; Merdeka (45,000) is second; Suluh Indonesia and Indonesia Raya (both with some 40,000) are next. Outside Djakarta, probably the most important paper is Waspada of Medan, with about 30,000 circulation.

Most newspapers of the Republic are small, poorly-printed sheets averaging from 4 to 8 pages. The typical Indonesian newspaper, regardless of language, seems to be a four-pager with news on the first page, more news

are used in the papers are very small--usually one column. Many of the papers have nine columns to the page. A good example of a nine-column daily is the Socialist party's lively Pedoman, whose make up and typography is quite attractive compared with many other Indonesian dailies, and which seems to use far more staff-written stories than its competitors. Merdeka is another nine-column daily; about the only things which break its vertical narrow-columned appearance is the editorial (set two columns) and one comic strip.

The English language Indonesian Observer of Djakarta fits the general Indonesian concept of a newspaper. It does, however, use its third page mainly as a children's section, with display advertisements confined to the last page.[2] A nine-column, four-pager with a rather sloppy appearance, this daily regularly uses Antara (the Indonesian news agency), AP, UPI, AFP, and Reuters news dispatches. Typesetting and proofreading on the English language papers appear to be very poor. Especially poor typography is found in the English language Times of Indonesia. In one issue the writers found that every story was speckled consistently with wrong-font letters. For example, a story of 160 words had 64 words containing wrong fonts, and many words had wrong fonts for every other letter.

GENERAL PRESS SITUATION AND PROBLEMS. Usually considered the boldest of the newspapers of Indonesia is the Indonesian language anti-Communist daily Indonesia Raya of Djakarta. During 1957 and 1958 it was shut down several times by the government of President Achmed Sukarno (usually considered sympathetic to Communism) because of its anti-Communist and anti-government articles. During these same years about 30 other Indonesian newspapers were suspended because of their critical editorials and antigovernment flavor. Sukarno's police stopped in to "maintain peace;" the papers, were out of business for varying intervals. In one ten-month period in 1957 at least a dozen editors were arrested for printing information which the Sukarno government did not like.

Many problems face the Indonesian press today other than the general political unrest. The culture is extremely heterogeneous (about fifty ethnic groups and some eighty regional languages and dialects), and publishers are hampered by cultural and economic factors. Newsprint is costly, advertising is scarce and rates are low. Many journals are sponsored by parties mainly because this is the only way the papers exist economically; this may in some part explain the strong political flavor of the Indonesian press. Printing equipment is old and there is not enough of it. Subscription prices are higher than they should be to reach many of the potential (literate) readers (about 42,000,000 of them). In general, there is just not enough political and economic stability, nor enough literate citizens, to support a strong and independent press.

In spite of all these handicaps, many observers say that the Indonesian press is vigorous, progressive, and in general, commendable. Typical of the comments by American visitors to Indonesia in recent years, is that of Hal O'Flaherty of the Chicago Daily News Foreign News Service, who after a recent trip through Indonesia, said: "I learned, first of all, what a strong bond of fraternal feeling exists between newspapermen....In every province I found able, intelligent, hard-working editors and reporters, all of them linguists fluent in the use of three, four or five languages....All editors are aware of the powerful part they play in keeping the public informed...."

Although this quotation may show something about the basic journalistic spirit and philosophy of Indonesian newspapermen, it should be remembered that during 1958 the Indonesian government was cloaking its activities behind a strict censorship; newspapers could publish only those items of a military nature which came from official sources. Those journals incurring the antagonism of the Army of the Government were closed and their editors jailed without trial. In the midst of the political unrest and censorship that has characterized Indonesia since 1957, it was virtually impossible for the press to do a good job of informing the people of what was happening regardless of the intentions of the publishers.

BRIEF PRESS HISTORY OF INDONESIA. Even though the Republic of Indonesia has existed little more than eight years,the history of journalism in the islands dates back to about 1900. During the Colonial Era, when the islands were ruled by Europeans, the authorities were deeply suspicious of the press, regarding it as subversive. No real freedom was enjoyed by vernacular publications. The Dutch had reason to be wary of the native press since most of the journals exerted every effort to further the nationalist movement which began in the Dutch East Indies about 1908. In these early years almost all Indonesian journalists were political leaders, and many of these journalists (Sukarno and Mohammed Hatta for example) became prominent government figures (President and Vice President respectively) when Indonesian independence was gained in the 1940's.

During the Dutch colonial period Indonesian journalists were marked men, often in trouble with the authorities. Newspapers were published irregularly because of the heavy censorship and the scarcity of money and newsprint. The Indonesian press passed from Dutch authority to Japanese domination in 1942 when Japan took over the islands. Privately-owned newspapers were banned, and only fourteen (all carefully regulated by the Japanese) were allowed to remain in operation. But even before the end of World War II, courageous Indonesian publishers were distributing nationalistic mimeographed papers from mountain and jungle retreats. This was the beginning of the nationalistic press which played a large part in gaining final independence from Holland in 1949.

NATIONAL NEWS AGENCY. Antara (founded 1937) is Indonesia's equivalent of the U.S.'s Associated Press. Most newspapers in the country get their news--particularly foreign news--from Antara. Another important source of news is the Dutch news agency, Aneta, or its Indonesian branch called Press Indonesia Aneta.

Japan

This island-nation of 96 million people has Asia's most progressive and elaborate press system. In most respects the Japanese press is like that of the United States--especially in its basic philosophy, commercial competition, and mechanical techniques. There are some 100 dailies in Japan[1] circulating a total of some 39 million copies. Japan trails only the United States (60 million) and the U.S.S.R. (57 million) in total circulation. Every Japanese household gets an average of two daily newspapers every day. There are about 400 copies of dailies circulated for every 1,000 Japanese citizens, a rate slightly higher than is found in the United States. The Japanese ABC has two methods of calculating circulations. Under one system all copies of each edition are counted separately and total 39 million. Under the other system the AM and PM editions that go into the same household are combined. This method gives a total circulation of 26,000,000.

The nation's biggest and most influential dailies are published in two large cities-- Tokyo and Osaka. There is no real distinction in Japan between "quality" and "popular" papers.[2] The nationals are the big papers circulating throughout the country and printing in several cities. Japan's three major national papers are the Asahi, Mainichi, and Yomiuri, each of which prints about six million copies each day. The Provincial Press might be divided into "regional" papers and smaller "local" papers. The regionals are such papers as the Chubu Nippon Shimbun of Nagoya, and the Hokkaido Shimbun of Sapporo; they are actually national papers circulating on a regional basis. Then there are many small "local" papers with circulations from 25,000 to 200,000.

Major Japanese newspapers such as Asahi, Mainichi and Yomiuri (the Big Three of Japan), and Sankei Shimbun publish both morning and evening editions seven days a week. The big papers also publish weekly and monthly papers and magazines and books from time to time. The Big Three dailies, in addition to their Japanese language editions, publish special English language dailies (Asahi Evening News, The Mainichi, and Yomiuri Japan News).

Newspapers are privately owned in Japan. Between 40 and 50 per cent of their income is obtained from advertising[3] and about 95 per cent of the copies (morning and evening editions) reaches the nation's readers through an extensive network of sales agencies. Because of this home delivery system, readers must be solicited each month, and this leads to a high degree of competition among the newspapers. Subscription rates are very low; for a little more than $1.00 in 1962 a family could receive both AM and PM editions of a daily paper for a month. Some newspapers are spending as much as ¥1,500 ($4.20) to get a month's subscription at ¥390 ($1.09).[4]

Very few Japanese newspapers make a profit. For example, in 1957 only three--Chubu Nippon (Nagoya), Hokkaido Shimbun (Sapporo) and Tokyo Shimbun--showed a profit,[5] and owing to Japan's heavy tax take, profits are not considered especially desirable. In late 1962, as for some years past, the economic position of the press was a major concern of Japanese newspaper executives. President Chikao Honda of the Japan Newspaper Publishers and Editors Association pointed out to the membership that since World War II "our costs have exceeded our revenues" and that "our excessive competition is like pulling the legs of a man who is hanging himself."[6] Japanese publishers place great importance in the sales and circulation phases of the business; this does not mean that advertising is ignored, but that it does not account for as large a proportion of the income as in the U.S. and certain other countries.

LEADING DAILIES. Asahi--considered the country's leading newspaper from the standpoint of accuracy, quality, and prestige. It provides good, thorough news coverage, both national and international. It is aimed mainly at the upper and upper middle classes of Japan.

Mainichi--also noted for its comprehensive news coverage and progressive outlook. It is read mainly by the middle class working people, and probably ranks next to Asahi in national and international prestige. It is also Asahi's nearest rival in circulation.

Yomiuri--the most sensational of the "Big Three." It was influenced by Hearst's policies in the U.S. Although more sensational and less a "national" newspaper than Asahi and Mainichi, it is enterprising and presents a relatively well-balanced news picture.

Nihon Keizai--probably the most highly-respected economic-newspaper in the country. Although it presents good general news, it specializes in financial-economic-commercial coverage. Like the "Big Three" above, it is a national with both AM and PM editions.

THE NEWSPAPERS: OVERVIEW. Every Japanese citizen believes in thorough news coverage--both foreign and domestic. This mainly accounts for the great number of newspaper employees on the average newspaper. For example, Asahi and Mainichi maintain staffs of almost 7,000 persons each.[7] Large staffs also result from the keen competition, the need to write copy by hand, the need to translate much of the foreign copy, and the desire to cover big stories from many angles. The newspaper plants are manned 24 hours a day; most newspaper buildings are equipped with dormitories.

Newspapers have ample newsprint, and the Japanese lead the world in color printing with more than two-thirds of their newspapers equipped to print in four colors.[8] Type is set by hand or by special complex mono-type machines. Most newspapers use a simplified Japanese "alphabet" consisting of about 2,000 syllabaries and ideographs. The awkward alphabet is one reason for the small (usually 4 to 8 pages) papers. This is a problem all over the Far East, where editors have to cope with alphabets with hundreds and thousands of characters that defy efficient mechanical typesetting.

The Japanese are assiduous readers and to them "reading" is more than simply skipping from comic strips to pictures. Some of the mass-circulation papers such as Asahi carry large numbers of serious economic and political articles. After the end of the occupation most of the papers steered a neutral road politically and seldom expressed opinions or espoused causes. As Time said in 1958, the press was "in the grip of impartiality gone haywire."[9] The only papers with a political viewpoint were Akahata (Communist, circulation 30,000) and the thrice-monthly Shakai Shimpo (Socialist; circulation 80,000). Until the riotous Tokyo demonstrations of 1960 most of the other papers limited themselves to straight news and criticism of the government.

Although most newspapers were not opposed to the revised Japan-U.S. Security Treaty (the Leftists' primary target) many editors criticized the "undemocratic" manner in which the Kishi government "ramrodded" the treaty through the Diet (parliament) --in itself, according to able observers, a questionable premise--then continued to carp about it.

At the same time, much of the Japanese press personnel, including reporters and rimmen, were generally to the Left of the public as a whole, and many papers printed (often in the name of "freedom of expression" for such personnel) slanted stories and slanted headlines. Moreover, the columns of many politically uncommitted papers were open to numerous Leftist "social commentators." Withal, the press was so antigovernment that Premier Kishi had occasion to moan, "It is all bad; is there nothing good?" Ironically, the Communists in the country continued to regard the press as reactionary and capitalist-controlled.[10]

As the violence of the riots against the conservative government increased[11] many Japanese editors began having second thoughts about the unbridled freedom given members of their staffs and about their own responsibility.

```
                        PRINCIPAL JAPANESE NEWSPAPERS*

Asahi (AM-PM) . . . . . . . . . . . . . . . . . . . . . . . about 6.6 million
            Tokyo, Osaka, Kokura, Nagoya, Hokkaido

Mainichi (AM-PM) . . . . . . . . . . . . . . . . . . . . . about 5.85 million
            Tokyo, Osaka, Moji, Nagoya, Hokkaido

Yomiuri (AM-PM) . . . . . . . . . . . . . . . . . . . . . . about 6 million
            Tokyo, Osaka, Hokkaido

Sankei Shimbun (AM-PM) . . . . . . . . . . . . . . . . . . about 2.85 million
            Tokyo, Osaka

Tokyo Shimbun (AM-PM) . . . . . . . . . . . . . . . . . . . about 1.25 million
            Tokyo

Nihon Keizei Shimbun (AM-PM) . . . . . . . . . . . . . . . about 1.25 million
            Tokyo, Osaka

Chubu Nippon Shimbun (AM-PM) . . . . . . . . . . . . . . . about 1.85 million
            Nagoya

Hokkaido Shimbun (AM-PM) . . . . . . . . . . . . . . . . . about 1.5 million
            Sapporo

Nishi Nihon Shimbun (AM-PM) . . . . . . . . . . . . . . . . about 632,000
            Fukuoka
```

*Circulations are totals for AM and PM editions as reported in Editor & Publisher 1962 International Year Book, pp. 513-514, and The Japanese Press 1962, pp. 142-153.

After a coed was trampled to death within the Diet compound, seven leading Tokyo dailies joined in publishing a manifesto--later printed by forty newspapers throughout Japan--condemning the violence and appealing for peace and order.

With the world-wide loss of face that followed the riots, Japanese editors indulged in considerable self-examination, both among themselves and in print. Some admitted having gone too far in "nonpartisanship" and anti-government criticism. Since then, most editorial comment has been more considered.[12]

Ownership of most Japanese papers,[13] like other sectors of the industrial economy, has long been characterized by cartelization by powerful zaibatsu (family groups), and while many of the industrial cartels were broken up during the occupation the press zaibatsu (because of the principle of press freedom) were untouched and control remains in the hands of men who have more interest in the business side of the newspaper than in the editorial side. All the big papers of Japan engage in "outside" business activities. Yomiuri, for example, owns one of Tokyo's most imposing news buildings, and engages in many nonjournalistic activities such as owning a baseball team, and dealing in real estate. The Asahi ("Rising Sun") publishes many publications,[14] owns a general store, a hotel, and a theater. This type of thing is not at all uncommon in Japan.

Newspapers are highly selective in hiring reporters and subeditors. Once a year each paper gives a qualifying examination to prospective journalists. Sometimes as many as 5,000 take examinations in one year on one paper. Applicants must be college graduates. Only a small percentage of the exam-passers are hired; those who are not may take examinations and try for positions on other newspapers. Reporters and journalists in general have a great deal of prestige in Japan, and pay is good, usually on a par with other professionals such as lawyers.

INTEREST IN FOREIGN NEWS.[15] Japanese readers have a great interest in foreign news, and in general prefer the news from special correspondents rather than from news agencies. So each big national daily has more than 20 correspondents abroad, and sends more when a big news event occurs. Asahi, for example, has foreign correspondents in New York, London,

Paris, Bonn, Singapore, Taipeh, Hong Kong,
New Delhi, San Francisco, Honolulu, Seoul,
Melbourne, and Istanbul. It also subscribes
to about 25 news services from outside Japan.
Many of the stories from abroad used in the
Japanese press are background and interpretive
pieces. More space is given to foreign news
in Japanese newspapers on the average than in
U.S. or European papers.

TYPICAL AM NEWSPAPER. Most of the morning
papers in Japan consist of eight pages of
standard size and most evening editions have
only four pages.[16] The managing editor has
charge of the news collection and the news
editor says what is to be used. The common
arrangement of material in a Japanese AM paper
follows:

Page 1 (the back page of a U.S. paper) generally carries only "hard" news--national and
world political and diplomatic news. Editorials
are found mainly on Page 2; features, editorials,
letters on Page 3; commercial-economic items on
Page 4; arts and literature on Page 5; sports
on Page 6; city news, human interest stories
on Page 7, and local community news on the back
page. Advertising, as in most newspapers of
the world, is carried at the bottom of the
pages. As might be expected since Japanese
read from right to left and from top to bottom,
the "column rules" of the newspapers run
horizontally on the page.

NEWS AGENCIES. Japan's main news agency is the
Kyodo Tsushin (Kyodo News Service), a cooperative organization founded in 1945. Its membership is composed of all leading Japanese newspapers and the Japan Broadcasting Corporation.
Headquarters are in Tokyo. Kyodo is a nonprofit agency, and receives no government or
private subsidy.

The Jiji Press (founded 1945) provides
mainly economic and commercial news service to
subscribers.

Radiopress (founded 1945) has offices in
Tokyo and Osaka, and distributes mostly foreign
news which it receives by its radio monitoring
system. It is without correspondents. It
distributes news via teleprinter and printed
handouts. For a fee it even provides service
to other news agencies.

PRESS FREEDOM. There is very little government interference with the press in Japan
today. The press, as is the case in the U.S.,
has freedom to publish but is held responsible
under the law. The Japanese prize their freedom of the press, and even though it is of
recent origin, are determined to keep the
government from interfering in press matters.

Article 21 of the 1946 Constitution guarantees
"freedom of assembly and association as well
as speech, press and others of expression."
One Japanese journalist said in 1958: "Japanese
journalists believe that the spirit of the
new Japanese Constitution recognizes freedom
of expression as the fundamental right of the
individual. They regard any law to limit
such freedom as antisocial and are opposed
to it."[17]

Even Japan's vigorous and often vehement
Communist party daily, Akahata ("Red Flag"),
enjoys freedom from government pressures.
Most of Japan's newspaper publishers and
editors realize their responsibilities to the
people, and in general the newspapers have
high ethical standards. In conclusion, it
may be said that the Japanese press is free
from government control and influence, and
has progressed rapidly under a combination
"libertarian" and "social responsibility"
theory of the press.

A REPORT ON JAPANESE NEWSGATHERING TACTICS.
"Not only do the overstaffed papers hardly
ever fire anyone, but, as a sort of national
face-saving gesture, they yearly hire unneces-
sary help from Japan's crop of new college
graduates. With such manpower on tap, the
Japanese press can turn loose hordes of newsmen, give the cops more trouble than the
rioters at demonstrations. Japanese photographers vault graves and straddle coffins
to get good shots of mass funerals. A reporter
once got into Premier Nobusuke Kishi's bed-
room. In addition, Japanese papers use flashy
modern trappings such as airplanes, walkie-
talkies and monotypes that can set some 2,200
Japanese syllabaries and Chinese ideographs."[18]

JAPAN'S PRESS BACKGROUND. About a hundred
years ago (January, 1862) a Japanese book-
seller, Yorozuya Heishiro published Japan's
first printed newspaper, the Batavia Shimbun.
Printed with wooden blocks it contained translations from Dutch papers published in the
East Indies--and appeared only once. By 1868,
the date of the Meiji (royal) Restoration,

Batavia Shimbun

several newspapers had appeared, primarily to take editorial sides in the struggle between the royalists and the Tokugawa Shogunate. With the restoration the royalists at first banned all newspapers, but in 1869 the press was permitted to resume operations under strict proscriptions.

In the ensuing years, Japan's early newspapermen often showed their strength of will. Hundreds of dispossessed samurai, the sword-wielding warriors of the feudal era, took over editorial posts. John Black, an Englishman editing a Japanese paper at the time, attributed much of the vitality of the press to the samurai. Calling them the "real brains of the country," Black in his book Young Japan, wrote: "....the same irrepressible boldness that they always possessed in action has displayed itself in their utterances. They will write; and regardless of all consequences, they refuse to avoid criticism of the government and the officials. It has never once been found that when one writer or editor had been incarcerated, there was no man of ability to step at once into his place...."

By 1890, newspapers--daily, weekly, monthly-- numbered nearly 500. As in the United States at about the same time, fierce competition resulted in an era of "yellow journalism." In Japan this sensationalism manifested itself in a "black third page," devoted to gossip and scandal about business and political leaders. In 1909, the government enacted a law empowering the Home Minister to "prohibit the sale or distribution of newspapers or to seize newspapers if articles are printed which he deems are inimical to peace and order or injurious to public morals" and the Army, Navy, and Foreign Ministers to "prohibit the printing of articles relating to military and diplomatic affairs." To accomodate themselves to this law, many newspapers employed "jail editors"--minor staff members registered as editors, whose principal function was to sit in jail when a newspaper was cited for violation of the law. By this and similar devices the press functioned with varying degrees of freedom until the 1930's.[19]

With the advent of the militarists in the 1930's, press control was made complete and remained so until occupation authorities abolished all restraints on freedom in 1945. Before the war, the press had little significance and the journalists almost no status. In 1936 overall press authority was placed in the hands of a Board of Information; also, Japan's two old news agencies (Rengo and Nippon Dempo) were merged into a new official agency--Domei. Domei was replaced after the war by the present national agency, Kyodo, patterned closely after the Associated Press of the U.S. During World War II, the government decreased the number of newspapers greatly, almost eliminating the PM press. After the war, General MacArthur's occupation government "freed" the press of Japan, although the Occupation did exercise "pre-publication censorship" in the country until 1948.[20]

The occupation censorship was completely lifted in 1952, and for a time there was a mad rush to publish gossip items, scandal, and anti-American rumor. This trend gradually disappeared as editors realized that readers were more interested in government activities, economic matters and foreign news. Since 1960 Japan's newspapers are showing that they are among the best balanced, most enterprising in the world.

Two of Japan's contemporary journalists are Matsutaro Shoriki and Shintaro Fukushima, both of Tokyo. The former, owner of Yomiuri, is by far the most distinguished of Japanese journalists and is often called "the grand old man of Japanese journalism."[21] This eighty-year-old newspaperman (1963) has been a member of the Japanese cabinet with the rank of Minister of State. Always a friend of the United States, it was he who introduced major league baseball to the country and brought television to Japan. Shintaro Fukushima, president of the Japan Times of Tokyo, is not only the foremost interpreter of Japan's press through articles such as that cited herein and a working paper submitted to the United Nations Seminar on Freedom of Information held in New Delhi in 1962;[22] he is also one of the clearest voices sponsoring freedom and the liberal-democratic ideal in Japan.

MAGAZINES AND PERIODICALS. With more than 1,100 periodicals and many specialized magazines of limited circulation, few countries publish more magazines than does Japan. The growth of weekly magazines published by the leading newspapers has been a striking development of recent years. The Sunday Mainichi, Shukan Yomiuri, Shukan Asahi, Shukan Sankei have been joined by a long list of newcomers to the field. How many of the latter will survive is problematical in view of the precarious life of magazines in Japan today.

Japanese magazines are for the most part well printed and attractively illustrated in black and white as well as in gravure and color. Subject matter of the magazines range over education, science, industry, politics, art, and culture to films and dressmaking. Many magazines carry special supplements in one of these fields as a special feature.[23]

RADIO AND TELEVISION. There are two types of
radio enterprise in Japan--the Japan Broadcasting Corporation (NHK--Nihon Hoso Kyokai),
a semigovernmental entity similar to the
British Broadcasting Corporation, and commercial broadcasting. Television is similarly
organized with NHK operating thirty-four TV
stations and commercial companies operating
forty-four. From the outset, many of Japan's
commercial radio and television stations
have been under the direct management or
supervision of the large newspapers and derive
substantial income from advertising.[24]

PROMOTION. In addition to publishing newspapers, magazines, and books, and operating
radio and television stations, the large newspapers with nationwide circulations maintain
"enterprise" departments that sponsor academic
research projects, cultural exchange programs,
symphony orchestras, ballet troupes, post-
season barnstorming tours by American major
league baseball teams, national judo champion-
ships, Himalayan expeditions, bathysphere
explorations and even flower arrangement com-
petitions. In Japan the newspapers are in
every phase of the national cultural life.[25]

Korea

In the Republic of Korea (South Korea) with its 25 million people, the press is small and unattractive, but is believed to exert strong influence in political, social, and economic life. The daily press is composed of some forty dailies with a circulation close to a million copies each day. At least half the people are illiterate. Of the dailies in the little nation, about a dozen of them are in the capital city of Seoul (Korean: "Kyongsong"). Seoul also accounts for nearly three-fourths of the country's total circulation. About thirty weeklies, most of which are very small and publish on the proverbial "shoestring," are scattered throughout the Republic. Newspapers appear in three languages: Korean, Chinese, and English.[1]

Important dailies, all of Seoul, are Chosen Ilbo, Tong-A Ilbo, Chunnam Ilbo, Hankuk Ilbo, Yunhap Shinmun, Sege Ilbo, and Kyung Hyang Shinmun. The largest daily (Tong-A Ilbo) circulates about 260,000 copies. Hankuk is next with about 220,000; Kyung Hyang Shinmun is third largest with about 150,000. No other paper circulates as many as 100,000 copies.

South Korean newspapers are basically political pamphlets, usually written in formal-- almost academic--prose. Many of them use Chinese ideographs which can be understood by university-level readers only. In most publications news is presented in a highly opinionated and slanted manner.

Although some observers, such as Professor Roscoe Ellard of Columbia University, may feel that newspaper writing style in Korea is characterized by a formal and esoteric language, others believe that the journalistic style is marked by its exuberance. For example, Professor Robert T. Oliver of Pennsylvania State University quotes a random sentence taken from a South Korean newspaper to indicate this lively style; he says the "style of their (Korean) journalism is typically represented" by the following sentence: "They were steaming up readiness of going into a sit-down struggle at the National Assembly hall, but as it turned out it started with the force of a rocket but fell with the impact of a stick."[2] Professor Oliver writes that in general the newspapers lack accuracy.

Koreans generally are avid readers of news-

papers. In addition to the million copies sold daily (no papers are published, however, on Sunday), probably a half million more are circulated each week by the nation's more than 30 weekly papers.[3] Newspapers are posted on bulletin boards and are displayed in other prominent places for further reading. They are also read aloud to small groups on farms and in villages by some literate member of the community. As is true in most parts of Asia, the number of persons actually having access to the press is impossible even to estimate. The most widely-read magazine among intellectuals in the country is Sasangge ("The World of Ideas"), founded in 1953 in Seoul.

The poor quality newsprint used by most papers, the oftentimes poor typography, printing and halftone reproduction all serve to give the South Korean press a rather shabby appearance. The Korean Republic,[4]

a news-packed English-language tabloid, is a notable exception to this generalization. A typical paper is a four-pager of tabloid size (about 11 x 17 inches). Most of the larger papers have about 25 per cent advertising, much of it movie advertising. The front page usually contains foreign news; the second page carries editorials and economic news; page 3 contains domestic news and features, and page 4 is a culture page. News stories, with the exception of certain press agency items, appear to be written in chronological style. There is some editorializing in the

news columns, a great tendency toward political
and literary matters, and a strong foreign
news emphasis (especially in the government
publications). In 1963 it had a circulation
of about 12,000.

The Korean press did not really come into
existence until the end of the nineteenth
century. Although there had been a couple of
official government gazettes previously, the
first real Korean paper was begun in 1896 with
help from Western missionaries; this paper,
Toknip Shinmun[5] or "Independence Press," was
published mainly as an inspiration to nationalistic Koreans against the colonial rule of
Japan. This paper and other early Korean
papers contributed much to the independence
movement which brought about freedom from
Japan. It might be said that the early Korean
press in its revolutionary tendencies could be
compared to the American press of the eighteenth
century.

Although there are several national news
agencies in South Korea today, (e.g., Haptong
Tongshin and Orient Press), the most important
is generally recognized to be the Donghwa News
Agency (Donghwa Tongshin-Sa). It was founded
in 1956 as a private stock company with the
purpose of providing the Korean press with a
nonsubsidized service. It has exchange agreements with AP and AFP. It uses teletype and
facsimile for news transmission. According to
Chung Jae Ho, president of the agency in 1958,
the DNA has never received subsidies and its
business is growing steadily; the president
has stated that his agency provides "speedy,
unbiased and accurate reporting" and has
"accomplished pioneering achievements for
public service in Korea."[6]

The South Korean press is "free" from government censorship and oppression, according to
most specialists on the press situation of the
country, but newspapers are often subjected
to various types of pressure from the authorities. One of the chief ways the press is "controlled" is through legislation enacted to
assure "security." Korean newsmen often complain that it is very difficult to get information from public officials and even from
ordinary nongovernment sources.[7] There are
also complaints of "red tape" and "over-classification" of government documents, and of
much evasion of newsmen within government
circles. However, these are common complaints
today throughout the world; they are certainly
heard often enough in the United States.

One main difference exists, however, in the
South Korean and the American press "freedom"
situations; in the U.S. the press may criticize
any public official (including the President)
and often does so--at times caustically; in
Korea the press must be extremely careful of
any journalistic barbs cast in the direction
of the government.

The South Korean President appears to be
above criticism, and so far as the press is
concerned his name is almost sacred. This
rather strange status of the President re-
minds one of the situation which exists in
some Latin American republics (depending to
a large extent on who is President). This
gives the South Korean press (as is true in
Latin America and in Nationalist China) a
"limited" brand of freedom. And while it
seems that South Korea is basically "democratic" (in the Western sense), its press is
forced--because of "security" and "respect"
for the President--to watch very carefully
what it prints. Perhaps--as is probably true
in the case of Nationalist China--the geographical "crisis-area" in which South Korea finds
itself (adjacent to Communist Asia) is responsible for the press system which is to a
large extent authoritarian decked in the
trappings of libertarianism.

RADIO AND TELEVISION. The electronic media
of radio and TV in South Korea are under the
Ministry of Public Information of the government. Part of this government ministry is the
Korean Broadcasting System (KBS), the sole
nation-wide, noncommercial network of the
country. It operates about sixteen radio
stations and one TV station. There are about
400 amplified radio villages, set up by the
government to spread reception; each village
has receivers connected to the nearest station
by wire. There are some 400,000 radio sets
in South Korea--about one set for every 60
persons. In 1963 there were probably 3,000
television sets in South Korea, but the government was predicting at least 20,000 sets by
1968.

In addition to these government outlets of
the KBS, there are some privately-controlled
radio and TV stations in the country--in 1962
eight radio stations and one TV station. Although the future looks relatively bright for
the commercial stations, government-controlled
radio-television facilities dominate the
nation's electronic communication.

Pakistan

In this relatively new nation (established 1947) of some 92 million people about 800 newspapers are published, about 100 of them dailies.[1] Most of these, however, are small, some so small that they would hardly be considered newspapers in many countries. Pakistani papers, especially the dailies, are almost always serious; the writing is usually considered good, and the papers as a rule contain little or no sensationalism. Many, however, do try to encourage circulation by running rather juvenile literary contests and puzzles. Only about one-half of one per cent of the population can read and understand English, yet English language publications (about 150) are the most influential and are quite widely distributed. The great interest in English and the English language press is found in the cities, the military, the colleges and big businesses, and in most of the professions. English is generally spoken by all the upper classes, and is a compulsory language in the schools, even through the university-level. Urdu language papers are next in importance, and are especially influential in the rural areas of Pakistan.

A MULTILINGUAL PRESS. Pakistan is a nation of many languages. Literacy is only about 15 per cent and is spread over the Urdu, Bengali, Pushto, Baluchi, Gujarati, and English languages. Urdu is the most common, and some 550 newspapers are published in this language. Printing equipment is set up for five different scripts, and this fact limits the moving about of compositors, reporters, and editors. The eight press languages, coupled with the low literacy rate (18 per cent), presents a serious obstacle to press expansion in the country.

Of the press languages, English is the most important even though the newspapers in this language reach only a very small segment of the population. The English language papers present more foreign news than Pakistani papers in other languages. Dawn, the country's second largest daily and semiofficial spokesman of the government, is the leading English language newspaper. The Urdu language papers are centered in Lahore, the country's second most important city (after Karachi, the federal capital) and cultural center. Afaq (Lahore and Lyallpur), Nawa-i-waqt (Lahore), and Zamindar (Lahore and Rawalpindi) are among the country's most influential Urdu dailies.

However, Jang (Karachi) and Anjam (Karachi) have the largest circulations among Urdu papers. Bengali papers circulate mainly in East Pakistan; they reach large populations in a restricted region and have large circulations among the vernacular papers.

GENERAL PRESS PICTURE. Pakistani newspapers are principally characterized by their political affiliations and philosophies. Personal columns in the papers are mostly political essays, and a majority of the news columns are filled with national activities or political items. Cultural, educational, and economic subjects are played down in the newspapers. Basic press philosophy in Pakistan does not accord the press a special status; rather the press to a considerable extent is considered an arm of the government. Pakistan, therefore, has a rather strict governmental censorship of the press and certainly would have to be classified as a nation with an "authoritarian" press system. This is true even though the country's constitution[2] provides for, and many of its governmental officials pay lip service to, the concept of freedom of expression.[3]

One way the government keeps papers in line is by withdrawal of official advertising, or by threatening to withdraw it. This method has been used in recent years against such prominent publications as the Pakistan Observer, Evening Star, and Dawn (of Karachi), and the Pakistan Economist, Variety, and the Mirror. "Conformist" and "friendly" journalists are accorded a favored position by the government; these progovernment journalists are likely to be asked to serve on government committees and to be a part of special delegations abroad. This method (used to some extent in all nations) is a common way of obtaining press support by the Pakistani government without resorting to more direct action.

Newspapers of Pakistan do not publish circulation figures, but it is estimated that the combined newspaper circulation does not exceed 175,000. There are about 85 dailies, probably accounting for most of this total circulation. These dailies produce about two copies for every 1,000 inhabitants of the country, a very low readership rate. The press is centered in Karachi and Lahore. Newspapers, especially the smaller ones, rise and fade rapidly in Pakistan. During elections many "dead" journals are reborn as polemic organs, only to disappear after the votes are counted.

Two of Pakistan's most popular magazines, both published in Karachi, are the Illustrated Weekly of Pakistan and the monthly Mirror (the country's leading social magazine). Probably

the most important Urdu magazine is the weekly
Quindeel of Lahore. Other important periodi-
cals are the fortnightlies Pakistan Economist,
Panorama, Variety, and the Pakistan News Digest
(all of Karachi), and the monthlies Pakistan
Today of Dacca, Vision and Pakistan Digest of
Karachi.

DAILIES. Some of the country's most influential daily newspapers are Dawn (Karachi),
Pakistan Times (Lahore), and the Civil &
Military Gazette (Lahore) which once had Rud-
yard Kipling as assistant editor. Other
important daily papers are the Times of
Karachi, Evening Star, Morning News, and Pakistan Observer (English language Karachi papers),
and the Urdu language Azad and Musalman of
Karachi, and the Gujarati language Dawn Gujarati
of Karachi. Two Bengali language dailies have
considerable prestige in their regions; they
are Azan of Chittagong, and Sangbad of Dacca.

WEEKLIES. Important English language weeklies
of Pakistan are the Star, Light, and Catholic
News of Lahore, the Sunday Tribune of Karachi,
and the Pakistan Post of Dacca. Principal
Urdu weeklies are Adakar, Chatan, and Wahdat
of Lahore, and Alamgir and Jaras of Karachi.
Two other prominent weeklies are the Gujarati
Mujahid of Karachi, and the Pushto language
Shahbaz of Peshawar.

PRESS FREEDOM IN PAKISTAN.[4] Article 8 of the
Constitution grants freedom of expression in
Pakistan. However, there are many press laws
in the country which state explicitly how the
press shall operate and just how far editors
can go with their freedom of expression. These
laws set up regulations for entry into newspaper publishing. They also specify in detail
the characteristics of "defamatory" articles
and illustrations. The country's Penal Code
says which actions by the press are "offenses
against the state," (Act XLV of 1860) or
against "public tranquility" (Act XLV of 1860).
Many special laws of more recent origin, such
as the Official Secrets Act (1923), the Public
Safety Ordinance (1949), and the Security of
Pakistan Act (1952), place a great number of
specific restrictions on the press. Like
many nations, Pakistan may be said to have
freedom of the press in theory, but not very
much in reality.

NATIONAL NEWS AGENCY. The country's chief
news agency is the Associated Press of Pakistan
(APP), founded in 1949. It is managed by a
trust called Eastern News Trust. Finances
come largely from papers subscribing to its
services and from its commercial news sales.
Headquarters are in Karachi, and chief branch
offices are in Lahore, Peshawar, Hyderabad,
Rawalpindi, Dacca, and Chittagong. It gets

its foreign news from Reuters (London) and
the Associated Press (New York) on the basis
of long term exchange agreements. APP also
has an exchange agreement with Indonesia's
Antara agency (Djakarta). Another national
agency in Pakistan is the United Press of
Pakistan (UPP), with main offices in Karachi.

BRIEF HISTORY OF THE PRESS. Pakistan's press
today is largely a remnant of the Moslem press
that flourished during the Moslem struggle
for the nation (1940-47). However, the Urdu
language press dates back to 1823 when the
first Urdu weekly was founded.[5] The first
real Urdu "news" paper was the Urdu Akhbar
("Urdu Gazette") founded in 1836 by Muhammad
Baqir, a famous literary figure. Other important Urdu newspapers making significant contributions to the development of the press
were Paisa Akhbar (f.1887), and Zamindar
(f.1903) which is still a prominent Pakistani
newspaper.

Until 1950 the press developed very slowly,
mainly due to the acute shortage of printing
facilities. It was not uncommon for several
papers to be printed in the same plant.
Until 1947 the only rotary press in Pakistan
was in the plant of the Civil & Military
Gazette (Lahore). By the end of 1950, however, Dawn, Evening Times, and the Pakistan
Times were using modern equipment imported
from the United States and Europe. Since
World War II several important Urdu papers
have begun, including the popular Shahbaz
and Nawa-i-Waqt. The main paper beginning
since the formation of the country has been
Imroz of Lahore. It gave the entire Urdu
press a new style of writing and page make up.

The press of Pakistan today is still handi-
capped by a lack of equipment and a scarcity
of newsprint. This is especially true of
the English language press; most of the vernacular papers, being printed by lithographic
methods, are not greatly affected by a shortage of equipment. Another problem plaguing
all newspapers is an inadequate supply of
well-trained newspapermen. Low salaries,
coupled with the fact that journalism education is not stressed, do not help this situation. Other barriers to press growth in
Pakistan are (1) the high illiteracy rate,
(2) predominance of a rural population, (3)
underdeveloped transportation and communications facilities.

In 1962 Pakistan had 10 radio stations,
with more in the process of being set up.
However, radio was not too important as a
means of news dissemination since the number
of receiving sets was extremely low--about
400,000.

Philippines

Twenty million people inhabit the Philippine Republic. They speak eight distinct languages and about 90 dialects, and approximately 35 per cent of them are illiterate. Some fifteen metropolitan daily newspapers in the country circulate more than 300,000 copies each day throughout the thousand-mile stretch of islands. Besides the dailies, there are about 175 weekly papers scattered through the Republic. These weeklies (mainly vernacular papers) have a rather difficult time existing, because most businessmen in the Philippines tend to limit their advertising to the big Manila dailies.

Most of the nation's dailies are published in the largest city and old capital, Manila (on the island of Luzon), and are published in English, Chinese, Spanish, and the official (since 1946) national language--Tagalog, a Malayan dialect. Daily newspapers average 12 to 20 pages and have formats much like their counterparts in the United States. Circulations for the most part range from 10,000 to 60,000. The English language Manila Times breaks the pattern with a daily press run of about 125,000.

While the majority of publications are in the four main languages named above, there are many (especially in the provinces) published in such dialects as Cebuano, Ilocano, Bicol, Ilongo, and Pampangan. Often a newspaper will be published with sections in two or three languages or dialects in an effort to reach the largest possible readership.

The country's sole national news agency is the Philippine News Service, which is organized and run like the AP of the United States. The PNS provides all domestic news to the press of the Philippines. Foreign news is supplied by Agence France-Presse, Reuters, and the U.S. agencies.

THE NEWSPAPERS.[1] The English language daily papers of Manila have the greatest circulations and are usually considered the most influential of the nation's periodicals. Especially outstanding are the Manila Times (f.1945 , especially noted for its lively international editorials; circulation about 125,000), Manila Chronicle (f.1945; also noted for its international editorials and commentaries; circulation about 50,000), Philippines Herald (f.1920

by the late President Manuel Quezon as a nationalistic journal; circulation about 90,000), Manila Bulletin (f.1912; pro-American and probusiness; has excellent commercial and financial page; circulation about 20,000).

The Spanish language press appears to be on the decline, and only two Manila dailies (they have very small circulations) are of any significance. They are El Debate, and Voz de Manila, both with circulations less than 10,000. Most of the Spanish language publications in the Philippines are small religious (Roman Catholic) or educational journals.

The vernacular press is centered in Manila, but is well entrenched throughout the islands. Most of these native language papers are weeklies which depend chiefly on circulation for existence since advertising is scarce in the country. These vernacular papers are mainly entertainment journals, splashing their pages with personality sketches, color illustrations, sob-stories, and comic strips. Vernacular weeklies range in circulation from 1,000 to about 80,000. The weeklies are popular in the provinces and many observers believe they contain some of the best writing being done in the Philippines today. The biggest circulation vernacular weekly is Liwayway (about 80,000), and its native language daily counterpart is Mabuhay, a Tagalog journal with about 25,000 circulation. The second largest Tagalog daily is Taliba, with about 20,000 circulation.

The Chinese language press is also centered in Manila, where the leading dailies are Kong Li Po, Fookien Times, and the Chinese Commercial News. All of these have circulations between 7,000 and 15,000, and support the Nationalist Chinese government on Formosa. Fookien Times is the largest of the Chinese dailies (circulation about 12,000) and is generally considered the best edited and most influential.

The provincial press is not considered to be on very solid financial ground, and it is not noted for its progressive tendencies or serious news coverage. In 1958 the typical provincial paper was a weekly tabloid of four pages, published on Saturday or Sunday. It was circulating from 1,000 to 2,000 copies and selling on the newsstands for the U.S. equivalent of about 10 cents. Publishers make little or no money from their papers and manage to survive only through income from commercial printing. Most of the provincials are published simply as a "public service" or for personal or political reasons. The leading provincials are published in the provincial capitals and important commercial towns. Some of these are the Bicol Star, the Mindanao Times, the Davao Herald-Tribune, and the Cebu Morning Times. Throughout the provinces are some ninety local dialects, and the rural publishers attempt to solve this problem by printing part of the paper in the local dialect and part in English, which is read by rapidly-growing numbers of Filipinos.

LEADING MAGAZINES. The nation's oldest existing weekly magazine is the English language Philippines Free Press (f.1907). It is most popular in the provinces, where its able social and political criticisms, exposés, and lively sports stories find a ready audience. Another important general weekly magazine is Kislap (begun as a Tagalog journal but now bilingual--Tagalog and English). It specializes in discussions of current events, education, social life, and home activities. The Weekly Women's Magazine, published by the Manila Times Publishing Co., is also quite popular, especially in the larger cities and towns.

PRESS FREEDOM. The press of the Philippines is one of the freest and most militant in the world, the only restrictions being libel laws and some quite serious economic problems. Filipino newspapers have shown great courage in exposing corrupt governmental practices, both in Quezon City (the capital), and in the various provincial capitals. Press freedom is granted in the Philippines Constitution.

Article III, Section 8 provides that "no law shall be passed abridging the freedom of speech, or of the press, or of the right of the people peaceably to assemble and petition the government for redress of grievance."[2]

WRITING. The average editor in the Philippines enjoys "editorializing" and goes about it vigorously in the same manner of the American "personal" journalists of a half-century ago.[3] There is much lively, colorful writing in the press, but this is balanced by serious, well-researched articles of an interpretive nature. Newswriting, however, is much like editorial writing--frank and simple, yet forceful and vivid. Although most journalists are "self-made," a school of journalism at the Catholic University of Santo Tomas is turning out increasing numbers of well-trained newspapermen. In addition, many Filipinos have been studying journalism in the United States in recent years.

PRESS PROBLEMS. Journalism is a vital factor in the growth and development of the Philippines and wields an important influence on the political scene. This is true despite the fact that the press is struggling to overcome a host of serious problems. Chief among them are (1) high production costs, especially in printing equipment and newsprint, (2) limited advertising, (3) the many languages of the island, (4) distribution and transportation handicaps, and (5) the small amount of money in circulation in the Philippines.

Thailand

Thailand (Siam) is rather typical of the smaller nations of Southeast Asia with its small, poorly-printed newspapers and its underdeveloped radio system. Reliable material is extremely difficult to get about the Thai press.[1] Only a few Americans have studied the press systems of Southeast Asia and of Thailand in particular; probably the best-informed students among them are Professor Albert G. Pickerell of the University of California and Professor Nathan Blumberg of Montana State University.

In 1962 there were 20 daily papers in Thailand, all published in the capital city of Bangkok. The country had some 75 radio stations, most of low quality, often operating on an experimental basis for some limited purpose. With the exception of one commercial station, the broadcasting stations were government-owned in 1962. Broadcasting was done in six languages.

In addition to the country's dailies, there are about a dozen weeklies, most of them published outside Bangkok, serving the provincial areas. Circulation figures cannot be obtained for the Thai papers, but Thai Embassy materials estimate the country's total daily circulation (with weekly circulations woven into the figure) at close to 500,000. About 80-90 per cent of all newspaper copies are sold on the newsstand.

Professor Pickerell has pointed out that overall public indifference to newspapers has been the chief factor in the extremely slow development of the Thai press. Even the better-educated citizen of Thailand, according to Dr. Pickerell, has a "difficult-to-explain aversion to reading." Although Thailand, a nation of some 20 million people, has a literacy rate of nearly 60 per cent (high for Southeast Asia), newspapers are tiny, poorly printed, and in most cases give the reader very little real news and interpretation.

A recent visitor to Thailand, Dr. Blumberg of Montana State University, listed in 1962 "extreme sensationalism and government censorship" as two of the main problems facing the Thai press. Dr. Blumberg reported that the Thai press had changed little since 1960.[2]

Bangkok is the center of the press and broadcasting. The nation's magazines are published

there. The radio stations have no degree of permanency; the newspapers and magazines are generally of low quality, and in general it may be said that UNESCO's statement that all information media are "underdeveloped" is valid.

THAI PRESS CHARACTERISTICS. Dailies are printed in Thai (14), Chinese (4), and English (2). The country's largest and smallest newspapers are in the Thai language. English is the country's second language for the educated Siamese. All newspapers are handset, and pages are gathered and folded by hand.

Journalists have very little formal training and salaries are very low. Time magazine points out, for example, that in 1958 the star photographer of the highly-respected World was once the editor's houseboy and the paper's general manager was a converted taxi driver, and that "gaudy and sometimes bawdy typos...regularly speckle" the paper.

Newspaper salaries are low, with new reporters getting about $40 a month. Even editors average only about $115 a month. This low salary scale leads many newsmen to work for several periodicals or for the electronic media to supplement their incomes. Many of the best writers are found in the Government's Public Relations Department, where salaries are better and prestige is greater.

The English-language World was the one which Time called the best daily in Thailand. With a circulation of only some 4,500, the World is edited by an American expatriate named Darrell Berrigan, who gives his readers news from the largest world news agencies, and spots the paper's ten pages with columns and comic strips from the United States.

Although none of Thailand's papers has a large circulation, the native-language papers are generally set off by unusually small circulations, lack of financial stability, and little sense of social responsibility.

There is practically no press freedom in Thailand; in 1958 about half of the country's newspapers were in the hands of government officials, and little criticism of the government could be expected. Editors generally steer clear of controversial issues and write practically no editorials; they mainly present straight news, human-interest stories, or just literary ramblings. Time gives an example of a "literary rambling" type describing the coming of dawn which was written for a Thai paper: "In the quiet hour before the sun bursts above the surrounding trees, and the mystery is burned from the sky, the

villager is closer to his God than when he
kneels in the temple." Newspaper reporting
is generally lively, resulting from the
scramble for circulation.

About 60 weeklies and other periodical publications appear in Thailand, all with small
circulations. Perhaps the most influential
daily is Siam Rath, a PM with nearly 30,000
circulation. This opinion paper publishes an
English-language weekly called the Siam Rath
Weekly Review. The Thai-language Phim Thai
(circulation about 28,000) is the leading
"yellow journal" of the country. Read by the
better-educated classes of the country is Siam
Nikorn, a PM of some 20,000 circulation. It is
the only paper that gives much attention to
foreign events, and was referred to in 1960 by
Dr. Pickerell as the "nearest thing to a newspaper" in the country. Sarn Seri, (AM), is the
mouthpiece of the government.

The two English-language dailies of Thailand
in 1962 were the Bangkok World, and the Bangkok
Post. In addition there was the weekly tabloid-size Standard. This last-named paper
(calling itself "a weekly newspaper for international readers") presents a good, solid
diet of serious articles in its editions
which often run to 34 and 38 pages.

A few of the leading Chinese-language papers
in Thailand are Hsing Hsien Jih Pao (AM),
Shih Chieh Jih Pao (AM), Ching Hua Jih Pao (AM),
and Hsin Jih Pao (AM).

The country has no national news agency and
foreign news is mainly supplied by the
international agencies--especially France's
AFP and the American UPI and AP. Most newspapers of Thailand are members of the Press
Association of Thailand, a professional
group of newspapermen.

Africa: Overview

The press of this vast continent is generally considered still in its infancy. European nations with territories or "protectorates" in Africa saw to it that their territorial press systems developed slowly but constantly; however, the vernacular press, at least up until about 1940 had made practically no progress. The native press of the new and emerging nations has expanded greatly since World War II, however, and vernacular publications have spread even into remote jungle villages whose populations were completely illiterate in the mid-1940's.

Throughout Africa today one may find many district and regional journals, none of them large, appearing in several local languages. A rather large number of these smaller sheets are mimeographed with nameplate and certain advertisements printed offset. Usually these newspapers run from six to ten pages and are stapled in the upper lefthand corner. One thing is certain about the African press: the stage of press development among (and within) different countries varies widely.

In some African countries (e.g., South African Republic) there are newspapers of high quality, while in others only small, poorly-printed bulletins exist. Facilities for mass communication are largely concentrated in the urban areas with about 80 per cent of the continent's 60 million people in rural areas receiving little or no service. Only about 10 per cent of the adults in Africa were literate in 1963--the lowest level of any of the world's principal land areas. This fact, of course, helps explain the underdeveloped status of the continent's press, and has placed the electronic media--especially radio--in a highly important position as news instruments.

Africa is definitely a continent in ferment, a tremendous land filled with fundamentally illiterate peoples speaking dozens of native languages. In some of these "emerging" nations of Africa, there are European languages (e.g., French, Spanish, English), but these are not read by enough of the African masses to make for a healthy communications situation.

Another communication barrier is an economic one. Most of the new republics of Africa are basically in the stone age of industry; certainly their economy may be termed unstable. Private capital is unable to create and sustain many newspapers, radio stations, or magazines. In spite of the great need for educating the masses through the news media, the economy just will not allow it to any extent. At present there seems to be nationalism without adequate communication to provide adhesion; this is obviously a bad situation.

It is quite possible that unless the economic situation gets better in the very near future, a large number of the African nations will have government-owned-and-controlled printed media as well as electronic media of mass communication.

Certain writers have pointed out that the climate for a free and healthy press in most areas of Africa is indeed poor, and that the future appears to indicate newspapers and magazines largely devoted to mirroring government philosophies. There is very little straight or objective news reporting outside a few countries. Most is of an economic, racial, religious, and political nature-- usually packed with emotion.[1]

It appears that the press of the African republics is becoming more and more one that (1) espouses nationalism, (2) sides with one of the nation's political factions, (3) creates internal tension, (4) criticizes colonialism, and (5) rejects a respect for objectivity. It is very difficult for a newspaper reader

in any of the new nations of Africa to get a
well-rounded view of the chaotic situation
which exists in many parts of this continent.
In such nations as The Congo, the printed
media seem to have little value; although the
situation appeared to be improving in 1963,
the press could not be relied upon to get the
word to the people. Radio, not only in the
Congo, but all through Africa is generally
considered much more important as a news
medium.

Radio can reach a mass audience over large
distances easily. This, in Africa, is very
important. Even so, the multiplicity of
languages used makes the radio communicator's
job difficult. Large segments of the African
populations are nomadic, ever-roving across
large expanses; this further complicates the
task of the printed media--and even of radio.
Newspapers generally receive their news file
from the world agencies by radio, and outgoing messages almost invariably travel via
the air waves. This, of course, is true only
of the larger papers of the principal metropolitan centers which use foreign news to any
extent. Besides using the world news agencies,
African newspapers in the dependencies and
former dependencies of Britain, France, Belgium, Portugal, and Spain get news daily from
their old home countries' national news
agencies. And, also, there are a few "purely"
African news agencies. Most local or area
stories come to the newspapers by mail, telephone, and telegraph. However, this service
is slow and uncertain. Often because of inadequate facilities, press telegrams are
carried from outlying or remote areas on 30
m.p.h. trains.

Actually newspapers throughout Africa reach
more people than the paltry circulations
(when they can be obtained) indicate. It is
common practice for newspapers to be passed
along by hand or posted in public places.
Many illiterates hear the newspapers read
aloud on the streets, in parks, in business
establishments, and in private homes. Even
so, only a small fraction of the total population of Africa is touched by the press. And
it appears that, even with rapid advances
being made, the press will not really take a
significant place in Africa until communication and transportation facilities develop
greatly, until the vernacular press increases
in quality and quantity, until political tensions are eased, until the economic situation
improves, and until illiteracy recedes further
into the still "Dark Continent."

Most of the African press systems are small
and underdeveloped; this is mainly due to the
tremendous distances, the slow development of

transportation and communications, the
sparsely-populated regions, and the overall
lack of capital. There is a serious scarcity
throughout most of the African press today
of men and machines with which to produce
newspapers and magazines. Every publication
needs capital to buy equipment and materials,
hire larger and better-trained staffs, and
to modernize methods of distribution.

Publications (especially newspapers) on
the continent today are generally:
(1) small with crude, outmoded equipment;
(2) understaffed and poorly staffed (salaries
    are poor, working conditions are far from
    satisfactory, trained newsmen are ex-
    tremely scarce, and in general there is
    little incentive for educated persons to
    enter the profession);
(3) hampered by poor communications and trans-
    portation;
(4) submitted to many pressures (from "non-
    African" nations, from local or provincial
    governments, from "nationalistic" parties
    and groups which are becoming ever more
    influential, and from religious factions).

Other than Egypt (discussed in the "Middle
East" portion of this book because it is the
center of that area's more progressive and
prosperous press system), no African state
has more than 20 daily newspapers. Those
African political units having the greatest
number of dailies follow (none has fewer
than eight dailies): Union of South Africa,
Nigeria, Ghana, Algeria, Tunisia, Morocco, and
the Congo Republic. Even in the areas where
the greatest number of papers exist, large portions of the population are illiterate. For
example, in Nigeria the more than 13 dailies
circulate a total of slightly less than 200,000
copies in a population which is 85 per cent
illiterate.

DAILIES

In 1962 there were some 230 daily papers
in Africa, circulating about 3 million
copies--providing only slightly more than one
copy per every 100 inhabitants. In North
Africa the governments owned a large segment
of the press, whereas in the South, East
(and to some extent in the West) a majority
of the most important papers were owned by
Europeans. African ownership in West Africa
seems to be growing very rapidly. Most of
the African dailies are small, with circulations ranging from about 1,500 to 8,000.
Many of the circulations are not made public,
but they are generally considered small, well
within the above range. Other than several
of the South African dailies, none of the
dailies of the continent (excluding Egypt)
has a circulation of as much as 150,000.
The Times of Lagos, Nigeria, comes the closest

with a circulation of about 110,000.

Vernacular dailies of Africa are generally small--in number of pages and in circulation. In fact, vernacular dailies (other than those in Arabic in the north and Afrikaans in the south) are so few as to be unimportant in the press picture. The only dailies of any real size and influence are printed in English, French, Arabic, and Afrikaans. Some of these contain certain columns printed in vernacular languages.

Some of the largest dailies in Africa (excluding those in South Africa) follow; they have circulations greater than 25,000 but less than 150,000: Daily Graphic, Evening News, and Ghana Times of Accra, Ghana; The Times and West African Pilot of Lagos, Nigeria; East African Standard of Nairobi, Kenya; L'Echo d'Alger of Algiers, Algeria; La Vigie Morocaine of Casablanca, Morocco, and Echo du Maroc of Rabat, Morocco. Only in the Union of South Africa are there dailies with circulations of 125,000 and upward.

WEEKLY PAPERS. Africa's weekly newspapers (nearly 1,000 in 1963) are usually considered better-edited than the dailies, and generally have larger circulations. And, in contrast to the daily press, there is a rather large and influential vernacular weekly press on the continent. Most of the larger weeklies are found in South Africa, where The Sunday Times of Johannesburg is the circulation leader among African newspapers, with a weekly press run of 300,000. Other prominent weeklies of South Africa are Johannesburg's Dagbreek and Die Brandwag, both published in the Afrikaans dialect. The largest vernacular weekly newspaper (other than those in Afrikaans) is Irohin Yoruba of Lagos, Nigeria (circulation about 60,000) which is published in Yoruba dialect. In French-Arabic North Africa the largest weeklies are Samedi Soir and Dimanche-Matin of Algiers, Dépêche-Dimanche of Oran, and L'Action of Tunis.

Other prominent weekly newspapers of Africa follow: Sunday Mirror of Accra, Ghana; The Sunday Times and Nigerian Catholic Herald of Lagos, Nigeria; Ethiopian Herald of Addis Ababa; Matalisi of Kampala, Uganda; Baraguma of Dar-es-Salaam, Tanganyika; Eastern Outlook of Enugu, Nigeria; Gaskiya Ta Fi Kwabo of Zaria, Nigeria; African Weekly of Salisbury, Rhodesia, and Die Huisgenoot of Cape Town, South Africa.

MAGAZINES. Some of Africa's most significant and largest magazines follow: Drum[2] (monthly news and general interest), Zonk (general interest) and Roci Rose Rose (monthly women's journal) of Johannesburg, South Africa; Outspan (weekly family) of Bloemfontein, South Africa; Mambo Leo (monthly general) of Dar-es-Salaam, Tanganyika; Pour-quoi Pas (weekly general and news) of Léopoldville, the Congo Republic; Kenya Today (quarterly illustrated) of Nairobi; Huna Tarablus Al-Gharb (bimonthly literary and feature) of Tunis; Simoun (bimonthly literary) of Oran, Algeria; Bingo (monthly government review, illustrated) of Dakar, West Africa; African Challenge (monthly Protestant journal) of Lagos, Nigeria; A Voz de Angola (monthly Protuguese review) of Luanda, Angola. In 1963 one of the best newsmagazines was the Reporter (f.1961), published in Kenya. With a circulation of about 8,000, it circulates largely in East Africa. This weekly is known widely in Africa for its honest and careful news coverage.

NATIONAL NEWS AGENCIES. Right at 20 countries of Africa had national news agencies by 1963, with others in the planning stage. This, of course, was largely the result of emerging nationalism and independence. This number showed a rapid increase over 1957 when only three African states had news agencies. Most of the national agencies in 1963, however, were still in their infancy and needed considerable development to provide adequate coverage--even in domestic news. Many of the African agencies have been created by the government and are dependent on government support for existence. Many so-called news agencies are nothing more than government information departments. African news agencies have a very long way to go before they can be considered on equal footing with national agencies in other parts of the world. At present they are generally poor, undermanned, and serve principally as propaganda spokesmen for their respective governments.

SOME LEADING AFRICAN DAILY NEWSPAPERS

Algiers, Algeria	L'Echo d'Alger (60,000)
	Dépêche Quotidienne (30,000)
Oran, Algeria	L'Echo d'Oran (75,000)
Elizabethville, the Congo	L'Essor du Congo (8,000)
Léopoldville, the Congo.	Le Courrier d'Afrique (15,000)
Casablanca, Morocco	La Vigie Morocaine (38,000)
	Le Petit Morocain (35,000)
Rabat, Morocco	Echo du Maroc (30,000)
Tunis, Tunisia	La Dépêche Tunisienne (20,000)
	La Presse de Tunisie (35,000)
	As-Sabah (10,000)
Addis Ababa, Ethiopia	Sendek Alamatchin (10,000)
	Addis Zemen (10,000)
Accra, Ghana	Daily Graphic (92,000)
	Evening News (60,000)
	Ghana Times (60,000)
Kumasi, Ghana	Ashanti Pioneer (25,000)
Nairobi, Kenya	East African Standard (35,000)
Tripoli, Libya	Journale de Tripoli (5,000)
Ibadan, Nigeria	Nigerian Tribune (15,000)
Lagos, Nigeria	Times (115,000)
	West African Pilot (45,000)
	Daily Service (30,000)
Khartoum, the Sudan	El Saraha (8,500)
Freetown, Sierra Leone	Daily Mail (15,000)

(Republic of South Africa and Central African Federation)

Cape Town	The Cape Argus (100,000)
	Cape Times (60,000)
	Die Burger (45,000)
Durban	Natal Daily News (65,000)
Johannesburg	The Star (170,000)
	Rand Daily Mail (125,000)
	Die Vaderland (60,000)
	Die Transvaler (45,000)
Pretoria	Pretoria News (30,000)
Salisbury	Rhodesia Herald (40,000)

THE ELECTRONIC MASS MEDIA. Great progress in radio has been made in recent years, and this medium seems destined to play a very important part in the development of the continent. The great number of languages in many parts of Africa is the main problem; nevertheless radio enjoys the advantage of being able to reach large numbers of illiterates in relatively inaccessible regions of Africa. Radio broadcasting is developing most rapidly in the continent's North and South. In 1962 broadcasting was found to be the major source of news for the peoples of Africa.[3] Another reason radio has not done even better in this respect is that there is a paucity of receiving sets. The British, in their parts of Africa, never considered wired radio systems or public-address systems practical; but they did loan "government sets" to coffee shops and did set up a few community sets in some villages.[4]

The Belgians have never been able to produce inexpensive sets. This has also been the case with the French, although they have done somewhat better.

Although television is still an infant in Africa, it promises to spread rapidly during the coming decade and aid greatly in the dissemination of news and views. In 1963 there were regular telecasts in Algeria, Rhodesia, and Nyasaland--and in the United Arab Republic. Television is certain to become an important medium of communication in Cameroun, Congo, Central African Republic, Bahomey, Ethiopia, Ghana, Ivory Coast, Kenya, Liberia, Senegal, Sierra Leone, the Sudan, Tanganyika, Togo, and Tunisia in the next few years.[5] As the young nations of Africa develop, they can learn to pull together when they are wired together.

Australia
and
Canada

The press systems of these two Commonwealth nations are in many ways patterned after the press of the United Kingdom, but with certain notable differences. In both Australia and Canada the local newspapers are the backbone of the press, and while in Australia more emphasis is given to international events than in Canada, the common local press orientation is probably the most significant feature. Neither nation has a newspaper of major "national" or "international" renown, and generally the circulations are small--reflecting again the "local" nature of the press. The Canadian press probably has more variety among its publications than does the press of Australia; this is mainly due to its proximity to the United States and the many French-language publications scattered throughout the country.

Australia

The press of this nation of some 10 million people (literacy about 99 per cent) is today in the midst of a period of great expansion and is enjoying unprecedented prestige. Some 50 daily newspapers with a total circulation of more than 3.5 million are published in Australia. About one-third of these are metropolitan papers. Nine Sunday papers are published in state capitals. There are right at 40 publications with circulations topping 100,000 in the country; nearly half of them are daily and weekly newspapers. The press system of Australia in general is patterned after that of Great Britain. For example, there are the serious and dignified dailies (e.g., The Age of Melbourne and West Australian of Perth), the sensational Sundays (e.g., Truth with editions in several cities), the

sensational popular dailies (e.g., the tabloid Daily Mirror of Sydney), and the semi-popular general dailies such as the Sydney Morning Herald. As is true in the United Kingdom, the Sunday papers have the largest circulations. Sydney's Sun-Herald, for example, circulates some 630,000 and the same city's Sunday Telegraph has a weekly circulation of nearly 600,000. Truth, published in several cities, has a weekly circulation of close to a million.

Canberra (population 35,000) is the seat of Parliament and is probably the most important political news center in Australia; however, its newspapers (the AM Canberra Times and the weekly official Commonwealth of Australia Gazette) are very small, and the nation's newspaper centers are Melbourne, Sydney, and Brisbane.

Melbourne is the home of Australia's two largest daily newspapers, Sun News Pictorial and The Herald. The first of these is a morning tabloid paper circulating some 565,000 copies, making it the nation's largest-circulation daily. The latter, an evening paper, is the country's largest regular-format (non-tabloid) daily with a circulation of about 455,000. The Herald is also one of Australia's oldest newspapers, having been founded in 1840.

There seems to be no great trend toward newspaper consolidation or chain-ownership in Australia as in certain other countries, although the weekly Truth publishes several editions in various cities. There are some 50 dailies and about 575 weeklies publishing in Australia today. Also in the country is a rather large number of semiweekly and tri-weekly papers--especially in towns of about 10,000 population. Many (nearly half) of the dailies are tabloids; the most influential of these are Brisbane's Telegraph, Perth's West Australian, Sydney's Daily Mirror and Sun, and Melbourne's Sun News Pictorial. These tabloids are not sensational by U.S. or British standards, and with the notable exception of the Mirror they do not give crime and sex major emphasis; in other words, they are "general" newspapers.

Australia has no definite "quality" press as does the United Kingdom; at least there are no papers to compare with several of the great dailies found in Britain such as The Times, The Daily Telegraph or the Manchester Guardian. However, there are several dailies which reach a high level of excellence. The Age of Melbourne, for example, is considered one of the best and most comprehensive of Australia's papers. This morning newspaper has more prestige and influence than its

170,000 circulation might suggest. Another
daily which seems to be one of the most influential is the Sydney Morning Herald, the

country's oldest. It is a well-edited paper,
which gives comprehensive coverage of domestic
and foreign news. Generally the newspapers of
the country carry very little interpretive
material. They play the most important stories
in the upper left corner of the page rather
than in the upper right as do newspapers in the
United States. Headlines in many of the papers
appear to be hastily written and little care
seems to be given to make up. Probably the
daily with the best-planned make up is Sydney's
Morning Herald, which presents its news and
pictures in a fashion resembling that of London's respected Daily Telegraph. The most
flamboyant make up techniques are used by the
Daily Mirror of Sydney.

Most Australian dailies have editions of
from ten to eighteen pages. Classified advertisements are very popular and often as many
as six or eight pages of a sixteen-page edition
will be filled with these ads. There appears
to be little attempt made by editors to keep
stories of one kind together in the papers,
and stories tend to be scattered without much
thought given to classification by page or
section as is true in many countries. By-lines

are seldom given to reporters or correspondents who write for Australian newspapers.

The Australian press, although possibly
having more than its share of editorial weaknesses, has a great amount of freedom. Newspapers are probably as free as any in the
world, and editors and publishers appear
determined to keep them that way. The main
complaint of Australian journalists is what
they call "censorship by request," whereby
authorities have attempted to put pressure
on the editors and publishers by appealing
to their "loyalty" when they would want something published or not published. Most
observers feel that the Australian press has
done a good job of convincing the populace
that press freedom is indispensable to the
freedom of the people. As evidenced in many
issues of Newspaper News and in other general
books on Australia, the press appears always
ready to fight against any type of governmental restrictions, secrecy, or oppression.

Freedom of the press in Australia is zeal-
ously guarded. There is no censorship and
criticism of government is quite common.
Press freedom is generally accepted as is
the principle that a person criticized in the
press has a right to reply. As in the United
States, editors can print anything they desire, but must be responsible before the law
for their publications. Truth is the most
important defense a newspaper can use against
alleged libel. And also as in the U.S.,
privilege is another important defense (e.g.,
Parliamentary proceedings are not actionable
although they may contain statements which
would out of that context be libelous).[1]

Although Australian papers give their
readers about the same kind and proportion
of news as an American would find in his own
papers, they contain far fewer personal columns,
interpretive journalistic essays, and gossip.[2]
It might be said, then, that Australian papers
generally are more accurately "news" papers
than their counterparts in the United States.
This does not mean, however, that Australian
papers have no editorial backbone; in fact,
their editorials are often more vicious than
are those in the U. S. It simply means that
subjective essays do not have a very prominent
place in the papers, and the few that are
printed are not syndicated offerings as is
so often the case in the American press.

All the big daily papers of Australia are
found in the important cities--capitals--of
the states. These big dailies account for
the bulk of the total daily circulation of
some 3.5 million for the country. The daily
press outside the big cities provides only

about a half million copies daily.

The most important press organization in Australia is the Australian Journalists Association, to which the nearly 5,000 practicing journalists belong--with only few exceptions. The A.J.A. is a union, founded in 1910, with central offices in Melbourne. This organization has done much to improve standards generally and to keep Australian press ethics about as high as can be found in any nation.

PRESS ORGANIZATIONS. Employees and employers of Australian papers have a number of organizations to which they belong. In the cities, employers have two groups: the Australian Newspaper Proprietors' Association and the Australian Newspapers' Council. In the provinces newspapers belong to the Australian Provincial Press Association, with sub-groups for each state. The APPA's motto is "one people, one destiny."

Australia is associated with other Commonwealth countries of Britain in the Commonwealth Press Union, an organization dating from 1909 when it was known as the Empire Press Union. This Union promotes the press of the Commonwealth in many respects, dealing with freedom largely, and holding conventions to discuss mutual problems.

Even Australian newspaper-sellers (called "newsagents") have their own organizations. The Australian Association of National Advertisers controls, for the most part, newspaper advertising. Printers belong to the Printing Industry Employees' Union. Editorial workers--writers, artists, and photographers have their group: the Australian Journalists' Association (AJA, founded 1910). Its activities range from promoting journalism courses in universities to the sponsoring of social events. It has written a code of ethics which all AJA members are pledged to keep.

In Australia there is the Audit Bureau of Circulations on the business side of publishing. Founded in 1932, it verifies circulation figures submitted to advertisers. It is largely patterned after the American organization by the same name.

BRIEF HISTORY. The four-page Sydney Gazette founded in 1803 by a government printer (George Howe) initiated Australia's newspaper history. This was really nothing more than an official bulletin board. It was not until 1824 that the earliest independent paper, The Australian, was founded in Sydney; it lasted twenty-six years. The Tasmanian, founded in Launceston in 1925, was the country's first country newspaper. On the mainland the first

provincial paper was the Hunter River Gazette of Maitland, founded in 1841. The Sydney Morning Herald, founded in 1831, is the oldest surviving paper in the country.

THE CITY PRESS. Metropolitan newspapers generally have up to 60 or 64 pages an issue. Newsprint cost and scarcity has accelerated the tendency toward tabloids and narrower columns in the city dailies. Today about half these papers are tabloids, the first being the Sun-Pictorial of Melbourne (1922). The majority of city papers are owned by public companies; many have played important roles in Australian history and have old family traditions. Most of the large metropolitan newspaper firms also publish magazines.

Morning papers are generally delivered to the homes by newsagents; most afternoon papers reach their readers on the streets. Copies of city papers, in some cases, are sent in bulk by air to rural areas at extremely high rates; however, most country distribution is handled by rail, bus, and truck. Circulations of city papers have jumped greatly in the last half century, even faster than the population. Estimates are that the total circulations have more than tripled since 1928. Sydney and Melbourne account for more than half the circulation of the country's city dailies.

THE PROVINCIAL PRESS. Nonmetropolitan or "grassroots" newspapers of Australia have played important parts in the development of communities throughout the country. It is the firm belief of Australian journalists that the force of the provincial press has had great impact on politics and business in particular. Community papers enjoy great prestige throughout Australia and New Zealand and generally provide well-balanced news coverage and intelligent editorial comment. By providing these services in the local context, plus the great service of community advertising, the provincial press has fought with much success the inroads of the big city newspapers upon its circulation. Emphasis on the sensational and the atypical aspects of the news are not nearly so great in the provincial press as in the city press.

Most provincial papers are privately owned, in contrast to their big brothers in the city. Most towns with a population of at least 20,000 have their own daily. Papers range from the well-printed daily of twenty-four pages to the small country paper of four pages.

Concentration among the provincial papers is on local news; this has been brought about by the frequency of radio and television

```
                          PRINCIPAL NEWSPAPERS

              Sydney:

     Herald (PM) . . . . . . . . . . . . . . . . . . . . . . . . . 450,000
     Sun (PM tab) . . . . . . . . . . . . . . . . . . . . . . . . 265,000
     Daily Telegraph (AM). . . . . . . . . . . . . . . . . . . . . 324,000
     Sydney Morning Herald (AM). . . . . . . . . . . . . . . . . . 310,000
     Daily Mirror (PM tab) . . . . . . . . . . . . . . . . . . . . 260,000
     Sun-Herald (Sunday) . . . . . . . . . . . . . . . . . . . . . 630,000
     Sunday Telegraph . . . . . . . . . . . . . . . . . . . . . . 595,000
     Truth (Weekly). . . . . . . . . . . . . . . . . . . . . . . . 520,000
     Sun News Pictorial (AM) . . . . . . . . . . . . . . . . . . . 560,000

              Melbourne:

     Sun News Pictorial (AM) . . . . . . . . . . . . . . . . . . . 565,000
     Herald (PM) . . . . . . . . . . . . . . . . . . . . . . . . . 455,000
     Age (AM) . . . . . . . . . . . . . . . . . . . . . . . . . . 170,000
     Truth (Weekly) . . . . . . . . . . . . . . . . . . . . . . . 225,000

              Brisbane:

     Courier-Mail (AM) . . . . . . . . . . . . . . . . . . . . . . 235,000
     Brisbane Telegraph (PM) . . . . . . . . . . . . . . . . . . . 160,000
     Sunday Mail . . . . . . . . . . . . . . . . . . . . . . . . . 300,000
     Truth (Weekly) . . . . . . . . . . . . . . . . . . . . . . . 200,000

              Adelaide:

     Advertiser (AM) . . . . . . . . . . . . . . . . . . . . . . . 185,000
     News (PM tab) . . . . . . . . . . . . . . . . . . . . . . . . 115,000
     Sunday Mail . . . . . . . . . . . . . . . . . . . . . . . . . 215,000

              Perth:

     West Australian (AM) . . . . . . . . . . . . . . . . . . . . 160,000
     Daily News (PM) . . . . . . . . . . . . . . . . . . . . . . . 100,000
     Sunday Times . . . . . . . . . . . . . . . . . . . . . . . . 122,000

              Auckland (New Zealand):

     New Zealand Herald (AM) . . . . . . . . . . . . . . . . . . . 180,000
     Auckland Star (PM) . . . . . . . . . . . . . . . . . . . . . 120,000
```

newscasts and the slowly-growing circulation of city papers in country areas. Oftentimes there is almost total exclusion of national and international news in the country press.

SUNDAY PAPERS. Sunday papers in Australia are patterned generally on their counterparts in Britain; they are very thick tabloids containing a potpourri of items--mainly feature articles, short stories, sports stories, children's pages and comics, and sections given over to other special areas. Sydney, the home of the country's first Sunday paper (1885), today is the publication site for three--the Sun-Herald, the Sunday Telegraph, and the Sunday Mirror. The Sun-Herald is the most widely-read.

Brisbane has the Sunday Mail and Truth. In Perth is published the Sunday Times. And in Adelaide also is the Sunday Mail. Truth is also a Sunday paper in Hobart.

PERIODICALS. A flourishing magazine press is found in Australia. They range from the high-circulation Australian Women's Weekly (nearly a million copies) to much smaller specialized journals. Magazines cover the gamut of subjects--sports, films, motoring, science, religion, literature, music, agriculture, politics, history, the press, radio-TV, and the professions.

One of the most interesting weekly journals is The Bulletin, founded in 1880. Although it is mainly a political journal of opinion, it reflects a wide range of intellectual interests and is marked by vigorous and imaginative prose. It also includes notable articles of literary criticism. Representative of the trade journals is Newspaper News, a biweekly magazine which is in general comparable to the U.S.'s Editor & Publisher or to Britain's World's Press News.

A few other important Australian magazines are Adam (monthly magazine of fiction and fact articles) of Sydney; Pix (national picture magazine circulating all through Australia and New Zealand), and Women's Day (high class women's weekly magazine) published in several cities.

NEWS AGENCIES. The two locally-controlled news agencies of Australia are the Australian Associated Press (AAP) and the Australian United Press (AUP). AAP was founded in 1935, replacing the old Australian Press Association. Its purpose: to provide a world news service for all but one of the capital city dailies who own it cooperatively. AAP has its main office in Melbourne. It is mainly responsible for the large amount of foreign news found in the bigger dailies; it has overseas offices in some ten cities, about half of them in the Far East. AAP works closely with Reuters and gets the benefit of the big British agency's excellent world news file. The agency also services radio and TV stations. AAP has more

than 100 full-time employees, half in Australia and half in other parts of the world.

The other agency, AUP was founded in 1932 when smaller agencies combined. It gathers and distributes national news and transmits AAP foreign news to the country press. Stockholders in the AUP are provincial newspapers. AUP has offices in Sydney, Melbourne, and Canberra, and correspondents in all parts of the country.

ELECTRONIC MEDIA. Some 170 radio stations exist in the country, about half of them belonging to the Australian Broadcasting Commission,[3] a national authority. There are about two million radio listener families in Australia. News broadcasts on radio grew rapidly during the Second World War. Although the Australian Broadcasting Commission is the main force in the country's broadcasting, the commercial radio and television stations give much-needed balance and are important. Most of these commercial stations are partly or wholly owned by newspaper companies.

Television began in Australia in 1956, and by 1962 fourteen TV channels served the country-- three each in Melbourne, Brisbane, Sydney, and Adelaide, and one in Hobart and Perth. Approximately one million TV sets were in use by 1962. Australian sources have indicated that, although TV (and radio) has hurt newspapers somewhat, brief broadcast news summaries on the electronic media have really created a demand for more detailed news reports furnished by the press.

Canada

This vast Dominion, with a land area larger than that of the United States, but with a population of 17,000,000, more than 80 per cent of whom live within 100 miles of the U.S. border, has a vigorous local and regional press.

There are 107 dailies (three-fourths of them afternoon papers) circulating 4.2 million copies, and 920 weekly newspapers with a total circulation of 3 million.[1]

The largest publication centers are Montreal, Toronto, Ottawa, Quebec, and Vancouver. By contrast, the weeklies wield great influence in local affairs by circulating in the many Canadian cities ranging from 10,000 to 20,000 population.

Biggest publisher of small and medium-size dailies is Roy H. Thomson, who at the beginning of 1963 owned 27 newspapers in five of the ten provinces of the Dominion:

British Columbia--Kamloops, Kelowna, Nanaimo, Penticton

Ontario--Barrie, Chatham, Cornwall, Galt, Guelph, Kirkland Lake, Orilla, Oshawa, Pembroke, Port Arthur, Sarnia, Sudbury, Timmins, Welland, Woodstock

Prince Edward Island--Charlottetown

Quebec--Quebec

Saskatchewan--Moose Jaw

Before the end of 1963, Thomson was expected to buy at least one paper in each of the other five provinces (Alberta, Manitoba, New Brunswick, Newfoundland, and Nova Scotia), as well as in cities other than those listed for the five provinces cited above.[2] Many of the Thomson dailies serve cities of 30-to 40,000.

In addition, Thomson owns newspapers, radio and television stations, and magazines in the United States, the West Indies, Britain, Australia, Africa, and Asia, having become the British Commonwealth's chief Press Lord.[3]

TORONTO'S STAR. Toronto's Weekly Star, published every Saturday, with a circulation of 900,000, is Canada's largest newspaper. The same city has the country's largest daily, the Toronto Daily Star, an afternoon paper with 350,000 circulation.

Toronto also has Canada's most influential daily, the Globe and Mail, with a circulation of 260,000. This morning paper, with excellent coverage of national and international news, is Canada's only truly "national" daily. In 1958 it became the first Canadian paper to publish an overseas edition, a weekly tabloid summary of its regular editions, printed in London for distribution throughout Europe.

MONTREAL'S NEWS SOURCES. Although Ottawa is the nation's capital, and Toronto has the biggest circulation dailies, Montreal is Canada's largest city, has its largest number of dailies. It is the news center for the Dominion's French-speaking population, and draws many of the newsworthy foreign visitors who come to Canada. Montreal is world headquarters for the International Civil Aviation Organization, a branch of the UN and a source of news about the various airlines of the world.

Montreal's evening La Presse, a comprehensive afternoon daily with an exceptionally fine weekend edition, is the largest daily in the French language in the Western Hemisphere; its circulation totals 270,000. Montreal has two morning dailies in French, Le Devoir and Montreal-Matin, and another afternoon French-language daily, Le Nouveau Journal, with a circulation of 100,000 even though it was started as recently as September, 1961.

A Sunday French-language newspaper, Le Petit Journal, circulates 260,000, and a Saturday paper in French, Photo-Journal, circulates 151,000. With the two English-language dailies, the Gazette in the morning and the Star in the evening, Montreal supports six dailies and three large weeklies. In addition to the Saturday and Sunday papers already mentioned, another Sunday French-language paper, Patrie du Dimanche, circulates 195,000.

BROADCASTING. Like newspapers, radio and television broadcasts in Canada are in both English and French. During Quebec's provincial election in November, 1962, the rival candidates for provincial premier debated each other for one hour and 45 minutes on a province-wide French-language telecast copied in format from the Kennedy-Nixon presidential television debates of 1960.[4]

Canada has 250 radio stations and 99 television stations,[5] the French-language broadcasts being in Quebec and the English-language ones in the other provinces, with some bilingual broadcasting in Quebec and Ontario.

In terms of economics as well as languages, Canada has a mixed broadcasting system. There are both publicly-owned and privately-owned television, radio, and even FM stations.[6] The responsible authority over all broadcasting activities is a governmental agency called the Board of Broadcast Governors. The Canadian Broadcasting Corporation operates the three radio networks--Trans-Canada, Dominion, and French--and two television networks (English and French).

These networks link CBC-owned and privately-owned stations. Unlike the British Broadcasting Corporation, which it resembles in some respects, the CBC accepts commercial announcements. In addition to money from a limited amount of advertising, the CBC also receives tax funds.

News broadcasts are prepared in the CBC central news room in Toronto as well as in various regional stations.

Canadian radio and television stations are free to contract for programs from the United States either tape recorded or fed live at the time such programs are being broadcast in the

U.S. Thus many Canadian stations are "Affiliates" of U.S. networks.

CANADIAN-U.S. NEWS FLOW. Journalistically, Canada is entwined both with the United States and Britain, and, as in its broadcasting, is often a composite of both. Politically, the U.S.-Canadian border not only remains peaceful but often almost nonexistent. One must look to the province of Quebec and the states of Maine, Vermont, and New York for the world of linguistic difference that separates French-language and English-language cultures.

United States television and radio programs have found outlets in Canada. U.S. make up, not British typography, shapes the appearance of Canadian newspapers. Canadian papers carry a large volume of United States news, whereas U.S. newspapers report little about Canada.[7]

As for magazines, three out of four magazines read in Canada are from the United States and 41 per cent of all Canadian advertising in magazines is in American-owned magazines. Despite pressures from Canadian magazine publishers during 1961-62 for governmental barriers to protect their product from the unrestricted flow of U.S. periodicals across the border, that flow of information continues.[8]

WESTERN CANADA. Canada's international news flow comes from the central and eastern listening posts of correspondents in Toronto, Montreal, and Ottawa. But some of the significant stories coming into these cities, to be condensed by foreign correspondents for transmission abroad are from western Canada.

Especially important is Vancouver, British Columbia, whose evening daily, the Sun, with 220,000 circulation, and whose morning daily, the Province, with 99,000 circulation, carry many significant stories of western Canada.

In Winnipeg, Manitoba, the Free Press, an evening daily with 121,000 circulation, has good coverage of central and western Canada.

TRAINING OF NEWSMEN. Most Canadian journalists have received no formal academic journalism training; however, increasing emphasis is being given journalism instruction in the classroom, and Canada now has four schools of journalism--at Carleton College (Ottawa), Ryerson Institute of Technology (Toronto), the University of Western Ontario (London), and the School of Journalism, Halifax, Nova Scotia. Generally, Canadian journalists exhibit skill and care in their writing and editing, and newspapers maintain high professional standards.

THE CANADIAN PRESS (CP). The CP, Canada's national cooperative news agency, was founded in 1917 under pressure of newspapers for news of the first World War. It is a nonprofit agency with its operating expenses being met by yearly assessment of members. This assessment is based mainly on the newspaper's location (the population of the area served). Membership is open to any daily paying an initial fee of $500 and willing to share in the annual expenses through its dues. The CP has always stressed accuracy over speed. Today CP delivers home and world news to about 100 Canadian papers and most of the radio and TV stations. It has exchange agreements with Reuters and the American AP, and covers Canada for them while receiving their foreign news file. Headquarters are in Toronto; in addition it has seven main offices--in Halifax, Quebec, Montreal, Ottawa, Winnipeg, Edmonton, and Vancouver. CP is especially well-known for the thoroughness of its Parliamentary coverage. The agency provides a French-language service (begun in 1951) for some members which had previously translated the copy from English.

GENERAL PRESS CHARACTERISTICS. Newspapers of Canada are mainly "local" journals due to the great distances with sparse populations, the language differences, and the varied assortment of news values found throughout the country.

Local incidents--especially crimes--will generally take the prominent places on the front pages of Canadian newspapers. However, some few dailies (e.g., Toronto's Globe and Mail) attempt to give considerable space to national and world news.

Most of Canada's dailies are afternoon papers, with those in the big cities having the large circulations. Local interest is the keynote of success, and national or world news must really be exceptional even to get on the front pages. In almost all Canadian newspapers (and especially in the PMs) the big human interest story which deals with a person or incident closest home is the one which gets the best play.

The morning papers give more space to world news than do the PMs; however, even in such big morning papers as the Globe and Mail and Montreal's influential La Presse, these stories must be of striking importance to get prominent play.

The two most important news agencies operating in Canada--the Canadian Press and the British United Press--are chiefly interested in supplying home news. The CP relies on Reuters and American AP for its world news, and the British UP tries to compete with CP in the domestic news picture. International events in Canadian newspapers find their main expression on the editorial page, not the news page. Foreign news in Canada, although minimized in the press, is far from ignored. It is available constantly via the air waves, since Canadian radio and TV stations give it prominent and repeated emphasis.

Part III

Aids for the Student

Notes

NOTES TO PART I

1 Lester Markel, "The Future of the Printed Word," Vital Speeches of the Day (April 1, 1956), 384. See also Markel, "Flow of News Among Nations: Editors Held Largely to Blame if Readers Don't Understand Our Foreign Stories," The Bulletin of the American Society of Newspaper Editors (April 1, 1955), 4; Hereinafter cited as the ASNE Bulletin; Carroll Binder, "An Obligation of the Press: To Provide Citizens With What they Need for an Understanding of World Affairs," ASNE Bulletin (April 1, 1955), 5-6. For a good discussion of the amount and nature of news passing among countries and its value, see International Press Institute, The Flow of the News (Zurich, 1953), parts A and B of chap. ii.

2 Quoted in Robert U. Brown, "Shop Talk at Thirty," Editor & Publisher (April 30, 1960), 112.

3 For good discussions of governmental relationships to the press, see Herbert Brucker, Freedom of Information (New York, 1949), chap. xvi; Robert W. Desmond, The Press and World Affairs (New York, 1937), chap. iv; IPI, Government Pressures on the Press (Zurich, 1955); Llewellyn White and Robert D. Leigh, Peoples Speaking to Peoples (Chicago, 1946), chap. iv.

4 Louis M. Lyons, in a speech at a Harvard Club dinner in 1958, leveled such an indictment at the press--especially the U.S. press--saying that the press in this country is largely a "mirror of a negative attitude" and that the "foreign news analysis of a great wire service reads as if it were written in Mr. Dulles' back office...." What the press needs, the speaker stated, is "reporting in depth, the full dimensions of the news...." As quoted in Frederick W. Roevekamp, "Friendly Critic Hits Press," Christian Science Monitor, April 25, 1958, p. 13.

5 Kent Cooper places the blame on the citizen in these words: "If the American layman continues to find himself comfortably borne along in the present current of change, in which his government does his thinking for him and decides his fate, he is not going to awaken to the necessity of resisting infringement by the government upon his Right to Know. Apparently he cannot be aroused from his languid disinterest in protecting that right...." Kent Cooper, The Right to Know (New York, 1956), 308.

6 "Voice of America Steps Up Air Time," New York Times, October 16, 1961. See UNESCO reports for 1962.

7 Robert B. Rhode, "News for a Nation," Nieman Reports (July-October, 1962), 3-5; Albert E. Norman, "Radio Australia," Christian Science Monitor, May 17, 1962; Robert J. McCleave, "Canadian Broadcasting," Gazette, V (1959), 323-29. Compare Canadian and Australian broadcasting, both of which allow privately-owned stations to exist alongside their BBC-type outlets.

8 Burton Paulu, British Broadcasting in Transition (Minneapolis, 1961); Paulu, British Broadcasting (Minneapolis, 1956).

9 "Unions to Black Out French Radio-TV," New York Times, November 5, 1962.

10 H. G. Franks, "Dutch Snub TV and Radio," Christian Science Monitor, October 18, 1962.

11 "Prosperous Belgium Torn by Language Dispute," New York Times, October 28, 1962.

12 Ram Nandan Singh, "The All India Radio," Freedom of Information Center Publication No. 52 (March, 1961), 1-6.

13 Donald K. Pollock and David L. Woods, "A Study in International Communication: Eurovision," Journal of Broadcasting (Spring, 1959), 101-16.

14 Fred Siebert, Theodore Peterson, and Wilbur Schramm, Four Theories of the Press (Urbana, 1956). This book contains an excellent bibliography of basic works which relate directly to the four theories.

15 Commission on Freedom of the Press, A Free and Responsible Press (Chicago, 1947); William Ernest Hocking, Freedom of the Press (Chicago, 1947).

16 Copies of 86 such documents were examined.

17 The best recent study discussing in detail the scope and types of these pressures is IPI, Government Pressures on the Press.

18 The best comparative study of the main types of regulations governing the information media is Fernand Terrou and Lucien Solal,

Legislation for Press, Film and Radio,
(UNESCO: Paris, 1951).

19 The oldest free press laws were enacted
during strong parliamentary periods in
Sweden (1766) and Denmark (1770). For a
translation and discussion of the former,
see Carter R. Bryan, " ' Enlightenment of
the People Without Hindrance': The Swedish
Press Law of 1766," Journalism Quarterly
(Summer, 1960), 431-34.

20 Basically this is the classification system
used by the IPI in Government Pressures on
the Press.

21 For a more detailed discussion of this sub-
ject, see Bryan, "Security and the News in
Liberal Countries," Journalism Quarterly,
(Autumn, 1961), 485-96.

22 For a good discussion of this type of law
common in Latin America, see E. P. Deutsch,
"Descato," Nieman Reports (July, 1957),
7-9.

23 The Japanese Press, 1959, Nihon Shinbun
Kyokai (Japanese Newspaper Publishers and
Editors Association), (Tokyo, 1960), 148,
150, 152.

24 For a more detailed discussion of economic
pressures, see Bryan, "Economic Intervention: Prelude to Press Control," Journalism
Quarterly (Winter, 1961), 67-75.

25 The best recent study, IPI, The Press in
Authoritarian Countries (Zurich, 1959).

26 For a more detailed discussion of the problem of secrecy, see James Russell Wiggins,
Freedom or Secrecy, (New York, 1956).

27 Marquis W. Childs, "The Press' Role in the
Struggle for Freedom," The Press and the
War of Ideas (Madison, 1955), 20, 24.

28 Kent Cooper calls censorship "any government's own worst enemy." His reason: "For
the poison that is censorship is so strong
when rigorously applied to suppress the
news that it benumbs government into a
false sense of security." Cooper, The
Right to Know, 316.

29 For a more exhaustive discussion of this
subject, see IPI, Professional Secrecy and
the Journalist (Zurich, 1962).

30 John Wigmore, Evidence in Trials at Common
Law, (3rd. ed.; Boston, 1940), 531.

31 For a brief analysis of these tests and

their applicability to the journalist by
Frederick S. Siebert, author of books on
the legal aspects of journalism and dean
of the College of Communication Arts of
Michigan State University, see IPI, Professional Secrecy and the Journalist, 175-77.

32 IPI, The Flow of the News.

33 Markel, "Flow of News Among Nations," loc.
cit., 7.

34 For a detailed discussion of these systems,
see White and Leigh, Peoples Speaking to
Peoples, chap. iii; several chapters of
Desmond, The Press and World Affairs, present good material on this aspect; Francis
Williams, Transmitting World News (Paris,
1953).

35 An excellent treatment of this alliance
and its dissolution is given in Cooper,
Barriers Down: The Story of the News Agency
Epoch (New York, 1942).

AUSTRIA

1 Probably the best general reference on the
Austrian press is the Handbuch Österreichs
Presse Werbung Graphik (Vienna, 1962).
Most of the basic facts and circulation
figures used in this section of the survey
were taken from this source and Editor and
Publisher International Year Book, 1962.

2 Many of the country's leading dailies, however, are listed as "independent." Among
them are Die Presse, Express, and Der Neue
Kurier of Vienna; Klein Zeitung of Klagen-
furt; Linzer Volksblatt of Linz; Kleine
Zeitung of Graz; Tiroler Tageszeitung of
Innsbruck, and what is regarded by many as
the best newspaper in the country, Salzburger Nachrichten of Salzburg. Handbuch,
11-20.

3 Joseph Wechsberg, "Letter from Vienna," The
New Yorker (October 4, 1958), 140; see also
Donald F. Graff, "In Austria: The Press
Walks a Tightrope," Montana Journalism
Review (Spring, 1962), 13-15. Cf. Maxi-
milian Feicher, "Self Discipline for the
Austrian Press," IPI Report (January, 1961),
10-11.

4 IPI, Professional Secrecy and the Journalist,
33.

5 Österreichisches Jahrbuch 1957 (Vienna,
1958), 110-11.

6 Ingo Mussi, Austrian Press Attaché, Austrian

Embassy, Washington, D. C. (December, 1962).

7 Handbuch.

8 Ibid.

9 Sample copies of Austrian newspapers were furnished by the Austrian Information Service.

10 Maurice Feldman, "Newspaper Keystone of Business Empire," Editor and Publisher (November 24, 1962), 62.

11 Editor's note, Atlas (November, 1962), 364.

BELGIUM

1 Although 54 daily newspapers are listed, circulation figures are given for only 35 in Editor and Publisher International Year Book, 1962, p. 475.

2 La Presse (Bulletin Trimestriel de la Federation Belges), No. 27 (August-October, 1960).

3 "Survey Assesses World FOI," Freedom of Information Publication (December, 1959), 4.

4 "Belgium Defines the Word 'Journalist,'" IPI Report (October, 1962), 11.

5 Copies of leading newspapers were sent the writers by the Belgian Information Center, 50 Rockefeller Plaza, New York 20, New York.

BRITAIN

1 Very useful basic source materials used in this discussion of the British press were Editor and Publisher International Year Book, 1962, and Central Office of Information, The British Press (London, 1958). The writers also received valuable materials and sample copies of British publications from the British Embassy, Washington, D.C.

2 For a more detailed account of the King-Thomson contest, see Allan Delafons, "British Eye King-Thomson Struggle," Editor and Publisher Year Book, 1962, pp. 442-43.

3 Charles Fenby, "The Real Threat to the British Press," IPI Report (October, 1962), 1-3. Cf. John Tebbel, "How the British View their Press," Saturday Review (December 8, 1962), 68-69; Editor and Publisher (September 22, 1962), 10, and Editor and Publisher (September 29, 1962), 14.

4 Editor and Publisher (November 24, 1962), 60.

5 IPI Report (September, 1958), 11. Cf. New Statesman (February 7, 1959), 176, for a good discussion of dropping circulations.

6 A good general history of the British press is concisely presented by Harold Herd, The March of Journalism: The Story of the British Press from 1622 to the Present Day (London, 1952).

7 Time (May 26, 1958), 53.

8 Francis Williams, "Fleet Street," New Statesman (August 16, 1958), 184. Cf. Circulation data published in Editor and Publisher Year Books through 1962.

9 Time (November 3, 1958), 77. See also, Jim Bedford, "English Version: Sensationalism on Trial--The Plaintiff's Case," The Quill (January, 1959), 8-9, 18.

10 Francis Williams, "Fleet Street Notebook," New Statesman (July 27, 1957), 109. In this article Williams takes issue with Sir Linton Andrews, saying in effect that "triviality" is relative and even such papers as the Times contain many stories which would certainly seem trivial to great numbers of readers.

11 The expression "Fleet Street" is almost synonymous in Britain with "the press." Actually, it is a rather shoddy street in London which contains many of the big national newspaper plants, advertising agencies, and offices for free-lance writers. A very good description of Fleet Street is provided by John Prebble's "London's News-paper Row," Holiday (June, 1957), 26 ff. passim.

12 Newsweek (October 6, 1958), 58.

13 Randolph Churchill, "Fleet Street Fracas," The Spectator (July 11, 1958), 52.

14 Joseph Whitt, "Englishman's Castle," ASNE Bulletin (June 1, 1957), 10. Whitt's indictment of the popular papers seems an unfair one. Such papers as the Daily Express, the Daily Mail and even the tabloid Mirror generally evidence sharp, clear, zestful writing; make up and typography of these papers (especially the Express) is anything but "amateurish" and "confused" as Whitt calls them; in fact, they show a sense of design, imagination, and planning often missing from their mass-appeal U.S. counterparts. For an opposite

view of the popular journals, see A. W. Parsons, "Putting Life into the City Page," IPI Report (October, 1962), 6-7.

15 "Role of British Popular Press" (a two-page advertisement), Editor and Publisher (May 24, 1958), 26-27.

16 Peter Bostock, "Fleet Street Letter," Editor and Publisher (August 9, 1958), 56.

17 H. F. Ellis, "The Times and Punch," Holiday (April, 1958), 28 ff. passim.

18 There are many good books on British journalism which provide excellent discussions of the Times. For the most thorough historical treatment of this great paper, see the Times's own four-volume series, The History of "The Times," London (London, 1935-52).

19 For a good recent discussion of the Times see "Establishmentarianism," Newsweek (October 1, 1962), 48-49.

20 J. D. Scott, Life in Britain (New York, 1956), 236.

21 Central Office of Information, The British Press, 20.

22 Francis Williams, "Fleet Street," loc. cit., 812, gives the main headlines as they appeared in British national daily papers when the first U. S. satellite rocket failed to fire in late 1957. Williams points out that the headline of the Daily Worker was most sedate of all the papers. It read: "America's Sputnik Launching Fails. Rocket Explodes." For comparison, here are heads placed over this same story by other papers: "Oh Dear!!! US Sputnik Blows Up on Ground!!! The Man from the Mirror (BLUSHING) Was There" (Daily Mirror); "US Rocket Explodes in Satellite Test" (the Times); "US Sputnik Goes Up In Smoke" (the Guardian).

23 For a good commentary on the Sunday press and its reading public, see Francis Williams, "Sunday Spice," New Statesman (August 30, 1958), 240-41.

24 The term "crisis" has become quite common in referring to the British press situation; it has been used often since 1957 when the situation began making news in the U.S. general press. E.g. see "The Fleet Street Crisis," Time (June 10, 1957), 84. Also for interesting insights on the "crisis," see Allan Delafons, "TV, Rising Costs, Plague British Press," Editor and Publisher International Year Book, 1958 (New York,

1958), 353-54; "Cheerful News Reporting Headlined by Macmillan," Christian Science Monitor, April 28, 1958, p. 12; "Rethink and Rethink," Newsweek (May 19, 1958), 64; "Fleet Street Has Big Drop in Circulation," Editor and Publisher (August 9, 1958), 56; "The Threat to the British Press," IPI Report (October, 1962).

25 Letter from H. C. Strick, Director of the National Council for the Training of Journalists, January 11, 1960. Cf. UNESCO, The Training of Journalists (Paris, 1958), 206-16.

26 "Rethink and Rethink," loc. cit.

27 J. Edward Gerald, "The British Press Council: A Summary and an Evaluation," Journalism Quarterly (Summer, 1959), 295-306.

28 See "'Tactical Desirability' of Press Council," IPI Report (April, 1953), 1-3. Cf. Peter Berenson, "The British Law and Press Freedom," IPI Report (September, 1961), 2; Bryan, "Security and the News in Liberal Countries," Journalism Quarterly (Autumn, 1961), 486-87.

29 The London Times, July 17, 1958, p. 6.

30 See Central Office of Information, The British Press, 33-36.

31 "Professional Secrecy and the Journalist," IPI Survey (1962), 161-62.

32 "British Reporter Must Tell Source, Court Rules," Washington Post, January 25, 1963, p. 8B.

DENMARK

1 Letter from the Danish Information Office, New York. Much of the information in this section is based on material in this letter and correspondence with the Danish Embassy in Washington.

2 Probably the best general book on the Danish press in recent years is Svend Thorsen's Newspapers in Denmark (Copenhagen, 1953). Also quite helpful to the student of the Danish press is Danmarks Blad-og Bogverden ("The World of Papers and Books in Denmark" with section headings in four languages--including English--to help the non-Danish reader) published by Politikens Forlag in 1955. An interesting summary article in the Danish press is Poul Graae's "A Popular and Quality Press Combined," Danish Foreign Office Journal (1957), 14-16.

3 An excellent sketch of Berling and his newspaper is given in the little booklet, Two Hundred Years Berlingske Tidende (Copenhagen, 1951). Also see Thorsen, Newspapers in Denmark, 69-73 passim.

4 "Security and the News in Liberal Countries," loc. cit., 494; material quoted from Thorsen, Newspapers in Denmark, 69-73 passim.

5 IPI, Professional Secrecy and the Journalist, 54.

6 Graae, "A Popular and Quality Press Combined," loc. cit., 15.

7 A good discussion of outstanding Danish journalists may be found in Thorsen, Newspapers in Denmark. A complete list of contemporary journalists and their newspapers is available in Danmarks Blad-og Bogverden.

8 Walter Schwartz, "Decorators of the Newspapers," Danish Foreign Office Journal (June, 1955), 22-25. This is a very good discussion of illustrations used in the Danish press with drawings selected from various of the country's newspapers accompanying the article.

9 For a more detailed discussion see "Joint Distribution Helps Danish Press," Editor and Publisher (January 16, 1960), 52.

10 Copies of Danish papers were supplied by the Danish Embassy, Washington, D.C.

FINLAND

1 Circulation data (December, 1961), provided by Finnish Embassy.

2 Axel Grönvik, "The Character of the Finnish Press" (1953, revised 1961); this mimeographed survey provided by the Finnish Embassy, Washington, D.C., served as the source of much of the information in the first part of this discussion. Cf. A. E. Pedersen, Jr., "Kekkonen and the Finnish Press," Journalism Review (Montana, 1962), 18. See also Jukka Miesmaa (ed.), Facts about Finland (Helsinki, 1960), 42.

3 Based on results of 1962 elections.

4 Foreign Ministry of Finland, "The Finnish Press," Yearbook of Finland (Helsinki, 1947), 344-45.

5 Foreign Ministry of Finland, "Form of

Government Act and Diet Act of Finland" (Helsinki, 1947), 5.

6 Grönvik, "The Character of the Finnish Press," 4. Cf. Gayle Waldrop, "The Daily Newspaper Press in Finland," Journalism Quarterly (Spring, 1957), 228-38, for an excellent, although in some respects dated, discussion of this and other aspects of the Finnish press.

7 "Survey Assesses World FOI," loc. cit., 3.

8 Ibid.; IPI, Government Pressures on the Press, 92, 111-12.

9 IPI, Government Pressures on the Press, 86.

10 "Survey Assesses World FOI," loc. cit. 3.

11 IPI, Professional Secrecy and the Journalist, 61-64.

FRANCE

1 For an interesting account of this experiment and for a good insight into the lively character of L'Express, see André Bonnefoy, "L'expérience de 'L'Express' quotidien," Gazette, II (1956), 78-85.

2 "Tabloid Makes Brassy Bow," Editor and Publisher (October 17, 1959), 68; Cf. Editor and Publisher Year Book, 1962, p. 429.

3 Editor and Publisher International Year Book, 1959, p. 328, and 1962, p. 479.

4 For a good discussion of the French press and the government crisis in France during 1958, see Genêt, "Letter from Paris," The New Yorker (October 4, 1958), 107-108. See also Ernest O. Hauser, "France Starts Over," Saturday Evening Post (November 15, 1958), 42.

5 There were from 28 to 30 dailies in Paris just prior to World War II; in 1946 there were 32; in 1959 Paris dailies numbered only 15.

6 For a good summary of the French press just prior to World War II, see Robert W. Desmond, The Press and World Affairs, 199-218.

7 Robert Salmon, "Successes--and Anxieties--Mark Growth of French Press," IPI Report (May, 1962).

8 Michel Logié, "The Provincial Press in

France," Gazette, I (1955), 226. This article gives an excellent survey of the provincial press until 1955.

9 Pierre R. Wolf, " 'News Discrimination' on a Provincial Paper," IPI Report (August, 1958), 2-3.

10 For a good discussion of the regional edition of the French provincial dailies, see Francois Pasqualini, "French Dailies Thrive on Regional Editions," Editor and Publisher (December 5, 1959), 48-49.

11 "La Presse Feminine," Revue Militaire d'Information (September-October, 1957), 54-55.

12 Sample copies of leading French newspapers and periodicals and other valuable materials on the French press were furnished the writers by Roger Vaurs, Director, French Press and Information Service, New York, N.Y. in October, 1958.

13 For a good discussion of the Catholic press in France, see "La presse confessionelle," l'Echo de la Presse et de la Publicité (Paris, 1958), 23-28.

14 Salmon, "Successes--and Anxieties--Mark Growth of French Press," loc. cit.

15 For a good summary of censorship see IPI Reports (June, 1958), 9-11 (July, 1960), 5-6.

16 Robert U. Brown, "Report on the French Press," Editor and Publisher (May 20, 1961), 90.

17 "The Toils of the Press," IPI Reports (April and October, 1962).

18 The Economist (March 22, 1958), 1017.

19 Genêt, "Letter from Paris," The New Yorker (November 26, 1960), 210.

20 Frank Luther Mott, ASNE Bulletin (October 1, 1957), 7.

21 "Interview with Adenauer," Atlas (May, 1962), 369.

22 Genêt, "Letter from Paris," The New Yorker (October 4, 1958), 108. See also Editor and Publisher (January 26, 1957), 65.

23 A good discussion of the French Leftist press is "La presse d'extreme gauche," l'Echo de la Presse et de la Publicité (April 1, 1958), 9-14, and (April 15,

1958), 19-22.

GREECE

1 Press Department, Ministry of the Prime Minister, Directory of Newspapers and Periodicals (Athens, 1962), 75-76.

2 This section is based on data provided by the Royal Greek Embassy, Washington, D.C. The embassy also furnished sample copies of leading Greek publications.

3 For a good discussion of this side of Greek journalism, see Wallace Graves, "Journalism in the First Democracy," Journalism Quarterly (Spring, 1959), 209-12.

4 Kenneth E. Olson, "Dean Olson Reports Press Privations," Editor and Publisher (May 16, 1959), 66.

5 "Duchess Keeps Fit With Long Morning Runs," Washington Evening Star, December 27, 1962, p. 2.

6 "Survey Assesses World FOI," loc. cit., 4-5.

7 Ibid.; Cf. Olson, "Dean Olson Reports Press Privations," loc. cit.

HOLLAND

1 Indicating the trend toward opinion papers is the fact that before World War II (in 1936) nearly half of the national circulation was of "information" papers, whereas by 1957 these papers accounted for only 23 per cent of the circulation. Maarten Schneider, "Some Aspects of the Netherlands Daily Press," Journalism Quarterly (Winter, 1957), 77. See also Schneider, "Dutch Press Reflects Political, Religious Groups," IPI Report (December, 1954), 4-5.

2 "La Diffusion des Opinions dans la Presse Les Examples Hollandais et Suisses," Gazette, IV (1958), 165.

3 Letter from D. J. van Wijnen, First Secretary for Press and Cultural Affairs (December 19, 1962). The writers were also furnished sample copies of leading Dutch newspapers by the Press Section of the Netherlands Embassy, Washington, D.C.

4 Holland is considered the country in which the periodical press originated. Le Journal des Scavans is known as the first magazine in the world of a scientific and literary

nature. It was founded in Amsterdam in 1665 by Dexis de Sallo.

5 Maarten Rooy as quoted in Joe B. Vogel, "Dutch Would Be in Dutch With U.S. News Tactics," The Quill (February, 1956), 12.

6 "Survey Assesses World FOI," loc. cit.

7 "Dutch Council to Judge Press," Editor and Publisher (November 28, 1959), 52. Cf. "Press Councils and Press Codes," IPI Report (August, 1961), 14.

ITALY

1 Ignazio Weiss, "The Distribution of Advertising Media in Italy," Gazette, VI (1961), 357-63.

2 Claire Sterling, "Transformation South of Rome," The Reporter (September 27, 1962), 32-34; Arnaldo Cortesi, "Italy Adds Roads to Develop South," New York Times, September 22, 1962, p. 8.

3 Weiss, "The Daily Press in Italy," Gazette, IV (1958), 255.

4 Italian Information Office, Ten Years of Italian Democracy 1946-1956 (Rome, 1957), 307.

5 One of the most popular of these magazines is Epoca with a format much like the U.S.'s Life. See Weiss, "The Illustrated News-weeklies in Italy," Gazette, VI (1960), 169-79. The weekly news magazine Oggi with a circulation of 980,000 outsells Epoca, whose weekly circulation totals 370,000. Il Borghese, a weekly published in Rome, is a popular magazine combining humor of the Punch (Britain) type and news of the Der Spiegel (West Germany) type.

6 Armistead S. Pride, "It's Uphill in Italy-- But U.S. Helps," The Journalism Educator (January, 1959), 7-10, 32.

7 Anna M. Cornetta, "Italy's Disappearing Dailies," Nieman Reports (July-October, 1962), 28-32.

8 See Malcolm S. MacLean, Jr. and Luca Pinna, "Mass Media in Scarperia," Gazette, IV (1958), for descriptions of a small Italian newspaper.

9 "Commercials Limited to 35 Seconds," U.S. News & World Report (November 30, 1959), 52.

10 Walter Lucas, "Italian Radio-TV Jolted,"

Christian Science Monitor, December 30, 1961, p. 10; "TV and Radio Censorship in Italy," New York Times, September 23, 1962, p. 3.

11 Weiss, "The Distribution of Advertising Media in Italy," loc. cit., 362-63.

12 Lucas, "'Play' Money Jingles in Italy," Christian Science Monitor, September 11, 1962, p. 8; Donald K. Pollock and David Lyndon Woods, "A Study in International Communication: Eurovision," Journal of Broadcasting (Spring, 1959), 99-117.

13 "La 'Terza Pagina'," Notizie e Commenti (April, 1958), 3.

14 For a review of how Italian papers treated the death of Pope Pius XII in late 1958, see Time (November 3, 1958), 76-77, and Editor and Publisher (October 25, 1958), 68.

15 See William E. Porter, "The Influence of Italy's Communist--Bloc Dailies," Journalism Quarterly (Fall, 1954), 473-80.

16 "Red Ink in Italy," Time (August 12, 1957), 44.

17 On December 22, 1947, the Constituent Assembly approved the new constitution. It became effective January 1, 1948.

18 ANSA is not yet a worldwide news agency to the extent that AP, UPI, Reuters, AFP, and TASS are. But it has crossed the Atlantic and has a few clients in Latin America, such as Radio Miraflores in Lima, Peru, and a few newspaper clients in Argentina.

19 These are the newspapers likely to be checked by a U.S. news correspondent covering Italy.

20 For an excellent commentary on L'Osservatore Romano, as well as for a recent survey of the Italian press situation, see Frank Brutto's "In Italy: The Word is Complicated," Montana Journalism Review (Spring, 1962), 10-12.

21 USIS contracts have broadened geographically too. Italy has 95 provinces and 7,850 municipalities. See Istituo Nazionale di Economia Agraria, La distribuzione della proprietà fondiaria in Italia (Rome, 1956).

NORWAY

1 Much of the information in this section is based on materials (including sample copies of leading publications) furnished the writers by Anders Komnaes, Cultural Attache' of the Norwegian Embassy, Washington, D.C. (December, 1962). Statistical data is from Editor and Publisher International Year Book, 1962.

2 For a fuller discussion of this subject see IPI, Professional Secrecy and the Journalist, 121-32.

3 Bjørn Bjørnsen, "Avisdøden pa naert hold," ("Death of a Newspaper"), Aktuell (August 30, 1958), 4-5. This article gives insight into the problems facing the small Norwegian newspaper; many of these are threatened by economic crises such as hit Vestfold of Sandefjord, a small provincial which had begun publishing in 1881. For a more recent picture of Norway's press see Bryan, "Norway's Weeklies Enter Third Century," Grassroots Editor (January, 1963), 24-25.

4 Collections of these interesting underground papers of World War II are housed at Hoover Library, Stanford University, and at the Oslo University Library.

PORTUGAL

1 Circulation figures are not audited in Portugal. Those given are either from Editor and Publisher International Year Book, 1962, or from recent estimates provided by U.S. and Portuguese government sources.

2 Sample copies of newspapers and other materials on the Portuguese press were provided by the Portuguese Embassy, Washington, D.C.

3 For a more comprehensive analysis of the conditions under which the press of Portugal operates, see IPI, The Press in Authoritarian Countries, 155-62.

4 Ibid., 155-56.

5 Richard Scott Mower, "Government Press Controls Capricious and Constant," IPI Report (September, 1958), 4.

6 As recently as November, 1962 the International Press Institute reported the

arrest of a Portuguese newsman, Mario Rodrigues, a journalist working for Diario Popular and Seara Nova. IPI Report (November, 1962), 6.

SPAIN

1 Marvin Alisky, "Spain's Press and Broadcasting: Conformity and Censorship," Journalism Quarterly (Winter, 1962), 63-69.

2 "Franco Crackdown," Hispanic American Report (August, 1962), 485-88; "Steps Toward a 'New' Spain," Hispanic American Report September, 1962), 582-83;"Franco's Spain," Look (July 31, 1962), 17-30; Time (January 11, 1963), 30-31.

3 "Orden: La Escuela Oficial de Periodismo," Boletin Oficial del Estado (November 19, 1941), 1.

4 "Orden Ministerial, Periodismo," Boletin Oficial del Estado (July 25, 1957), 1.

5 Direccion General de Prensa, Registro Oficial de Periodistas (Madrid, 1961), I.

6 "Press Law in Spain," America (National Catholic Weekly Review for April 8, 1961), 47-48; "Illusions of Freedom, IPI Report (January, 1961), 11.

7 Claire Sterling, "Spain Without Franco: Will We Be Ready?" The Reporter (March 30, 1961), 17-20.

8 "Spain: the Second Effort," Fortune (May, 1960), 99-100, 105; Arthur P. Whitaker, Spain and the Defense of the West (New York, 1961), 2-20.

9 Alisky, "Spain's Feature-Filled Weeklies," Grassroots Editor (January, 1962), 9-10.

SWEDEN

1 June, 1962 circulation data were obtained from Tiden No. 7 (1962), 443-44. Time magazine (April 13, 1959), 82, provides a good summary of Expressen's policy and operations. An IPI Report (February, 1959), provides an excellent article on Dagens Nyheter.

2 Tiden No. 7 (1962), 443-44, for daily circulations.

3 Time (April 13, 1959), 82.

4 Thomas Harris, "Something for Everybody in

Sweden's 'Dagens Nyheter'," IPI Report
(February, 1959), 7.

5 Sweden's oldest paper (f. 1645 under a
different name) today is Stockholm's Post-
och Inrikes Tidningar ("Mail and Domestic
News") which is an official government
paper carrying mainly official notices.
Aftonbladet of Stockholm (f. 1830), one of
the country's oldest existing dailies, is
usually regarded as Sweden's first modern
daily.

6 Presbyrån (Information about AB Svenska
Presbyrån), an information brochure pro-
vided by the Swedish Embassy, Washington,
D.C.

7 The Communist press is firmly bound to the
Party. Circulations are unknown for the
Communist papers; however, it is estimated
that their total circulation is less than
50,000 daily. The main Communist daily is
the morning Ny Dag of Stockholm, begun in
1930. Two other leading Red dailies are
Norrbottens-Kuriren (Luleå), and the afternoon Arbetartidningen (Göteborg).

8 Sample copies of leading Swedish newspapers
and valuable information on these pages
were furnished by the Swedish Embassy,
Washington, D.C.

9 Anders Yngve Pers, Newspapers in Sweden
(Stockholm, 1954), 15.

10 For a more detailed discussion of Sweden's
provincial press see Bryan, "Local Pride
and Social Responsibility Keep Sweden's
Grassroots Press Alive," Grassroots Editor
(April, 1961), 15.

11 Manchester Guardian Weekly, February 27,
1958, p. 5.

12 For a more detailed discussion of the
Swedish Press Law of 1766, see Bryan,
"'Enlightenment of the People Without
Hindrance': The Swedish Press Law of 1766,"
Journalism Quarterly (Summer, 1960), 431-34.

13 Pers, Newspapers in Sweden, Appendix I,
53-55, gives a good summary of the Press
Fair Practices Commission's make up and
functions.

14 Sven Boman, "Sweden Has 'Court of Honor',"
IPI Report (January, 1953), 2-3.

15 Gerard Fay, "Sweden's Decorous Press,"
Manchester Guardian Weekly, February 27,
1958, p. 5.

16 Earl H. Voss, "Sweden Has a Plan to Prevent Newspaper Strikes," Washington Sunday
Star, January 27, 1963, p. 3B.

17 IPI, Professional Secrecy and the Journalist, 145-49.

SWITZERLAND

1 An excellent recent discussion of the
Swiss newspapers, their characteristics
and circulations, is "La Diffusion des
Opinions dans la Presse les Exemples
Hollandais et Suisses," Gazette, 1V (1958).
Another is Hans Mehlhorn's "Die Entwick-
lung der Zeitungen und Zeitschriften im
Jahre 1957," Zeitungs-Verlag und Zeit-
schriften-Verlag (May 1, 1958), 256-64.
Although dated in some particulars, still
probably the best general survey of the
Swiss press is Karl Weber's The Swiss Press:
An Outline (Berne, 1948).

2 Weber, The Swiss Press, 37.

3 Cited in "The Freedom of the Swiss Press,"
(Swiss Embassy mimeographed report by
Pierre Cordey), 5-6.

4 For a fuller discussion of Swiss journalists'
right of secrecy, see IPI, Professional
Secrecy and the Journalist, 151-60.

5 For an excellent discussion of the Neue
Zürcher Zeitung, see Melanie Staerk,
"Neue Zürcher Zeitung," Swiss Review of
World Affairs (May, 1959), 22-24. Although this article gives some interesting
information on the newspaper in its own
right, it is actually a review of a book
by a British historian--Elizabeth Wiskemann's A Great Swiss Newspaper. The Story
of the Neue Zürcher Zeitung (London, 1959).

6 IPI, The Flow of the News, 249-50.

WEST GERMANY

1 Albert Dusenberg, The Press in Germany
(Bonn, 1960).

2 For an excellent recent discussion of the
German mass media of communication, see
Gazette, V (May, 1959). See also Evelyn
J. Williams, "The West German Press,"
Gazette (March, 1960), 1-8.

3 Dusenberg, The Press in Germany, 40; Hans
J. Merkatz and Wolfgang Metzner (eds.),
Germany Today (Frankfurt, 1954). This
book presents a good general description

of the West German press in its "Press"
section (pp. 196-204). About the non-
party press it says, "it has become
apparent...that German newspaper readers
today prefer to read big, politically independent newspapers in contrast to the
period prior to 1933, when the official organs
of the political parties were more popular,"
196.

4 West German journalist Karl-Heinz Abshagen,
"Germany's Press Since the War," the
London Times, September 25, 1958, p. 6.

5 Three articles giving excellent treatment
to this period are Richard Straus, "Postwar Development of the German Press,"
Department of State Bulletin (February 23,
1953); Ernst Meier, "The Licensed Press
in the U.S. Occupation Zone of Germany,"
Journalism Quarterly (Spring, 1954), and
C. Jacobi, "The New German Press," Foreign
Affairs (January, 1954).

6 Peter Liebes, "The Post-Licensed German
Press," Journalism Quarterly (Winter, 1956),
67. Cf. Bryan, "Ten Years after Licensing
West German Press Flourishes," Editor and
Publisher (August 15, 1959), 11, 56.

7 For a good discussion of the German
"Illustrateds" see Sherilyn C. Bennion,
"Mass Magazine Phenomenon: the German
'Illustrierte,'" Journalism Quarterly
(Summer, 1961), 360-62; Time (January 25,
1960), 56.

8 UNESCO, News Agencies, Their Structure and
Operation (Paris, 1953); article by Fritz
Sanger, IPI Report (October, 1955); Die
Deutsche Presse 1954 (Berlin, 1954).

9 Dusenberg, The Press in Germany, 54.

10 IPI, Professional Secrecy and the Journalist,
77-87.

11 Bryan, "Security and the News in Liberal
Countries," Journalism Quarterly (Autumn,
1961), 493.

12 IPI, Press Councils and Press Codes, 25-30.

13 "Talking in the Mirror," Time (November 24,
1958), 14.

14 "Dispute over Magazine Shakes Adenauer
Regime," New York Times, November 4, 1962,
p. 5E.

15 For a good discussion of the Frankfurter
Allgemeine and its predecessor, Frankfurter
Zeitung, see Der Grosse Brockhaus (Wiesbaden,

1954), IV, 204-206. Also see Time (November 11, 1957), 76-78, for a summary-com-
mentary on Die Welt and other Axel Springer
publications, and Joseph Wechsberg, "Letter
from Berlin," The New Yorker (December 13,
1958), 161. Wechsberg states without
qualification: "The three leading German
newspapers today are the Frankfurter
Allgemeine, the Süddeutsche Zeitung of
Munich, and Die Welt of Hamburg."

16 Karl W. Deutsch and Lewis J. Edinger,
Germany Rejoins the Powers (Stanford, 1959),
especially chap. viii, "Gate Keepers of
Opinion: Influential Editors and Publishers,"
111-23.

U.S.S.R. AND
EUROPEAN COMMUNIST NATIONS

1 The student interested in the tactics and
devices of the Communists in penetrating,
and ultimately taking over the press systems
in Bulgaria, Czechoslovakia, Estonia,
Hungary, Latvia, Lithuania, Poland, Rumania,
and Yugoslavia should read Communist Penetration and Exploitation of the Free Press
(Committee on the Judiciary, U.S. Senate)
published by the U.S. Government Printing
Office, Washington, D.C., and released in
November, 1962.

2 "Advertising in the Communist Press," East
Europe (September, December, 1959).

3 A thorough discussion of advertising in
the Communist press is provided by Bryan
in two articles: "Red Economists See Need
of Advertising," Editor and Publisher
(October 20, 1962), 18, 50, and "Communist
Advertising: Its Status and Functions,"
Journalism Quarterly (Autumn, 1962), 500-506.

U.S.S.R.

1 Forty Years of Soviet Power in Facts and
Figures (Moscow, 1958), 267. See also
W. J. Jorden, "Fit to Print, Moscow's
Formula," New York Times Magazine (December
29, 1957), 10.

2 Editor and Publisher International Year
Book, 1962.

3 A student can easily detect these recurrent
themes as they manifest themselves in all
U.S.S.R. propaganda outlets, and especially
in the press. He may specifically see them
in the press if he keeps up with Soviet

newspaper content through weekly transla-
tions of selected articles from some sixty
Soviet publications; these translations
are done by the Joint Committee on Slavic
Studies of the American Council of Learned
Societies and the Social Science Research
Council in New York City and published in
the weekly Current Digest of the Soviet
Press.

4 Cooper, The Right to Know, 320.

5 Robert Ergang, Europe in Our Time (New
York, 1953), 799; Carl J. Friedrich and
Zbigniew K. Brzezinski, Totalitarian Dictatorship and Autocracy (Cambridge, 1956),
116; The Land of Soviets: The Country and
the People (Moscow, 1957), 230. For a
good popular discussion of Soviet newspapers by a Russian journalist, see Mark
Arkadyev, "Soviet Newspapers," USSR (May,
1959), 24-29.

6 Alex Inkeles in his Public Opinion in
Soviet Russia (Cambridge, 1950), 156, says
of the "wall" newspapers: "There is a
strong temptation for an outside observer
of the Soviet Union to pass over a phenomenon like a bulletin-board or wall newspaper as a matter of no significance. To
do so would actually involve a serious over-
sight. The wall newspaper, like the
Bolshevik agitator, represents one of the
striking examples of the Communist party's
vigor in utilizing meager local resources
to extend the coverage of the more formal
media of mass communication, to increase
their penetration, and to enhance their
effectiveness."

7 Many sources were used for the list of
Soviet publications which begins on this
page. Among the most useful were these:
unpublished material furnished the writers
by Nicolai G. Bagrichev of the Soviet
Embassy, Washington, D.C. (November, 1958);
Newspapers and Magazines of the U.S.S.R.
for 1959 (Moscow, 1958), 3-6; Walter H.
Mallory (ed.), Political Handbook of the
World (New York, 1958), 194-95; Editor and
Publisher International Year Book, 1962;
John Gunther, Inside Russia Today (New York,
1958), 303; Howard M. Norton, "Soviet News-
papers are Deadly Serious; Their only Task:
to Sell Communism," ASNE Bulletin (February
1, 1958), 13-14; Time (June 9, 1958), 69;
Mitchell K. Stanley, "Journalism in Soviet
Subjected to Change," Editor and Publisher
(November 24, 1956), 32-34; Bolshaya
Sovetskaya Entsiklopediya ("Large Soviet
Encyclopedia") (2nd ed., Moscow, XXIII.)

8 A good profile of Pravda in 1960 was given

by CBS's Sam Jaffe in "U.S. Newsman Draws
Portrait of Pravda," Editor and Publisher
(November 12, 1960), 36, 38.

9 Iskra, the first Bolshevik newspaper, lasted
only five years, ceasing publication in 1905.

10 More than any other paper it makes use of
many quotations and speeches made in Western
countries and reported in the press of
these countries; these reprints, of course,
consist only of those critical of non-
Communist nations or persons or those which
fortify the Soviet "line" at the time. For
a good discussion of this aspect of the
Soviet press, see Andrew H. Berding (Assistant Secretary for Public Affairs), "The
Battlefield of Ideas," Department of State
Bulletin (June 23, 1958), 1045-46.

11 Friedrich and Brzezinski, Totalitarian
Dictatorship and Autocracy, 116.

12 The Current Digest of the Soviet Press (May
25, 1955).

13 John Gunther says that "of all dull things
in the U.S.S.R. the dullest are the great
newspapers," and points out that Pravda
once gave nearly an entire issue to the
full text of a play. Gunther, Inside
Russia Today, 303.

14 According to Henry Shapiro, long-time U.S.
correspondent in Moscow, newspapers are
hard to read because they have no "leads"
in the Western sense. He says, "You may
read a dull six-column article and in the
last paragraph find an item of headline
news in the U.S." Ray Erwin, "Moscow
Dateline," Editor and Publisher (February
9, 1957), 14.

15 Nicolás Gonzáles Ruiz (ed.), El Periodismo:
Teoría Y Práctica (Barcelona, 1955), 466.

16 The Soviet Press (June 6, 1958), 2.

17 Cooper, The Right to Know, 61.

18 V. I. Lenin, Collected Works (London, 1927),
114.

19 Quoted in The Soviet Press (April 26, 1958),
2.

20 Quoted in Inkeles, Public Opinion in
Soviet Russia, 136.

21 N. S. Khrushchev, "Khrushchev Lays Down
the Line on the Arts," The New York Times
Magazine (September 29, 1957), 68.

22 Besides the newspapers, several of the political journals which are leaders in in carrying on this work are the semi-monthly Komsomolskaya Jizny (Komsomol Life) and Partiyinaya Jizny (Party Life), the weekly Novy Vremya (New Times) and Getopisy Gazety Statiye (Chronicle of Newspaper Articles), and the monthly Molodoye Kommunist (The Young Communist), and Kultura i Jizny (Culture and Life).

23 Ergang, Europe in Our Time, 798.

24 Constitution (Fundamental Law) of the Union of Soviet Socalist Republics (Moscow, 1947). Brucker, Freedom of Information, 227-28; also see Serge L. Levitsky, "Soviet Law and the Press," Journalism Quarterly (Winter, 1957), 51-57.

25 Inkeles, Public Opinion in Soviet Russia, 137.

26 Leo Gruliow, "How the Soviet Newspaper Operates," Problems of Communism (March-April, 1956), gives an excellent insight into the activities of the Soviet papers.

27 Brown, "Shop Talk at Thirty," loc. cit., 72. Actually only the "low level" journalists are assigned by the University faculty; "editors" (especially of the national papers) are appointed by the Central Committee of the Party; all editors, even on regional and local papers, are actually placed by the Party organization which concerns itself with the publication of the paper.

28 E. J. Kahn, Jr., "A Reporter at Large," The New Yorker (December 20, 1958), 44. Kahn reports in a second article on the U.S.S.R. in the same magazine the following week (December 27, 1958), 32, that the Moscow News belies its name. He said all the "spot news we got out of it was the number of times Sputnik III had cruised around the earth at press time." Mostly feature articles of the "nonpersonality" type (sample headline: "Chicks to be Hatched All Year Round") fill the paper, according to Kahn.

29 Gunther, Inside Russia Today, 305. The pay for other journalists does not seem to be so good; for example, in 1958 a visitor to Izvestia reported that the paper's "editors" (evidently not the "senior editors" referred to by Gunther) make about $140 a month, and that local correspondents outside Moscow made about $250 a month. Joe Grossman, "A Visit With the Editor of Izvestia" (a letter), Editor and Publisher

(February 22, 1958), 7. Reports from a number of sources in 1962 and 1963 indicated that salaries had risen 8 to 10 per cent. Cf., James W. Markham, "Effects of 'The Thaw' on the Soviet Press," Journalism Quarterly, (Autumn, 1961), 511-19.

30 Norton, "Soviet Newspapers are Deadly Serious; Their only Task: to Sell Communism," loc. cit., 13; Cooper, The Right to Know, 61.

31 An indication that Soviet newspapers carry little important news in the U.S. sense of the word is cited by E. J. Kahn, Jr., a visitor to the Soviet Union in 1958. He mentions that on one day when (as he later found out) the New York Times was having difficulty getting "all the events that were shaking the globe" onto its front page, the only newsstory in Pravda dealt with a hydroelectric station in Kuibyshev which was beginning full-scale operations. E. J. Kahn, Jr., "A Reporter at Large, " loc. cit. (December 27, 1958), 32.

32 An interesting, though brief, recent discussion of some of the aspects of TASS's operation, as well as other general information pertaining to the Soviet press, may be found in an article by Lee Hills in The Quill (October, 1962), 10-15.

BULGARIA

1 One of the best recent discussions of the Bulgarian press is Dafin Todorov, "The Press in Bulgaria," Gazette, VIII, 3 (1962), 246-50.

2 "Bulgaria's Press: A Study of Control," East Europe (November, 1959), 30-41, and J. Sylla, "The Bulgarian Press After the Second World War," Gazette, IV, 4 (1958), 299-304. These articles give a good insight into the entire Bulgarian press situation.

3 An excellent discussion of Bulgaria's broadcasting media is provided by Todorov, "Press and Broadcasting in Present-day Bulgaria," Journalism Quarterly (Spring, 1962), 212-15.

4 All published in the capital city of Sofia.

EAST GERMANY

1 Political Handbook of the World, 84. Information contained in this section was also gleaned from many sources, letters, and conversations too numerous to mention.

2 Hans J. von Merkatz and Wolfgang Metzner
(eds.), Germany Today, 197-98. Political
Handbook of the World also lists the Freie
Erde ("Free Earth") of Neubrandenburg with
a circulation of some 225,000 as one of the
principal dailies outside Berlin.

3 For a good discussion of East German journalism, see Peter Grothe, To Win the Minds
of Men: The Story of the Communist Propaganda War in East Germany (Palo Alto,
1958), chaps, iv, v.

4 "Better Dead than Ulbricht Red," translated from Vita, Rome; Atlas (December,
1962), 453-54.

HUNGARY

1 Information about this newspaper and about
other aspects of the Hungarian press was
obtained from Andras Csagoly and Andras
Torok, students from Hungary attending
Texas A&M, 1962-63.

POLAND

1 Good surveys of the Polish press situation
can be found in Ryszard Dyoniziak, "Research
on Mass Media," Polish Perspectives, No. 7
(1961), 66-72, and Karol Schindzielorz,
"Becoming a Journalist in Poland," Journalism Quarterly (Fall, 1959), 460-68.
For the Polish radio situation, see Henry
Cendrowsky, "Sound Broadcasting in Poland,"
Gazette, VI, 3 (1960), 273-80.

2 By the end of 1957 there were about 100
cultural and political periodicals in
Poland. Z. Jolies, "Czytelnictwo i rozwoj
prasy w r. 1957," Prasa Polska (May, 1958),
11-16. This article is a good overview of
the press as of late 1957.

3 Time (February 11, 1957), 62.

4 Editor and Publisher (August 24, 1957), 80.

5 "Poland's Angry Young Men," The Manchester
Guardian Weekly, July 24, 1958, p. 14.
See also, "Trends in Polish Culture," East
Europe (February, 1959), 12-19.

YUGOSLAVIA

1 Ilija Uzelac, Publishing Activity, The
Press, Broadcasting and Cinematography in
Yugoslavia (Belgrade, 1955), 15.

2 Circulation figures used in this section
come from a number of sources and are
adjusted here and there in accordance with
the latest or what the writers believe to
be the most realistic figures. Helpful in
this respect were materials (and sample
copies of leading Yugoslav publications)
sent by the attaché of the Yugoslav
Embassy, Washington, D.C. This information
dealt with circulations and other aspects
of the Yugoslav press picture and has been
used in passim in this section. Cf.
Editor and Publisher International Year
Book, 1962.

3 Information from Yugoslav Embassy, Washington.

4 This main national Communist party organ
also publishes an edition in Zagreb each
morning except Friday; it also runs separate
editions in the Cyrillic and Latin alphabets in the Serbian and Croatian languages
and also an edition in the Slovene language.
Its total daily circulation is probably very
close to a million copies. It is technically the nation's finest paper, with a
modern plant and good machinery.

5 One principal difference, however, between
the Yugoslav dailies and the dailies of
the Soviet Union is the number of pages.
Yugoslav papers, especially the big ones
like Politika and Vjesnik, generally publish editions of 16 to 24 pages, whereas
in the U.S.S.R. even the biggest dailies
never publish more than 16 pages (and even
a 16-page Soviet edition is extremely
unusual).

LATIN AMERICA OVERVIEW

1 James W. Markham, "Foreign News in the
United States and South American Press,"
Public Opinion Quarterly (Summer, 1961),
249-62.

2 "Plans Ready for Mill in Central Chile,"
Editor and Publisher (October 13, 1962).
This mill is being built by a Canadian
company, Sandwell of Vancouver.

3 "World's Newsprint Demand is Booming,"
Editor and Publisher (December 15, 1962), 28.

4 Brown, "Growth and Progress," Editor and
Publisher (November 24, 1962), 70.

5 Marvin Alisky, "Hablemos," Gazette, VI, 2
(1960), 199-201.

6 Audit Bureau of Circulations, Life En
Español Publisher's Statement (Chicago,

June 30, 1962), 1-4.

7 "Peru Slum Series Wins IAPA Award," Editor and Publisher (May 5, 1962), 51.

8 International House, Primer Seminario Panamericano de Prensa (New Orleans, 1962), 4-25.

9 "Mexican PR Seen Coming Up Rapidly," Editor and Publisher (July 21, 1962), 38.

10 Inter-American Press Association, Estatutos y reglamento de la OCC (New York, 1958), 1-29.

11 "N.Y. Times Int'1. Edition Pushes on Into Latin America," Advertising Age (December 4, 1961). "Ratings Warfare Breaks Out in Mexico," Advertising Age (September 10, 1962), 88.

12 Brown, "Shop Talk at Thirty," loc. cit., 72.

13 "The News from Latin America," Columbia Journalism Review (Fall, 1962), 49-60. This section contains the reports from Hal Hendrix, Al Marlens, Joseph P. Lyford, Frank K. Kelly, Frank Starzel, Earl J. Johnson, Clifton Daniel, and Emanuel Freedman.

MEXICO

1 Official listings until 1957 often lumped dailies with papers appearing two or three times a week. Thus, for 1956, one finds 188 as the total, but that included semi-weeklies and triweeklies. See Marvin Alisky, "Mexico's Crusading Weekly News-papers," Grassroots Editor (October, 1960), 11-12.

2 Medios Publicitarios Mexicanos (February 15, 1960), 7-52.

3 Medios Publicitarios Mexicanos (November 15, 1962), 9-56.

4 Marvin Alisky, "Growth of Newspapers in Mexico's Provinces," Journalism Quarterly (Winter, 1960), 79.

5 Marvin Alisky, "Mexican Newscasts Link a Nation," The Quill (September, 1953), 12-14; Secretaría de Economía, Dirección General de Estadística, Compendio estadís-tico (Mexico, D.F., 1957).

6 Secretaría de Educación Pública, Memoria (Mexico, D.F., 1962); for a description of how these Missions use mass media see Marvin Alisky, "Radio's Role in Mexico," Journalism Quarterly (Winter, 1954), 69.

7 Howard F. Cline, Mexico: Revolution to Evolution, 1940-1960 (New York, 1962); Marvin Alisky, State and Local Government in Sonora, Mexico (Tempe, 1962).

8 "Dos Visitas," Tiempo (August 8, 1960), 4.

9 Reports for 1962 from Asociación Inter-americana de Radiodifusores. See Marvin Alisky, "Mexico City's Competitive Radio Market," Inter-American Economic Affairs (Winter, 1953), 19-27.

10 Cine-Sistema, Tarifa Número 3B (November, 1962).

11 "Gilberto Figueroa of Excelsior Dies," Editor and Publisher (November 17, 1962), 69; "Gilberto Figueroa," Tiempo (November 19, 1962), 12.

12 John C. Merrill, "The Image of the United States in Ten Mexican Dailies," Journalism Quarterly (Spring, 1962), 203-209.

13 Victor Alba, "Frontier Journalism in Mexican Provincial Press," IPI Report (March, 1957), 6.

14 The most serious attack on a Mexican editor in recent years was the murder of Alberto Altamirano, 32, of the small crusading daily, El Diario, in Poza Rica, Veracruz in August, 1960. See "Oil-Town Murder," Time (August 15, 1960), 15.

15 "Gran pérdida para el mundo de las letras," El Regional (December 22, 1962), 1. This Hermosillo daily and Mexican papers all across the republic made front-page news of García Naranjo's death, and radio stations issued news bulletins.

16 Marvin Alisky, "Early Mexican Broadcasting," Hispanic American Historical Review (Novem-ber, 1954), 515-26.

17 Joe Belden and Associates, Radiómetro (Mexico, D.F.), reports for 1953 through 1962. The Belden company of Dallas and Mexico City conducts Mexico's most reliable audience surveys.

18 Marvin Alisky, "Mexican Tax Now Limiting U.S. Publications," The Quill (May, 1962), 19.

CENTRAL AMERICA

1 James L. Busey, "Central American Union," Western Political Quarterly (March, 1961), 49-63; Busey, "Foundations of Political Contrast: Costa Rica and Nicaragua," Western Political Quarterly (September, 1958), 627-59. See the plea of former Costa Rican President José Figueres, "North Americans, Share Your Democracy with Us," Reader's Digest (August, 1961), 45-51.

2 Marvin Alisky, "The Mass Media in Central America," Journalism Quarterly (Fall, 1955), 479-86.

3 Alisky, "Press and Radio Serve Central America," The Quill (May, 1955), 5-15.

4 James S. Copley, Mission to San Salvador (San Diego, 1960). Copley also sent Taylor to Costa Rica in 1962 to modernize the typography and make up of the San Jose daily La Prensa Libre.

5 Letter from Mary Gardner to Marvin Alisky, December 10, 1962.

6 Marvin Alisky, "Central American Radio," Quarterly of Film, Radio and Television (Fall, 1955), 51-63; Alisky, "The End of Nicaragua's Radio Freedom," Journal of Broadcasting (Fall, 1961), 311-14.

7 Marvin Alisky, "Our Man in Managua," The Reporter (December 22, 1960), 26-27; Alisky, "Candle in the Dark," Washington Daily News, November 14, 1960, p. 29; Alisky, "La Prensa Leads Fight Against Nicaraguan Censorship," The Quill (March, 1961), 15-16, 19.

8 Alisky, "Journalism Instruction in a Dictatorship," Editor and Publisher (October 29, 1960), 7, 56.

CUBA

1 Alisky, "Havana Havoc," Nieman Reports (April, 1956), 16-18.

2 George Marvin, "Keeping Cuba Libre," World's Work (September, 1917), 553-67; C. E. Chapman, A History of the Cuban Republic (New York, 1927), 426-39; Graham H. Stuart, Latin America and the United States (New York, 1943), 224-26.

3 "Cuba Printers Ask Control Editorials," Washington Post, May 19, 1959, p. 1.

4 "Last 4 Havana Papers Serve Castro's Line," Editor and Publisher (August 11, 1962), 62.

5 Alvin Austin, "Throttling of the Free Press in Latin America," Freedom of Information Report (Chicago, 1962), 47-51. See "Prensa Latina Denies It's Castro Owned," Editor and Publisher (December 12, 1959), 73; "Castro's News Service Hews Closely to Line," Editor and Publisher (November 28, 1959), 46; "Castro Uses Press to Berate the U.S.," Editor and Publisher (March 19, 1960), 12.

The 1961 and 1962 meetings of the Inter-American Press Association had valuable reports on the Cuban press and its news agency. See various issues of the IAPA monthly, Press of the Americas. Also, Claude E. Erbsen, "Cuban Press Plight Laid to Communism," Editor and Publisher (October 22, 1960), 14.

6 Marvin Alisky, "Confused Cuba," Nieman Reports (April, 1960), 12-13; Alisky, "The Cuba Nobody Knew," Nieman Reports (April, 1959), 2, 29.

7 José I. Rivero, "When the Paper Died," Guideposts (April, 1962).

8 "Cuba," IPI Report (October, 1962), 10.

9 Roscoe Lewis, "Cuban Radio Cuts in on U.S. Broadcasts," Los Angeles Times (October 30, 1962), 4; "News Breaks on Castro's Late Show," Editor and Publisher (November 24, 1962), 10.

10 Mervin Block, "The Night Castro 'Unmasked,'" Columbia Journalism Review (Summer, 1962), 5-10.

ARGENTINA

1 Gladys Delmas, "The Argentine Mess," The Reporter (January 3, 1963), 18-20. Contrast current reports with early post-Perón optimism. See Arthur P. Whitaker, "Argentina: Recovery from Perón," Current History (April, 1957), 210-11.

2 Mary Gardner, "The Argentine Press Since Perón," Journalism Quarterly (Summer, 1960) 426-30.

3 James Montagnes, "Letter," Editor and Publisher (May 21, 1960), 7.

4 Tía Vicenta ("Aunt Vicenta"), the national Argentine humor magazine never used to be

listed among the news magazines. But in-
asmuch as it now stresses lampooning of
national public officials, Tía Vicenta has
become must reading for foreign correspondents in Buenos Aires. The magazine
uses many cartoons, trick composite photographs, and drawings, especially when
military leaders are targets. See "Argentine Magazine Laughs at Political Crisis,"
New York Times, May 6, 1962, for a summary
of subtle, off-beat captions the magazine
uses.

5 A rare exception to the lack of adequate
profits in television is the company "Pro-
ducciones Telefilms," whose half-hour
features on music and noncontroversial
subjects sell not only inside Argentina
but are exported to Mexico City for re-
broadcast there.

                    BRAZIL

1 "Brasil--demográfica," Conjuntura Econômica
(April, 1962), 39-46. This gives the results of Brazil's 1960 general census.

2 Peter T. White, "Brazil, Oba!" National
Geographic (September, 1962), 299-353.

3 "Crisis in Brasília," Atlas (February,
1962), 120-25. This detailed report has
been translated from Portuguese into
English. Originally it appeared as two
stories in the Rio daily, Jornal do Brasil,
November 14 and 15, 1961. Built from the
ground up a few years ago, Brasília has a
population of 48,000, with 75,000 living
in nearby suburbs or "satellite cities,"
as Brazilians call them.

4 William L. Schurz, Brazil (New York, 1961),
127.

5 "Brazil Press Honors Moses in 25th Year,"
Editor and Publisher (June 9, 1956), 66.

6 "Divided Empire," Time (May 25, 1962), 43;
"AP Service Now in Rio to 4 Papers, 3
Stations," AP World (Autumn, 1956), 6.

7 Louis L. Wiznitzer, "Which Revolution for
Brazil?" New Republic (March 19, 1962),
18-19. Wiznitzer, U.S. correspondent for
Folha da Manhã of São Paulo and Diário
Carioca of Rio, is Latin American editor
of Atlas, the U.S. magazine which digests
and translates the press of the world. See
also "Waiting for Quadros," New Republic
(March 12, 1962), 7.

8 Danton Jobim, Espírito do jornalismo (Rio

de Janeiro, 1959).

9 Alisky, "Educational Broadcasting in Latin
America," Journal of the AERT (January,
1956), 23-27. The AERT Journal is now
the NAEB Journal, published by the National
Association of Educational Broadcasters.

10 David B. Richardson, "Brazil: Troubled
Giant of the Americas," U.S. News and
World Report (February 29, 1960), 38.

11 "Belo Horizonte Gets TV," Brazilian
Bulletin (October 15, 1956), 5.

12 "Carioca's Revenge," Time (October 20,
1961), 49.

13 Tad Szulc, "Kubitschek Ends Brazil Censoring," New York Times, February 2, 1956,
p. 8.

14 A. E. Austin, "The Situation in Latin
America," Report of Sigma Delta Chi Freedom of Information Committee (September,
1962, 10.

15 H. Stuart Morrison, "Brazilian Regulation
Hits Hiring Practices," Editor and Publisher (August 18, 1962), 62.

16 Ibid. Also "Censorship Condemmed," Press
of the Americas (November-December, 1961), 2.

17 Morrison, "Foreign Newsmen Can't Cover
Brazil Congress," Editor and Publisher
(June 9, 1962), 101.

18 Jobim, "French and U.S. Influences Upon the
Latin American Press," Journalism Quarterly
(Winter, 1954), 61-66.

19 Hadley Cantril and Lloyd A. Free, "Hopes
and Fears for Self and Country," American
Behavioral Scientist (October, 1962 Supplement), 13-14. See the section on "Rising
Expectations among Brazilians."

                    CHILE

1 Dorothea Smith, "Press Commission in Other
Countries," Freedom of Information Center
Publication No. 35 (University of Missouri:
August, 1960), 5.

2 Frederick B. Marbut, "Chile Has Law to
Enforce Code of Ethics," The Quill (April,
1960), 16.

3 James S. Copley, With a Mission to Chile
(San Diego, 1961), 1-14.

4 Edward C. Burks, "Urchin Problem Vexes Santiago," New York Times, November 18, 1962, p. 40.

5 Diane Stanley, "The Press in Chile," Nieman Reports (January, 1961), 29.

6 Raúl Matas, "Chilean Radio," Américas (October, 1955), 6-9.

7 Ted Morello, "Chile's Journalism School," The Quill (July, 1955), 10, 14-15.

8 Margaret V. Campbell, "The Chilean Press: 1823-1842," Journal of Inter-American Studies (October, 1962), 545-55.

COLOMBIA

1 David F. Belnap, "Freedom of the Press Returns to Colombia," Editor and Publisher (May 25, 1957), 11, 80; John D. Martz, Colombia: A Contemporary Political Survey (Chapel Hill, 1962). For a glimpse of El Siglo's most demagogic editorials, see the late Vernon L. Fluharty's Dance of the Millions (Pittsburgh, 1957).

2 Algunas preguntas sobre las escuelas radio-fónicas de Colombia (Bogota, 1958).

3 Susana Amaya, "Radio Helps Eradicate Mass Illiteracy in Rural Colombia," Gazette, V, 4 (1959), 403-408.

ECUADOR

1 Raymond B. Nixon, "UNESCO Program for Media Outlined," Editor and Publisher (May 7, 1960), 54.

2 J. David Bowen, "Ecuador on a Tightrope," The Reporter (March 29, 1962), 30-33.

PERU

1 Ministerio de Hacienda y Comercio, Dirección Nacional de Estadística y Censos, Anuario estadístico del Perú (Lima, 1955); Ministerio de Trabajo, Memoria (Lima, 1955).

2 Marvin Alisky, "The Peruvian Press and the Nixon Incident," Journalism Quarterly (Fall, 1958), 411-19; Alisky, "Peruvian Press Shows American Influence," The Quill (July, 1959), 15-16, 20.

3 Stands for American Revolutionary Popular Alliance or Alianza Popular Revolucionaria, founded in 1924 by Haya de la Torre. See

M. O. Hudson, "Haya de la Torre Case," American Journal of International Law (January, 1952), 8-12.

4 "Limit of Tolerance," The London Economist (July 21, 1962), 221.

5 Andrés Henestrosa and José Fernández, Periodismo y periodistas de Hispanoamerica (Mexico, 1947), 71, 136.

6 El Comercio, I, No. 1, Saturday, May 4, 1839, p. 1.

7 Marvin Alisky, "Broadcasting in Peru," Journal of Broadcasting (Spring, 1959), 118-27; Correos y Telecomunicaciones del Perú, Subdirección de Telecomunicaciones, Radioemisoras (Lima, 1960), 1-3.

URUGUAY

1 Asociación Nacional de Broadcasters Uruguayos, Memoria Andebu (Montevideo, 1960).

VENEZUELA

1 Ministerio de Fomento, Octavo censo general de población (Caracas, 1957), XII A, 39-40. See also Dirección General de Estadística, Boletín mensual (December, 1960), 7-11.

2 Edwin Lieuwen, Venezuela (New York, 1961), 14-16.

3 P. N. Tablante Garrido, Periodismo merideño (Venzuela, 1959); Rafael Ramón Castellanos, Historia del periodismo trujillano en el siglo XIX (Caracas, 1957).

MIDDLE EAST OVERVIEW

1 Francis Williams in New Statesman (July 12, 1958), 37.

2 Letter to the writer from Mohamed Habib, press attaché of the Embassy of the United Arab Republic, Washington, D.C. (November 20, 1958).

3 Most Arab papers have circulations under 10,000 throughout the Middle East; even Al Bilaad of Jeddah, Saudi Arabia's only paper of any importance, barely reaches this figure. Circulations of as much as 8,000 or 10,000 are considered significant in this region; for example, on the island of Cyprus (in the city of Nicosia) are three papers

which have considerable local and regional prestige even with such small circulations. They are Eleftheria (Greek), and the English-language Cyprus Mail and Times of Cyprus.

4 Michael Adams, "Iraq's Unfinished Revolution," the Manchester Guardian Weekly, December 28, 1958, p. 5. Cf. Freedom of Information Center Publication No. 21, p. 5.

5 For a good discussion of Lebanon's press since the revolt in 1958, see Welles Hangen, "Arab World's Last Free Press," IPI Report (November, 1958), 4-5.

ISRAEL

1 Several good articles have appeared in recent years relative to the Israeli press. A few, felt by the authors to be most helpful, are: Ted R. Lurie, "Press Freedom and Responsibility in Israel," Gazette, VII, 2 (1961), 189-92; Moshe Zak, "The Contemporary Press in Israel," Gazette, VII, 1 (1961), 1-8; Dan Pines, "The Dynamic Press of Israel," IPI Report, X, No. 1, pp. 1-2; Rafael E. Gill, "Journalists in Israel: A Statistical Portrait," Journalism Quarterly (Winter, 1959), 57-62; and Chaim Isaak, "The Training and Recruiting of Journalists in Israel," Gazette, VII, 1 (1961), 123-27.

2 Sample copies of leading daily newspapers of Israel were furnished by Hugh Y. Orgel, press attaché, Embassy of Israel, Washington, D.C.

3 Williams, New Statesman (July 12, 1958), 37.

4 An excellent survey of ITIM is Hayin Balstan, "ITIM--An Experiment in National News Agency Reporting," Gazette, VII, 1 (1961), 109-21.

TURKEY

1 A Reuters dispatch from Istanbul (September 18, 1962) reported the stopping of sales of four Turkish papers by the government because some photographs displeased authorities. Cf. "Turkey," Time (January 18, 1963), 29-30.

2 Time (March 31, 1958), 20.

3 Editor and Publisher (December 10, 1960), 71.

4 A good insight into the part played by the Turkish press in the transformation of the country from the old Ottoman Empire to the

new Turkish Republic is given in the autobiography of the editor of Istanbul's Vatan, Ahmed Emin Yalman, Turkey in My Time (Norman, Oklahoma, 1956).

UNITED ARAB REPUBLIC

1 Letter from Mohamed Habib, press attaché, UAR Embassy, Washington, D.C.

2 "Nasser's Iron Grip on Press," IPI Report (May, 1960), 9-10.

FAR EAST AND SOUTHEAST ASIA OVERVIEW

1 See Wilmott Ragsdale, "A Program for Developing the Media of Southeast Asia," Journalism Quarterly (Spring, 1960), 275-79.

BURMA

1 Information on the Burmese press and sample copies of leading newspapers were furnished by the Embassy of Burma, Washington, D.C. Probably the best recent discussion of the Burmese press is Milton Hollstein's "The Press in Burma: Its Hopes and Problems," Journalism Quarterly (Summer, 1961), 351-59.

Former Prime Minister U Nu delivered the graduation address at commencement exercises in the Spring of 1957 at the Burma Translation Society's School of Journalism in Rangoon. In his speech he said: "...there can be no true democracy in any country unless there is a free and responsible press....The power of the press is enormous and unlimited. But it must be used wisely and responsibly. On the press lies the heavy and arduous responsibility of shaping not only public opinion and people's outlook, but also the very character and calibre of the entire nation....You should write without fear or favour; but you should not put the interests of your paper or your own personal satisfaction or gain above considerations for your nation or for the welfare of humanity....Journalism would be an ugly profession to follow, if you have to make a living by other people's tears.... The most successful journalists, and the best ones, have been those who are patriotic, human, and humane...." "Premier's Address to Budding Journalists," Burma (July, 1957), 1-3.

COMMUNIST CHINA

1 See Milton Shieh, "Red China Patterns Controls of Press on Russian Model," Journalism Quarterly (Winter, 1951), 74-80 for a good discussion of press structure in Communist China.

2 Propaganda has no sinister meaning in Red China, where it is considered synonymous with "journalism" or "literature." According to Mao Tse-tung, "Any person engaged in talking with another person is engaged in propaganda." Peter S. H. Tang, Communist China Today (New York, 1957), 358. Chapter ix, "The Propaganda Machine," gives an excellent overview of the concept of the press in Red China. See also Gerald Clark, Impatient Giant: Red China Today (New York, 1959), 41-56, chap. iv, "Persuasion and Indoctrination"; and Franklin W. Houn, "Chinese Communist Control of the Press," Public Opinion Quarterly (Winter, 1958-59), 438-39.

3 Houn, "The Press in Communist China: Its Structure and Operation," Journalism Quarterly (Fall, 1956), 503-505. See also "La Presse Chinoise," l'Echo de la Presse et de Publicité (Paris, 1957), 21; Richard L. Walker, China Under Communism: The First Five Years (New Haven, 1955). This book by Walker in part eight ("Culture and the Intellectuals") contains twelve pages of cartoons, posters, and pictures from Red Chinese newspapers of a typical propagandistic nature.

4 Kwangming Jih Pao until 1958 had been the most popular non-Communist party journal and was heavily subscribed to by intellectuals; it is now a state paper but still stresses literature and the arts. Ta Kung Pao (of both Peiping and Tientsin) is the main business-economic paper of the country; Chung Kuo Shao Nien Pao is a youth newspaper of national popularity, and Kung Jen Jih Pao or "Daily Worker" is the principal trade union publication.

5 "The Voice of Red China," Time (June 23, 1958), 77.

6 Robert Guillain, 600 Million Chinese (New York, 1957), 148.

7 Ibid., 147.

8 Journalism Quarterly (Winter, 1958), 6.

9 For a good historical summary of the development of the Red Chinese press, and also for a fine treatment of the basic structure of the Communist press system, see "Press in Communist China," IPI Report (May, 1952), 4-5. See also a brief history of the Chinese press by Stanley D. Bernstein, Chinese Communist Press (Freedom of Information Publication No. 84, 1962).

NATIONALIST CHINA

1 For a good discussion of the Nationalist Chinese Press, see Shen Shan, "Taiwan and Its Press," Nieman Reports (July, 1960), 17-21. Some information contained in this section was supplied by Hwei Choung Fu, student at Texas A&M, 1962-63.

2 China News and China Post, the two leading English-language dailies on Formosa, have long been noted for their courageous, outspoken editorial policies. China News, although a mimeographed journal, is very influential.

3 Carlton Culmsee, "Formosan Press Is Still Under Kuomintang Thumb But is Winning Freedom," The Quill (June, 1957), 15.

4 James Morris, "Formosa Under the Skin," The Manchester Guardian Weekly (October 9, 1958), 5.

5 Carlton Culmsee, "How Free is the Press in 'Free China'?" Journalism Quarterly (Fall, 1956), 501.

6 Information from Y. Y. Bao (Chinese Embassy, Washington, D.C.). Central Daily News, a Chinese language paper, is a well-printed paper usually running four pages. It uses small pictures and drawings and red ink (for additional color) on its front page. The paper prints an island and an international edition.

7 Hsin Sheng Pao is a stock company in which the government is the largest stockholder; it is Free China's second largest newspaper. Chung Hua Jih Pao, probably the best of the island's dailies in its news coverage, prior to 1949 was the sole Kuomintang paper on Formosa. Information from Y. Y. Bao; also China Handbook 1956-57 (Taipeh, 1956), 213.

8 For a good report on President Chiang's views on government-press relations, see Howard R. Long, "Chiang Kai-shek Outlines Conditions for Freedom of the Press in Formosa," The Quill (July, 1958), 8-10, 21.

INDIA

1 No two sources seem to agree on the number
of languages and dialects found in India.
For example, the number 723 is given by
Ed Hirschmann in "Babel in Bombay," Penn
State Journalist (June, 1962), 1; 782 is
given by Nadig Krishna Murthy, "The Weekly
Press of India," Grassroots Editor (April,
1962), 16, while only 190 are mentioned by
Asad Husain, "The Future of English-
Language Newspapers in India," Journalism
Quarterly (Spring, 1956), 213. However,
it is generally agreed that the country
has fourteen main languages.

2 Much of the basic information for this
section was furnished by Pramod Desai,
Debabrata Ghosh, and Dharam Dev Malik,
Indian students at Texas A&M 1962-63.
Also, valuable references are Chancel
Sakar, "New Dimensions of the Indian Press,"
Nieman Reports (January, 1961), 25-27, and
Jerome P. Kline, "Illiteracy Adds Complexity
to Bizarre Indian Press," News Workshop
(June, 1959), 8, 10.

3 New Statesman (August 16, 1958), 187.

4 Roland Wolseley, "How India Could Improve
its Press," The Quill (February, 1953),
8-10. See also for elaboration on these
problems: Wolseley (ed.), Journalism in
Modern India (Bombay, 1953), and H. P.
Ghose, The Newspaper in India (Calcutta,
1952).

5 Letter to the editor "Indian Journalism,"
by A. Hariharan of the Free Press Journal,
Bombay, in Editor and Publisher (November
16, 1957), 7.

6 Asad Husain, "The Future of English-Language
Newspapers in India," loc. cit., 216-17.

7 "Does Nehru Want to Punish Newspapers for
their Success?," Saturday Evening Post
(June 29, 1957), 10.

8 Ibid.

9 Murthy, "The Weekly Press of India," loc.
cit., 16.

10 For a good discussion of All India Radio,
see Arthur Bonner, "India's Masses: The
Public That Can't be Reached," The Atlantic
(October, 1959), 48-51.

11 Gene D. Overstreet and Marshall Windmiller,
Communism in India (Berkeley, Calif., 1959),

chap. xviii, 446-65, "The Agit-Prop
Instrument," gives a good survey of Communist periodicals of India.

INDONESIA

1 Much of the material in this section was
supplied by Zainal A. Abbas, an Indonesian
student at Texas A&M 1962-63.

2 The authors are indebted to the Embassy
of Indonesia (Kedutaan Besar Indonesia),
Washington, D.C. for pertinent and recent
materials on the Indonesian Press.
Particularly useful were sample copies of
principal Indonesian newspapers furnished
by the embassy.

JAPAN

1 Shintaro Fukushima, "100th Anniversary of
Japanese Press," Editor and Publisher
(April 21, 1962), 21, 126, 128, 130;
Nihon Shimbun Kyokai (The Japanese News-
paper Publishers and Editors Association),
The Japanese Press, 1962 (Tokyo, 1962).

2 One daily, however, does stand out because
of its general excellence, prestige and
accuracy; this is the Asahi, which is
usually called Japan's "quality" daily.
For an excellent insight into this paper's
high standing, see Hessel Tiltman, "Success
Secrets of Japan's 'Asahi'," IPI Report
(November, 1958), 6-9.

3 The Japanese Press, 1962, p. 8.

4 Ibid., 6. Also see, Mitsugi Kondo, "Newspaper Competition in Japan," Gazette, II,
2 (1956), 97-112. This is an excellent
summary of this phase of the Japanese
press picture.

5 Gordon Walker, "Japanese Press Out of
Chaos into Solid Achievement," ASNE
Bulletin (September 1, 1957), 10.

6 Fukushima, "100th Anniversary of Japanese
Press," loc. cit., 128.

7 Asahi ("Rising Sun") and Mainichi ("Every
Day") each has some 500 staff members who
are reporters and photographers.

8 Editor and Publisher (May 16, 1959), 50.

9 Time (October 20, 1958), 61.

10 "Japan's Second Century," The Economist
(March 8, 1958), 12. See also, Fukushima,

"100th Anniversary of Japanese Press,"
<u>loc</u>. <u>cit</u>., 130.

11 The conservative government of Japan is
run by the powerful Liberal Democrat party
which is the product of a 1955 merger of
two conservative groups. In the same year
the rightwing and leftwing Socialists
joined into one (Socialist) party. Except
for a short period of coalition government
in 1947-48, the conservatives have been in
power since the new constitution became
effective in 1947. "Japan's Second Century,"
<u>loc</u>. <u>cit</u>., 12, 16. See also, Edward P.
Whittemore, <u>The</u> <u>Press</u> <u>in</u> <u>Japan</u> <u>Today</u>...
<u>A</u> <u>Case</u> <u>Study</u> (South Carolina, 1961); this
book contains a detailed study of the role
of the press in the political turbulence
in Japan.

12 Fukushima, "100th Anniversary of Japanese
Press," <u>loc</u>. <u>cit</u>., 130.

13 Bryan, "Economic Intervention: Prelude to
Press Control," <u>Journalism</u> <u>Quarterly</u>
(Winter, 1961), 70.

14 Such as <u>Shukan</u> <u>Asahi</u> (circulation 1.5
million in 1960; similar to <u>Time</u> or <u>News-
week</u>) and <u>Fujin</u> <u>Asahi</u> (women's monthly).
Cf. Hisashi Maeda, "A National Newspaper
in Japan," <u>Nieman</u> <u>Reports</u> (April, 1956),
9-13; Hessel Tiltman, "Success Secrets of
Japan's 'Asahi'," <u>loc</u>. <u>cit</u>., 6-9.

15 Valuable information on the Japanese press
and sample copies of leading Japanese newspapers were furnished by Hirozo Ushida,
Special Assistant, Information Office, The
Consulate General of Japan, New York, N.Y.

16 See Yashiro Kawanaka, "Analysis of the
Japanese Dailies," <u>Gazette</u>, VI, 1 (1960),
2-7.

17 Susumu Ejiri (Nihon Shimbun Kyokai, Tokyo)
in <u>IPI</u> <u>Report</u> (April, 1958), 10. See also
Hideo Ono, "Thirty Years Study of Journalism
in Japan," <u>Gazette</u>, VI, 1 (1960), 11-21.

18 <u>Time</u> (October 20, 1958), 61.

19 Fukushima, "100th Anniversary of Japanese
Press," <u>loc</u>. <u>cit</u>., 12.

20 An excellent discussion of the Japanese
press during the American occupation is
William J. Coughlin, <u>Conquered</u> <u>Press</u>: <u>The</u>
<u>MacArthur</u> <u>Era</u> <u>in</u> <u>Japanese</u> <u>Journalism</u> (Palo
Alto, Calif., 1952).

21 Barry Faris, "Japanese Practice 'Blanket
Coverage'," <u>Editor</u> <u>and</u> <u>Publisher</u> (July 27,

1957), 48.

22 The text of this paper is published in
full in <u>The</u> <u>Japanese</u> <u>Press</u>, <u>1962</u>, pp.
95-103.

23 Japan Information Service, <u>Facts</u> <u>about</u>
<u>Japan</u> (New York, 1960), 5.

24 <u>Ibid</u>., 5-7.

25 Fukushima, "100th Anniversary of Japanese
Press," <u>loc</u>. <u>cit</u>., 128.

KOREA

1 Information and sample copies of leading
South Korean publications were furnished
by the Korean Embassy, Washington, D.C.
Additional information was supplied by a
Korean newspaperman, a journalism graduate
student at the State University of Iowa
in 1962, Yong Hoon Rhee, and by a student
at Texas A&M 1962-63, Jai Hak Hong. South
Korean circulation figures were reported
for the first time in <u>Editor</u> <u>and</u> <u>Publisher</u>
<u>International</u> <u>Year</u> <u>Book</u>, <u>1962</u>. See also
for a good survey of the Korean press,
Kwon-Sang Park, "South Korean Press Puts
its House in Order," <u>IPI</u> <u>Report</u> (May, 1961),
10.

2 Robert T. Oliver, "Present-Day Newspapers
in the Republic of Korea," <u>Journalism</u>
<u>Quarterly</u> (Winter, 1957), 85. Professor
Oliver is here quoting from the English-
language <u>Korea</u> <u>Times</u>, which as an anti-
government paper has long been known for
its brisk, lively reporting. One wonders
if its style is really typical of the
Korean press. In fact, Professor Ellard's
point concerning the heavy, academic style
was mainly in reference to the vernacular
press. However, let us take a lead sentence
from the English-language <u>Korean</u> <u>Republic</u>
(September 24, 1958, p. 3) as one further
illustration: certainly a rather heavy
style will be noted here: "The nation will
consume 892,339 tons of chemical fertilizer
during the year ending July 31, 1959,
according to a plan recently finalized by
the Agriculture-Forestry Ministry."

3 Many of the weekly papers (and some dailies)
are only one-sheet journals printed on both
sides.

4 The <u>Korean</u> <u>Republic</u> is an extremely neat,
well-edited and well-printed newspaper.
Its editorial page and page opposite
(containing features and opinion pieces)
are especially attractive. This government-

sponsored newspaper is usually eight pages, sometimes running to ten and twelve. The Korean Republic in its technical aspects is in direct contrast to the country's other English-language daily, the Korea Times, a poorly-printed four pager of Seoul.

5 Independence Press was published thrice weekly in the Korean language. In the same year this paper was founded (1896) the first Korean daily was begun by Syngman Rhee, who was just beginning his political career. This was Maiyil Shinmum, printed partly in Korean and partly in English. For a good summary of Korean press development, see Kyung Cho Chung, Korea Tomorrow (New York, 1956).

6 Editor and Publisher (August 16, 1958), 43.

7 D. Wayne Rowland of Southern Methodist University's journalism faculty, a recent student of the South Korean press, believes that the greatest threat to press freedom in the country does not come from governmental secrecy or restraints, but from the general economic insecurity of the press. Most papers, he says, are losing money. Professor Rowland says that the Korean press is making progress, but points to many problems which the newspapers face (e.g., poor plants and equipment, low-quality newsprint, not enough advertising, awkward alphabet, over-staffed newspapers, and insufficient number of trained journalists). D. Wayne Rowland, "The Press in the Korean Republic: Its Status and Problems," Journalism Quarterly (Fall, 1958), 450-54.

PAKISTAN

1 Especially useful in the discussion of Pakistani newspapers has been information provided by the Embassy of Pakistan, Washington, D.C. In addition, useful background data were furnished by the following Pakistani students at Texas A&M 1962-63: A. H. M. Nuril Ula, Muhammed Wahed, Syed Zoha, Hossain Sarkar, and Molla Fazluz Huq.

2 Pakistan Press Year Book, 1956, p. 35.

3 Prime Minister Mohammad Ali stressed in 1956 that the government should not "stifle freedom of expression" and he contended that if it did so, this was "evidence of lack of wisdom." Ibid., 36-37. A serious discussion of press freedom and press responsibilities is a speech by A. K. Brohi, Pakistan's Minister of Law, Information, and Broadcasting. This speech was published

in a little pamphlet called Freedom of Information (Karachi, 1954). In connection with this subject, see also Kenneth Allen, "Free Press on Trial in Pakistan," The Quill (March, 1959), 12-14.

4 Good discussions of press freedom in Pakistan may be found in Pakistan Press Year Book, 1956, pp. 36-37, and in Brohi's speech as published in Freedom of Information, 10-12. Another article touching on the attitude of the authorities toward the press (and presenting other highlights of Pakistan's press situation) is Herbert Feldman, "The Press in Pakistan," Gazette, II, 2 (1956), 92-96.

5 The Urdu press is excellently treated in S.M.A. Feroze's "The Evolution of Urdu Press," Pakistan Quarterly (Autumn, 1954), 18-23, 62-63.

PHILIPPINES

1 Especially useful in this discussion of the newspapers of the Philippines has been material furnished by the Embassy of the Philippines, Washington, D.C. Also useful was material furnished by three Filipino students at Texas A&M in 1962-63--Sotero Salac, Damaso J. Paculdo, and Ramón A. Ibarbia.

2 Embassy materials.

3 Mason Rossiter Smith, "Journalism in Philippines Retains Old Hell and Brimstone Tradition," The Quill (February, 1957), 7. This interesting article by a New York weekly newspaperman who visited the Philippines gives an illuminating picture of the Filipino journalist, his character, philosophy, and writing style.

THAILAND

1 For example, the Thai Embassy in Washington, D.C. was able to furnish little information (and what was furnished was of a general nature) concerning the country's press. Some data was provided by a Thai student at Texas A&M in 1962-63--Tanongchit Wongsiri. Undoubtedly the best source for information on the Thai press can be found in Albert G. Pickerell's article, "The Press of Thailand: Conditions and Trends," Journalism Quarterly (Winter, 1960), 83-96.

2 Nathan B. Blumberg, "Report on the Thai Press," Montana Journalism Review

(Spring, 1962), 30-32.

AFRICA

1 Most all recent information concerning
the press of Africa stresses the limita-
tions of the news media and the danger of
press nationalization. A few of the
sources used in developing this section
follow: Esuakema U. Otom, "Development of
Journalism in Nigeria," Journalism Quarterly
(Winter, 1958); Helen Kitchen (ed.), The
Press in Africa (Washington, 1956); Charles
A. Hayes, "Press Report from Kenya,"
Nieman Reports (April, 1962); William
Gordon, "In Newest Africa," Nieman Reports
(July, 1959); Bob Warner, "An Emerging
Press: The African Story," Editor and
Publisher (August 27, 1960); Abiodun Aloba,
"Journalism in Africa: I. Nigeria," Gazette,
V, 2 (1959); Esuakema Udo Oton, "The Press
of Liberia: A Case Study," Journalism
Quarterly (Spring, 1961); Adam Clymer,
"The Divided Press of South Africa,"
Nieman Reports (July, 1960); "South Africa:
A Press in Chains," IPI Report (May, 1960);
"Menace to Freedom Remains in South Africa,"
IPI Report (March, 1962); "The Press in
Asia and Africa," IPI Report (August, 1961);
Louis M. Lyons, "Press Notes from Africa,"
Nieman Reports (July-October, 1962); James
W. Carty, Jr., "The African Press," Grass-
roots Editor (July, 1962). Information was
also received from Krishan Shaunak, student
from Kenya at Texas A&M in 1962-63.

2 This Life-size monthly resembling the U.S.'s
Ebony in format and content is Africa's
leading magazine. Each month more than
250,000 copies are distributed across
Africa. Drum was founded in 1951; from
its headquarters in Johannesburg it reaches
into at least ten African countries. In
Lagos, Nigeria, alone, some 20,000 copies
go on sale early in the morning and by sun-
down the kiosks are empty. Drum regularly
beats forth a dedication to the equality of
man, recognizes no color line--even on its
150-man staff. The magazine's more than
40 pages of pictures serve up a rich diet
of society, scandal, politics, sex, and
sports. An excellent book by a former
staff member who puts the magazine's
founding and development in an interesting
perspective is Anthony Sampson, Drum: The
Newspaper That Won the Heart of Africa
(Boston, 1957).

3 UNESCO, Reports and Papers on Mass Communication (1962), No. 37.

4 See Leonard W. Doob, "Informational

Services in Central Africa," Public
Opinion Quarterly (Spring, 1953), 13-14.

5 UNESCO, Reports and Papers on Mass Communication (1962), No. 37.

AUSTRALIA

1 Particularly helpful information pertaining to press freedom and other aspects of
the Australian press can be found in
"The Australian Press," a 25-page mailing
piece of the News and Information Bureau
of Australia's Department of Interior.
See also, IPI, Government Pressures on
the Press, 92-93, and W. Sprague Holden,
Australia Goes to Press (Michigan, 1962).

2 Holden, "Newspapers in the Land Down Under
are Much Like American Counterparts,"
The Quill (March, 1958), 6. This article
provides a good survey of Australian
papers.

3 See Robert Rhode, "News for a Nation,"
Nieman Reports (July-October, 1962), for
a good discussion of the A.B.C. See also
Hugh Elliot, "The Three-Way Struggle of
Press, Radio and TV in Australia,"
Journalism Quarterly (Spring, 1960), 267-74.

CANADA

1 "Canada's Changing Weeklies," Grassroots
Editor (October, 1962), 10-12.

2 Roy H. Thomson, "Communications Business--
International Aspects," Editor and Publisher (November 3, 1962), 12-66.

3 "Anything Bigger?" Newsweek (December 11,
1961), 58; "Roy Thomson Sees Service in
Expansion," Editor and Publisher (October
27, 1962), 10; "'Good Citizen' Roy Thomson
May Have Too Much Power," Editor and Pub-
lisher (November 18, 1961), 46; Charles
Fenby, "Fleet Street's Crisis--and the
Moral," IPI Report (March, 1961), 1.

4 Tania Long, "Quebec TV Debate to Spur Election," New York Times, November 11, 1962,
p. 15.

5 Philip N. Schuyler, "Canadian Papers Can
Beat Airwave Media," Editor and Publisher
(November 3, 1962), 17.

6 Of 99 TV stations, 21 are CBC publicly-
owned and 78 are privately-owned commercial
outlets. Of 250 radio stations, only 36
are CBC, 214 are privately owned.

7 Robert A. Farquharson, "The Imbalance in
  Canada-U.S. News Flow," <u>Nieman</u> <u>Reports</u>
  (January, 1961), 24.

8 Louis M. Lyons, "Canada Reads American
  and Worries Over It," <u>Nieman</u> <u>Reports</u>
  (October, 1961), 38-40.

Selected Source Materials

I. SPECIAL PUBLICATIONS AND YEARBOOKS

Alisky, Marvin. Latin American Journalism Bibliography. Mexico, D.F.: Fondo de Publicidad Interamericana, 1958.

Asociacion Nacional de Broadcasters Uruguayos. Memoria Andebu. Montevideo: Asociacion Nacional de Broadcasters Uruguayos, 1960.

Czechoslovakia Foreign Institute in Exile. Situation in the Czechoslovak Periodical Press. Chicago, 1953.

Danmarks Blad-og Bogverden ("The World of Papers and Books in Denmark"). Copenhagen: Politikens Forlag, 1955. (Text in Danish, German, French and English). Edited by Folmer Christensen.

Die deutsche Presse 1956: Zeitung and Zeitschriften. Berlin: Freien Universitat, 1956.

Direccion General de Prensa. Registro Oficial de Periodistas, Vol. 1. Madrid: Ministerio de Informacion y Turismo, 1961.

Directory of Newspapers and Periodicals. Athens, Greece: Press Department, Ministry of the Prime Minister, February, 1962.

Editor and Publisher International Year Book (New York). Annual.

Facts About Finland (Helsinki: Otava, 1956). Edited by Jukka Miesmaa.

The Foreign Correspondent: His Problems in Covering the News Abroad (No.1, Iowa Studies in Mass Communications; State University of Iowa, 1954).

Forty Years of Soviet Power in Facts and Figures (Moscow: Foreign Languages Publishing House, 1958).

Freedom of Information (Karachi: Ferozsons, 1954). Address delivered by A. K. Brohi, Minister of Law, Information and Broadcasting, Government of Pakistan, September, 1954.

Freedom of Information Publications (School of Journalism, University of Missouri).

General Council of the Press. The Press and The People (London, 1954).

Guide to the New Zealand Market (Advertising Rates and Mechanical Details of Newspapers as of January 1, 1962). Wellington: Newspaper Proprietors Association.

Handbuch Österreichs Presse Werbung Graphik (Vienna: Verband österreichischer Zeitungsherausgeber; Wiener Verlag, 1962).

Hero, A. O. Mass Media and World Affairs. Boston: World Peace Foundation, 1959.

History of Indian Journalism. Part II of the Report of the Press Commission, Publications Division, Delhi, 1955.

Hungary Today (Budapest, Central Statistical Office, 1958).

Husain, Asad. Bibliography of a Century of Indian Journalism, 1858-1958. (School of Journalism, University of Minnesota, 1960).

Internationales Handbuch Für Rundfunk und Fernsehen. Hamburg: Hans Bredow-Institut, 1959.

I.P.I. As Others See Us (International Press Institute, Zurich, 1954).

I.P.I. Government Pressures on the Press (Zurich, 1955).

I.P.I. Improvement of Information (Zurich, 1952).

I.P.I. The Flow of the News (Zurich, 1953).

I.P.I. The News from the Middle East (Zurich, 1954).

I.P.I. The News from Russia (Zurich, 1952).

I.P.I. News in Asia (Zurich, 1956).

I.P.I. Press Councils and Press Codes (Zurich, 1961).

I.P.I. The Press in Authoritarian Countries. (Zurich, 1959).

I.P.I. Professional Secrecy and the Journalist (Zurich, 1962).

Jahrbuch der Öffentlichen Meinung 1947-1955 (Allensbach: Verlag für Demoskopie, 1956).

Janssens, Bertrandus. Het pers probleem. Antwerp: Studiecentrum voor zielezorg en predicatie, 1951.

The Japan Annual--1958 (Japan Annual Publica-
    tions, Tokyo, 1958). May be obtained from
    the Tokyo News Service, Ltd., Kosoku Doro
    Bldg., 10 Ginza Nishi 8-chome, Chuo-ku,
    Tokyo.

Japanese Press (Tokyo: Japan Newspaper Pub-
    lishers and Editors Association; annual).

Johnson, Elmer D. Communication (a concise
    introduction to the history of the alphabet,
    writing, printing, books and libraries).
    New Brunswick, N.J.; Scarecrow Press, 1955.

Kayser, Jacques. One Week's News (UNESCO,
    Paris, 1953). This is a comparative study
    of 17 major dailies for a seven-day period.

The Land of Soviets: The Country and the
    People. Moscow: Foreign Languages Publish-
    ing House, 1957.

Merrill, John C. Gringo: Mexican Journalists
    Look at the U.S. (School of Inter-American
    Studies, University of Florida, 1963).

Nafziger, Ralph O. (compiler). International
    News and the Press (an annotated biblio-
    graphy). New York: H. H. Wilson, 1940.

Newspaper Press Directory and Advertisers'
    Guide (London). Annual.

Newspapers and Magazines (Wellington, N.Z.,
    Revised 1960).

Newspapers and Magazines of the U.S.S.R. for
    1959 (Moscow: "Mezhdunarodnaya Kniga,"
    1958).

Österreichisches Jahrbuch 1957 (Vienna: Druck
    und Verlag der Österreichischen Staats-
    druckerei, 1958). (See especially the
    section "Die österreichische Press," pp.
    110-111.)

Pakistan Press Yearbook (Karachi: Express
    Publishers). Annual.

The Polish Journal of Press Research (Warsaw:
    Press Research Institute, 1959).

Problèmes et Techniques de Presse. Paris:
    Fondation Nationale des Sciences Politiques,
    1950.

Report of the Royal Commission on the Press,
    1947-1949. London: H. M. Stationery Office,
    1949.

Ten Years of Italian Democracy 1946-1956. Rome:
    Information Office, Documentation Center,
    1956. (See especially "Press, Entertainment
    and Sport," pp. 304-320.)

Ulrich's Periodicals Directory: A Classified
    Guide to a Selected List of Current
    Periodicals, Foreign and Domestic (Edited
    by Eileen C. Graves). New York, 1956.

UNESCO. Basic Facts and Figures (Paris, 1960).

UNESCO. Legislation for Press, Film and Radio
    (Paris, 1951).

UNESCO. Meeting of Experts on Development of
    Information Media in Latin America (New
    York, 1961).

UNESCO. News Agencies: Their Structure and
    Operation (Paris, 1953).

UNESCO. The Problems of Transmitting Press
    Messages (Paris, 1956).

UNESCO. Professional Association in Mass Media
    (Paris, 1959).

UNESCO. The Training of Journalists (Paris,
    1958).

UNESCO. World Communications: Press, Radio,
    Film, Television (Paris, 1956).

Union Catalogue of New Zealand Newspapers
    (Wellington, 1961).

Weber, Karl. The Swiss Press: An Outline.
    Berne: Herbert Lang & Cie., 1948.

Wheeler, Urban G. (ed.). Propaganda and
    International Relations. San Francisco:
    Chandler, 1960.

Williams, Francis. Transmitting World News
    (UNESCO, Paris, 1953).

Yearbook of Finland. Helsinki: Foreign
    Ministry of Finland.

II. BOOKS

Acción Cultural Popular. Algunas preguntas
    sobre las escuelas radiofónicas de Colombia.
    Bogotá: Acción Cultural Popular, 1958.

Alexanderson, Nils. Svensk Tryckfrihet
    ("Freedom of the Press in Sweden"). Stock-
    holm, 1950.

Alisky, Marvin. State and Local Government
    in Sonora, Mexico. Tempe: ASU Bureau of
    Government Research, 1962.

Assante, A. Il Giornale--Libertà di Stampa e

Giornalismo in Italia e nella legislazione mondiale. Naples: Morano, 1952.

Bahia, Juarez. Tres, Fases da Imprensa Brasileira. Santos, S. Paulo, Brazil: Editora Presenca, 1960.

Ballester, Eliel. Derecho de Prensa. Buenos Aires: El Ateneo, 1947.

Barghoon, Frederick. The Soviet Image of the United States. New York: Harcourt, Brace, 1950.

Barghoorn, F. C. The Soviet Cultural Offensive. Princeton: Princeton University Press, 1960.

Bell, William M. (ed.). Press, Radio and World Affairs. Melbourne: Melbourne University Press, 1938.

Beltrán, Oscar. Historia del Periodismo Argentino. Buenos Aires: Sopena, 1943.

Bisbee, Eleanor. The New Turks. Philadelphia: University of Pennsylvania Press, 1951.

Blanksten, George I. Perón's Argentina. Chicago: University of Chicago Press, 1953.

Bloch, Pierre, Liberté et Servitude de la Presse en France. Monte-Carlo: Editions du livre, 1952.

Boivin, Emile. Histoire du journalisme, Paris: Presses universitaires, 1949.

Borrego, Salvador E. Periodismo Trascendente. Mexico, D.F.: Editorial Jus, 1958.

Borton, Hugh. Japan's Modern Century. New York: Ronald Press, 1955.

Bowman, William D. The Story of the Times. London: Deal, 1931.

Brinton, Crane. The Shaping of the Modern Mind. New York: New American Library, 1953.

Brucker, Herbert. Freedom of Information. New York: Macmillan, 1949. (See especially chaps. X and XVI.)

Buchanan, William, and Cantril, Hadley. How Nations See Each Other. Urbana: University of Illinois Press, 1953.

Carrasco Puente, Rafael. La prensa en México. Datos históricos. Mexico: Universidad Nacional Autónoma de Mexico, 1962.

Castellanos, Rafael Ramón. Historia del periodismo trujillano en el siglo XIX. Caracas: Imprenta Nacional, 1957.

Catlin, George. The Story of Political Philosophies. New York: Tudor Publishing Co., 1939.

Christensen, Folmer (ed.). Danmarks Blad -- og Bogverden. Copenhagen: Politikens Forlag, 1953.

Christiansen, Arthur. Headlines All My Life. New York: Harper & Brothers, 1961.

Cline, Howard F. Mexico: Revolution to Evolution, 1940-1960. New York: Oxford, 1962.

Codding, G. A., Jr. Broadcasting Without Barriers. Paris: UNESCO, 1959.

Collins, Irene. The Government and Newspaper Press in France, 1814-1881. New York: Macmillan, 1959.

Commission on Freedom of the Press. A Free and Responsible Press. Chicago: University of Chicago Press, 1947.

Cooper, Kent. Barriers Down: The Story of the News Agency Epoch. New York: Farrar & Rinehart, 1942.

_____. The Right to Know. New York: Farrar, Straus and Cudahy, 1956.

Copley, James S. Mission to San Salvador. San Diego: Copley Press, 1960.

_____. With a Mission to Chile. San Diego: Copley Press, 1961.

Coughlin, William J. Conquered Press: The MacArthur Era in Japanese Journalism. Palo Alto, Calif.: Pacific Books, 1952.

Cretzianu, Alexandre (ed.). Captive Rumania: A Decade of Soviet Rule. New York: Praeger, 1956.

De Anda, F. Ibarra. Las Mexicanas en el Periodismo. Mexico, D.F.: Imprenta Mundial, 1935.

De Palma, Samuel. Freedom of the Press--An International Issue. Washington, D.C., 1950.

Desmond, Robert W. The Press and World Affairs. New York: Appleton Century Crofts, 1937.

Deutsche Presse Agentur (DPA). Hamburg, 1950.

Doob, Leonard. Communication in Africa. New

Haven: Yale University Press, 1961.

Dresler, Adolphe. Geschichte der Italienischen Presse. Berlin: Oldenbourg, 1934.

Duarte, Jacinto. El Diario Moderno. Montevideo: Imprenta Talleres Gráficas Sur, SA., 1948.

Duesenberg, Albert. The Press in Germany. Bonn: Buchdruckerei M. Scholl, 1960.

Fainsod, Merle. How Russia is Ruled. Cambridge: Harvard University Press, 1953.

Ferón, Bernard (ed.). Feu la Presse Libre. Paris: Temoignage Chretien, 1954.

Fitzsimons, Thomas (ed.). Iraq. New Haven: HRAF Press, 1958. (See chap. 9).

Fliess, Peter J. Freedom of the Press in the German Republic, 1918-1933. Baton Rouge: Louisiana State University Press, 1955.

Fluharty, Vernon L. Dance of the Millions. Pittsburgh: University of Pittsburgh, 1957.

George, Alexander L. Propaganda Analysis: A Study of Inferences Made From Nazi Propaganda in World War II. Evanston, Ill.: Row-Peterson, 1959.

Gerald, J. Edward. The British Press Under Government Economic Controls. Minneapolis: University of Minnesota Press, 1956.

Ghose, Hemendra Prasad. The Newspaper in India. Calcutta: University of Calcutta, 1952.

Gollin, Alfred M. The Observer and J. L. Garvin, 1908-1914. London: Oxford University Press, 1960.

Gonzáles Ruiz, Nicolás (ed.). El Periodismo: Teoría y Práctica. Barcelona: Editorial Noguer, 1955. (See especially Part IV.)

Gramling, Oliver. AP: The Story of News. New York: Farrar and Rinehart, Inc., 1940.

Grothe, Peter. To Win the Minds of Men. Palo Alto: Pacific Books, 1958. (See chap. 4.)

Guillain, Robert. 600 Million Chinese. New York: Criterion Books, 1957.

Gunther, John. Inside Russia Today. New York: Harper, 1958. (See especially chap. XIV.)

Hagemann, Walter (ed.). Die deutsche Zeitung.

Münster, 1949.

Halecki, Oscar (ed.). East-Central Europe Under the Communists: Poland. New York: Praeger, 1957. (See especially chap. 6 "Propaganda.")

Hanazono, Kanesada. Development of Japanese Journalism. Nichi, 1934.

Helmreich, Ernst C. Hungary. New York: Praeger, 1957.

Henestrosa, Andrés, and José Fernández. Periodismo y periodistas de Hispanoamerica. Mexico, D.F.: Secretaría de Educación Pública, 1947.

Herd, Harold. The March of Journalism: The Story of the British Press from 1622 to the Present Day. London: George Allen & Unwin Ltd., 1952.

Hitler, Adolf. Mein Kampf. New York: E. P. Dutton, 1950.

Holden, W. Sprague. Australia Goes to Press. Detroit: Wayne State University Press, 1961.

Iguchi, Ichiro. Masu Kominyukeishion ("Mass Communication"). Tokyo: Kobunsha, 1951.

Inkeles, Alex. Public Opinion in Soviet Russia. Cambridge: Harvard University Press, 1950. (See especially Parts 1, 2, and 3.)

Inkeles, Alex and Raymond Bauer. The Soviet Citizen. Cambridge: Harvard University Press, 1959.

Jobim, Danton. Espírito do Jornalismo. Rio de Janeiro: Livraría São José, 1959.

Jones, Robert V. The Challenge of Liberty. Chicago: Heritage Foundation, Inc., 1956.

Khudiakov, E. L. Theory and Practice of the Party-Soviet Press (in Russian). Moscow: Moscow University Press, 1957.

Kisch, E. E. Klassicher Journalismus. Berlin: Kemmerer, 1923.

Kitchen, Helen (ed.). The Press in Africa. Washington, D.C.: Ruth Sloan Associates, 1956.

Kottyar, A. Newspapers in the USSR. New York: USSR Research Council, 1955.

Koyama, Elizo. Hikaku Shimbungaku. Tokyo: Yuhikaku, 1951.

Kruglak, Theodore E. The Foreign Correspondents. Geneva: Librairie E. Dorz, 1955.

_____. The Two Faces of TASS. Minneapolis: University of Minnesota Press, 1962.

La Prensa, editors of. Defense of Freedom. New York: John Day, 1952.

Lenin, Vladimir I. Collected Works. New York: International Publishers, 1927.

Lieuwen, Edwin. Venezuela. New York: Oxford, 1961.

Linebarger, Paul; Chu Djang, and Burks, A. W. Far Eastern Governments and Politics. Princeton: D. Van Nostrand Co. Inc., 1956.

Lin Yutang. A History of the Press and Public Opinion in China. Chicago: University of Chicago Press, 1936.

McFadden, Tom J. Daily Journalism in the Arab States. Columbus: Ohio State University Press, 1953.

Markert, Werner. Jugoslawien (Osteuropa-Handbuch). Cologne: Böhlau-Verlag, 1954.

Martínez Dominguez, Guillermo. 15 años de Periodismo al Servicio de México. Mexico, D.F.: Ediciones Asociacion Mexicana de Periodistas, 1958.

Martz, John D. Colombia: A Contemporary Political Survey. Chapel Hill: University of North Carolina, 1962.

Mathews, Joseph J. Reporting the Wars. Minneapolis: University of Minnesota Press, 1957.

Matthews, Herbert L. The Yoke and the Arrows: A Report on Spain. New York: George Braziller, Inc., 1957.

Mead, Margaret. Soviet Attitudes Toward Authority. New York: McGraw-Hill, 1951.

Meier, Ernst. Zeitungen auf Gronland. Berlin: Duncker & Humblot, 1960.

Merkatz, Hans J. and Wolfgang Metzner (eds.). Germany Today: Facts and Figures. Frankfurt am Main: Alfred Metzner Verlag, 1954. (See especially "The Press," pp. 196-204.)

Merrill, John C. A Handbook of the Foreign Press. Baton Rouge: Louisiana State University Press, 1959.

Mills, William H. The Manchester Guardian: A Century of History. New York: Henry Holt, 1922.

Mizami, Majib. The Press of Pakistan. Lahore, Pakistan: University of Punjab, 1958.

Morison, Stanley. The English Journalist. New York: Macmillan, 1932.

Morris, Joe Alex. Deadline Every Minute: The Story of the United Press. New York: Doubleday, 1957.

Mott, Frank L. Jefferson and the Press. Baton Rouge: Louisiana State University Press, 1943.

Ovink, G. W. Het Aanzien van een eeuw. The Hague, Netherlands: Martinus Nijhoff, 1959.

Paulu, Burton. British Broadcasting in Transition. Minneapolis: University of Minnesota Press, 1961.

_____. British Broadcasting. Minneapolis: University of Minnesota Press, 1956.

Pepper, W. M., Jr. Dictionary of Newspaper and Printing Terms. New York: Columbia University Press, 1959.

Pers, Anders Yngve. Newspapers in Sweden. Stockholm: The Swedish Institute, 1954.

Pound, R. and G. Harmsworth. Northcliffe. New York: British Book Service, 1959.

Price, R.G.G. A History of Punch. London: Collins, 1957.

Pridonoff, Eric L. Tito's Yugoslavia. Washington D.C.: Public Affairs Press, 1955.

Rauch, Walter J. Presse und Volkstum der Lausitzer Sorben. Wurzberg: Holzner-Verlag, 1959.

Robbins, Alan P. Newspapers To-day. London: Oxford University Press, 1956.

Ronblom, H. K. Tryckfriheten i Sverige ("Freedom of the Press in Sweden"). Stockholm, 1940.

Rostow, W. W. The Dynamics of Soviet Society. Cambridge: Technology Press, 1952.

Sampson, Anthony. Drum: The Newspaper that Won the Heart of Africa. Boston: Houghton Mifflin Co., 1957.

Schneider, Maarten. The Netherlands Press Today. Leiden: E. J. Brill, 1951.

Schramm, Wilbur (ed.). One Day in the World's Press. Palo Alto: Stanford University Press, 1959.

Schurz, William L. Brazil. New York: L. Dutton, 1961.

Scott, John D. Life in Britain. New York: Morrow, 1956.

Siebert, Fred; Peterson, Theodore, and Schramm, Wilbur. Four Theories of the Press. Urbana: University of Illinois Press, 1956.

Smith, Bruce L., and Smith, Chitra M. International Communication and Political Opinion. Princeton: Princeton University Press, 1956.

Sparrow, Geoff (ed.). Crusade for Journalism. Melbourne: Australian Journalists' Association, 1960.

Stalin, Joseph. Problems of Leninism. Moscow: Foriegn Languages Publishing House, 1940.

Storey, Graham. Reuters: The Story of a Century of News-Gathering. New York: Crown Publishers, 1951.

Stuart, Graham H. Latin America and the United States. New York: Appleton Century, 1943.

Suaree, Octavio de la. Socioperiodismo. Havana: Cultural S.A., 1949.

Tablante Garrido, P. N. Periodismo merideño. Merida, Venezuela: Universidad de los Andes, 1959.

Tang, Peter S. H. Communist China Today: Domestic and Foreign Policies. New York: Praeger, 1957. (See especially Chap. IX-- "The Propaganda Machine.")

Taylor, H. A. The British Press--A Critical Study. London: Arthur Barker, Ltd., 1961.

Thorsen, Svend. Newspapers in Denmark. Copenhagen: Det Danske Selskab, 1953.

The Times (London). The History of "The Times," London. Four volumes: I(1935); II(1939); III(1947); IV(1952).

Torres, Teodoro. Periodismo. Mexico: Ediciones Botas, 1937.

Ullstein, Hermann. The Rise and Fall of the House of Ullstein. New York: Simon & Schuster, 1943.

Vinciguerra, M. Stampa e Democrazia. Rome: Bussola, 1956.

Walker, Richard L. China Under Communism: The First Five Years. New Haven: Yale University Press, 1955. (See especially Part 8--"Culture and the Intellectuals.")

Waples, Douglas. Los Problemas de la Comunicación Pública en el Perú. Lima: Instituto Relaciones Humanas y Productivad, 1959.

Weber, Karl. Profil der Schweizer Presse. Bern: H. Lang, 1948.

Weed, Katherine K. Studies of British Newspapers and Periodicals from their Beginning to 1800. Chapel Hill: University of North Carolina Press, 1946.

Westerstahl, Jorgen and Carl-Gunnar Janson. The Political Press. Sweden: Political Science Institute, University of Gothenburg, 1958.

Whitaker, Arthur P. Spain and the Defense of the West. New York: Harper, 1961.

White, Llewellyn, and Leigh, Robert D. Peoples Speaking to Peoples (A report on international mass communications from the Commission on Freedom of the Press). Chicago: University of Chicago Press, 1947.

Whittemore, Edward P. The Press in Japan Today...A Case Study. Columbia: University of South Carolina Press, 1961.

Wiggins, James Russell. Freedom or Secrecy. New York: Oxford University Press, 1956.

Wilgus, A. Curtis (ed.). The Caribbean: Contemporary Trends. Gainesville: University of Florida Press, 1953. (See especially Part III.)

Williams, Francis. Dangerous Estate. London: Longmans, Green and Co., 1957.

Williams, Raymond. Britain in the Sixties: Communications. Baltimore: Penguin Books, 1962.

Wiskemann, Elizabeth. A Great Swiss Newspaper. The Story of the Neue Zürcher Zeitung. London: Oxford University Press, 1959.

Wolseley, Roland E. (ed.). Journalism in Modern India. Bombay: Asia Publishing

House, 1953.

Yalman, Ahmed Emin. *Turkey in my Time*. Norman: University of Oklahoma Press, 1956.

Ziesel, Karl. *Das verlorene Gewissen (Hinter den Kullisen der Presse, Literatur und ihrer Machtträger von heute)*. Munich, 1957.

Index

251

EL MERCURIO   CORRIERE DELLA SERA   LE MONDE   LE FIGARO   FRANKFURTER
JE ZURCHER ZEITUNG   MANCHESTER GUARDIAN   THE TIMES   THE SCOTSM
ENDE   EXPRESSEN   DAGENS NYHETER   PRAVDA   IZVESTIA   TIMES OF IN
THE AGE   MANILA TIMES   ASAHI   MAINICHI   PEOPLE'S DAILY   L'OSSERVAT
AFRIQUE   KENYA DAILY MAIL   GHANAIAN TIMES   FRANKFURTER ALLGEMEINE
BERLINER MORGENPOST   TELEGRAF   DER TAGESSPIEGEL   BILD-ZEITUNG   W
MEINE   HAMBURGER ABENDLATT   MANCHESTER GUARDIAN   DAILY TELEGRAPH
DAILY HERALD   DAILY MAIL   DAILY MIRROR   DIE PRESSE   DER NEUE KURI
LINZER VOLKSBLATT   SALZBURGER NACHRICHTEN   LE SOIR   HET LAATSTE
EURE   BERLINGSKE TIDENDE   POLITIKEN   BORSEN   FRANCE-SOIR   LE PA
ORE   OUEST-FRANCE   LE PROGES LYON   LA VOIX DU NORD   HET VRIJE VO
DE TELEGRAAF   CORRIERE DELLA SERA   CORRIERE D'INFORMAZIONE   IL TEMP
A   L'OSSERVATORE ROMANO   AFTENPOSTEN   DAGBLADET   ARBEIDERBLADE
RIO DE NOTICIAS   DIARIO DE LISBOA   ABC   ARRIBA   INFORMACIONES   E
DAGENS NYHETER   EXPRESSEN   AFTONBLADET   GOTEBORGS-POSTEN   STO
ARBETET   JOURNAL DE GENEVE   ZERI I POPPULIT   RABOTNICHESKO DELO
S DEUTSCHLAND   NEPSZABADSAG   TRYBUNA LUDU   SCINTEIA   BORBA
YA PRAVDA   KROKODIL   MA'ARIV   HAKOL   DAVAR   BAMA KHIT   JEN MIN
CHUNG YANG HUA PAO   THE HINDU   THE STATESMAN   THE TIMES OF INDIA
TRIKA   VISHWAMITRA   MERDEKA   KUANG PO   INDONESIA RAYA   AS
OMIURI   SANKEI SHIMBUN   TOKYO TIMES   KOREA REPUBLIC   DAWN   AFIA
LE   WORLD   O GLOBO   EL MERCURIO   LA CRONICA   EL TIEMPO   SUN-HE
NG HERALD   SUN-NEWS PICTORIAL   LA PRESSE   RAND DAILY MAIL   ATHINA
CUMHURIYET   DEMOCRACIA   EVENING STAR   FRIHETEN   GLASGOW HERALD
SALEM POST   KRISTALL   LIBERATION   MAAKANSA   NOVO VREME   OVAC
QUICK   RAZON   SWIAT   TA NEA   ULUS   VOZ OBRERA   WIENER ZEITUNG
NDAR   GLOBE & MAIL   EXCELSIOR   EL UNIVERSAL   EL TIEMPO   O GLOBO
ENSA   LA NACION   EL MERCURIO   CORRIERE DELLA SERA   LE MONDE   LE
ALLGEMEINE   NEUE ZURCHER ZEITUNG   MANCHESTER GUARDIAN   THE TIMES
BERLINGSKE TIDENDE   EXPRESSEN   DAGENS NYHETER   PRAVDA   IZVESTIA
E HINDU   THE AGE   MANILA TIMES   ASAHI   MAINICHI   PEOPLE'S DAILY
ANO   LE COURIER D'AFRIQUE   KENYA DAILY MAIL   GHANAIAN TIMES   FRANK
BERLINER ZEITUNG   BERLINER MORGENPOST   TELEGRAF   DER TAGESSPIEGE
WESTDEUTSCHE ALLGEMEINE   HAMBURGER ABENDBLATT   MANCHESTER GUAR
EXCELSIOR   EL UNIVERSAL   EL TIEMPO   O GLOBO   O JORNAL   LA PR
EL MERCURIO   CORRIERE DELLA SERA   LE MONDE   LE FIGARO   FRANKFUR
JE ZURCHER ZEITUNG   MANCHESTER GUARDIAN   THE TIMES   THE SCOTS
ENDE   EXPRESSEN   DAGENS NYHETER   PRAVDA   IZVESTIA   TIMES OF
THE AGE   MANILA TIMES   ASAHI   MAINICHI   PEOPLE'S DAILY   L'OSSERV
AFRIQUE   KENYA DAILY MAIL   GHANAIAN TIMES   FRANKFURTER ALLGEMEIN
BERLINER MORGENPOST   TELEGRAF   DER TAGESSPIEGEL   BILD-ZEITUNG
MEINE   HAMBURGER ABENDLATT   MANCHESTER GUARDIAN   DAILY TELEGRAPH
DAILY HERALD   DAILY MAIL   DAILY MIRROR   DIE PRESSE   DER NEUE KURIE
LINZER VOLKSBLATT   SALZBURGER NACHRICHTEN   LE SOIR   HET LAATST
EURE   BERLINGSKE TIDENDE   POLITIKEN   BORSEN   FRANCE-SOIR   LE PA
ORE   OUEST-FRANCE   LE PROGES LYON   LA VOIX DU NORD   HET VRIJE VO
DE TELEGRAAF   CORRIERE DELLA SERA   CORRIERE D'INFORMAZIONE   IL TEM
A   L'OSSERVATORE ROMANO   AFTENPOSTEN   DAGBLADET   ARBEIDERBLADE
RIO DE NOTICIAS   DIARIO DE LISBOA   ABC   ARRIBA   INFORMACIONES
DAGENS NYHETER   EXPRESSEN   AFTONBLADET   GOTEBORGS-POSTEN   STO
ARBETET   JOURNAL DE GENEVE   ZERI I POPPULIT   RABOTNICHESKO DELO
S DEUTSCHLAND   NEPSZABADSAG   TRYBUNA LUDU   SCINTEIA   BORBA
YA PRAVDA   KROKODIL   MA'ARIV   HAKOL   DAVAR   BAMA KHIT   JEN MIN
CHUNG YANG HUA PAO   THE HINDU   THE STATESMAN   THE TIMES OF INDIA